# THE BASIC VALUES IN LAW
## A Study of the Ethico-legal Implications of Psychology and Anthropology

THOMAS E. DAVITT

*Professor of Jurisprudence, School of Law, Marquette University*

Revised Edition

Marquette University Press
Milwaukee, Wisconsin 53233
United States of America

To

Those Men And Women To Whose Lot It Falls
To Make World Law

MARQUETTE UNIVERSITY PRESS
MILWAUKEE, WISCONSIN
U.S.A.

# PREFACE

This is a book about values in law. The main purpose of the book is to show that there are certain values which are in law necessarily. These are the values which give law its distinctive contours by furnishing it with its over-all goals.

For some time now there have been those who have asserted that there are no values necessarily in law. The values which are in law, according to this theory, are in law simply because lawmakers choose to recognize and serve these values. The dearest aim of this group is to keep necessary values out of law so that law can be said to be scientific in its concern for facts and not for values. In this view, there are no value judgments which men make of necessity and there are no values which law necessarily and predictably protects and furthers.

This picture of men and their law, however, is grossly distorted. The findings of psychology show that there are certain value judgments which are necessarily present in the thinking of all men and consequently in the laws of all men. These findings receive support from the data of anthropology. These data indicate that there are certain value judgments which are universally present in the laws of all known societies of men. Not that this universality is evidence of the necessity of these value judgments. Such evidence comes from psychology. But this universality is solid corroboration of the findings of psychology that men form these value judgments necessarily. There are also value judgments which, although all individual men cannot be said to make them universally, are found in the laws of all known societies of men. There are further value judg-ments which are not found universally in the laws of all societies but are present in varying degrees of prevalence.

That there are such findings of psychology and such data of anthropology is not a new thought, but it is an ignored one. Sufficient account of this evidence has not been taken. Instead it has been disregarded, passed over, left unexamined and unrelated to the functioning of values in law. What is needed is a restatement of this evidence. An analysis and examination of it is called for. To such a task this book is addressed. In carrying out this analysis and examination, this book in its own way builds a bridge between the disciplines from which this evidence comes and the discipline of law itself.

My thanks are due to the American Philosophical Society for grants from the Johnson and Penrose Funds and to the Committee on Research of Marquette University for matching grants. My appreciation is also due to the library staff of Harvard University Law School, especially Mr. George Strait, for their most helpful cooperation. My grateful thanks are owed further to Professor Paul Bohannon, Chairman of the Center of Social Science research of Northwestern University, for reading a preliminary draft of the anthropological data and making many important suggestions. Finally, my deep gratitude must be expressed to Professor Iredell Jenkins, Chairman of the Department of Philosophy of the University of Alabama. To the generous help of his incisive criticisms I am very greatly indebted.

THOMAS E. DAVITT

# THE BASIC VALUES IN LAW
## A study of the Ethico-legal Implications of Psychology and Anthropology

Thomas E. Davitt

## CONTENTS

PAGE

Introduction ........................................ 6

Part One: Values and Law ........................ 7

Chapter 1. Values .................................... 7
I. Basic values from basic drives .................. 7
  A. Fundamental meaning of value ................ 7
    1. Values from drives ........................ 7
    2. Values a prerequisite to motivation ......... 9
    3. Values given and constructed .............. 10
  B. The nature of drives ........................ 11
    1. Drives are not instincts ................... 11
    2. Drives are plastic tendencies .............. 12
      a. Shaped by knowledge and decision ......... 12
      b. Fountainhead of cultures .................. 13
    3. The basic drives ......................... 13
      a. Opinions regarding basic drives ............ 13
      b. Position taken regarding basic drives ....... 14
II. Obligation and rights from basic values ............ 16
  A. Obligation ................................. 17
    1. Obligation from value-relation of means to end 17
    2. Absolute and relative necessity in value-relations 17
    3. Hypothetical and categorical value-relations .... 17
      a. Obligation from master drive .......... 17
      b. "Ought" from demands of "is" ............. 18
  B. Rights ..................................... 18
    1. The basis of rights ........................ 19
      a. Given relations of title .................. 19
      b. Constructed relations of title ............ 19
    2. The viability of rights .................... 20
    3. Property .................................. 21
    4. Rights and the content of law ................ 22

Chapter 2. Laws .................................... 22
I. The concept of law ............................ 22
  A. Law is a directive judgment ................. 22
    1. Directive versus command ................. 23
    2. Values common to all the people ........... 23
    3. Directive judging .......................... 23
      a. The people themselves ................... 23
      b. The people's delegates ................... 24
  B. Obligation of law from means-end relation ....... 24
    1. Absolute and relative necessity of law's content 24
    2. Means-end necessity precedes law .......... 24
    3. Obligation in law not from command or coercion 24
      a. Kant .................................... 25
      b. Austin .................................. 26
      c. Gray ................................... 27
      d. Kelsen ................................. 28
      e. Hart ................................... 29
      f. Root kinship ........................... 30
    4. Obligation and values necessarily in law ........ 30
      a. Data of psychology and anthropology ........ 30
      b. Process of law-making .................... 31
      c. Just law ............................... 32
      d. "Science of law" ........................ 32

PAGE

II. Laws unwritten and written ...................... 34
  A. Regulations may or may not be laws ............ 34
  B. Unwritten regulations may be laws ............ 35
III. Values self-evident and not self-evident in law ...... 36
  A. Values which are self-evident ................... 36
  B. Values which are not self-evident ............. 37

Part Two: Value-Areas in Law .................... 38

Chapter 3. Values in unwritten law ................ 38
I. Lists of universal values ........................ 39
II. Regulations and obligation are universal ............ 40
III. No societies without regulations which are law ...... 41

Chapter 4. Life and sex ............................ 42
I. Preserving life ................................. 42
  A. Universal value judgments in all societies ........ 42
    1. Self-defense ............................. 43
    2. Regulations regarding title to life ............ 43
    3. Failure to respect title to life: murder ........ 43
  B. Less than universal value judgments ............. 44
    1. General ................................... 44
      a. Killing in self-defense—war ............. 44
      b. Abortion ............................... 45
      c. In-group versus out-group killing .......... 46
    2. Common: Suicide .......................... 47
    3. Occasional: infanticide and senilicide ........ 49
II. Uniting sexually ............................... 50
  A. Universal value judgments ..................... 50
    1. In all societies ........................... 50
      a. Regulations regarding title to sexual union .. 50
      b. Selectivity and permanence ................ 50
      c. Marriage and the family ................... 51
    2. In all societies with rare exceptions .......... 52
      a. Polyandry .............................. 52
      b. Failure to respect spouse's title to sexual
        union: adultery ......................... 54
      c. Incest ................................. 55
  B. Less than universal value judgments ............. 56
    1. General ................................... 56
      a. Premarital intercourse and premarital child-
        birth .................................. 56
      b. Exchange of items at marriage ............. 57
      c. Failure to respect title to sexual integrity:
        rape ................................... 59
      d. Divorce ................................ 59
    2. Common ................................... 60
      a. Polygyny ............................... 60
      b. Monogamy .............................. 61

Chapter 5. Knowledge and decision ................. 62
I. Knowing ....................................... 62
  A. Universal value judgments in all societies ........ 64
    1. Regulations concerning title to know .......... 64
    2. Failure to respect title to know: unjust repres-
      sion of thought .......................... 64

|                                                                        | PAGE |
|------------------------------------------------------------------------|------|
| 3. Communicating                                                       | 65   |
|    *a.* Language                                        | 65   |
|    *b.* Art                                             | 65   |
| 4. Learning                                                            | 67   |
|    *a.* Oral instruction                               | 67   |
|    *b.* Example                                         | 68   |
|    *c.* Initiation rites                               | 69   |
| 5. Explanations of life                                                | 70   |
|    *a.* Life principle                                 | 70   |
|    *b.* Life after death                               | 71   |
|    *c.* Suprahuman power                               | 72   |
|    *d.* Relationship with suprahuman power             | 73   |
| B. Less than universal value judgments                                 | 75   |
|   1. General: control of events                             | 75   |
|   2. Common                                                 | 76   |
|    *a.* Lying                                          | 76   |
|    *b.* Other-than-human spirits                       | 76   |
|    *c.* Supreme being                                  | 77   |
|    *d.* Origin of man and world                        | 78   |
| II. Deciding                                                           | 79   |
| A. Universal value judgments in all societies                          | 80   |
|   1. Regulations concerning title to decide                 | 80   |
|   2. Failure to respect title to decide: unjust repression of action | 80 |
|   3. Individual responsibility for decisions                | 80   |
|   4. Decision to violate regulations—reactions              | 81   |
| B. Less than universal value judgments                                 | 81   |
|   1. General                                                | 81   |
|    *a.* Intention versus accident                     | 81   |
|    *b.* Hot blood versus cold blood                    | 83   |
|    *c.* Collective responsibility for decisions        | 83   |
|   2. Common                                                 | 84   |
|    *a.* Insanes and inebriates                        | 84   |
|    *b.* Negligence                                     | 85   |
| Chapter 6. Mine and thine                                              | 86   |
| I. Universal value judgments                                           | 86   |
| A. In all societies                                                    | 86   |
|   1. Regulations regarding title to things                  | 87   |
|   2. Failure to respect title to things: theft              | 87   |
|   3. Ways of establishing relations of title                | 88   |
|    *a.* Labor                                          | 88   |
|    *b.* Exchange agreements                            | 91   |
|    *c.* Gift-giving                                    | 91   |
| B. In all societies with rare exceptions: title by occupation         | 92   |

|                                                                        | PAGE |
|------------------------------------------------------------------------|------|
| II. Less than universal value judgments                                | 93   |
| A. General                                                             | 93   |
|   1. Keeping agreements                                      | 93   |
|   2. Title by inheritance                                   | 93   |
|   3. In-group versus out-group taking of things             | 94   |
| B. Common: land                                                        | 95   |
| Chapter 7. Association for protection and security                     | 96   |
| I. Universal value judgments                                           | 101  |
| A. In all societies                                                    | 101  |
|   1. Protection and security                                | 101  |
|   2. Cooperative effort                                     | 102  |
|   3. Regulative judging                                     | 103  |
|    *a.* Self-government                                | 103  |
|    *b.* Making custom law                              | 104  |
|    *c.* Removal of leaders                             | 104  |
|   4. Sanctions                                              | 105  |
|   5. Judging cases                                          | 106  |
| B. In all societies with rare exceptions                               | 107  |
|   1. Distinguishing offenses directly and indirectly against common values | 107 |
|    *a.* "Crimes" and "torts"                          | 108  |
|    *b.* Lists of offenses                             | 109  |
|   2. Respect for the elderly                               | 110  |
| II. Less than universal value judgments                                | 110  |
| A. General                                                             | 110  |
|   1. Councils                                               | 111  |
|   2. Witnesses and ordeals                                 | 111  |
|   3. Ridicule and shame                                    | 113  |
|   4. Death                                                 | 115  |
|   5. Compensation                                          | 116  |
|   6. Enforcement                                           | 118  |
| B. Common                                                              | 119  |
|   1. Leaders                                               | 119  |
|   2. Self-help                                             | 121  |
|   3. Proportionate retaliation                            | 122  |
|   4. Exile                                                 | 124  |
|   5. Confessions                                           | 125  |
| C. Frequent: oaths                                                     | 125  |
| D. Occasional                                                          | 126  |
|   1. Changing custom law                                   | 126  |
|   2. Equitable fictions                                    | 127  |
|   3. Mutilation—wounding—combat                            | 128  |
|   4. Imprisonment                                          | 128  |
| CONCLUSION                                                             | 129  |
| BIBLIOGRAPHY                                                           | 131  |
| INDEX                                                                 | 136  |

# INTRODUCTION

This inquiry proceeds in two parts. In part one, models of values and of law are presented. The models are developed from an analysis of the accepted findings of psychology in regard to values, and of the observed data of regulated order in relation to law. The importance of the models is that they indicate the loci, within a unified conceptual framework, of the various value judgments which will be later encountered. They also present a definite affirmation concerning the necessity and prevalence of certain value judgments in law.

In part two, the data reported by anthropologists and ethnologists regarding patterns of value judgments in preliterate law will be examined in an effort to find support for this affirmation. Such support is not difficult to find in written laws. In order that this support can be said to be universal in all law, the unwritten law of preliterates has to be investigated. This inquiry will follow the guidelines furnished by the models. The various value-areas marked out for examination in this second part are a reflection of the distinctive areas which are developed in the models.

PART ONE

# VALUES AND LAW

CHAPTER 1

## VALUES

"Value" has many different meanings. In our model of value, we must first isolate the particular meaning which the word will have in our present context before proceeding to a discussion of the origin and function of values.

### I. BASIC VALUES FROM BASIC DRIVES

"Value" has to do with the evaluation we make of something in itself or as a means to an end. I evaluate my car or my next-door neighbor for what they are worth in themselves. I also evaluate my health-caring actions for what they are worth as a means to my general well-being. To the degree that these various value-objects measure up to the standards I hold concerning them, I appraise them one way or another. These value judgments which I make will find utterance in such terms as good or bad, right or wrong, justifiable or unjustifiable, approvable or disapprovable, acceptable or unacceptable, noble or ignoble, and the like. I say that my car is a good or bad car. I affirm of my neighbor that he is noble or ignoble. I assert of my health-caring actions that they are right or wrong, justifiable or unjustifiable, and so forth. Running throughout these evaluations are the norms I hold concerning mechanical construction, personal character, and human activity.[1]

#### A. FUNDAMENTAL MEANING OF VALUE

The "value" which immediately concerns us here is not the value of things or persons in themselves. Our particular interest is in the value of our actions which we choose as means to an end. Not that there is no interrelation between these various kinds of values. The actions a person performs are related to the kind of character he eventually develops. But the value of which there is question in law is the value of our actions and their objects. More specifically, it is the value of our actions and their objects which relate to the common needs of all the people. This is the value on which our obligation to obey or not to obey a law rests, and it is the value from which derive our fundamental personal rights, as we shall see. This value of human actions has perennially been referred to as ethical or moral value. So also has the character of a person been similarly spoken of which develops as the result of these actions. The value of things, on the other hand, may be economic, sentimental, or otherwise, but it is not ethical or moral.[2]

### 1. *Values from Drives*

When the fundamental standard is sought according to which men's actions are evaluated, it will be found to be men's basic drives. Men have elementary needs.[3] They lack objects which will be suitable and helpful to them. They have drives to fulfill these needs. Drives are appetites or tendencies or inclinations toward objects which will be beneficial once they are possessed. "Tendencies . . . remain the 'indisputable postulates of all psychology.'"[4] A drive, therefore, is a tendency towards an object which upon attainment will reduce the drive. It is an inclination toward an object I somehow evaluate as "the thing for me" in so far as it will reduce my drive. The object may be designated as "desirable for me," inasmuch as there is this awareness of its suitability. It may be termed "good for me" or anything else evaluative.[5]

My value judgments are related, therefore, to my needs and tendencies. "[A]ction tendencies must be linked with values."[6] My basic values take their

[1] "Value implies a code or a standard which has some persistence through time, or, more broadly put, which organizes a system of action. Value, conveniently and in accordance with received usage, places things, acts, ways of behaving, goals of action on the approval-disapproval continuum." Clyde Kluckhohn, "Values and Value-Orientations in the Theory of Action: An Exploration in Definition and Classification," in: Talcott Parsons and Edward Shils, eds., *Toward a General Theory of Action* (Cambridge, Mass., 1959), p. 395.

[2] See William Frankena, *Ethics* (Englewood Cliffs, 1963), p. 9. See also Michael Polanyi, *Personal Knowledge* (Chicago, 1958), pp. 214–215.

[3] For a listing of primary, secondary and tertiary needs, see Edward Tolman, "A Psychological Model," in: Talcott Parsons and Edward Shils, eds., *Toward a General Theory of Action* (Cambridge, Mass., 1959), pp. 321–322.

[4] Gordon Allport, "Traits Revisited," *Amer. Psychologist* 21 (1966): p. 8; quoting William McDougall, "Tendencies as Indispensable Postulates of All Psychology," *Proc. XI International Congress on Psychology* 1937: pp. 157–170. "We have, each one of us, an essential inner nature which is instinctoid, intrinsic, given, 'natural'. . . . This inner core shows itself as natural inclinations, propensities or inner habit." Abraham Maslow, *Toward a Psychology of Being* (New York, 1962), p. 178.

[5] See Raymond McCall, "Invested Self-Expression: A Principle of Human Motivation," *Psychol. Rev.* 70 (1963): p. 291. Needs related to the basic drives are obviously not coextensive with acquired wishes. If need "is nothing more than an acquired wish, the list would be unlimited, and certain prominent persons could be said to possess a 'need' to become President of the United States." Robert Faris, *Social Psychology* (New York, 1952), p. 19.

[6] Henry Murray, "Toward a Classification of Interaction," in: Talcott Parsons and Edward Shils, eds., *Toward a General Theory of Action* (Cambridge, Mass., 1959), p. 463. "I have come to believe (after identifying myself with Dr. Allport) that action tendencies must be linked with values, which means that both values and tendencies should be classified. . . . I am calling the action tendencies vectors, each vector being defined as a direction of transformation. Every vector may be combined with every value, giving us a large but manageable number of value-vectors, each of which is a certain kind of need." Murray, *ibid.*

meaning from my basic drives and what is demanded by them, as we shall see shortly. Value, consequently, is that quality of my action and its object according to which it is appraised as capable of satisfying or frustrating my basic drives. It is these drives which determine what will be basically satisfying to me and will thereby be contributive to my development. Men's basic drives are the points of departure for ascertaining human values.[7] The basic drives are norm-indicators which give us a running start on judging what are the elementary values in the lives of men.[8] Such value judgments, which have to do with actions which are means to the ends of the drives, are verifiable and predictable in the lives of men.

This necessity of the basic drives as the anchor of our evaluations of actions has long shown itself in explanations of what is meant by "good" as the opposite evaluation of "bad."[9] In the mainstream of ethical thinking, "good" has consistently been related to appetite or tendency. "Good" has been described as that which is the object of our striving or seeking.[10] Since

what satisfies desire relates to the development of the person having the desire, "good" has frequently been described as that which promotes progress toward a goal.[11] This goal-related aspect of "good" and "bad" is specifically denoted by the terms "right" and "wrong."[12] It is on the recognition of the relation of "good" and "bad," of "right" and "wrong," to the basic drives that any hope of agreement on the elementary meaning of these terms appears to depend.[13]

A word may be in place here parenthetically, though it hardly seems necessary, regarding the much discussed "naturalistic fallacy." This "fallacy" has been said to be the attempt to "define the good" as that for which men have a natural desire.[14] This charge would be justified if a description of the way men commonly refer to objects which satisfy their drives or desires was intended to be taken as a definition from which values could be deduced. But such is not the case. To call the object "good" which satisfies a drive is not to define the "good," nor is it to predicate "good" of the drive or the desire itself. "Good" is coterminus with being and as such is indefinable. It cannot be reduced to genus and species. Nor can the drive or desire itself be termed "good" except in the ontological sense that all things which exist are in some sense good. Rather, and this is the central point, "good" is an arbitrary term assigned to the non-arbitrary and verifiable quality which some objects have of reducing drives, of fulfilling needs, of satisfying desires.[15] The solution to the problem of "good" lies not in an ethics deriving from logic, but in an ethics grounded on psychology and experience. Seen in this perspective, "good" is what completes the incomplete.[16]

Basic values, then, are related to basic drives. Values have their root in what is indicated by the drives. Drives are, to repeat, norm-indicators of basic values. Values derive from what is demanded by the drives. In such a situation, as we shall have occasion to recall

---

[7] "Even to speak in biological terms of tissue needs—such as hunger, thirst, maintenance of temperature—is to assume survival of the organism as a good. The idea of fundamental psychological needs . . . implies some kind of force or operative organization in human beings—the dynamic element traditionally embodied in the drive concept. . . . The investigation of the way in which fundamental needs function in human life shows that they provide raw material for many values, often serve as structural components of values, and enter into numerous value-configurations." Abraham Edel, *Ethical Judgment* (Glencoe, 1964). pp. 167, 170.

[8] "[A]t the core of most prescriptive norms there is usually found some fundamental tendency of the human organism." Bronislaw Malinowski, "Introduction" to Ian Hogbin, *Law and Order in Polynesia* (New York, 1934), p. xxxvi. "Value is so fundamental in human life that its true character can be seen only against the background of human nature. If the intrinsically good is that which this nature finds in itself attractive, it is reasonable to suspect that its atractiveness has something to do with its answering that nature's needs and demands." Brand Blanshard, *Reason and Goodness* (New York, 1961), p. 292.

[9] In regard to the words "good" and "value," it should be noted that "good" is of a more ancient lineage than "value." "Good" is representative of the thinking of men who consider that something can be known by the human mind about the nature of men and the direction in which their true self-development lies. "Good" in this way of thinking designates a quality which actions have when they promote this self-development. "Value," on the other hand, is of more recent origin. It characterizes the thinking of men who hold that the human mind can know little about men's nature and their development. One cannot speak about what is truly "good" for men, but only about what appears to be useful for them or what is of "value" to them. Although this is the history of these terms, "value" has acquired other commonly accepted meanings. The "value" of an action can refer to its goodness or badness, rightness or wrongness. An action can also be of "value" to me in the sense that it is "good" for me.

[10] "The good has rightly been declared to be that which all things seek." Aristotle, *Nicomachean Ethics*, Book I, chap. 1, 1094ª2-3, trans. by W. D. Ross, Richard McKeon, ed., *The Basic Works of Aristotle* (New York, 1941), p. 395. See

also Thomas Aquinas, *Summa Theologiae,* Part 1-2, Question 94, Article 2 (Ottawa ed., Ottawa, 1941), pp. 1224–1226.

[11] "[W]e find that increase of knowledge, increase of control, increase of autonomy, increase in emotional capacity and enjoyment, increase in will and purpose, increase in individualization, are all good since they make for progress." Thomas Huxley and Julian Huxley, *Touchstone for Ethics* (New York, 1947), p. 251.

[12] See Ralph B. Perry, *Realms of Value* (Cambridge, Mass., 1954), pp. 3, 107, 108.

[13] "If we are to talk of good and evil we need some working conception of their meaning. There is, fortunately, some minimal linguistic agreement among most ethical theories. They tend to define 'good' to some extent in terms of the direction of human striving or aspiration, and 'evil' as the object of aversions or at least what profoundly frustrates the good." Abraham Edel, *Ethical Judgment* (Glencoe, 1964), p. 79.

[14] G. E. Moore, *Principia Ethica* (Cambridge, 1903), chap. 1.

[15] The relation of this verifiability to the charge that our value judgments are not rational and cognitive but emotional and non-cognitive will be discussed later.

[16] For a discussion of the "naturalistic fallacy," see Henry Veach, *Rational Man* (Bloomington, 1962), p. 203.

later, the value of the means of fulfilling a drive is interrelated with the value of the end of the drive which is its fulfillment. Food has a value because self-preservation has a value. The ends of the basic drives themselves have value inasmuch as they, in turn, are means to the end of the master drive of self-realization which we will discuss later. Self-preservation is a means necessary for men's personal self-development. It is this value of the basic drive which is the guide for correction when aberrations occur. Psychiatry attempts to change a person's suicidal tendencies only because self-preservation itself is desirable and is a value to be sought.

### 2. Values a Prerequisite to Motivation

Values and value judgments are implied in all motivation. Motives are described as tendencies toward or away from objects which are evaluated as good or bad for us.[17] The close relation between basic drives, values and motives becomes evident. Values motivate our decisions concerning these objects as ends or as means to ends. "A value is a conception, explicit or implicit, distinctive of an individual or characteristic of a group, of the desirable which influences the selection from available modes, means, and ends of actions."[18]

Basic values are basic motives. Men are motivated to follow the demands of their basic drives by the obvious benefits to be gained by satisfying the drives. Human motivation denotes human drives and their evaluated goals.[19] Goals or ends are by supposition attainable. If an object is desired but is unattainable, it cannot be a goal which motivates actions as means to the end. Such a desired but inaccessible object remains merely an unattainable "ideal." The ends of the drives are attainable goals which are constant. "[W]e must accept the importance of drives as motivating factors throughout life. [They are] 'absolutely dependable motives'—found in all men and in all cultures . . . . Drives, then, form the *starting point* for our theory of development."[20]

The basic drives, then, are the font from which all of men's actions spring. Their needs are the first which must be fulfilled. Inasmuch as the objects demanded by the basic drives are evaluated as suitable and helpful, they become the initiating goals which set in motion all action.[21] The basic drives "give" initial values and final values, as we shall see more in detail in a later section. But from the standpoint of psychological effectiveness and well-being, in between our first and last goals there must be other goals or values which we "construct," presupposing the "given" values. These intermediate values are prerequisite if we are to live not aimless and drifting but directed and integrated lives.

To be alive, to unite sexually, to possess something as "mine" and to live in association with others, are beginning values. To accomplish the maximum of self-actualization or happiness is an ultimate value. But to attain prestige, wealth, artistic creation, service, learning, comfort and the like, are necessary intermediate or penultimate values. They are goals which guide most of our preferential judging. "Man . . . has an expanding image of himself (a conception of what he would like to be), and the pursuit of this goal directs much, if not most of his conduct."[22] This is why I am motivated by some values more than by others.[23] At the heart of preferential judging and its motivation, and presupposed by them, is the process of evaluation.[24]

Not all motives, as is obvious, are directly related to the basic drives. Those values and motives which are given, as we shall explain, are thus closely related. The constructed values and motives are not. A man may desire one or more of the intermediate values such as learning, prestige, and comfort. These are not directly relatable to the basic drives and values, although they may be indirectly connected with them. The motives for such desires come rather from values whose construction presupposes the given values.[25] Nor are all

---

[17] "A human motive is . . . a felt tendency toward or away from an object cognized as in some sense desirable or undesirable, good or bad for us as we see it." Raymond McCall, "Invested Self-Expression: A Principle of Human Motivation," *Psychol. Rev.* 70 (1963): p. 291.

[18] Clyde Kluckhohn, "Values and Value-Orientation in the Theory of Action: An Exploration in Definition and Classification," in: Talcott Parsons and Edward Shils, eds., *Toward a General Theory of Action* (Cambridge, Mass., 1959), p. 395.

[19] "The study of motivation must be in part the study of the ultimate human goals or desires or needs." Abraham Maslow, *Motivation and Personality* (New York, 1954), p. 66. "Goals [are the] centering principle in motivaton theory. . . . It has been proven sufficiently by various people that this is the most suitable point for centering in any motivation theory." Abraham Maslow, "A Theory of Human Motivation," *Psychol. Rev.* 50 (1943): pp. 370, 392.

[20] Gordon Allport, *Pattern and Growth in Personality* (New York, 1961), p. 91.

[21] Magda Arnold, *Emotion and Personality* (New York, 1960), pp. 232, 233. See also Edward Murray, *Motivation and Emotion* (Englewood Cliffs, 1964), p. 50.

[22] Gordon Allport, *Pattern and Growth in Personality* (New York, 1961), p. 251. See also *ibid.*, p. 223.

[23] "When I am motivated in properly human fashion I am aware of myself as motivated, and this awareness enables me to evaluate the motive in relation to the well-being (or values) of that self as I see it. It is the evaluation of the motive in relation to the cognized self that lends to the motive its degree of ego-involvement or self-investment. . . . We are moved by some goals much more than by others because we see them as closer to the needs or values of the self." Raymond McCall, "Invested Self-Expression: A Principle of Human Motivation," *Psychol. Rev.* 70 (1963): p. 301.

[24] "Evaluating has, of course, always been implicit in deliberate preferential judgment or in configurations of individual and group life-goals, just as length measurement and counting are implicit in judging one thing to be greater than another or one group to be larger than another." Abraham Edel, *Ethical Judgment* (Glencoe, 1964), p. 122.

[25] "[I]t has too often been assumed that . . . motive corresponds to a specific . . . drive. However, because all normal adults want to wear clothing, it does not follow that there is a specific and dependable clothing drive." Theodore Newcomb, *Social Psychology* (New York, 1950), p. 138.

of men's actions motivated. The association of ideas, for instance, or conditioned reflexes are among the many examples of non-motivated actions. But the great majority of our actions are performed with some degree of knowledge and freedom of decision and are therefore motivated.[26]

In sum, the implications of motivation for law are clear. In motivation there are evaluated goals, hence in the motivation of lawmaking there are also evaluated goals. These are the purposes of a law's enactment. The content of a law is chosen precisely because of the value it has as a means of bringing about the ends which the law is intended to accomplish. Such evidence stands directly against the claim that there are no values in law. Further, certain basic values derive from men's basic drives. These values, as we shall see more in detail shortly, cannot but function in the minds of all men including the minds of those who make law. It is these given values which impart to law its essential features which make it identifiable as the law of men and the law for men. The data of the basic drives take dead aim at the claim that there are no values necessarily in law.

### 3. Values Given and Constructed

Some values are "given" and others are "constructed," as we have intimated. A man's basic drives are given and so are the value judgments he makes according to their demands without a reasoning process.[27] The evidence indicates, as we shall see more in detail shortly, that every man judges that the goals of his basic drives are in themselves good and that he should seek to fulfill them as a means of satisfying his basic needs. Every man judges that preserving his life is in itself good and not evil, that it is desirable and not undesirable. He also judges that what contributes to this end is also

good and not evil. These given value judgments are the non-reasoned points of departure for all further judging about values. Unless there are some un-reasoned judgments from which reasoning processes can begin, reasoning could never get started.

Other value judgments, however, are not given or formed without a reasoning process. They are "constructed." Starting with the basic value judgments which are given, we construct other values both by logical deduction and by factual induction. The amount of reasoning involved ranges from the minimal to the maximal. The given value judgments are the same in all normal men. The constructed value judgments may vary in normal men. Some constructed value judgments are found in all societies of men. In all societies, for example, protection and security are so obviously needed for the fulfillment of other needs that there is a consensus of constructed value judgments that protection and security are good and desirable. Other constructed value judgments, as the evidence will show, are by no means this prevalent in all societies.

Constructed value judgments may even be contrary to the given value judgment of a basic drive. A normal man judges that preserving his life is good and desirable in itself. But, for certain reasons which seem to him to be over-balancing such as ill-health, he may reason rightly or wrongly that taking his life is better and more desirable. The forming of such a judgment does not connote that his drive to preserve his life, and the concomitant value judgment that it is good to do so, cease to function vitally. It only means that because this drive and judgment continue to operate and make themselves felt, there is a tension and struggle set up within the man as a result of these two conflicting value judgments.[28] For this reason, the man's constructed judgment to kill himself takes on more than ordinary significance if it ultimately prevails. The need felt by the suicide himself, or his survivors, to explain or justify the act is evidence of this.[29]

---

[26] Abraham Maslow, *Motivation and Personality* (New York, 1954), pp. 76, 102.

[27] How such judgments are formed without a reasoning process has been the subject of some discussion. One explanation is that, in contradistinction to non-value judgments which are object-related, these given value judgments are drive-related. Thus, the judgment I make that "This is a tree" is related to an object which is designated as "tree." On the other hand, the judgment I make that "Preserving my life is good" is related to my drive for self-preservation. The assumption here is that, the unity of man being what it is, men's apprehensive powers are aware of the functioning of the appetitive powers. Men are somewhat aware of their drive for self-preservation. This means that my mind being aware however vaguely of my drive for self-preservation judges immediately and without any reasoning that self-preservation is good and something to be striven for. The same would hold for the given value judgments concerning the other basic drives. This type of value judgment has been called "judgment by inclination," "judgment according to drive," or "co-natural judgment." The concepts involved in this drive-related judgment are imprecise, for instance, "self-preservation." The concepts entailed in object-related judgments are relatively clear and definite, for example "tree." See Jacques Maritain, *Man and the State* (Chicago, 1951), pp. 16–17.

[28] "[T]he fact that some individuals or even some groups commit suicide by no means proves that it is as 'natural' to wish for death as for life." Otto Klineberg, *Social Psychology* (rev. ed., New York, 1954), p. 69.

[29] The suggestion has been made that along with men's "life instinct" there is also a "death instinct." This supposed instinct, which shows itself especially in hostility and aggression, is said to be basically a tendency in organic matter to revert to the state in which it was before external forces started it on a process of evolution. Sigmund Freud, *Beyond the Pleasure Principle*, trans. by C. J. M. Hubback (London, 1924), pp. 24, 44, 83. Protection against this tendency to destroy oneself can be had, it is claimed, by being hostile and agressive and by destroying other things and other persons. Sigmund Freud, *New Introductory Lectures on Psychoanalysis*, trans. by W. J. Sprott (London, 1933), pp. 144–145. The "death instinct," however, has obviously never won wide acceptance. The death of a living being is obviously explained by other causes than by a drive to die which is on a par with the drive to live. Hostility and aggression can be ways of striving for life-preserving aims which can be, besides the removal of anxiety and guilt, the acquiring of various kinds of possessions.

The distinction between value judgments which are given and those which are constructed is of importance in determining whether value judgments are grounded on variable emotions or on verifiable facts. If men's value judgments are based on arbitrary and changing emotions, these values are not constant, verifiable, and predictable. Hence, they would not be rational and cognitive, and ethics would have no chance of being a science. But if these value judgments are based on given and unchanging drives, they are constant, verifiable, and predictable. They are cognitional and ethics can be a science.

The basic drives, however, are observable constants. As such, they are the foundation of a science of values.

[W]e can, in principle, have a descriptive, naturalistic science of human values; . . . the age old mutually exclusive contrast between "what is" and "what ought to be" is in part a false one; . . . we can study the highest values or goals of human beings as we study the values of ants or horses or oak trees, or, for that matter, Martians. We can discover (rather than create or invent) which values men trend toward, yearn for, struggle for, as they improve themselves.[30]

The given values are as much given facts as are the given facts of physical nature. By observing the demands of men's basic drives we can know in a scientific manner what some of the fundamental requirements are for men's advancement. The matter of knowing elementary values is not emotional conjecture.

In principle, a scientific basis for values is discoverable. Some values appear to be as much "given" by nature as the fact that bodies heavier than air fall. . . . We don't have to rely upon supernatural revelation to discover that sexual excess achieved through violence is bad. This is as much a fact of general observation as the fact that different objects have different densities. The observation that truth and beauty are universal, transcendental human values, is as much one of the "givens" of human life as are birth and death.[31]

The difference between given and constructed value judgments will also be of significance when we come to explain the plasticity of the basic drives. The drives have fixed area-goals, but under the influence of knowledge and decision admit of a great variability of means to be employed in reaching these goals. The "immense diversity within regularity"[32] which is encountered everywhere can be explained only in terms of given and constructed value judgments and their relations to the drives with their inflexible-flexible aspects. It is this rational plasticity of the drives which accounts for the variety of cultures observable among all peoples but which have a universal strain of values present in them all.

[T]he broad outlines of the ground plan of all cultures are and have to be about the same because men always and everywhere are faced with certain unavoidable problems which arise out of the situation "given" by nature. . . . [T]he "givens" provide foci around which and within which the patterns of every culture crystallize.[33]

Lawmaking, to recap, implies evaluated goals and evaluated means to these goals. These evaluations are not limited to constructs which lawmakers are free to make or not to make. They include the evaluations which are given by the basic drives which lawmakers cannot help but make. The basic values of life or sex or the other human activities, which we shall discuss later, is not a matter of decision of lawmakers. The basic value of life is predetermined by men's basic drive before legislators consider enacting statutes regarding its preservation.[34] Likewise, the value of two sexes and their interrelationship preexists before courts come to adjudicate the regulations of sex in marriage, adultery, incest, and the like.[35] Such values necessarily determine the main outlines of law.

### B.  THE NATURE OF DRIVES

A basic drive, as we have seen, is an inclination towards an object which upon attainment is capable of satisfying it. In order to understand drives better, it must be seen how drives differ from instincts and how drives are characterized by a flexible plasticity.

### 1.  Drives Are Not Instincts

Needs and drives are described by some psychologists almost exclusively in terms of the organic. Drives in this sense are the correlative of organic need. In this view basic needs and drives are limited to the homeostatic. An equilibrium between excess and defect must

---

[30] Abraham Maslow, *Toward a Psychology of Being* (New York, 1962), p. 157.

[31] Clyde Kluckhohn, *Mirror for Man* (New York, 1949), pp. 285–286.

[32] Paul Bohannon, *Social Anthropology* (New York, 1963), p. v.

[33] Clyde Kluckhohn, "Universal Categories of Culture," in: Sol Tax, ed., *Anthropology Today: Selections* (Chicago, 1962), p. 318.

[34] "If we remember the broad definition of 'good' in terms of striving and aspiration . . . it becomes possible at least to recognize the scientific character of the question whether life is a good. Here the evidence provided by the biological perspective lends a basic bias towards an affirmative answer. All forms of life are seen as struggling to maintain and extend themselves and to continue life. The intensity and persistence of the effort toward survival on the widest scale is such that one is not surprised to find philosophies making respect for life the basic ethical commandment." Abraham Edel, *Ethical Judgment* (Glencoe, 1964), p. 125.

[35] "From the fact that there are different sexes, giving rise among human beings to a union that is *sui generis*—an actual datum of the first rank—, the question arises concerning the juridicial regulation of this union. If the fact itself cannot determine the rules of marriage, at least it clearly indicates that a similar union could not exist with its own proper character among beings of the same sex, regardless of the rules assigned to it." François Geny, *Science et Technique en Droit Privé Positif* (4 v., Paris, 1922–1924) **2**: p. 372. My translation.

be maintained for the development of the organism itself.[36] Emphasis on the organic, however, easily leads to a description of drives which is hardly distinguishable from that of instincts.[37] But drives are not instincts.

Instinct is an inborn impulse to behave in a fixed pattern which is connected with anatomical structures keyed to organic needs and which manifest a general uniformity throughout the species. Instincts at one time were thought of as operating more or less after the manner of a stimulus-response bond.[38] But this almost mechanical notion of instinct has been abandoned.[39] It has been replaced by an idea of instinct which allows for activities which are set in motion not only by external stimuli but also by internal impulse, and for activities which are much more complex than simple reflexes such as the sneeze and the knee jerk.

One of the best examples of this more perceptive concept of instinct is that of the nest-building of some birds. The Baltimore Oriole, for instance, which is hatched artificially out of its nest and away from other birds and without any opportunity to see another nest, at a certain age and without any example or coaching will build the dangling nest which is characteristic of its species.[40] The word "instinct," however, still is open to varying interpretations. For this reason tendencies toward such clear goals as self-preservation, sexual union and association are more accurately referred to by the word "drive."[41]

## 2. Drives Are Plastic Tendencies

Drives differ from instincts inasmuch as drives allow for the molding and shaping influence of knowledge and decision. The mark of instinct is a fixed pattern of behavior. The characteristic of drive is plasticity regarding which means will be used to attain the end of the drive, as well as flexibility concerning the form the end will take when attained or even whether the end itself will be effectively sought. Whether and how a man will actually aim at the goals of the drives will depend on his knowledgeable decision. Ideas and desires contrary to the ends of the drives can inhibit the full seeking of their goals. Such a plasticity is found only in human drives.

### a. Shaped by Knowledge and Decision

A man has a drive for self-preservation. This is a fixed area-goal inasmuch as all normal men exhibit this

drive. The means he will employ throughout his life to accomplish this goal are many and variable. He has a wide range of choices, say in regard to food and drink, in directing himself in this area. How his specific behavior will be shaped concerning the specific actions of his self-preservation is to a great extent up to him. He will form habits concerning these specifics. This is inevitable once he begins to give specificity to the over-all drive for self-preservation by coming into contact with particular satisfying objects and being motivated by them.[42] The basic drives are, therefore, plastic and allow for the supervening of knowledge and decision upon them in the molding of habits concerning the means which will satisfy their over-all ends. In the use of means which will fulfill the area-goals of our basic drives, the satisfactions and pleasures which we will enjoy, or the dissatisfactions and sorrows we will suffer, are to a large extent determinable by our knowing decisions.[43]

The ends of the basic drives are plastic in so far as the form they will actually take when they are attained is shaped by our knowledge and decisions. A man may direct himself in such a manner that he preserves his life but does so as a self-declared derelict living a broken and meaningless existence on skid-row. Or he may direct himself in such a way that he preserves his life as a devotee of physical health and pursues an integrated and purposeful life in his respected community. The ends of the basic drives are likewise plastic regarding the attainment itself of their ends. A man has the drive to preserve his life, once again, and forms the given value judgment that it is good to do so. But he may, as we have said, reason to a constructed value judgment that it is better to end his life in suicide because he concludes, rightly or wrongly, that his life has been a failure. Such a value judgment constructed contrary to the demands of his basic drive does not of itself imply that the drive has ceased to function or that the man is abnormal, as we shall discuss later.[44] It merely indicates that the drive as it functions in the attainment of its end is plastic to the point where it can be effectively inhibited by knowledge and decision. This process of given value judgments and constructed counter value judgments, *mutatis mutandis,* may also take place in regard to the other basic drives.

---

[36] Robert Woodworth and Harold Schlosberg, *Experimental Psychology* (rev. ed., New York, 1954), pp. 657, 683.

[37] John Gillin, *The Ways of Men* (New York, 1948), p. 227.

[38] William McDougall, *Introduction to Social Psychology* (London, 1908), *passim*; Wilfred Trotter, *Instincts of the Herd in Peace and War* (London, 1916), p. 94.

[39] Luther Bernard, *Instinct: A Study in Social Psychology* (New York, 1924), *passim*.

[40] Robert Faris, *Social Psychology* (New York, 1952), p. 12.

[41] Gordon Allport, *Pattern and Growth in Personality* (New York, 1961), p. 87. See also Theodore Newcomb, *Social Psychology* (New York, 1950), p. 86.

[42] "Needs are at first objectless or goalless. To bring the condition of hunger into relation with the objects that satisfy it a specific form of experience is necessary. The organism must encounter the object and feel its pleasurable or painful effects. Such an encounter is the necessary condition for establishing the properties of the object as a goal or its relevance to the need. When the relevance has been experienced and has altered the organism by establishing a trace of itself, we observe the transition from a condition of need to a state of motivation." Solomon Asch, *Social Psychology* (New York, 1952), p. 83.

[43] "Nature leaves more to learning and less to prior appointment as it goes up the animal scale." Brand Blanshard, *Reason and Goodness* (New York, 1961), p. 296.

[44] See chap. 4.

The basic drives, then, leave room for a moldability not only regarding the means which will be used in fulfilling the goal of a drive but also concerning how and whether the end of the drive will be actually sought. Considered in the context of its plasticity, then, a drive can be described as an innate inclination or tendency to direct one's actions in certain areas of human living in such a manner that needs basic to these areas will be satisfied.[45]

### b. Fountainhead of Cultures

The plasticity of the drives, as shown in the interplay of value judgments which are given and constructed, makes possible and accounts for the fact of culture with its constants and variables. Culture is the manifest working out of men's basic needs and drives. It is possible because some of his needs and drives are not acquired but are innate.[46]

There are apparent counterparts of men's basic drives in animals concerning life, sex, knowing and deciding, property and association. But these are resemblances only. The similarity between men's basic drives with their relatively high degree of plasticity and an animal's basic drives with their comparatively fixed behavior is superficial. A man's drives are under the control of himself as a knowing and deciding being, that is, of an individual person. A man's knowledge, as we shall see later, is abstract and symbolic. There is no evidence that an animal's knowledge is such. This knowledge makes possible men's accomplishments in science, in art, and in all the areas of human living which make up what we call culture. It is through such abstract and symbolic knowledge, mainly communicated to us by others, that men direct their activities and thereby form various cultures.[47]

In a word, the uniqueness of men's given and constructed values as the font of culture is not explainable by the physiological alone in man. Only the psychological can offer an explanation of why the physiological serves cultural purposes in men and not in animals.[48] To repeat, it is the psychological in man—the knowledge he has and the decisions he makes—which is the source of all culture.[49] The part that value judgments have played and play in the evolving of men in all areas of human living should not be overlooked. "The function of ethicizing is to mediate the progress of human evolution, a progress which now takes place mainly in the social and psychological sphere."[50] "Man's sense of right and wrong has always influenced the course of history, as we call that sector of the evolutionary process that has occurred in our species since written records began."[51]

### 3. The Basic Drives

But which of men's drives are to be taken as basic? Many opinions have been advanced regarding drives, as is well known.

### a. Opinions Regarding Basic Drives

Some have said there is only one basic drive be it regarding sex, economics, will-to-power, or inquiry. Some have claimed there are two drives, feeding and breeding. Some have said there are three drives, self-preservation, reproduction, and gregariousness; or feeding, breeding and inquiring. Others have said there are four fundamental drives, hunger, thirst, sex, and seeking physical well-being; or self-maintenance, self-perpetuation, self-gratification, and religion; or self-preservation, procreation, organized cooperation, and religion; or the visceral, the active, the esthetic, the emotional; or avoidance of injury, maintenance, reproduction, and creativity; or self-preservation, nutrition, sex, and gregariousness. Still others have maintained there are five basic drives which stand in hierarchical relation to each other, namely, the physical, safety, love, esteem, and self-actualization.

Not a few authors distinguish primary or biological drives which men share with animals such as food, sex, and the like, from secondary or acquired drives which are uniquely human such as learned cultural patterns. Some divide the drives into primary and secondary with further distinctions. The primary are physiological such as air, nourishment, water, pain, sex, urination, defacation, cold, heat, fatigue, and psychic such as new experiences, responses from others, frustration, or elementary anger; the secondary are the acquired habit complexes which are ultimately based on the primary drives. Some include among the innate drives individual survival, sex, and post-maternal care; and among the acquired drives, acquisitiveness or possessiveness and affiliation. Others include among the innate drives the organic or visceral, activity and the esthetic drives; while among the acquired drives are gregariousness,

[45] "Even the drives that, biologically considered, are most fundamental are inhibited or redirected under the influence of ideas." Brand Blanshard, *Reason and Goodness* (New York, 1961), p. 354.

[46] Ashley Montagu, *Man: His First Million Years* (Cleveland, 1957), p. 109; Clark Wissler, *Man and Culture* (New York, 1923), p. 265; David Bidney, *Theoretical Anthropology* (New York, 1953), p. 64.

[47] Walter Goldschmidt, *Man's Way* (Cleveland, 1959), pp. 20–21; Robert Lowie, *An Introduction to Cultural Anthropology* (2nd ed., New York, 1940), chaps. XVII–XX; Ashley Montagu, *Man: His First Million Years* (Cleveland, 1957), p. 215; David Bidney, *Theoretical Anthropology* (New York, 1953), p. 125; Melville Herskovits, *Man and His Works* (New York, 1948), p. 38.

[48] Robert Faris, *Social Psychology* (New York, 1952), p. 32.

[49] John Gillin, *The Ways of Men* (New York, 1948), p. 176.

[50] C. H. Waddington, *The Ethical Animal* (London, 1960), p. 59.

[51] Thomas Huxley and Julius Huxley, *Touchstone for Ethics* (New York, 1947), p. 257.

acquisitiveness, and self-submission. Still others, relating drives to values, list as many as twelve drives and fourteen values.

These various listings of drives have not been immune from criticism. Concentration on one single drive, it has been pointed out, fails to provide a foundation for making obvious distinctions that later must be made. Further, it is difficult to see how visceral needs can be put in the same classificatory system with self-preservation, procreation, or inquiry. The homeostatic needs of hunger, thirst, elimination and the like, while more flexible in their functioning than strict instincts, are far less plastic than other drives. Organic needs would seem rather to be of a class of function that is contributive to the over-all need of self-preservation. Besides, to limit the basic drives to homeostatic needs is to fail to take account of other experimentally proven drives that cannot be reduced to the organic. To hold that there are only two drives, feeding and breeding, fails to allow for other needs and drives especially that of intelligent direction. Again, those who limit the basic drives to feeding, breeding, and inquiry, assume that other drives such as distinguishing mine from thine are not innate but are acquired through inquiry. But the cases which are cited as exceptions to the innateness and even universality of these drives, as we shall see when we treat of these drives individually, can hardly be said to be supported by evidence which is scientific in any sense. On the other hand, some of the drives listed, such as esthetic and activity drives, are obviously functions of more basic drives.[52]

### b. Position Taken Regarding Basic Drives

The above listings of drives manifest varying grounds of classification. They emphasize the underlying problem of locating a fundamental, taxonomic principle.

Such a classifying principle can be found in the existence of a being, that is, in the different degrees or levels of a being's existence. Nothing is more fundamental than the existence of a being. On the ground of the levels of existence of men, their basic drives can be functionally classified. Those drives are basic the fulfillment of whose goal-areas satisfies the needs of these levels of existence.

When the above listings of drives are viewed according to men's existence levels, they fall into the following classification within which they can all be contained. There is the drive for the continued existence of the individual through his self-preservation. There is the drive for the continued existence of the human race through sexual union. There are the drives for a distinctively humane existence through the acquiring of knowledge and making decisions, through distinguishing mine from thine in justice, and through associating and communicating with others in social and political union. There is finally the master drive for a level of existence which exceeds the levels of mere living, procreating, possessing, knowing, deciding, and associating. This is the drive for the ever greater actualization and realization of all the capabilities with which a man is endowed.[53]

This master drive for self-realization is the dynamism behind all the other basic drives, and it is the anchor of obligation, as we shall see shortly. Even when the needs of the lower levels of existence appear to be satisfied, the needs of this higher level make themselves felt.

Growth motives . . . lead to self-actualization . . . . [A]ll motivation (of whatever type) partakes of this character.[54]

Behind and sustaining all or virtually all particular human motives there is an *élan to maximize*: not merely to maintain life—though that of course is basic to the enterprise of maximization—but to live it as fully as possible, to develop one's capacities, extend and deepen experience, exercise one's powers in the highest; in a word, to achieve for one's self the greatest possible self-enrichment psychologically speaking.[55]

---

[52] Opinions regarding basic drives: James Feibleman, *The Theory of Human Culture* (New York, 1946), pp. 9, 14; Brand Blanshard, *Reason and Goodness* (New York, 1961), p. 354; Walter Goldschmidt, *Man's Way* (Cleveland, 1959), p. 21; William Sumner and A. G. Keller, *The Science of Society* (4 v., New Haven, 1927) 1: p. 21; Ralph Piddington, *An Introduction to Social Anthropology* (London, 1950), pp. 15, 16; Gardner Murphy, Lois Murphy and Theodore Newcomb, *Experimental Social Psychology* (rev. ed., New York, 1937), *passim;* Robert Faris, *Social Psychology* (New York, 1952), p. 19; Wilfred Trotter, *Instincts of the Herd in Peace and War* (London, 1916), p. 47; Abraham Maslow, "A Theory of Human Evolution," *Psychol. Rev.* **50** (1943): pp. 370–396; Melford Spiro, "Human Nature in Its Psychological Dimensions," *Amer. Anthropologist* **56** (1954): p. 20; John Gillin, *The Ways of Men* (New York, 1948), pp. 227–229; Theodore Newcomb, *Social Psychology* (New York, 1950), pp. 134–136; Otto Klineberg, *Social Psychology* (rev. ed., New York, 1954), pp. 164–165; Henry Murray, "Toward a Classification of Interaction," in: Talcott Parsons and Edward Shils, eds., *Toward a General Theory of Action* (Cambridge, Mass., 1959), p. 463; Graham DuShane, "The Proper Study of Mankind," *Science* **135** (1962): p. 697; Gordon Allport, *Pattern and Growth in Personality* (New York, 1961), p. 213.

[53] For a similar classification of the basic drives see Raymond McCall, "Invested Self-Expression: A Principle of Human Motivation," *Psychol. Rev.* **70** (1963): pp. 289–303. Here the drives, paralleling our own division, are classified as the homeostatic drive for the maintenance of biological equilibrium or homeostasis; the pre-emptive drive in which the biological goal of sex may take precedence over more fundamental drives; the anastatic drives for going beyond the mere existence of the individual and the race to new and more enriching conditions of existence, among which would be knowing, deciding and possessing; the affiliative drive for living with other human beings; and the maximizing drive for self-expression, the drive to realize as fully as possible all one's capabilities. A classification along these same general lines but with some differences is to be found in Abraham Maslow, "A Theory of Human Motivation," *Psychol. Rev.* **50** (1943): pp. 370, 382.

[54] Gordon Allport, *Pattern and Growth in Personality* (New York, 1961), p. 215. Abraham Maslow, "A Theory of Human Motivation," *Psychol. Rev.* **50** (1943): pp. 370, 382.

[55] Raymond McCall, "Invested Self-Expression: A Principle of Human Motivation," *Psychol. Rev.* **70** (1963): p. 302.

Because this master drive is all-encompassing, it has been referred to as the "one major principle of motivation."[56]

The self-actualization or self-development of a man should not be thought of as implying a concentration on self to the exclusion of others. On the contrary, any true self-realization of all of a man's capabilities connotes the inclusion of others and their values. "A man helps himself by helping others" as the adage has it. For, a man is a social person. He has a basic drive to associate with others, as we shall see. Any decision that he makes which is motivated by values which pertain solely to him is a denial of the fact-situation in which he finds himself, namely, a necessary dependence on others. If such self-centered development were to become widespread, it would spell the end both of orderly, cooperative social living and of the individual's own well-being.

It is to be noted, though, that the drive for the total self-development of the individual person is related to one of the drives and its goal more directly than it is related to the others. The drives for self-preservation, sexual union, distinguishing mine from thine and living in society can be satisfied but with a new discontent, restlessness, and desire soon developing. Men still have a drive for further goals which distinctively relate to their power of knowing and creating.[57] Men's capacity for knowing, being the unique power it is, appears to be endless. The more men know, the more they want to know. On this basis it would follow that until men know all things knowable this drive will never be fully satisfied nor will men be completely happy. In this perspective, the goals of the other drives are but means to the goal of knowledge which is not encompassed by any of them. These means-goals have added value in relation to their promotion of the end-goal of knowledge and its value.

This master drive to exist with the greatest possible satisfaction of all desires is another way of saying that we have a master drive for happiness. "Happiness" is but the psychological state we attain when we enjoy the satisfaction of fulfilling our desires. And complete happiness would be the secure and permanent satisfaction of all of our desires. True, happiness is not the direct object of a drive as are the other objects of drives. A man does not strive for happiness in the same manner in which he strives for self-preservation or knowledge. He seeks, rather, the objects which upon attainment will fulfill his desires and thereby render him satisfied and happy.[58] But inasmuch as a man has a drive for the secure fulfillment of all of his capabilities which will result in his total satisfaction, he has a drive for complete happiness.

*i. Normal men.* These basic drives are present in greater or less degree, as we have said, in all normal men. The normal man in this context is the medically normal man. He is the man who functions according to accepted standards of psychology and psychiatry regarding the kind of behavior expected of men in society. The full thrust and meaning of the drives can best be seen in their malfunctioning in men who do not behave according to these criteria. A suspicion of abnormalcy is raised by the man who value-judges that preserving his life is wrong in itself and continually tries to take it; or who value-judges that all sexual activity is in itself evil and continuously tries to prevent it wherever he can; or who constantly value-judges that knowing in itself is wrong and will not even look out of the window, for instance, to learn whether the sun is shining; or who persistently value-judges that making decisions is in itself wrong and will not, for example, decide even to take a step; or who habitually value-judges that it is wrong to make any distinction between what belongs to him and what belongs to others and haphazardly appropriates whatever he comes into contact with; or who value-judges that associating with others is in itself wrong and resolutely shuns the company of others. Such actions would be indications of at least incipient psychosis. They are not the behavior of a "normal" man and the standard is based on the natural functioning of men's basic drives.[59]

It is sometimes said that in normal men the basic drives are not constant and therefore are not an invariant source of necessary values. This can mean that men, as they are now constituted, have no fixed drives but only variable desires. Or it can mean that, although they have fixed drives at the present time, men may eventually evolve into beings which have other drives or no drives at all.

---

[56] Raymond McCall, "Invested Self-Expression: A Principle of Human Motivation," *Psychol. Rev.* **70** (1963): p. 302. See also Harold Overstreet, "The Growth Imperative," in Salo Baron, Ernest Nagel and Koppel Pinson, eds., *Freedom and Reason* (Glencoe, 1951), *passim;* and Hadley Cantril, *The "Why" of Man's Experience* (New York, 1950), *passim.*

[57] James Feibleman, *The Theory of Human Culture* (New York, 1946), p. 14.

[58] "There are many difficulties with the concept of happiness as motive. Most serious of all is the simple fact that one cannot aim directly at the achievement of happiness. It is therefore not a concrete motive. . . . Happiness is at best a by-product of otherwise-motivated activity. One who aims at happiness has no aim at all." Gordon Allport, *Pattern and Growth in Personality* (New York, 1961), p. 200.

[59] As has been appositely pointed out concerning a man who would have the habit of pushing pins into other people, who was insensitive to the suffering of others' pain, and who value-judges that it was good to do such pin-pushing: the "recognition of some values—however general and however few—enter into the normal definition of what constitutes a sane human being. . . . [B]eings totally lacking such ends can scarcely be described as human; still less as rational. In this sense, then, pursuit of or failure to pursue, certain ends can be regarded as evidence of—and in extreme cases part of the definition of—irrationality." Isaiah Berlin, "Rationality of Value Judgments," *Nomos* **7** (1964): p. 22.

Men are said, for instance, not to desire to preserve their lives because they have a permanent drive to do so. They desire to survive merely because they desire to survive.[60] Such statements, however, run directly counter to accepted scientific opinion. They ignore certain observable facts: the continuity of the drive in men to survive with the drive in other species of living beings to survive, the biochemical and physiological basis of this drive, and the universality of this drive among all individual men. There are basic drives therefore, and the drive for self-preservation is one of them, which are fixed and "absolutely dependable."[61] They are part of our lives. "[W]e must accept the importance of drives as motivating factors throughout life . . . . Although drives cannot account for all later motivation, they are with us all our life."[62] In the face of such evidence, it seems purely gratuitous to assert that men have no basic drives which are stable and permanent.

If men have no fixed drive for self-preservation, it should be further noted, an even greater problem arises. How explain why all normal men do actually and universally desire survival if survival is not the object of a basic drive? Why do all men, regardless of their philosophy or theology of life, have a desire to preserve their lives even though they may eventually decide to take their lives? It could be maintained, of course, that on purely intellectual grounds and unrelated to any fixed drive most men consider that the advantages to be gained by preserving their lives are greater than the values to be gained by taking their lives. But, while this explanation may hold for certain groups of men, it would hardly be valid for all men taken indiscriminately as the whole human race. Such universality demands an explanation more radical than chance unanimity of intellectual conviction.

To maintain that at some future time the basic drives may change and not remain an invariant source of necessary values, is not relevant here and now. The problem concerning men's basic drives concerns men as they are at the present time. This is the man psychology analyses, anthropology investigates, and law directs. Research attempts to know the facts about men as they now are. Science can inquire into only what exists. In the event that men's basic drives would change, our root problem would change. There would no longer be a question of values which relate to men as they are now. In this new situation, the values pertinent to this new being would be different from the values which now refer to men. If and when such a new entity came into existence, a new book would have to be written about the values which would control the life and laws of this new entity.

*ii. Innate—acquired.* There is general agreement that the drives for self-preservation, sexual union, and knowledge and decision are innate and not acquired. There is some disagreement whether the drives to distinguish mine from thine and to associate in society are innate or acquired. Some regard them as acquired. But the evidence for holding them to be acquired is by no means beyond question, and in the absence of solid data to the contrary the time-tested conviction will be followed here that these drives as well as the others are innate. As a matter of fact, however, it is immaterial to our general purpose in this book whether these last two drives are innate or acquired. Even though only the drives for self-preservation, sexual union, and acquiring knowledge and making decisions were the only innate basic drives, this would be sufficient grounds for establishing that there are some basic values which are given and which necessarily must be in all law. Whether the drives for distinguishing mine from thine and for associating with others are innate or acquired, they are found along with the other basic drives in all men in all societies. They are in this sense basic. Besides, the gap sometimes depicted between the innate and the acquired is seen as substantially narrowed when it is recognized that whatever is acquired is acquired because of a disposition to acquire which is innate.[63]

*iii. Inclusiveness.* The fact that the basic drives are separately listed with differing area-goals should not be interpreted as meaning that they and their goals are of equal rank or that they function in isolation from one another. One drive may be the channel through which several other drives express themselves. The drive for sexual union may operate together with the drive to know. Under the direction of reason, one drive may be subordinated to another. The drive for self-preservation may be dominated by the drive for knowledge. Also, the drives may operate with varying degrees of conscious motivation. The drive for self-preservation may accomplish its goal with less attention than the drive for knowledge.[64]

## II. OBLIGATION AND RIGHTS FROM BASIC VALUES

The importance of the basic values given by men's basic drives is further shown by the axial position they have in relation to obligation and our personal rights.

60 "[W]e can, in referring to survival discard, as too metaphysical for modern minds, the notion that this is something antecedently fixed which men necessarily desire because it is their proper goal or end. Instead we may hold it to be a mere contingent fact which could be otherwise, that in general men do desire to live and that we may mean nothing more by calling survival a human goal or end than that men do desire it." Herbert L. A. Hart, *The Concept of Law* (Oxford, 1961), pp. 187–188.

61 Otto Klineberg, *Social Psychology* (rev. ed., New York, 1954), pp. 69, 164.

62 Gordon Allport, *Pattern and Growth in Personality* (New York, 1961), pp. 90–91.

63 David Bidney, *Theoretical Anthropology* (New York, 1953), p. 64.

64 See Abraham Maslow, *Motivation and Personality* (New York, 1954), p. 70.

This interrelationship will be implicit in our later treatment of the patterns of values which are observable in the practical areas of law.

### A. OBLIGATION

Obligation has the general connotation of being bound to do something or of having the duty to do it. Obligation means that a person ought to do something. We oftimes say that a person has to do something, must do it, or should do it. But obligation, duty, and ought have a more precise meaning than these other expressions, as we shall see. Obligation does not carry the connotation of being constrained to do something, of being compelled or coerced or forced to do it. Obligation is of a different nature and rests on a different foundation than constraint, compulsion, coercion or physical power.

### 1. Obligation from Value-Relation of Means to End

Obligation functions only within a means-end context of values. It comes into play when there is question of my obtaining some valued end through the employment of a valued means which will accomplish this end. If I desire to live, I am obliged to decide to eat as a means necessary for living. I am necessitated to choose this means in order to accomplish this end. The object which I desire must be attainable, otherwise it cannot inspire action regarding means necessary for the end. The unattainable object remains an ideal which is incapable of initiating any means-end action, as has been pointed out.

Obligation, then, is a particular kind of necessity or determination. It is not the type of necessity dictated by the make-up of a thing, such as a man being determined to having skin more penetrable than steel by the very fact that he is a man and not processed iron. Nor is it the kind of determination that comes from force and compulsion which excludes the exercise of free-determination. A man is necessitated to remain face down on the ground when someone stronger than he holds him there. Obligation, rather, is the type of necessity which derives from the supposition of a valued end which is practically attainable and the relation of valued means to the attaining of this end. Obligation in this sense leaves the exercise of self-determination free.

### 2. Absolute and Relative Necessity in Value-Relations

The manner in which means are value-related to ends varies. Some means are related absolutely. This is the case in the example we have just used regarding eating and living. Further, this is the relation of drive-fulfillers to drive-fulfillment in general. This value-relation specifically, however, is not absolute but relative. The plasticity of the basic drives being what

it is, we have a choice of the specific foods with which we will sustain our lives. I am not absolutely necessitated to eat parsnips. This difference in the manner in which means can be related to ends runs the entire range of human activities. In law, it is often the subject of debate by legislatures whether certain means are necessary, absolutely or relatively, for the common welfare. For this reason they are "deliberative bodies." If the means under deliberation are not necessary in some sense, they do not belong in the content of law, as we shall see later.

### 3. Hypothetical and Categorical Value-Relations

When obligation is seen as deriving from the value-relation of means to end, the question arises as to whether obligation is not in the last analysis merely hypothetical. I am obligated to eat, *if* I desire to live. On the supposition that I do not desire to live, I have no obligation to eat. Unless obligation is made fast to an end which is fixed and about which I have no choice, I am "obliged" only by what I desire. The question of whether there is anything I cannot help but desire is therefore controlling in regard to obligation.

### a. Obligation from Master Drive

It is the master drive all men have for their own self-realization or happiness which is the anchor that makes all obligation ultimately categorical. For, as noted above, the motivation of all the basic drives is implicitly aimed at the total self-development of the individual person. I have no choice about having this drive or about its goal. It is part of me. When I perceive, again however vaguely, that a certain means is necessary for my self-development, I am obliged categorically to pursue it. The end of my drive for self-preservation, to remain in existence, is itself a means to the end of my self-realization. Unless I continue to live, I can never realize all of my potentialities. Hence, I am obliged to eat, if I desire to live and I am obliged to live because living is a means to my self-development and happiness about which I have no choice.

It is in the master drive for self-realization, then, that is contained the root of obligation. For in recognizing however vaguely and without a reasoning process that I ineluctably desire to attain my greatest development and happiness, I implicitly judge that I ought to use whatever means are necessary for the attainment of this end. This is every man's first contact with the necessity of using means for an end. It is his first acquaintance with obligation. In the "is" of his master drive is contained the seed of "ought." Implied here also, however inchoately, is the judgment that the means which lead to this end are different from those which do not. A difference is recognized, in other words, between what we call, in short-hand fashion, right and wrong means. Implicit here too is the judgment, formed in the same rudimentary manner, that the norm of distinguishing right from wrong means is whether they lead to the end. Inherent in obligation are norms of telling right from wrong means.

In a word, my master value judgment that my self-development, the object of my master drive, is good and ought to be sought, is accompanied by two other value judgments. One is that it is good to distinguish right from wrong. The other is that it is good to have norms according to which this difference can be told.

If these judgments are formed by all men, we should expect to find evidence of them. The "inner urge" which all of us experience that we ought to do what is right is a manifestation of the dynamism of these judgments. Such an encounter with "ought" inevitably follows from our "is." [65] Obligation is recognized early in the lives of children. Research has shown that, without any external pressure being applied by adults, awareness of obligation progresses through phases as the child grows older. A child is admonished by his parents not to tell a lie. He feels obliged not to lie first because of respect for his parents. Soon, however, the child begins to think about what a lie is. He then feels he is obliged not to lie because of what a lie is in itself. Upon more reflection, finally, the child sees that truthfulness is necessary if he is to be believed by the other children. He now feels obliged not to lie because he sees that truthfulness is a means necessary for gaining the respect of the other children. [66]

These given judgments concerning obligation and values, right and wrong, are recognizable in all normal men. "[N]ormal human beings have a 'moral sense' or feeling of ethical obligation, of values in terms of right and wrong." [67] Preliterates as well as literates, as we shall see later, give evidence of forming these judgments.

### b. "Ought" from Demands of "Is"

To see obligation as arising from the value-relation of the means which will lead to the end of the master drive, is not to derive "ought" from "is" or value from fact. It is rather to recognize that "ought" arises from what is demanded by an "is" situation, that value comes from what is required by a fact condition. The "is" of the master drive for its satisfaction, or of any drive for that matter, is a demand for some object not yet possessed which will bring about its satisfaction. This object is needed for the fulfillment of the drive and to this extent is needed for the completion of the whole

person who has the drive. This is the human condition —a state of incompleteness and need, with continuous attempts to bring about greater fulfillment of need and greater completeness. The "is" condition of a drive is one of incompleteness and of needing an object which will complete it to some degree. The necessary relation between the completing object as means and the state of completion as end is the root of "ought." Psychology and experience, not logic as we said before, proffer the key to the solution of the so-called problem of "is" and "ought," of fact and value. [68]

### B. RIGHTS

Men's fundamental personal rights are also related to men's basic drives and the valued actions these drives demand. These basic rights are grounded on the unique relation of title which exists between the demanded actions and my self, and they are made viable by others fulfilling their obligation to respect these unique relations of title. My personal rights may or may not be regulated by law depending on whether they do or do not have a proximate relation to the common welfare of all the people.

Preliminary to a consideration of the unique relations of title established by the drives is a recognition of the unique relation of title existing between my body and my self. I am aware that this body is uniquely related to me and not to someone else. Because of this unique relation I conceive of this body as "mine" and the bodies of others as "thine." Such a concept is one of the earliest workings of the drive to distinguish mine from thine. [69] Underlying the recognition that this body as "mine," is the distinction I naturally make between "body" and "self." [70] In this context, the "self" can be

[65] Arnold Brecht, *Political Theory* (Princeton, 1959), p. 367; "The Myth of Is and Ought," *Harvard Law Rev.* **54** (1941): p. 811.

[66] See Jean Piaget, *The Moral Judgment of the Child,* trans. by Marjorie Gabain (Glencoe, 1948), pp. 1–2, 193–194.

[67] George Simpson, "Naturalistic Ethics and the Social Sciences," *Amer. Psychologist* **21** (1966): p. 28.

[68] "Such a link, as we know, is never a logical necessity, nor is its acceptance justified by operations of a merely logical nature. Breakable or not, any link between Is and Ought can be only factual, not logical. The intertwining fact in this case is that apparently all human beings do feel and think that way, that they are unable to feel and think otherwise, even if they want to, or to imagine, concretely and realistically, that they could feel and think otherwise." Arnold Brecht, *Political Theory* (Princeton, 1959), p. 415.

[69] "My own body and what ministers to its needs are thus the primitive object, instinctively determined, of my egoistic interests. Other objects may become interesting derivatively, through association with any of these things, either as means or as habitual concomitants; and so, in a thousand ways, the primitive sphere of the egoistic emotions may enlarge and change its boundaries. This sort of interest is really the meaning of the word *mine*. Whatever has it, is, *eo ipso*, a part of me." William James, *The Principles of Psychology* (2 v., New York, 1890) **1**: pp. 319, 324.

[70] "Important as the bodily sense is, it is not the whole of one's self. Those who have suffered extreme torture report that while feeling pain, they also feel a detachment. 'This,' they say, 'is happening to my body, not to me.' I shall come through this somehow, and continue to be the same self I have always been. And so the sense of self depends on more than the bodily me." Gordon Allport, *Pattern and Growth in Personality* (New York, 1961), p. 114.

taken as the same as the "ego."[71] It is because of this unique relation between this body and my self, however vaguely perceived, that I have grounds for claiming it as "mine."[72]

Another example of the rudimentary recognition of unique relations of title is had between those who generate and those who are generated. The mother considers the child to whom she has given birth as "mine." The father looks on this son as "mine." Together they say the son is "theirs." Conversely, the child eventually looks on this man and woman as "my" father and mother. This recognition of the unique relationship of "mineness" is carried on down the line of blood and legal relationships. I speak of "my" brothers and sisters, uncles and aunts, cousins and in-laws because I consider them to be in some unique sense related to me.

### 1. *The Basis of Rights*

The unique relations of title with which we are here concerned, however, are not those pertaining to things such as bodies. They are, rather, the relations of title which relate to actions such as self-preservation, sexual union, and other objects of the basic drives.

#### a. *Given Relations of Title*

My drive to preserve my life, for instance, establishes a unique relation between the actions which will lead to this end and myself. These actions relate to me and to no one else. I have a unique relation of title to them which no one else has. This title is given to me. These actions are "mine" in the doing and "mine" when done. My recognition of their value motivates me and no one else. Because of the necessity of these actions for my self-preservation, I alone am obliged to perform them. Others are obliged to respect this unique relation of title which I have to these actions at the price of all of us being otherwise reduced to a state of animal struggle, a point which we will discuss in a moment. This respect is constructed by others.

The source of my personal rights, therefore, lies in the unique relation of title which my basic drives establish between what they demand and myself. This is the source of my personal rights to self-preservation and to sexual union, to knowing and deciding, to distinguishing mine from thine, and to associating with others socially and politically. Consequently, I have a claim on others to be allowed to direct myself, with relative freedom, in the fulfillment of the demands of my basic drives for these objects. This authority which I have over myself is the basis of any delegation I may later make of it in political living.

#### b. *Constructed Relations of Title*

Besides the unique relations of title which are given by my elementary drives, other unique relations are constructed by me. This is done both by my creative actions and by my enterprising activities.

I can create intangibles. On my own I can create ideas. These ideas may take many forms. They may be ideas for a poem, for a drama, for a television program, for building a supersonic aircraft and so on indefinitely.[73] These ideas may not yet be externalized. But I have created them in my mind and, provided they are truly created by me, they are uniquely related to me and to no one else. I therefore have a title to them. They are "mine."

Or I can create tangibles. I may not only create an idea but I may create its external expression. I may create an idea of what I want a figurine to look like which I intend to carve out of a piece of ivory which is already "mine." The idea of the form it will take is "mine." When I externalize this idea by patterning the figurine after it, a unique relation of title is established between the entire product and my self and it is "mine." If the ivory is not mine but belongs to someone else, the "mine" of the eventual product is obviously shared. But my title to a share is grounded principally on the fact that it is my idea which is part of the figurine.

If neither the pattern idea nor the material elaborated are "mine," there is still a part of me in the product which is more basic than the time and energy I expend in my labor on the figurine. Inasmuch as no animal could make the contribution to the figurine which I am making, there is something of human ideas in the process of production. There is still something of my ideas, human ideas, guiding the productive processes which go into the making of the figurine. In the event that I waive my claims to what is "mine" in the product for a flat hourly wage rate, as regularly occurs, my title to the wages remains the same. It is principally the ideas, at some level, which were "mine" and which I have contributed to the end product. In a word, the wage contract is based on my unique relation of title to a part of the product.

My labor, in other words, is a process by which I extend part of myself, my ideas, to what I produce. This extension of self to the object I make is an ex-

---

[71] "The term *self* is used in a great many ways by a great many theorists. Often the term *ego* is employed instead. And since no clear and consistent distinction has been made between *ego* and *self,* we shall need to treat them as equivalent." Gordon Allport, *Pattern and Growth in Personality* (New York, 1961), p. 111. See Theodore Sarbin, "Preface to Psychological Analysis of the Self," *Psychological Rev.* 59 (1952) : p. 21.

[72] Attention has been called to an example which shows the importance of this unique relation between an object and the self. When saliva is in my mouth, I consider it part of me and call it "mine." But when I expectorate and the saliva is on the ground in front of me, I am much less inclined to look upon it as part of me and "mine." See Gordon Allport, *Pattern and Growth in Personality* (New York, 1961), p. 114.

[73] "A person's fantasies, while private, and supposedly subjective, may be treated as an object. The person, by virtue of his cognitive organization, may identify and evaluate his fantasy reactions in the same way that he identifies and evaluates external objects." Theodore Sarbin, "Preface to Psychological Analysis of the Self," *Psychological Rev.* 59 (1952) : p. 18.

tension of the "mineness" I have over myself.[74] Such an extension can result in near identification. We have a tendency to look upon what we have produced as almost a part of ourselves.[75] This is exemplified in the artisan's view of his finished product. He can accurately say that he stamps his product with his own ideas, with his own person.[76] The clearness of this stamp will be in proportion to the singularity of the contribution made. This singularity diminishes in the range from hand-crafted to machine-made.[77]

The enterprising actions by which I construct unique relations of title are discovery and occupation of something to which no one has a relation of title, and exchange agreements such as contracts, gifts, and inheritance.[78] Of these, contract is the most frequent. Occupation does not presuppose previous relations of title to the thing involved. Contracts, gifts and inheritance obviously do presuppose such a relation.

To be noted is the fact that the relations of title which are established by my creative actions are intrinsic to the thing created. My ideas are embodied in it. The relations of title set up by my enterprising actions, however, are extrinsic to me and the thing to which I acquire title. There is no part of me either in the thing I find and occupy, in what I contract for, or in what I acquire by gift or inheritance. Worth nothing, too, is the fact that the titles created by labor are of a more fundamental economic nature than those caused by contract. The laborer creates objects of value and in doing so creates unique relations of title to them. Those who contract for goods or services, such as psychiatrists and law professors, do not create value in this fundamental sense. They merely exchange relations of title to things already pre-existing.

## 2. *The Viability of Rights*

It is because of the unique relation of title which I have to the objects of my drives that I can expect others to allow me to do what is required to fulfill them. I can lay claim on others to permit me to use whatever means are needed, for instance, in preserving my life. Unless I am allowed the freedom to perform the actions I judge necessary for continuing my life, my entire psychological processes of drive, valuation, motivation, and obligation are nullified and rendered meaningless. I cannot live as a human being. If such a condition should become general, men would be reduced to living not according to the demands of rational life but according to the exigencies of animal existence.

My claims are centered, then, in the obligation of others towards me. Depending on whether others fulfill their obligation to respect my relations of title, my claims and expectations have viability. My claims or expectations take on meaning from what others are willing to do towards me. Either others will do their duty towards me regarding my relations of title and my claims will therefore be viable, or I will have to bring physical power to bear on these others and force them to respect my relations of title if I am able to do so.[79] Either right will be done by them or force will be used by me. Either what is "mine" will be respected humanely, or it will be protected animally.[80]

Because respect for my relations of title is due to me by others for the reasons given, their obligation is one

[74] "[T]he proprietary sense is a sort of extension of the sense of ego or selfhood: the ego expands beyond the limits of its mental domain to the ownership of the mind's body and beyond it to those things which are owned by the individual. This is best illustrated by the ease and universality with which ownership is claimed in things produced by one's hands, and only a little less markedly, to the things worn or used by a person. A thing that owes its existence to the labour of our hands sucks in the personality of its maker during the very process of its becoming. When it is done it is part of you, its maker." Alexander Goldenweiser, *Anthropology* (New York, 1937), p. 50.

[75] "It is clear that between what a man calls *me* and what he simply calls *mine,* the line is difficult to draw. We feel and act about certain things that are ours very much as we feel and act about ourselves. Our fame, our children, the work of our hands, may be as dear to us as our bodies are, and arouse the same feelings and the same acts of reprisal if attacked." William James, *The Principles of Psychology* (2 v., New York, 1890) 1: p. 291.

[76] "In making the object my own, I stamped it with the mark of my own person; whoever attacks it attacks me; the blow struck it, strikes me, for I am present in it. Property is but the periphery of my person extended to things." Rudolph Von Jhering, *The Struggle for Law,* trans. by John Lalor (Chicago, 1879), p. 55.

[77] The idea of a relation of title established between the laborer and his product as here delineated should be carefully distinguished from the "labor theory of value" which was prevalent during the eighteenth century. According to this notion, which was somewhat promoted by Marx, the laborer had a right to the whole product of his labor. This position was rightly criticized not for maintaining that there is an intrinsic relation between the product of labor and the laborer but for not taking into account certain economic factors. Among these factors are demand and cost of production as dependent not only on quantity of time as Marx has asserted but also on quality of labor and reserves necessary to aid labor. See Anton Menger, *The Right to the Whole Produce of Labor,* (London, 1899), pp. 15–16; and Alfred Marshall, *Principles of Economics* (2 v., 9th ed., London, 1961) 2: pp. 420–421.

[78] Prescription or adverse possession and accession are other ways of establishing relations of title to things. They will, however, not be of relevance here.

[79] "The fact that in all human societies individuals are secured against the necessity of being constantly on the alert to defend such objects from others by physical force alone is one of the prime contributions of the institution of property to a *human* social order and the security of the individual. A. Irving Hallowell, "The Nature and Function of Property as a Social Institution," *Jour. Legal and Political Sociology* 1 (1943): p. 138.

[80] "[W]e cannot properly speak of rights, obligations, privileges, etc., among animals. . . . [A]n individual animal, or group of animals, must be prepared to meet any threat to food, nest or territory by the exertion of physical force. A dog will fight any other dog who tries to take his bone. No other remedy is possible, for this is the inevitable result in circumstances where there is no institutionalization of claims to objects of value." A. Irving Hallowell, "The Nature and Function of Property as a Social Institution," *Jour. Legal and Political Sociology* 1 (1943): p. 137.

of justice. For justice is the habit of will which disposes us to give to a man what is due to him.[81] Further, because justice is the concern of man-made law, the obligation which others have of showing me respect for my relations of title is incorporated into all legal systems. The law directs others to show this respect to me and when they fail to do so, and only after they fail to do so, the law brings to bear physical force and punishment. In sum, my claims are backed by law inasmuch as law demands that others fulfill their obligation in justice to respect my relations of title. When others fail to do this, the law takes forceful action.

"Right" is, therefore, not simple but complex in its connotations. It is a triadic concept, as has been frequently pointed out. It supposes myself and my drives, an object, and other persons. It contains the unique relations which exist between an object and myself, as well as the relations of justice maintained by others between themselves and me concerning these unique relations. "Right," then, is actually the web of relations which exist between persons regarding some object. Implied are my title, others' obligation to respect it, and my claim on them to do so.

### 3. *Property*

From the analysis we have just made of right, a workable concept of "property" emerges. Seen in this perspective, "property" is not merely an ethnocentric expression used to describe what is only one of many relational situations in which men find themselves *vis-à-vis* objects.[82] "Property" is much more than this. It is basically the inevitable relations which result from the fact that one human being living among other human beings establishes titles to things.

The word "property" is sometimes used to denote the object with regard to which relations exist between persons, as when it is said that this figurine is my "property." This is a natural usage since the word "property" expresses what is "proper" to me.[83] But this dyadic concept of "property" is much too simple and it has been the cause of much ambiguity and confusion.[84] "Property," rather, refers to the relations which exist between an object, myself and other persons, as does "right," but with the added connotation of at least relative exclusiveness of use and disposal of what is "mine." For this reason, it has long since been suggested that the term "property" not be used to refer to objects alone.[85] It should be used to refer to objects and relations. It is this meaning of the word "property" which is employed in our present man-made law of property.[86]

The possession of what is "mine" is not of itself ownership. Added to possession must be at least relatively exclusive use and disposal of what is "mine" if I am to have ownership. Only then will what is "mine" be my own. This exclusive use and disposal is brought about not by me but by others fulfilling their obligation to respect my unique relations of title. It is others doing their duty, and not myself using force, which gives me such exclusiveness.[87] In this manner, what is "mine" is made my "own," it is made "proper" to me, it is made my "property." "Property," then, is a social institution. It is what it is because of the relations persons living in society establish between themselves regarding objects.[88] We shall see this exemplified later among preliterates.

"Property" is not coextensive with "mine." "Mine" refers both to things which are impersonal and to human beings who are personal. "Property," on the other hand, can properly refer only to impersonal objects. Thus, a man can appropriately refer to his automobile as "mine" and to his wife as "mine." But, while he

---

[81] See Justinian, "De Justitia et Jure," *Digest*, Book I, chap. 1, Theodore Mommsen and Paul Krueger, eds., *Corpus Juris Civilis* (3 v., 17th ed., Berlin, 1963) 1: p. 1.

[82] Paul Bohannon, *Social Anthropology* (New York, 1963), p. 366.

[83] From the Latin word "proprium" meaning what is one's own or what is special or peculiar to one.

[84] "It seems likely that the oversimplified conceptualization of the property relation in dyadic rather than triadic terms, is at the root of the essential ambiguity which has characterized the term property in common speech and sometimes in law. For property is a term commonly applied to both *objects* that are said to be owned as well as the *rights* exercised over such subjects. While this ambiguity has been noted for decades and is assumed to be clearly understood in legal parlance, at the same time it has repeatedly called for comment down to the present day." A. Irving Hallowell, "The Nature and Function of Property as a Social Institution," *Jour. Legal and Political Sociology* 1 (1943): p. 120.

[85] "[I]t would seem from the point of view of both legal and economic analysis that the use of the term property to denote external objects is misleading and should be abandoned." Huntington Cairns, *Law and the Social Sciences* (New York, 1935), p. 59.

[86] "The word 'property' is used sometimes to denote the thing with respect to which legal relations between persons exist and sometimes to denote the legal relations. The former of these two usages is illustrated in the expressions 'the property abuts on the highway' and 'the property was destroyed by fire.' This usage does not occur in this Restatement. When it is desired to indicate the thing with regard to which legal relations exist, it will be referred to either specifically as 'the land,' 'the automobile,' 'the share of stock,' or generically, as 'the subject matter of property' or 'the thing'. . . . The word 'property' is used in this Restatement to denote legal relations between persons with respect to a thing." American Law Institute ed., *Restatement of the Law of Property* (5 v., St. Paul, 1936) 1: p. 3.

[87] "[A]lthough an individual may be the possessor of some valued object, some *res nullius* that he has picked up, occupied, or created, that object does not become property until the members of the society at large agree, tacitly or explicitly, to bestow the property attribute upon the object by regulating their behavior with respect to it in a self-limiting manner." E. Adamson Hoebel, "Anthropology of Inheritance," *Social Meaning of Legal Concepts* 1 (1948): p. 9.

[88] "The genuine nature of property is found in its qualities as a social institution. Property in its full sense is a web of social relations with respect to the utilization of some object (material or nonmaterial) to which a person or group is tacitly or explicitly recognized to hold quasi-exclusive and limiting connections to that object." E. Adamson Hoebel, *Man in the Primitive World* (New York, 1949), p. 329.

could properly refer to his automobile also as his "property," he could not fittingly refer to his wife as his "property." The reason is that "property" connotes, as just indicated, relatively exclusive use and disposal of what is owned. In any free society, human beings, who are persons, cannot be used and disposed of as can impersonal objects. Persons have a unique dignity which comes from their being endowed with powers of knowing and deciding. When persons are used and disposed of as impersonal objects conditions of human slavery prevail. We shall allude to this later in our discussion of whether wives are considered among some preliterates to be chattels.

Among animals, birds and fish it is sometimes said that there is "ownership" and "property." Cited as evidence are the well-known examples of fish, birds and animals living within certain areas which they defend as their "property" against intruders. Cited also are examples relating to the gathering and storing of provisions.[89] If these facts are approached with a dyadic notion of "property" in mind, they can easily be misconstrued as connoting animal "property." The nest appears to be the "property" of the bird who built it. But when these facts are interpreted according to a triadic concept of "property" such as outlined above, it becomes clear that among animals, birds and fish there is no "property." For if whatever viable meaning "property" has derives from others fulfilling their obligation in justice to respect my unique relation of title to a thing, there is no "property" among animals, birds or fish. They give no evidence of recognizing relations of title to things nor of an obligation in justice to respect such relations.[90] On the contrary, whatever can be called respect for the territory or provisions of others among them, is actually avoidance in the face of possible violent and forceful reaction.

#### 4. *Rights and the Content of Law*

The content of law is concerned supposedly with the rights of citizens and their protection. But, as we have seen, my right which the law protects actually refers to others' obligations. When I say "I have a right to do this and the law protects it" what I am factually saying is that "You have an obligation to allow me to do this and the law sees to it that you do so." What is controlling is not civil rights but civil obligations. Because obligation arises from means-end value relationships which derive in the first place from the basic drives, the content of law is a focal point for the converging of the implications of drives, values, obligations and rights. The content of law represents the basic drives expressing themselves practically in the context of everyday life.

Our analyses of drives, values, obligations, rights, and property will be supposed and their implications will be seen when we examine the content of the unwritten law of preliterates as recorded in anthropological reports. There will be seen preliterates' emphasis on obligation instead of on rights, their views on rights in sexual matters, their conceptions of property, their attitude towards wives being chattels, and their many other value judgments which make up the content of unwritten custom law.

### CHAPTER 2

### LAWS

Laws are concerned with the values, obligations and rights of the people which relate to their common needs. These form the content of law and give to law its overall purposes.

#### I. THE CONCEPT OF LAW

Law is an instrument for directing the people in those things which pertain to the fulfillment of needs common to them.[1] In all known societies of men there are regulations which guide the members towards this common goal. A model of law, to be functional, must have relevance to such data. It must be applicable to all known systems of regulated order and must be able to interpret these regulations, written and unwritten, in reference to other systems throughout the world.

##### A. LAW IS A DIRECTIVE JUDGMENT

All known societies of men have regulations. Some of these regulations regard values which relate to the members' individual welfare and are not laws. Other regulations are concerned with values which pertain to the member's common welfare and are laws. Law's province, to repeat, is the values which are common to all the members of a society.[2]

Law is what its regulations are. Attempts to explain what law is, are attempts to explain what its regulations are. These endeavors have been numerous, as is well known.[3] A main observation concerning law is that wherever its regulations are considered by the people to

[89] Franz Boas, *The Mind of Primitive Man* (rev. ed., New York, 1938), p. 162.

[90] A. Irving Hallowell, "The Nature and Function of Property as a Social Institution," *Jour. Legal and Political Sociology* 1 (1943): p. 136.

[1] "The law of a people is the instrument by which its orderly activity is maintained and protected." Arthur Diamond, *The Evolution of Law and Order* (London, 1951), p. 303.

[2] "[L]aw comprises all those rules of conduct which regulate the behaviour of individuals and communities, and which by maintaining the equilibrium of society are necessary for its continuance as a corporate whole." Jack Driberg, "Primitive Law in East Africa," *Africa* 1 (1928): p. 65.

[3] On the various meanings given to law see, Thomas Davitt, *The Elements of Law* (Boston, 1959), pp. 8–10; T. Olawale Elias, *The Nature of African Customary Law* (Manchester, 1956), pp. 41–63; Bronislaw Malinowski, "A New Instrument for the Interpretation of Law—Especially Primitive," *Yale Law Jour.* 51 (1942): pp. 1237–1254; E. Adamson Hoebel, "Primitive Law and Modern," *Trans. New York Acad. Sci.* 5 (1942): pp. 33–35.

be obligatory, these regulations are concerned with the needs of the people.[4] When regulations are not concerned with the needs of the people, there is unrest, resistance, rebellion, and revolution. It is this relation between the demands of the regulations and the common needs to be fulfilled which is the controlling fact of the law.[5]

### 1. *Directive versus Command*

Law is primarily a pointing out or a declaring of what has been judged to be necessary for the common good of the people. The use of any kind of force or pressure as a threat or punishment to deviators is secondary. The model of law which best accounts for these facts presents law as a directive judgment of those with authority regarding means necessary for the common welfare of the people.[6] This concept of law is applicable to all law, written or unwritten. Municipal, international and preliterate regulations are seen in the light of this model to have the essential features of law.

There is a radical difference between this model of law which explains law's regulations as directive judgments and other models which explain them in other ways, such as commands, which we will examine later. Directive judgments are impersonal communications of what is objectively needed for the common welfare of the people.[7] This is oft-times measurable as in the case of pure food and drug regulations. Commands are personal orders regarding what is subjectively desired by the superior which may or may not be for the good of the people. Such were the commands of the Nazis ordering the extermination of the Jews. The directive judgment declares that "It is wrong to do this" and derives its authority from the objective necessity of what is directed for the common good. The command says "Do this" and it gets its authority either from the personality of the one commanding or from the physical power he has at his disposal.[8]

### 2. *Values Common to All the People*

The regulations which are law should be concerned only with the values which relate proximately to the common needs. The values which pertain first and foremost to their individual needs and refer only remotely to common needs should not become part of the content of law.

The difference between values which are common to the people and the values which are proper to them turns on the communicability of the valued objects. Common values such as protection, order, security, and peace are objects which are communicable to all the members of a society and they all can participate in them. These include the law itself, courts, police and other parts of the legal system. Comprised here also are those actions which relate directly to the common welfare such as murder, adultery, robbery, arson ("crimes"), and those which pertain to the common welfare indirectly such as breaches of contract and various kinds of personal injury ("torts").

Proper values which foster the individual welfare of the members of a society should not become part of the content of law. They are personal and individualistic and are not communicable. Such are my food, drink, mate, knowledge, occupation, religion, and convictions. These pertain to common needs only remotely.

### 3. *Directive Judging*

The directive judgments which are law are made by those who have the authority to do so. For, authority is the right to direct means necessary for an end.

#### a. *The People Themselves*

Those who have the fundamental right to direct the people are the people themselves. As we saw above, the obligation is imposed on me to attain my end of self-realization. Others have the obligation on their part to allow me to direct myself freely in the quest of this end. This is my claim to self-direction. This is my authority for governing myself.

Instances of the people governing themselves are well known. The New England town meeting and the

---

[4] Law is "any rule of human conduct which is recognized as being obligatory." Arthur Goodhart, "The Importance of a Definition of Law," *Jour. African Admin.* 3 (1951): p. 109. "The law of a given community is the body of rules which are recognized as being obligatory." Elias, *The Nature of African Customary Law* (Manchester, 1956), p. 55. One of the oldest ways of describing law is in terms of obligation. "Law is a rule and measure of acts whereby man is induced to act or restrained from acting. For law [*lex*] is derived from ligate [*ligare*], because it binds to act." Thomas Aquinas, *Summa Theologiae*, Part 1–2, Question 90, Article 1 (Ottawa ed., Ottawa, 1941), p. 1270. My translation.

[5] "[T]he essence of law is that it develops within society of its own vitality. . . . [L]aw is spontaneous, growing upwards, independently of any dominant will." Carleton K. Allen, *Law in the Making* (5th ed., Oxford, 1951), pp. 64, 1.

[6] The promulgation of a law has sometimes been said to be part of it. But this is not so. Promulgation is a prerequisite condition for the law being known by the people and for their recognition of the obligatory nature of its content. Like a road map, a law is complete in itself before it is given out as a guide. Distributing the road map does not make the map what is it.

[7] Carl Friedrich, *Man and His Government* (New York, 1963), pp. 224, 226.

[8] "'Do this' in many contexts frequently provokes a counter response which defeats its own purpose. But 'It is wrong to do this' removes the arbitrary decisional aspect of the explicit personal command or imperative. So understood, the moral judgment derives its authority neither from the emotional tone of the speaker nor from his physical presence alone. As such it appeals not to the private inclinations of the listener but to the socialized dispositions which he possesses as a member of society. The speaker pronounces the judgment, as it were, not as an agent, but as a carrier of meanings whose effective appeal is determined elsewhere." Henry Aiken, *Reason and Conduct* (New York, 1962), p. 120.

elections of the Swiss cantons are examples. So also are the examples we shall cite later of the members of preliterate societies governing themselves, even without the guidance of a leader.

### b.  The People's Delegates

What with the size of political societies being what they are, however, most people govern themselves through those to whom they have delegated some of the right they have to govern themselves. Delegated authority is, by and large, the source of the directive judgments which are law. Such is the delegated authority of legislators, of judges when their decisions are law, and of executives when they make law by executive order. But even within the context of delegated lawmaking authority, the people still continue to make law. This is evidenced in the customs the people make which attain the status of law. Customs established by workers in the building trades, in mining, in railroad work and in other occupations, are accepted by courts as guides on a level with law in making decisions in these areas.

Delegated authority should be distinguished from substitutional authority. Delegated authority is not absolutely required for government. The examples just cited of government by the people themselves, directly and without any delegation, are evidence of this. Substitutional authority, on the other hand, is required by the nature of things. Thus the parent's judgment is a necessary substitute for the judgment the child would make if he were able. Delegated authority has a permanent aspect about it which substitutional authority does not. Where there is substitutional authority, it is assumed that the time will come when the judgment of the parent will no longer be required and the child will have developed to the point where he can form his own judgment. The authority which the colonial powers wielded over the colonies, many of which contained some of the preliterates we will study, was maintained by many to be substitutional.

#### B.  OBLIGATION OF LAW FROM MEANS-END RELATION

The obligation of law derives from the same source as all obligation, namely, the necessity of a means for an end. It arises from the relation between what law's regulations specify and the fulfillment of the needs common to all the people. If these demands are necessary, the law fulfills its purpose and it obliges. If these demands are not necessary but are needless, the law fails in its pledged mission and does not oblige. In such a case, the law is a medium of harm and not of help to the people. It is an instrument of tyranny and dictatorship.

### 1.  Absolute and Relative Necessity of Law's Content

This necessity, which is the heart of obligation, ranges between what is absolutely necessary and what is rela-

tively necessary. We referred to this distinction above.[9] An object is absolutely necessary for the common welfare of the people when without it not even their basic common needs would be fulfilled. Police protection is absolutely necessary, men being what they are, for the protection of people's basic rights to life, sex, knowledge, and other fundamental values in life. Without police protection, these rights could not be protected. An object is relatively necessary for the common welfare of the people when without it important needs could not be fulfilled, even though the more basic ones were fulfilled. Regulation of air and water pollution may have been relatively necessary for the protection of the health of the people at one time, but not as necessary as was protection against murder, rape, and robbery. What was formerly only relatively necessary, however, may later become absolutely necessary. Protection against the pollution of air and water appears now to be one such example.

By contrast, not only should what is harmful to common needs be excluded from law but also what is merely useful to the common welfare. It is useful, for instance, for members of a community to accompany blind persons in dangerous areas. But because such an action has not been considered either absolutely or relatively necessary for the common welfare of all the people, it has not been incorporated into law.

### 2.  Means-end Necessity Precedes Law

The necessity implied in a means-end factual situation exists before the enactment of a law regarding it. The necessity of controlling air and water pollution exists before a law is passed regulating such pollution. It is this necessity which causes agitation for the enactment of such legislation. It is this objective need which causes the people to say, "There ought to be a law" controlling air and water pollution. Hence, the obligation of law arises from an observable need which preexists before a law is enacted.

### 3.  Obligation in Law Not From Command or Coercion

The locating of obligation in the objective necessity of means for an end is, obviously, opposed to those theories of obligation which find it elsewhere. The grounding of obligation on the means-end relationship presupposes an analysis of men which recognizes in them certain basic drives which dynamically express what is fundamentally necessary for men's self-development. Such an interpretation of what men are, however, has not always been followed by those concerned with obligation and its meaning. When men's drives are overlooked or rejected as the means-end ground of values and obligation, other grounds evidently have to be sought. These have been in the main either the nobility of obligation contained in an absolute command

---

[9] See "Obligation."

as expressed in the phrase "duty for duty's sake," or the very command of the will itself of the lawmaker, or the coercion used to enforce the command of the lawmaker.

The proponents of these positions have been many. We will discuss only those who have a special relevance for us here. Their works, to which we will refer, are well known and speak for themselves. Suffice it here merely to sketch their thinking in so far as it has a bearing on our analysis of drives, values, obligation and law in part one, and our examination of reported data in part two.

### a.　Kant

Few men, if any, have been more influential regarding a ground for obligation other than a means-end one than Immanuel Kant (1724–1804). Kant's approach to the practical problem of obligation is through his approach to the epistemological problem of knowledge, of what we can know of things and men. Kant maintained, for reasons which he fully developed but which are not relevant here, that we cannot know what a thing is in itself, that is, what the nature or essence of a thing is.[10] We can know only its appearances. Hence, we cannot know from experience such interrelations between things as cause and effect, means and end. These categories are given by the mind *a priori* and are applied to the appearances when experienced.

This being the case, any attempt to find starting points for value or obligation in men's nature and the means-end relationships indicated by it, is vain and illusory.[11] All thinking about values and obligation must be divorced from the empirical.[12] No position could be more opposed to taking men's nature and experience as the basis of human values and obligation.[13] As far as drives or inclinations are concerned, everything connected with them "automatically falls away" from any consideration of values and obligation.[14] For, the drives or inclinations are at war with reason and intention and any following of the inclinations can only be debasing and dangerous to men.[15] Consequently, not only does obligation not come from the means-end relationships connoted by the inclinations but obligation and the inclinations stand in opposition to each other. Obligation has nothing to do with inclinations.[16]

The basis of values and obligation in Kant, then, is not to be found in men's drives operating in specific situations but rather in the "higher" sphere of reason and intention.[17] It is on respect for the absolute command or the categorical imperative of the law of men's reason and will that obligation is founded.[18] This command is that every man should so act that the maxim of his will could be a universal law for all men.[19] In other words, if I preserve my life because I have a drive to do so, my action is bemeaning and of no moral value. But if I preserve my life because I have an obligation to do so, that is because I must respect the absolute command of the law of my reason, then and only then does my action have moral worth. The essence of obligation for Kant is not objective right but subjective duty. The inclinations are empirical and may be taken as a practical rule, but for the same reason they may never be taken as the expression of a law. For law comes from obligation and obligation comes only from pure reason.[20]

The inclinations demand actions which can be said to be obligatory only in the sense that they are conditions for obtaining an end.[21] But actions have to be com-

---

[10] See Immanuel Kant, *Critique of Pure Reason,* trans. by N. K. Smith (London, 1956), *passim.*

[11] "We cannot too much or too often warn against the lax or even base manner of thought which seeks principles among empirical motives and laws, for human reason in its weariness is glad to rest on this pillow. In a dream of sweet illusions (in which it embraces not Juno but a cloud), it substitutes for morality a bastard patched up from limbs of very different parentage, which looks like anything one wishes to see in it, but not like virtue to anyone who has ever beheld her in her true form." Immanuel Kant, *Foundations of the Metaphysics of Morals,* Second Section, trans. by L. W. Beck, *Immanuel Kant: Critique of Practical Reason and Other Writings in Moral Philosophy* (Chicago, 1949), p. 84.

[12] "Is it not of the utmost necessity to construct a pure moral philosophy which is completely freed from everything which may be only empirical and thus belong to anthropology." Kant, *ibid.,* Preface, Beck translation, *ibid.,* pp. 51–52.

[13] "Applied to men, it [moral philosophy] borrows nothing from knowledge of him (anthropology) but gives him, as a rational being, a priori laws. . . . All practical principles which presuppose an object (material) of the faculty of desire as the determining ground of the will are without exception empirical and can furnish no practical laws." Immanuel Kant, *Foundations of the Metaphysics of Morals,* Preface, trans. by L. W. Beck, *Immanuel Kant: Critique of Practical Reason and Other*

*Writings in Moral Philosophy* (Chicago, 1949), p. 53; Kant, *Critique of Practical Reason,* Part I, Book I, chap. i, Beck translation, *ibid.,* pp. 53, 132.

[14] Kant, *Foundations of the Metaphysics of Morals,* Second Section, Beck trans., *ibid.,* p. 85.

[15] Kant, *Critique of Practical Reason,* Part I, Book I, chap. 2, Beck trans., *ibid.,* p. 179.

[16] "Duty! Thou sublime and mighty name that . . . holdest forth a law . . . before which all inclinations are dumb even though they secretly work against it: what origin is there worthy of thee, and where is to be found the root of thy noble descent which proudly rejects all kinship with the inclinations." Kant, *Critique of Practical Reason,* Part I, Book I, chap. 3, Beck trans., *ibid.,* p. 193.

[17] "The ground of obligation here must not be sought in the nature of man or in the circumstances in which he is placed but sought a priori solely in the concepts of pure reason." (Kant, *Foundations of the Metaphysics of Morals,* Preface, Beck trans., *ibid.,* p. 52.

[18] "Duty is the necessity of an action done from respect for the law." Kant, *Foundations of the Metaphysics of Morals,* First Section, Beck trans., *ibid.,* p. 61.

[19] Kant, *Critique of Practical Reason,* Part I, Book I, chap. 1, Beck trans., *ibid.,* pp. 142–143.

[20] Kant, *Foundations of the Metaphysics of Morals,* Preface, Beck trans., *ibid.,* p. 52.

[21] Kant, *Foundations of the Metaphysics of Morals,* Third Section, Beck trans., *ibid.,* p. 86.

manded absolutely and not merely conditionally if obligation is to have more than a relative meaning.[22] Obligation must be rooted in an end which is necessary in itself. The only end which is necessary in itself and can be commanded absolutely is the end of so acting that the maxim of your will can be taken as a universal law for all. This is the necessary end of every absolutely good will and such is the absolute command, the categorical imperative, of reason itself.[23]

A cleavage between morals and law is inevitable once men's outward actions are conceived as being completely distinct from their inward intentions and as being in a different sphere. Men's obligation regarding these two areas would obviously be different.[24] At this point a shift in meaning occurs from the obligation of internal reason and intention to the "obligation" of the external action, as Kant clearly saw, is actually coercion.[25] Kant, however, was too great a mind not to see that obligation was not coercion and that obligation if it does not come from the means-end relationships demanded by the inclinations had to come from respect for the interior command of pure reason. But the stage was set for those who would come after Kant and who would by-pass Kant's noble concept of obligation and instead would emphasize "obligation" as synonymous with exterior coercion and force.

For Kant, then, inclinations or drives could not be the source of values and obligation. Values had to come from another source. Because of this view, Kant was never in a position to see the importance of men's master drive for self-realization as demanding an end which is necessary in itself. He was not disposed to see obligation fixed in such an end as absolute and categorical. Men's actions for him were not good because they satisfied drives and led toward this goal. They had value, in his opinion, because of their relation to a good will.

This formalism would show itself later in theories of "pure law" some of which we shall see shortly.

Morals and law, values and facts, were each of prime importance in their own area in Kant's thought. In making the distinction he made between them, it is doubtful he ever intended that law should be considered as being indifferent to one set of values as compared with another. But the manner in which he separated the interior sphere of intention and obligation (morals) from the exterior world of actions and coercion (law), opened up the possibility of such thinking. This gap would later be widened to the point where, from the standpoint of law, only facts and coercion were kept in view while values and obligation were allowed to recede into the background. For this reason, the ideas of Kant have been characterized as "a half-way house on the road to positivism." [26]

### b. Austin

Influence concerning the ground for obeying a law was exercised especially on Anglo-American thinking by John Austin (1790–1859). The practical approach of Austin the lawyer to this problem was not on the profound speculative level of Kant the philosopher. Austin was influenced by Kant as well as Hobbes. A key concept in Austin's thinking was sovereignty which he borrowed, with minor changes, from Hobbes.[27] Austin, following Kant, respected moral values and thought they should be recognized by law.[28] This relationship of moral value to man-made law, Austin points out, is often lost sight of.[29] In fact, he says, without bringing in values he would be unable to explain man-made law.[30] But Austin was concerned with analyzing law as it is rather than as it ought to be and he was at pains to keep law and morals separate in such an analysis. It was not that he had a theory of obligation which demanded this separation, as was the case with Kant. It was, rather, that he was convinced that a law could be perfectly valid without having to be judged just or unjust according to certain extra-legal values.[31] One set of values was as preferable as another as far as law was concerned. And because, as Austin and his teacher Bentham saw it, a particular code of values was em-

[22] Kant, *An Inquiry into the Distinctness of the Principles of Natural Theology and Morals*, Fourth Reflection, Beck trans., *ibid.*, p. 283.

[23] Kant, *Foundations of the Metaphysics of Morals*, Third Section; Beck trans., *ibid.*, pp. 94–95.

[24] "This separation [between morals and law] is grounded on this, that the idea of freedom, common to both these, renders necessary a distinction of duties into the offices of outward, and those of inward liberty, whereof the latter are alone moral." (Kant, *The Metaphysics of Ethics*, trans. by J. W. Semple (Edinburgh, 1836), p. 242.

[25] "For since law respects that only which is external and phenomenal in an action, strict law, i.e. law in which no ethical consideration is introduced, can require no internal, but merely external, determinators of choice, even although coaction be required to do so. All law whatever rests, it is true, on the consciousness of obligation under the moral law itself; but pure or strict law, in the sense now taken, does not expect that this consciousness should be the spring of conduct; but supports itself as a legislation for external actions, on its principle of coaction. . . . Law, strictly so called, always implies the power to co-act." Kant, *The Metaphysics of Ethics*, trans. by J. W. Semple (Edinburgh, 1836), pp. 195, 197.

[26] Frederick Copleston, *A History of Philosophy* (8 v., Westminster, 1946–1966) **6**: pp. 433–434.

[27] See John Austin, *Lectures on Jurisprudence* (2 v., Robert Campbell ed., 5th rev. ed., London, 1875) **1**: pp. 155–163.

[28] John Austin, *The Province of Jurisprudence Determined* (London, 1954), Lecture V, p. 162, n. 10.

[29] Austin, *ibid.*, pp. 162–163.

[30] "[I]t was not a deviation from my subject to introduce the principle of utility. . . . I . . . should often be unable to explain distinctly and precisely the scope and purport of a law, without having brought the principle of utility directly before you." Austin, *The Province of Jurisprudence Determined* (London, 1954), Lecture III, p. 59.

[31] John Austin, *The Province of Jurisprudence Determined* (London, 1954), Lecture V, p. 184.

bodied in "natural law," it was this bugbear to which especially a wide berth had to be given.[32]

With no certain values included in law, Austin had to say that men were "obliged" to obey the law for the reason that if they did not obey they would be subject to compulsion or force, as Kant had said before him. In this view, "obligation" became sanction, the only difference being that sanction referred to the punishment which would be inflicted in case of disobedience, and "obligation" was the liability to undergo this punishment.[33] This is the meaning of every law and every law is a command of the sovereign who has the power to enforce sanctions on his subjects.[34] The command of law is actually the expression of the sovereign's wish that subjects perform certain actions or they will have punishments inflicted upon them.[35] This is precisely the difference between superiors and inferiors, namely, that superiors are the persons who have the power of inflicting punishment.[36] To say that a person is "obliged" by the command of the sovereign, therefore, is for Austin the same as saying that the person will be punished by the superior if he does not obey.[37]

Austin does speak of the content and ends of law, which are universal to all systems of law, as "bottomed in the common nature of man."[38] But the possibility of Austin seeing this "common nature of man" as expressing itself dynamically through basic drives, and thereby indicating certain basic values which inevitably had to be present in all man-made law, was remote indeed. He was too much under the influence of Kant's rejection of inclinations as indicative of values and too convinced that the command of the sovereign is law regardless of whether it is just or not, to ever attain this insight.

Austin's concern was with "positive" law as distinguished from "moral" or "natural" law. The word "positive" in this context derives from the distinction between *lex a Deo aut natura data* and *lex ab hominibus posita*, that is, between law given by God or nature and law laid down by men. This distinction in itself did not carry the connotation that man-made laws did not recognize certain values. It only indicated that there were laws given to men and laws made by men.

The word "positive" in the context of "positivism," however, came to mean the professed exclusion of ethical values from scientific research of facts. Comte (1789–1857) distinguished between theological, metaphysical, and scientific knowledge and referred to these three areas as, respectively, the fictitious, the abstract, and the positive.[39] The key idea in Comte's thinking was that only empirical sciences are reliable sources of knowledge about things and their interrelations. Only the observable data of sense experience are scientifically verifiable and therefore intelligible.[40] Mill (1806–1873), who admittedly was influenced by Comte, also embraces this position.[41] Although Mill knew the writings of Kant, Comte did not. It is worth noting, then, that Comte came to the same conclusion as Kant regarding the separation of morals and values from laws and facts.[42] The remaining authors we will consider—namely Gray, Kelsen and Hart—are "positivists" in the sense that they hold there are no values necessarily in law.

### c. Gray

Both Kant and Austin have had a shaping effect on later thinking concerning obligation and the place of values in law. A good example is John Chipman Gray (1839–1915) who applied these ideas to courts. Gray followed Kant in separating morals and law. Men's internal intentions could not be regulated by external legislation, but their outward actions could be so regulated. Law recognized values but not this or that set of values.[43] Gray considered that Austin's final fixing of law as that which is and morals as that which ought

---

[32] "Now, to say that human laws which conflict with the Divine law are not binding, that is to say, are not law, is to talk stark nonsense." Austin, *The Province of Jurisprudence Determined* (London, 1954), Lecture V, p. 185. "The law of nature [is] a vague expression, and productive of a multitude of inconveniences." Jeremy Bentham, *The Principles of Morals and Legislation*, Chap. XVI, sect. 5, no. 9, n. 6 (New York, 1948), p. 303.

[33] "The difference between Sanction and Obligation is simply this. Sanction is evil, incurred, or to be incurred by disobedience to command. Obligation is liability to that evil, in the event of disobedience." John Austin, *Lectures on Jurisprudence* (2 v., Robert Campbell ed., 5th rev. ed., London, 1875) 1: p. 311.

[34] "A law, in the literal and proper sense of the word, may be defined as a rule laid down for the guidance of an intelligent being by an intelligent being having power over him." Austin, *ibid.*, p. 3. See also *ibid.*, pp. 12 and 116.

[35] Austin, *ibid.*, pp. 12–13.

[36] Austin, *ibid.*, pp. 19, 20–21.

[37] "Being liable to evil from you if I comply not with a wish which you signify, I am bound or obliged by your command, or I lie under a duty to obey it." Austin, *ibid.*, p. 13.

[38] Austin, *Uses of the Study of Jurisprudence* (London, 1954), p. 373.

[39] Auguste Comte, *The Positive Philosophy of Auguste Comte*, trans. by Harriet Martineau (2 v., London, 1893) 1: p. 2.

[40] "[N]o proposition that is not finally reducible to the enunciation of a fact, particular or general, can offer any real and intelligible meaning." A. Comte, *The Positive Philosophy of Auguste Comte*, Martineau trans. (1893) 2: p. 425.

[41] John S. Mill, *Auguste Comte and Positivism* (London, 1866), p. 6.

[42] "Wholly unrelated to Kantianism, the positivism of Comte nonetheless leads to a similar philosophical conclusion." Etienne Gilson, Thomas Langan, and Armand Maurer, *Recent Philosophy* (New York, 1962), p. 272.

[43] "According to Kant, moral philosophy is divisible into two parts: (1) the metaphysical principles of Jurisprudence, and (2) the metaphysical principles of ethics. Jurisprudence has for its subject-matter the aggregate of all the laws which it is possible to promulgate by external legislation. All duties are either duties of justice or duties of virtue. The former are such as *admit* of external legislation; the latter are those for which such legislation is not possible." John C. Gray, *The Nature and Sources of the Law* (2nd ed., New York, 1921), p. 95.

to be was an accomplishment of the first order. He even thought that Austin himself at times did not distinguish sharply enough between the "is" and the "ought" of law and morals.[44]

The basis of "obligation" in law for Gray is the same as it was for Kant and Austin, namely, coercion. It could not be based on certain values in law because there were none. Gray prefers to make a distinction between "obligation" and "duty," saying that it is "obligation" which carries the stronger legal connotation of external coercion. But regardless of the meaning given to "obligation" and "duty," "ought" according to Gray is present in all societies of men with the connotation of coercion.[45]

One of the main consequences of distinguishing between what the law is and what it ought to be, as Gray sees it, is the recognition of the pre-eminent place courts hold in the process of lawmaking. Any norm of justice which the courts do not recognize and enforce is factually not a part of the law. To think otherwise is not to make progress. This means that it is the rules which the courts create for the government of the people, and only these rules, which are law. Statutory legislation is not law until its meaning has been decided by the courts. Gray says that Austin was right in maintaining that only the rules laid down by judges are law.[46]

The practical consequences of Gray's thinking was to elevate the courts to the prime position of lawmaking in any legal system.[47] The judges were the ones who actually made the law. Holmes (1841–1935) and Cardozo (1870–1938) appear to have been influenced by his emphasis on the lawmaking position of courts.[48] Gray's thinking on this point did not receive widespread acceptance, but it did cause difficulties for field researchers, as we shall see. But because of the manner in

---

[44] *Ibid.*, pp. 16, 94, 304, 306.

[45] *Ibid.*, pp. 7, 309.

[46] "The Law of the State or of any organized body of men is composed of the rules which the courts, that is, the judicial organs of that body, lay down for the determination of legal rights and duties. . . . [L]egislation has to be interpreted by the courts before it becomes a part of the Law." (Gray, *ibid.*, pp. 84, 94–95, 268.)

[47] It has been said that Gray was motivated to take this extreme position because of the questionable quality of the law which some state legislatures were making during his time. Granting that this was the situation, the solution would not have been to adopt an astereoptical theory of law that lost sight of the whole nature and function of legislation and its relation to adjudication. The answer would have been to take the necessary political steps to improve the quality of legislator who made the law and thereby raise the standard of law produced.

[48] "The prophecies of what the courts will do in fact, and nothing more pretentious, are what I mean by the law." Oliver W. Holmes, "The Path of the Law," *Harvard Law Rev.* **10** (1897): pp. 457–461. "A principle or rule of conduct so established as to justify a prediction with reasonable certainty that it will be enforced by the courts if its authority is challenged, is, then, for the purpose of our study, a principle or rule of law." Benjamin Cardozo, *The Growth of the Law* (New Haven, 1924), p. 52.

which he conceived morals to be separated from law, and values to pertain to the internal and facts to the external life of men, he, like Kant, was hardly of a mind to recognize that certain basic values are inevitably in law. Nor was he able to view obligation as related to the necessity of means for fulfilling the common needs of the people.

### d. *Kelsen*

The thought of Kant and Austin concerning values, obligation and law has been given systematic organization and form by later writers. Such has been the work of Hans Kelsen (1881–    ). Kant's attempt to keep the command of "pure reason" free from anything empirical is faithfully reflected in Kelsen's endeavor to keep his "pure theory of law" free from values which are extraneous to the scientific method. This kind of thinking, which tries to keep any definite desires and values at arm's length from law and science, prefers to be known as "legal positivism." It is obviously opposed to any kind of "natural law." Its general position, according to Kelsen, is that of the analytical jurisprudence of Austin. Kelsen's thought also agrees in the main with that of Gray, although he disagrees with Gray on his theory that the courts alone make law.[49]

Kelsen refers to his position as both "legal positivism" and "analytical jurisprudence," although there is a difference between the meanings of the two phrases. Analytical jurisprudence is concerned with an analysis of the language used in law and not with explaining what law is. Values are kept out of this analysis not because they are not respected and some of them acknowledged but because it is the factual words and phrases of law which are the object of analysis. Moreover, values are based on emotions and therefore are non-intellectual and non-cognitional. Kelsen says that all moral value judgments, as distinguished from juristic value judgments, are determined by emotions and hence are not verifiable factually. Moral value judgments are not valid constructs deriving from reason and factual experience. Hence, they have no place in what is intended to be a scientific explanation of law.[50]

"Obligation," for Kelsen, derives directly from the legal norm itself and has no meaning apart from it. For Kelsen, however, the "ought" implied in "obligation" refers to what the government "ought" to do by way of applying a sanction to a violator rather than to what the violator himself ought to have done. Observance of the law is looked upon not so much as doing what is required by the law as performing the kind of actions which will avoid the infliction of sanctions. To say that legal norms are valid is the same thing as saying they "ought" to be obeyed. This validity derives

---

[49] Hans Kelsen, *General Theory of Law and State*, trans. by Anders Wedberg (Cambridge, Mass., 1946), pp. xiv–xv, 151–152, 435.

[50] Kelsen, *ibid.*, pp. 7, 48.

not from any objective value-basis but from the subjective way certain persons have created it, which way is hypothetically assumed to be valid. Norms are created by commands and commands are the expression, as for Austin, of the will of a superior that subjects behave in a certain way.[51]

"Obligation," because it derives from legal norms, ultimately derives from the source of the validity of these norms—the basic norm. The foundation of all law, according to the pure theory of law, is not extralegal values or an objective means-end relationship. It is the *grundnorm*.[52] This basic norm refers not to the first law created in any legal system but to the validity of this first law. This validity rests on the relation of the content of this law to the exigencies of the historical condition of the time. This postulate, which appears to be much like a Kantian *a priori* category, is the prerequisite to all valid lawmaking.[53] Kelsen's concept of "obligation," then, comes to the same thing as the sanction of coercion and is ultimately founded on the assumption that the basic law in any system was validly established.

The separation of morals from law, of values from facts, in the pure theory of law has the inevitable effect of turning obligation into sanction and coercion. Not that the pure theory of law does not make a place for the presence of values in law, even though they are non-intellectual and non-scientific.[54] The point to be made is that when law is considered scientifically for what it is in itself, there is no place for any definite values. Law may have any value-content.[55] Kelsen is apparently so influenced by Kant's rejection of the empirical in general and the drives in particular that he cannot see them as the source of values and obligation. As a consequence, the content of law and its obligatory aspect is not necessarily related to the practical demands of men's everyday values but to the theoretical assumption of a basic norm which supposedly came into existence long ago. As has been aptly remarked, the pure theory of law has clean hands because it has no hands.

### e. Hart

Prominent among contemporary legal positivists is Herbert L. A. Hart (1907–     ).[56] His thinking shows the influence of Kant, Austin, Gray, and Kelsen. Hart, like his predecessors, holds for the separation of morals and law saying that it was Kant's differentiation between juridical and ethical laws which was the source of this distinction. Hart, however, thinks that stating this difference in terms of internal motives and external actions is too simple. It can be misleading, although it does state a truth.[57] This truth is that the separation between morals and law is so complete that law does not necessarily contain any certain values. This is the meaning of legal positivism. Law may incorporate into itself moral values which it deems necessary for a workable stability.[58] But the point to be stressed is that, to repeat, there is no *necessary* connection between law and particular moral values. The assertion that there are no necessary given values in law, along with the contention that law is a command and that values are non-cognitive, are declared to be identifying marks of legal positivism.[59]

Hart's concept of "obligation" starts where Austin's did, namely, with the fact that where there is law the behavior of subjects is no longer optional but it is obligatory. But Hart immediately parts company with Austin's theory that law is simply a coercive command. The inadequacies of this theory have been pointed out, he says, regarding international law and preliterate law. Hart shows its deficiencies concerning various aspects of municipal law. The principal short-coming of the theory, according to Hart, is that it lacks the concept of a rule. Without such an idea, it is impossible to understand even rudimentary examples of law.[60]

Hart makes a distinction between "was obliged" and "had an obligation." To say that I "was obliged" to

---

[51] Kelsen, *ibid.*, pp. 30–31, 59–60, 394.

[52] "The pure theory of law . . . seeks the basis of law—that is, the reason of its validity—not in a metajuristic principle but in a juristic hypothesis—that is, a basic norm, to be established by a logical analysis of actual juristic thinking." Hans Kelsen, *General Theory of Law and State,* trans. by Anders Wedberg (Cambridge, Mass., 1946), p. xv.

[53] "The basic norm is . . . valid because it is presupposed to be valid; and it is presupposed to be valid because without this presupposition no human act could be interpreted as a legal, especially as a norm-creating, act. . . . The basic norm is not valid because it has been created in a certain way, but its validity is assumed by virtue of its content." *Ibid.,* pp. 116, 401.

[54] "It is, however, possible for the legal order, by obliging the law-creating organs to respect or apply certain moral norms or political principles or opinions of experts, to transform these norms, principles, or opinions into legal norms and thus into true sources of law." Kelsen, *ibid.,* p. 132.

[55] "[T]he concept of law has no moral connotation whatsoever." Kelsen, *ibid.,* p. 5.

[56] Hart has been classified among the "new analytical jurists." Listed among the older group are Austin, Gray, Hohfeld, and Kocourek. Among the later group are included Hart, Williams, Hughes, Dworkin, Fried, Morris and Wasserstrom. The "new" group is characterized as "broader in scope, more sophisticated in methodology, less doctrinaire and positivistic, and more likely to be of practical utility." Robert Summers, "The New Analytical Jurists," *New York Univ. Law Rev.* **41** (1966) : pp. 862–863. What "less positivistic" means would appear still to need further clarification.

[57] Herbert L. A. Hart, *The Concept of Law* (Oxford, 1961), pp. 168, 252, n. 168.

[58] "No 'positivist' could deny that these are facts [the myriad ways law mirrors morality], or that the stability of legal systems depends in part upon such types of correspondence with morals. If that is what is meant by the necessary connexion of law and morals, its existence should be conceded." Hart, *ibid.,* pp. 199–200.

[59] "[W]e shall take Legal Positivism to mean the simple contention that it is in no sense a necessary truth that laws reproduce or satisfy certain demands of morality, though in fact they have often done so." Hart, *ibid.,* pp. 181–182; see also p. 253, n. 181.

[60] Hart, *ibid.,* pp. 78, 80.

hand over my money to a hold-up man who is pointing a gun at me is different from saying that I "had an obligation" to hand over the money. "Was obliged" upon analysis means coercion. If I don't hand over the money, I will suffer harm. "Had an obligation," however, has an entirely different meaning. It means that there is a law or rule demanding that I act in a certain way and that social pressure is being brought to bear on me to do so.[61] The grounds for this pressure by the people is their judgment and conviction that the action in question is necessary for the preservation of their social life.[62]

Hart separates morals from law the same as did Austin. There are those values in law which law chooses to serve—a minimal number—but there are no certain values in law which are there necessarily. But Hart does not want to go to the logical conclusion of this separation which is that "obligation" is coercion. With perceptive insight, he wants to give obligation a different meaning. In order to do this, he has recourse to the necessity of some actions for the maintenance of the social life of the people. These indispensable values relate to the protection of persons, property, and promises. The people recognize these needs and demand that laws regarding them be obeyed. They bring pressure to bear on possible or real violators. It is because Austin's and others' formal concept of law failed to take account of these social needs of the people, Hart points out, that it has proved so inadequate. Assuming survival as a goal, he says, law must include this minimum value-content. Survival according to Hart, however, cannot be taken as a value which derives from any basic drive which causes men to desire it necessarily as a given end, as we have already noted. It is merely assumed as a controlling value.[63] Hence, the minimum value-content of law, of which survival is the assumed anchor value, is in law not necessarily but for the sake of expediency. In other words, there are no necessary values in law which are related to necessary needs of the people. This point will be adverted to later in our discussion of whether an unjust law can be law.

---

[61] Herbert L. A. Hart, *The Concept of Law* (Oxford, 1961), pp. 80, 84.

[62] "What is important is that the insistence on importance or seriousness of social pressure behind the rules is the primary factor determining whether they are thought of as giving rise to obligation. . . . The rules supported by this serious pressure are thought important because they are believed to be necessary to the maintenance of social life or some highly prized feature of it." (Hart, *ibid.*, pp. 84–85.) In terms of our analysis above, "was obliged" would indicate the necessity of using the means of handing over the money to save my life. This "obligation" would be overridden by "had no obligation" which would mean that the robber had no title to the money which it was necessary for me to respect. On the contrary, he was not fulfilling his obligation to respect my title to the money thereby reducing us both to a state of physical contention.

[63] Herbert L. A. Hart, *ibid.*, pp. 187–195.

## f. Root Kinship

A word may be in place here regarding the kinship which exists between voluntarism, scholasticism, and positivism. Protestations to the contrary notwithstanding, these positions have all been characterized by a shunning of observable facts and things as they are. In law, the preoccupation of these groups is not with the necessary, factual needs of the people but with the command of a superior, or formalized rules, or the coercion which can be brought to bear on the people.

What is of relevance here is the cognitional and perhaps emotional kinship between ancient voluntarism, deteriorating scholasticism, and modern positivism. A predisposition for form rather than for facts is the indicating sign. "Hoc volo, sic iubeo, sit pro ratione voluntas" was the expression of this mentality in classical antiquity.[64] Scholasticism in its deterioration from the heights of the thirteenth century to the depths of the seventeenth century shifted from the intellectualistic relation of objective means to end, as the basis of obligation and law, to the voluntaristic command of the subjective will of the lawmaker.[65] The sharp distinction it made between the "moral order" and the "legal order" was only another way of stating the complete separation of "ought" from "is." This is already a step toward positivism.[66] Positivism, paradoxically and in spite of its air of factualism, has not recognized the observable and necessary needs of the people as the basis of obligation and law. It does not see that the necessary needs of the people are necessary facts, and that these necessary needs imply necessary values in their fulfillment.

## 4. Obligation and Values Necessarily in Law

The main assumptions of positivism, as far as our present concern goes, are that inclinations or drives are not a source of values and that there are no certain values in law necessarily. In law, according to this position, there can be any values or there can be minimal values which law itself chooses to acknowledge and serve for the sake of expediency. But in order to hold these assumptions the data of psychology and anthropology have to be ignored, and the internal working of the law-making process has to be disregarded.

### a. Data of Psychology and Anthropology

It is of psychological necessity, as we saw, that certain values be in law. These definite values are in law necessarily because they derive from the basic drives

---

[64] "This I will, thus I command, let my will be the reason." Juvenal, *Satires*, Satire 6, line 233 (A. D. 116, my translation).

[65] See Thomas Davitt, *The Nature of Law* (St. Louis, 1951), pp. 9–108.

[66] "The voluntarist interpretation of the natural law tends to carry over into a positivist interpretation of law in general." Francis Oakley, "Mediaeval Theories of Natural Law: William of Ockham and the Significance of the Voluntarist Tradition, *Natural Law Forum* **6** (1961): p. 83.

which all normal men have. These given values, along with others which are constructed, are present in all motivation and this includes the motivation for making law. In other words, in order to hold that there are no certain values in law the validity of these scientifically established data have to be denied.

Further, to maintain that the values which the laws of all peoples actually serve are any values at all or that they are only those minimal values which relate to the protection of property, persons, and promises, goes dead against the current of anthropological data. While it is undoubtedly true that the number of values which the evidence indicates all peoples hold is relatively not large, this number is unquestionably greater than such a minimal number. The evidence which we shall adduce in the second part of this study shows that the values which the laws of all peoples actually reflect are considerably more extensive than this.

These considerations have a relation to explanations given of obligation and law. "Having an obligation," as we have seen, is described as connected with the values law chooses to recognize as needed for the maintenance of the social life of the people and with the people's reaction to violations of law which threaten it. But in the light of the data of both psychology and anthropology, there are certain of these values which are given, constant, and more extensive than recognized. Likewise when law is described as being grounded on a "basic norm," the validity of this *grundnorm* is assumed from its value-content at the time of its inception, as we also saw. This assumption implies that the value-content which the basic norm had at that time must have had a relation to the needs and values of the people if it was to be practical and not fictional. But again from the point of view of both psychology and anthropology, these values actually were not just any values. They were certain definite values which necessarily related to the common needs of the people.

## b. Process of Law-making

If the values in law can be any set of values or can be those only which law itself elects to recognize, the separation of moral values from legal facts should be an easy matter. The "ought" of law should be easily distinguishable from its "is." But in the lawmaking process, especially the judicial, drawing this distinction is not such plain sailing. There are some areas in statutes, for instance, which are clearer than others. As far as judicial interpretation is concerned, there are "zones of certainty" as they have been called.[67] Other areas in statutes are not clear and are "zones of uncertainty." In deciding how to apply the "zones of uncertainty" a problem arises. The judge in making his decision has

to bring to bear values which are not in the law but which are his own. The fact or "is" of the statute will have to be interpreted according to the values or "ought" of the judge. Nor are his values just any values. As the anthropological data show, the values which all normal men make—and this includes judges—run in patterns which are universal or almost universal, as well as general, common, frequent, and occasional.

The penetration of these values into law is well exemplified, for example, in divorce actions. The statute's definition of mental cruelty may be such that there is question of whether the conduct of the instant parties comes under it. The judge is confronted with a statutory "zone of uncertainty." He will have to make a decision. His directive judgment will not be controlled by the fact or "is" of the statute because it is too vague. The construction the judge finally puts on the statute will be determined by what he value-judges the law "ought" to be according to the values he holds personally.[68]

In like manner, the interchange of moral values and legal facts also shows itself in cases where a court has overruled itself and the dissenting values or "ought" of a previous decision now become the fact or "is" of the later decision. A good example of this, as has been pointed out, is the decision in the so-called "flag-saluting" cases.[69] In the years preceding World War II many states enacted statutes requiring pupils in schools to salute the flag of the United States and recite the pledge of allegiance. Children of Jehovah's Witnesses refused to comply on the grounds that their religion forbade such action. In 1939 the Supreme Court of the United States decided, with one lone dissent, that these statutes did not interfere with religious freedom and that they should stand.[70]

But when after much agitation the case was reheard by the same court in 1943, the court reversed itself and decided that the statutes were an infringement on religious liberty and that they not be allowed to stand.[71] The lone dissenting value-judgment or "ought" of the 1939 decision now became the legal fact or "is" of the 1943 decision. Obviously in these cases, as well as in the divorce cases just mentioned, the values on which the judges based their decisions went beyond any bare minimal values which the law could be said to have freely taken unto itself before their decisions. Nor were the values held by the judges, willy-nilly, this or that set of values. At bottom, they were values, to repeat, which the data will show follow certain patterns among all men.

---

[67] Harry Jones, "Legal Realism," in M. P. Golding, ed., *The Nature of Law* (New York, 1966), p. 273.

[68] Harry Jones, "Legal Realism," in: M. P. Golding, ed., *The Nature of Law* (New York, 1966), pp. 271, 274.

[69] Jones, *ibid.*, pp. 272–274.

[70] *Minersville Bd. of Education* v. *Gobitis*, 310 U. S. 586 (1939).

[71] *West Virginia Bd. of Education* v. *Barnette*, 319 U.S. 624 (1943).

*c. Just Law*

The inevitable result of looking upon law's regulations as obligatory if they fulfill the needs common to the people is, obviously, to look upon them as not obligatory if they do not fulfill these needs. And if regulations are not obligatory, they are not law. In other words, regulations which do not fulfill the common needs of the people are not law. Put another way, regulations which do not fulfill the common needs of the people are unjust and hence are not law. This means, in its usual verbal formulation, that "An unjust law is no law."

Those who hold there are no certain values necessarily in law do not easily abide such a conclusion. From their point of view, logically, there are no grounds for talking about the justness or unjustness of a law if there are no certain values necessarily in law. Much less is there any reason for saying that a law is not a law because it is unjust. To a thoroughgoing positivist, anxious to go all the way downwind with his convictions, such a statement is so much nonsense. A law is a law regardless of whether it is just or unjust. Legal validity does not depend on ethical value. What should be said, according to him, is that a law is a law even though it is "too iniquitous to be obeyed." [72] Austin goes out of his way to show that Hobbes didn't mean what he said when he states that "No law can be unjust." What Hobbes meant according to Austin was that "No positive law is legally unjust." [73]

The issue is clear enough. If all values of rightness and justness (according to the accepted meaning of these words) are extra-legal and belong necessarily to ethics and not to law, it makes good sense to talk about a law which is unjust according to ethical standards only. It would make little sense to talk about a law which was "unjust" according to legal norms. But values of rightness and justness are not extra-legal alone. They are inevitably in law and are its heart. The people of necessity have certain basic needs and values which are common to them and which it is the function of law to fulfill. Promoting the fulfillment of these needs through law is right and just and it signifies good government. Preventing the fulfillment of these needs by means of law is wrong and unjust and it connotes bad government. The fulfillment of the common needs and values of the people pertains to law as well as to ethics. A law which does not fulfill the needs of the people is not what it is supposed to be. Or, to say the same thing, a law which is unjust is not a law.

*d. "Science of Law"*

When law is considered to be free of all values except those which it chooses to serve, the temptation is to look upon law in itself as concerned only with facts and to say that law is a science. Many have resisted this temptation and made the distinction between lawmaking (which includes law's chosen values) and jurisprudence (which examines what is factually to be found in law including its chosen values whichever they may be). [74] If what is examined are the rules and values found in law, jurisprudence can be called the science of law. [75] And if what is examined are the underlying bases of the rules and values found in law, jurisprudence can be called the philosophy of law. But it has been found that it is impossible to consider jurisprudence apart from statutes and decisions. [76] Hence, the central issue of whether there are certain values which are necessarily in law is not settled by distinguishing between lawmaking and jurisprudence.

Law is not science. It is prudence. [77] But even if law were a science there would be values in it. For science, which supposedly deals only with facts, is surrounded and permeated by values many of which are related to motivation and drives.

Science is knowledge we have about things as they are. More specifically, science is a habitual way of proceeding mentally with ease and accuracy to reach conclusions concerning the nature of things. This may occur deductively. A nuclear physicist may deduce particular conclusions from general premises about what will happen when experiments with uranium are conducted. Or it may occur inductively. This nuclear physicist may reason from the particular reactions observed in the experiments to general conclusions about nuclear fission. The data regarding this kind of scientific knowledge is constant and invariable. It is based on the nature of uranium. Hence, predictions with a high degree of accuracy can be made as is proven by subsequent controlled explosions.

Law, however, is not primarily concerned with the nature of things or their interrelationships. It may use such knowledge as background for lawmaking, but this is not its main preoccupation. Law's main concern is with human actions which will promote the common needs of the people. Although a certain number of these values are constants and givens, the great majority of them are variables and constructs. What per cent of

---

[72] "This is law; but it is too iniquitous to be applied or obeyed. . . . [I]t does not follow from the proposition that a rule is too iniquitous to obey that it is not a valid rule of law." Herbert L. A. Hart, *The Concept of Law* (Oxford, 1961), pp. 203, 204.

[73] John Austin, *Lectures on Jurisprudence* (2 v., Robert Campbell ed., 5th rev. ed., London, 1875) 1: p. 155, n. 251.

[74] Hans Kelsen, *General Theory of Law and State,* trans. by Anders Wedberg (Cambridge, Mass., 1946), pp. 163–164.

[75] John C. Gray, *The Nature and Sources of the Law* (2nd ed., New York, 1921), p. 133.

[76] John Austin, *Lectures on Jurisprudence* (2 v., Robert Campbell ed., 5th rev. ed., London, 1875) 1: p. 217. Langdell's "case method" was an attempt to be scientific in the study of law. The facts of a case supposedly were to be found in Appellate Court decisions.

[77] Thomas E. Davitt, *The Elements of Law* (Boston, 1959), pp. 47–48, 315–316.

a man's income should be taxed in order that the government be supported cannot be determined with a knowledge which is scientifically exact. Only a prudential judgment can be made based on knowable facts. Such directive judgments are good law if they hit within a reasonable band or range of what is necessary for the common needs of the people. For, prudence too is a habitual way of proceeding mentally but its concern is the means which lead to an end. These means, as was evident from the plasticity of the basic drives, are many and variable. Although the ends too are plastic in the sense explained, they are also constants as far as their over-all goal-areas are concerned. In regard to these constant goal-areas scientific judgments can be formed. But in regard to the means which will lead to these ends, only prudential judgments can be made.

But science itself is encompassed by values, as is being recognized more and more. Values are present in the purpose which motivates the research and in the uses to which the results of the research can be put. Values are present also in the hypothesis which directs the research, in the standards which are followed during the research, and in the knowledge of the over-all purpose of the whole if research is being done on a part. Further, there are values in the communication of the results of research, in truth-telling concerning these results, in belief in the communications of those reporting, and in the freedom which has allowed the researcher to do the work he is doing.

*i. Purposes—hypotheses—standards.* All scientific research is motivated by a purpose. This is only another way of saying, as we saw above, that research is always motivated by values. It is value which initially launches any research. Closely related to this motive, or perhaps in some cases identical with it, is the social use to which the results of the research will be put. Because of these values, research can be put to good or bad use. It can also be right to utilize research for the good of society and wrong not to use it.[78]

Scientific research is also guided by the value of the hypothesis which the facts, once researched, are supposed to verify.[79] Research can answer only the questions put to it. The value of research depends directly on the value of these hypothetical questions. The whole of research, in other words, proceeds within a matrix of value assumptions.[80] In addition, there are values in the standards which are set up in all areas of research.

The physicist has standards of perfection, the physiologist has standards of functions, the animal psychologist has standards of problems to be solved, and so forth. Likewise, there is value in knowing the over-all purpose of the whole when a part is being researched. My understanding of a part of a machine, for instance, is incomplete as long as I do not also have an understanding of the purpose of the machine as a whole. So also in regard to an organism. Research on any of its functions cannot be completely assessed until it is known what the purpose of the whole organism is.[81]

*ii. Communication—truthfulness—faith—freedom.* Scientific knowledge, however, breathes the air of communication. Communication is the milieu in which scientific knowledge exists and grows. It is of the greatest value to science. Communal living is a prerequisite for scientific knowledge, for such knowledge is the product of the interchange of ideas. If men lived alone and out of touch with each other there would be no systematized knowledge of the various areas which we designate as sciences. Our knowledge is a "social construct" and the verification of any hypothesis depends on records, instruments, and ideas which others have provided.[82] Communication, then, must be put high on the list of values in science.

Truthfulness, in like manner, is a prerequisite value for scientific knowledge. It is on the supposition that scientific researchers are telling the truth that their reports are read and accepted. Truthtelling is a prime value to science. It is on this score that positivism's stand on the verifiability of facts or the "is" has also been criticized. In holding that the "is" is verifiable, positivism is implicitly holding that everyone "ought" to tell the truth about what "is" in order that it be verifiable. This "social nexus" is but another example of the latent interrelation between the "is" and the "ought." Failure to see this social implication of the "ought" in verifying the "is" has been said to be a reason why some have not recognized this close relation of "is" and "ought."[83]

Faith in the reports of scientific research is another value assumed by scientific endeavor. Information passed on to us by others who have conducted scientific research becomes profitable to us only when we have accepted it and made it our own. Such an acceptance can occur after we have individually repeated the same experiments and come to the same conclusions as those

[78] Bentley Glass, *Science and Ethical Values* (Chapel Hill, 1965), pp. 69, 76.

[79] "The view that science can begin without ideas, hypotheses, or anticipations of nature and proceed first of all to gather the facts, is nothing less than silly. For what facts are we to gather as relevant for our inquiry? Indeed, to find out what are the facts is the very purpose of scientific investigation. It is an illusion to suppose that we can build up a legal system or science of law by simply gathering all the cases together." Morris Cohen, *Law and the Social Order* (New York, 1933), p. 190.

[80] Cohen, *ibid.,* p. 188.

[81] Michael Polanyi, *The Study of Man* (Chicago, 1959), pp. 52, 74, 80.

[82] "[A]ll our knowledge has been built up communally; there would be no astrophysics, there would be no history, there would not even be language, if man were a solitary animal." Jacob Bronowski, *Science and Human Values* (rev. ed., New York, 1965), p. 57; Bentley Glass, *Science and Ethical Values* (Chapel Hill, 1965), pp. 82–83.

[83] Jacob Bronowski, *Science and Human Values* (rev. ed., New York, 1965), pp. 56–58.

reported. But ordinarily we do not follow this procedure. If each one had to do this individually, little progress would be made. What we regularly do is believe in the trustworthiness of a report and have confidence in it. We accept and trust the report on the authority of the reporter.[84] Those who claim that science is "pure" and free of all values, must face the part belief plays in the origin and growth of scientific knowledge.[85] Such an acceptance on faith of the world of scientific activities constitutes what has been called the "spiritual foundations of scientific life."[86] In a word, the assumption that scientific knowledge is impersonal is illusory and deceptive. Scientific knowledge is, like all knowledge, eminently personal.[87]

Freedom of research and publication is another value without which scientific knowledge is impossible. Such freedom relates to the very source of new knowledge and the dissemination of what knowledge is had.[88] Freedom is necessary for the manifestation of that adventurous, "sublime daring" which is part of all pioneer work at the outer edge of discovery. No scientist, or positivist for that matter, should overlook the value of freedom which is so necessary for creative research.

There are values necessarily in law and science, then, which it appears difficult to deny once the substance and context of law and science have been critically examined.[89] Positivism's mistake is to question the place of any necessary values in law, especially certain scientifically establishable, given values, instead of questioning the place of this or that imposed code of constructed values which could be highly unscientific and emotional. A scientific study of law and of the values which are necessarily in it can be made, as was noted. But, if law is a directive judgment of what is for the good of the

people, this study could hardly avoid the issue when it found laws with values in them, whatever they were, which worked against the good of the people. To hold otherwise would be an admission that the science of law was indifferent to the common values of the people. Unless this is to be merely an exercise in formalism the question should immediately be raised as to what values such a science actually serves.

## II. LAWS UNWRITTEN AND WRITTEN

The laws of men who have not learned to write are perforce unwritten. These laws are expressed principally in regulative customs which relate to the common welfare of the people.

Our main concern in this work, as noted above, is with the prevalence in all law of those patterns of value judgments which psychology indicates are there necessarily and which consequently should be found there universally. The identification of these patterns in all known written law is not too great a task, as we already noted. In order to make the claim that these patterns of value judgments are universal among all men, preliterate as well as literate, the laws of preliterate men have to be examined.

### A. REGULATIONS MAY OR MAY NOT BE LAWS

Regulations may be for the individual welfare of the members of a society or they may be for their common welfare, as we have seen. Rules of etiquette are for the individual good of the members. Regulations controlling the killing of human beings are for the common good of the members. In the context of preliterate regulations, this means that there are some customs which relate to the common good of the people and which are laws, and there are some customs which do not relate to the common good of the people and are not laws. All customs, of course, have some remote relation to the common welfare. But it is only those customs which have a proximate relation that are laws. This proximate relation may be direct as in the case of arson, or it may be indirect as in the instances of accidental injury or breach of agreement. It will be the relation of customs to the common needs of the people, then, which will be our norm of judging whether a preliterate custom is custom law or not. "As soon as his actions have a bearing upon the well-being of his fellows a customary behavior is demanded which may be designated as customary law."[90]

[84] "It is a fallacy to assume that one can test what is true and what is false unaided. But then it must follow that all verification, all science, depends upon communication with others and reliance upon others. Thus we come straight to the *ought* of science, for we must be able to trust the word of others." Bentley Glass, *Science and Ethical Values* (Chapel Hill, 1965), p. 83.

[85] "Each person can know directly very little truth and must trust others for the rest. Indeed, to assure this process of mutual reliance is one of the main functions of society." Michael Polanyi, *The Study of Man* (Chicago, 1959), p. 68. See also Polanyi, *Personal Knowledge* (Chicago, 1958), pp. 240, 266.

[86] Michael Polanyi, *The Study of Man* (Chicago, 1959), pp. 60–61.

[87] "The participation of the knower in shaping his knowledge . . . is now recognized as the true guide and master of our cognitive powers. . . . The ideal of a knowledge embodied in strictly impersonal statements now appears self-contradictory, meaningless, a fit subject for ridicule. We must learn to accept as our final ideal a knowledge that is manifestly personal." Michael Polanyi, *The Study of Man* (Chicago, 1959), pp. 26–27.

[88] See Bentley Glass, *Science and Ethical Values* (Chapel Hill, 1965), pp. 89, 90, 92.

[89] "Men may go on talking the language of positivism, pragmatism, and naturalism for many years, yet continue to respect the principles of truth and morality which their vocabulary anxiously ignores." Michael Polanyi, *Personal Knowledge* (Chicago, 1958), p. 233.

[90] Franz Boas, "Culture," *Encyc. of the Social Sciences* 2 (1930): p. 88. From what has been said, it is obvious that preliterate law is not "the totality of the customs of the tribe" (E. Sidney Hartland, *Primitive Law* [London, 1924], p. 5) nor "the patterns of interaction for all the members of a group" as distinguished from patterns for some members of the group. Eliot Chapple and Carleton Coon, *Principles of Anthropology* (New York, 1942), p. 658. Some have said that customs and laws are norms that are not distinguishable on the basis of con-

Among the Ifugao, for example, if a pregnant woman violates the custom regarding how she should dress, there is no public reaction. But theft, murder, arson, adultery, and defamation are reacted to by punishment. With the Tswana, if a man violates the custom regarding sleeping with a menstruating woman, even if she is his own wife, no sanction will be exerted against him. But if a man causes an unmarried woman to be pregnant, or commits adultery, or rapes a woman, he is liable to damages according to custom law. In some African societies the drumming and feasting at a marriage ceremony are customary, but the promise to make the marriage payment by the groom pertains to custom law. This promise is considered to be of the essence of the marriage contract.[91]

### B. UNWRITTEN REGULATIONS MAY BE LAWS

The unwritten custom law of a preliterate society is an expression of the directive judgments made by those with lawmaking authority for the common welfare of the people.[92] Included are the judgments made by leaders,

judges, councils, and the people themselves. Together these constitute preliterate custom law. It should be noted, as we shall see later, that leaders are considered to speak for the people and council members are looked on as representative of the people. This is shown by the people's action in removing from office those whom they deem guilty of wrongdoing. For preliterates, law-making authority resides primarily in the people.

Customs which relate to the common needs of the people are distinguished from those customs which refer only to their individual needs by the reactions of the people themselves to violations of these customs. When there is no common response either physical or non-physical by the members of a society to the violations of a custom, it can be assumed that the content of the custom in question does not proximately bear on their common welfare. This custom is not a law. When, on the other hand, there is a public reaction by the people to the violation of a custom, it is a clear indication that the content of the custom is considered by the people to have a bearing on their common welfare.[93] The rationale of the people's common reaction to actions injurious to their common welfare is that such actions threaten their very union itself. It menaces the common matrix within which they live their individual lives.[94] The type of reaction or sanction which the people bring to bear on violators varies. It may be physical or it may be psychological.[95] Ridicule or loss of face can be a more effective sanction than corporal punishment, as we shall see in part two.

To say that custom law can be recognized by the sanctions which the people impose is not to say that there must be sanctions in order that there be law. Sanction or coercion does not constitute law. There are written laws which have no sanction attached, as witness the Constitution of the United States, treaty agreements of International Law, and certain criminal statutes which we will note later.[96] There is no doubt

---

tent. They are differentiated according to the type of sanction attached. See Alfred Radcliffe-Brown, "Social Sanctions," *Encyc. of the Social Sciences* 13 (1935) : pp. 531–534. But such a position overlooks the only possible rationale for the type of sanction put forth—the content of the rule and its relation to the common welfare. See E. Adamson Hoebel, "The Political Organization and Law-ways of the Comanche Indians," *Mem. Amer. Anthropol. Assoc.* 54 (1940) : p. 46.

[91] Ralph Barton, "Ifugao Law," *Amer. Archaeology and Ethnology* 15 (1919) : pp. 11–13; Isaac Schapera, *A Handbook of Tswana Law and Custom* (London, 1938), p. 38; T. Olawale Elias, *The Nature of African Customary Law* (Manchester, 1956), p. 294.

[92] "The basic source of Kirghiz law was represented by their steppe customs. . . . Juridical customs comprise the main source of Buriat law." Valintin Riasanovsky, *Customary Law of the Nomadic Tribes of Siberia* (Tsiensin, 1938), pp. 20, 59. The phrase "custom law" seems better suited to designate the unwritten laws of preliterate peoples than "customary law." "Customary law" has long been used in international law to denote those practices and customs which are common among certain nations and which they agree by treaty will have the force of law among them. "Custom law," on the other hand, while admittedly a hybrid expression, does seem to express more accurately the unique type of law with which we are here concerned, namely, a *"custom-of-a-people-which-has-a-proximate-relation-to-their-common-welfare-and-is-by-that-fact-law."* This type of law is sometimes referred to as "adat-law" from the Arabic word "adat" which means custom or customary.

Because of the difference between those customs which are not law and those that are, some authors have adopted the distinction of "merely customs" v. "customs" (Ralph Barton, "Ifugao Law," *Amer. Archaeology and Ethnology* 15 [1919] : p. 13) or "neutral customs" v. "customs" (Bronislaw Malinowski, "Introduction," to H. Ian Hogbin, *Law and Order in Polynesia* [New York, 1934], p. xxvi; William Seagle, "Primitive Law and Professor Malinowski," *Amer. Anthropologist* 39 [1937] : p. 281; Leopold Pospisil, *Kapauku Papuans and Their Law* [New Haven, 1958], p. 289). Some preliterate groups have several expressions to denote the differences in their customs, but always retaining the difference between those whose breaches will not be punished and those that will. See Isaac Schapera, *A Handbook of Tswana Law and Custom* (London, 1938), pp. 35–36; Anthony Allott, *Essays in African Law* (London, 1960), p. 62.

[93] "All people have law in the broad sense of the term. . . . [These laws] may not be codified and are certainly not written. . . . Nevertheless, they are laws in the sense that they are agreed-upon modes of behavior, the breach of which calls for such sanction as the community has the means of applying." Walter Goldschmidt, *Man's Way* (Cleveland, 1959), p. 101. "By considering rules in their integral relationship to the sanctions which support them, it is possible to differentiate between various aspects of custom, and in particular between legal and non-legal rules of behaviour." Ralph Piddington, *An Introduction to Social Anthropology* (London, 1950), p. 353.

[94] "[T]he sanction of primitive law resides in the constitution of purposeful, organized, and effectively working systems of human activities. . . . [A]ny failure to maintain the rules makes an end to the institution." Bronislaw Malinowski, "A New Instrument for the Interpretation of Law—Especially Primitive," *Yale Law Jour.* 51 (1942) : pp. 1237–1254.

[95] "[A] legal sanction does not need to be corporal punishment or a deprivation of property. The form of a sanction is relative to the culture and to the subgroup in which it is used; it may be physical or psychological." Leopold Pospisil, *Kapauku Papuans and Their Law* (New Haven, 1958), p. 268.

[96] See "Association for Protection and Security."

about the existence of such laws, for they are written. Among preliterates who do not write down their laws, however, there is the problem of determining which customs are laws. Here sanction indicates law, it does not constitute law.[97]

## III. VALUES SELF-EVIDENT AND NOT SELF-EVIDENT IN LAW

Our value judgments, as we have seen, are either given or constructed. The result of this two-fold source of value judgments shows itself in all man-made law. In all law there are those value judgments which are accepted as self-evident and there are those which are not so regarded.

### A. VALUES WHICH ARE SELF-EVIDENT

The values which are self-evident may be self-evident absolutely; that is, they may be obvious to all men. Or they may be self-evident relatively; that is, they may be obvious to most men. Such are the universal or almost universal value judgments of which we shall see more later. They are postulated in every system of law. From these starting points all value-judging in law is done.[98]

Self-evident to all are the given value judgments which all men make without a reasoning process. These value judgments, because they are formed without reasoning, are understood and are meaningful to all normal men. They are so obvious that they are taken for granted and are not even expressed in man-made law.[99] Reference was made above to the fact that the given value judgments are so much a part of the normal men's mental processes that their absence raises a presumption of abnormalcy.[100] Consequently, laws formed according to the opposites of these given value judgments would

be abnormal and inconceivable.[101] The basic drives, as we have noted, are norm-indicators of certain basic values. Evidence of the functioning of these indicators is had in the given value judgments which are postulated in all law as self-evident. Lawmakers, as any other men, do not consider it necessary to prove that men's self-realization or self-preservation are good in themselves and not evil. "This category [of universals] also includes the association and values which lie, for the most part, below the level of consciousness but which are, at the same time, an integral part of culture."[102]

Self-evident to most men are also the value judgments which are formed with a minimal amount of reasoning. These are the elementary constructs which the evidence will show are formed by all men with few exceptions. They also are so evident that they are postulated by all law either implicitly or explicitly. Thus, the values of human association for the fulfillment of common needs, giving to others what is their due, the peace which thereupon ensues, self-protection, and ensured freedom may be postulated implicitly with no explicit mention being made of them in man-made laws. Or these postulate values may be explicitly stated. The Preamble of the Constitution of the United States of America names as values to be sought: union and a more perfect form of it, justice and its establishment, domestic tranquility and its insurance, common defense and provision for it, the general welfare and its promotion, and liberty and the securing of it. These values are merely listed and no attempt is made to show that they are good and desirable rather than evil and undesirable. They are assumed to be self-evidently good to most men and not in need of being proved or justified.

The presence of self-evident value judgments is seen in every culture. All cultures are a development of these originally assumed values.[103] In fact, the general direction which the laws of any culture take derives from these self-evident value judgments. According to the demands of these judgments, man-made law is shaped and reshaped.[104] The fundamental ideas of any culture

[97] It is perfectly true that a law without attached penalties gives a judge no means of enforcing the law. But this does not mean that it is not a law or that it does not oblige. It merely means that when the question arises of imposing penalties for the enforcement of the law, no provision has been made for them in the law.

[98] "Inasmuch as the members of a society ordinarily accept their basic propositions as self-evident truths and work upon them as if they were truths, and because they do reason from them, if not with perfect logic, they may best be called postulates. The particular formulations of specific customs and patterns for behavior that go into a given culture are more or less explicitly shaped by the precepts given in the basic postulates of that specific culture." E. Adamson Hoebel, *The Law of Primitive Man*, (Cambridge, Mass., 1954), p. 13. See Max Gluckman, "Natural Justice in Africa," *Natural Law Forum* **9** (1964) : p. 36.

[99] "Anthropologists must [recognize] the values lying behind the stated norm, and ultimately the propositions about the nature of society, the world, and God which are the unstated postulates of any set of laws. Legal anthropology . . . must also . . . ask how it is that the rules or laws reflect the most basic values, often so basic that they cannot be uttered by the people who hold them." Paul Bohannon, *Social Anthropology* (New York, 1963), p. 288.

[100] See "The Basic Drives" above.

[101] "[I]t becomes obvious that the values embodied in the universal components of legal systems cannot be replaced by the opposites of these values. Otherwise human life in society would become unbearable." Edgar Bodenheimer, "The Case Against Natural Law Reassessed," *Stanford Law Review* **17** (1964) : pp. 37, 45.

[102] Ralph Linton, *The Study of Man* (New York, 1936), p. 272.

[103] "Anthropology can lay bare the internal logics of each culture. It can sometimes show how the economic theory, the political theory, the art forms, and the religious doctrine of each society are all expressive of a single set of elementary assumptions." Clyde Kluckhohn, *Mirror for Man* (New York, 1949), p. 262.

[104] "[M]ost laws are the expression of some sound biological reality, of some important and functionally founded trend of culture." Bronislaw Malinowski, "Introduction," Hogbin, *Law and Order in Polynesia* (New York, 1934), p. lxvi. "[E]very culture has its definite postulates of law, and it is the duty of society, from time to time, to shape the law according to these

offer a lead to their source which is these postulated values.[105] These value judgments have been recognized by those who have "worked down" to them from man-made law, as well as by those who have "worked up" to them from men's basic drives and given values. "The jural postulates . . . are generalized statements of the tendencies actually operating . . . . They are ideals pre-supposed by the whole social complex, which can thus be used to bring the law into harmony with it."[106] The jural postulates are the presuppositions of life in any society.[107] In other words, the postulated values are

rules which basically govern the law and culture of society. Here we have "the idea of a rule imposing itself on man in society, over and above the contingency of facts, capable as such of restraining divergent wills and alone qualified to justify the fundamental direction of positive law."[108]

## B. VALUES WHICH ARE NOT SELF-EVIDENT

The remaining value judgments in law are not self-evident. They need reasoning and justification. They are constructed with more than minimal reasoning. They are not, on the evidence, universal or almost uni-versal. They are, rather, general, common, frequent and occasional. The value judgments to be formed re-garding the law of selective military service, for instance, are not thought of as self-evidently good or bad, right or wrong, desirable or undesirable. They are considered to be matters for reasoned value-construction.

requirements." Joseph Kohler, *Philosophy of Law,* trans. by A. Albrecht (Boston, 1914), p. 4.

[105] "A study of the key basic concepts of any culture . . . reveals that these key concepts not merely provide the ideas in terms of which the people of that culture conceive the facts of their existence but also define their values." F. C. S. Northrop, "Jurisprudence in the Law School Curriculum," *Jour. Legal Education* 1 (1949) : p. 489.

[106] Julius Stone, *Province and Function of Law* (Sidney, 1950), p. 337.

[107] Roscoe Pound, *Jurisprudence* (5 v., St. Paul, 1959) 3: pp. 7–8.

[108] François Geny, *Science et Technique en Droit Privé Positif* (4 v., Paris, 1921–1927) 2: p. 253.

PART TWO

VALUE-AREAS IN LAW

CHAPTER 3

VALUES IN UNWRITTEN LAW

According to our model of values, there are value judgments which are formed with psychological necessity in the areas of basic drives, obligation, rights and regulations. These are given. Other value judgments are constructed. It is to be expected, then, that wherever normal men are in society their laws will be found to contain certain given value judgments which are universal in all known societies. Further, on the assumption that some value judgments are formed more easily than others, because their objects are more evident, some constructed value judgments can be expected to be universal or almost universal in all societies. On the same assumption, the remaining value judgments can be expected to be general, common, frequent or occasional in all known societies.

*Categories.* "Universal" will here refer to those value judgments which are found without exception in all individuals or in all societies. "Almost universal" will mean universal in all societies with rare exceptions. It has been the practical wisdom of both ancients and moderns when treating of the category of "universal" to treat along with it the category of "almost universal." They are different to be sure, but the "almost universal" has an underlying connotation which remaining categories do not have.[1] It is the "universal" and "almost universal" in which we are primarily interested and concerning which only we will make statements which are factually verifiable. The universal and the almost universal are certain, constant, and predictable.

"General" will denote for us wide prevalence or what is found among the majority of the people. "Common" will refer to ordinary occurrences or to what has a like number approximately on either side. "Frequent" will mean encountered at times but as in a minority. "Occasional" will indicate happening irregularly or among a small minority. The lines between these categories which are less than universal or almost universal are not hard and fast as is obvious. These classifications, in contradistinction to the universals and almost universals, admit of a high degree of relativeness and are presented as such. Nor is there always certainty regarding

the category in which some value judgments belong. The locating of value judgments in one or other category has, at times, been the result of a considered estimate of whatever evidence has been available.

These categories, however, can give some notion of how widespread certain value judgments appear to be which are neither universal nor almost universal. They can also serve to show how some value judgments which speculatively have been said to be universal or almost universal are factually in neither of these categories. They can exemplify, in areas we will discuss at some length later, the varying appraisals which go into the formation of many constructed value judgments. They can also indicate areas where much research still remains to be done—among literates as well as preliterates— before we can know with any degree of accuracy what the prevalence of many value judgments actually is. Clarification of the place these less than universal value judgments have in these categories on the grounds of factually verifiable evidence is most cordially invited.

*Evidence.* The data we shall examine are contained in the reports of anthropologists, ethnologists, and researchers in custom law regarding the prevalence of various value judgments among preliterate peoples. These reports include data originating from field observations, as well as summaries of data made by recognized authorities. References are not needlessly multiplied where one or two reliable sources attest to the prevalence of a certain value judgment. The reliability of this evidence is in proportion to the correctness of the reporting. Insufficient or inaccurate reports have in the past contributed to many false statements, inferences, and conclusions. A time also had to be awaited, perhaps, when some degree of self-examination was possible on the part of various peoples themselves. Hence, the greater part of the reporters from whom we shall draw our evidence have done their work during the past generation or so. It is in this period that great and more dependable progress has been made.[2] The fact that preliterates are gradually decreasing in number is all the more reason for examining their custom law to show that certain value judgments were always present in the laws of men whether these laws were written or unwritten.[3]

---

[1] "If the universality is disturbed by no more than a few exceptions which may be explained in the light of special circumstances operative in those communities, the behavior may still have a fundamental basis." Otto Klineberg, *Social Psychology* (rev. ed., New York, 1954), p. 69.

[2] A. Irving Hallowell, "The Nature and Function of Property as a Social Institution," *Jour. Legal and Political Sociology* 1 (1943) : p. 115.

[3] "Often . . . I have used the present tense as if the Nupe kingdom of pre-British days still existed. . . . [Tribal Principles] are still valid and still mould society to-day as they moulded it thirty, fifty, or even a hundred years ago. . . . The

Our concern is with the prevalence of value judgments among preliterate peoples. Data concerning this prevalence are ample and reliable. Knowledge of the functioning and comparison of these values among preliterates is undoubtedly of great value. But reporting regarding these aspects of values among preliterates is scanty and insufficient to warrant treatment here.[4] Besides, such a knowledge of value functions and comparisons is not necessary in order to know what the value judgments are which peoples make and whether all peoples make them universally or otherwise. Indeed, it must first be known what value judgments people actually make before these values can be considered functionally and comparatively.[5] Hence, the reports of reliable anthropologists and ethnologists regarding those value judgments preliterates make and their prevalence will be an adequate source of data for our purposes.[6]

*Inferences.* The value judgments which we shall hold as universal in all societies are reported data. Other less than universal value judgments may be reported data or may be inferred from reported data. The licitness or illicitness of such inferences depends on the ground on which it rests. That certain groups of preliterates state they consider adultery to be wrong, is a reported datum. That some preliterate groups make no statement about the wrongness of adultery but do nonetheless punish it, is a reported datum from which it may be licitly inferred that they consider adultery to be wrong. Medically normal people do not inflict punishment without a reason. That a group of preliterates is reported as not physically punishing adultery is a datum from which it would be illicit to infer they do not consider adultery to be wrong.[7] Other types of punishment such as loss of reputation, avoidance, ridicule, and ostracism may be in practice.

Theft is reported to be encountered in all societies. This is a datum, however, from which it would be illicit to infer that all these societies value-judge theft to be good and acceptable. For, other data show that men are quite capable of doing things they know to be wrong. The value judgment all societies make regarding theft has to be ascertained more directly than by inference. That war is reported to be prevalent in human societies is also a reported datum. But, for reasons which we shall see, it could be licit to infer from this datum that war is judged by those who engage in it to be good rather than evil.

Furthermore, that a people is reported as having no word for, say, theft, is a datum from which it would be illicit to infer that they had no ideas of theft or that theft was wrong. There are peoples who live among ice and trees who are reported as having no word for "ice" and "tree."[8] But it would be inadmissible to infer from this fact that they had no ideas of "ice" and "tree." That a people had an idea of theft could be ascertained from their observable reactions to the taking of things by others without approval.[9]

## I. LISTS OF UNIVERSAL VALUES

The fact has long been recognized that there are certain human characteristics, many of them the value judgments with which we are concerned, which are universal in all known societies of men. "There are known and knowable principles of human behavior which are universal . . . . All human societies, from the 'most primitive' to the 'most advanced,' constitute a continuum."[10] So obvious is this fact that many have remarked on "the appalling monotony of the fundamental ideas of mankind all over the globe" which are "so trite as usually to be taken for granted."[11]

What with this universality of certain traits so evident, it has not been too difficult to draw up various schemata of them. Some lists contain such general categories as communication, thought, and tools; or artifacts, social institutions, language, and traditions. Others set down religion, socio-political structure, material equipment, art, morality. Several follow categories such as communication; material facts such as goods, shelter, utensils and the like; the family; social organization;

Nupe kingdom and its society still exist, not only very vividly in the memory of the people but to a very large extent in concrete reality. This is not denying the force of social changes, but stressing the tenacity of a social structure that survives although its contents have changed materially. . . . [A] stronger proof of the tenacity of the Nupe social system is the fact that where the Administration had departed from it and tried to make way for a new development the old trend broke through, undeflected." Siegfried Nadel, *A Black Byzantium* (Oxford, 1942), p. 157.

[4] Robert Spencer, "The Nature and Value of Functionalism in Anthropology," in: Donald Martindale, ed., *Functionalism in the Social Sciences* (Philadelphia, 1965), p. 3; Paul Bohannon, *African Homicide and Suicide* (Princeton, 1960), pp. 235, 252.

[5] I. C. Jarvie, "Limits of Functionalism and Alternatives to It in Anthropology," in: Donald Martindale, ed., *Functionalism in the Social Sciences* (Philadelphia, 1965), p. 19.

[6] Useful maps of preliterate peoples are to be found in Robert Lowie, *An Introduction to Cultural Anthropology* (2nd ed., New York, 1940) and Paul Bohannon, *Social Anthropology* (New York, 1963).

[7] Robert Redfield, "Maine's Ancient Law in the Light of Primitive Societies," *Western Polit. Quart.* 3 (1950): pp. 574, 580.

[8] Ashley Montagu, *Man: His First Million Years* (Cleveland, 1957), p. 117.

[9] H. Ian Hogbin, "Social Reactions to Crime: Law and Morals in the Schouten Islands," *Jour. Royal Anthropol. Inst.* 68 (1939): pp. 223, 226.

[10] Clyde Kluckhohn, *Mirror for Man* (New York, 1949), p. 266.

[11] "[I]t has become increasingly apparent that there are some basic categorical similarities in human culture the world over." A. Irving Hallowell, "The Nature and Function of Property as a Social Institution," *Jour. Legal and Polit. Sociology* 1 (1943): p. 115. Adolph Bastian, *Ethnische Elementargedanken in der Lehre vom Menschen* (Berlin, 1895), *passim.* See also Alexander Goldenweiser, *Anthropology* (New York, 1937), p. 455.

government; religion; explanations of natural phenomena; property; art; war.

Other schemata classify universal traits under general and special aspects. The general aspects are: geographical environment, demography, human ecology; material substratum; knowledge and belief; normative system; language; social-organization; life-cycle of the individual. The special aspects are: economic; political; legal; educational; magico-religious, art, recreation and ceremonial. Still other schemata classify the universal values in the order of their dependency, with the first existing solely for the purpose of supporting the last; family; transportation; communication; economics; education; politics; practical technologies; decorative arts; pure sciences; pure arts; philosophy; religion. Other universals, upwards of seventy, have simply been listed in alphabetical order.

These various attempts to classify human traits, including universal human values, only point once again to the underlying taxonomic problem. These schemata have been referred to as a "rough plan of convenience." [12] The only completely non-arbitrary principle of classification of value is the one given to us by the basic drives. According to the various basic drives, we have a fundamental classification of universal and other value judgments. [13]

## II. REGULATIONS AND OBLIGATION ARE UNIVERSAL

Regulations are universal in all known societies of men. A prime characteristic of men is that they do not live haphazard and promiscuous lives in society. [14] Men are guided and directed by rules, codes, and sets of customs which distinguish between what is acceptable and what is unacceptable, what is good and what is bad, what is right and what is wrong. Instead of random living, there is regulated and controlled action. Implied here is a certain amount of self-discipline and self-control. All cultures are regulative processes which demand certain ways of acting. Regulations and restraint are the price which is paid for the freedom which is enjoyed within these systems. In the formation of these patterns of regulations, it is the needs of the people which are controlling. "In any society human relations must be ordered so that basic interests are recognized and secured." [15] This relation between the needs of the people and the regulations of law, as we noted above, is the controlling fact about law. [16] On this basis, some regulations are not law because they do not relate to the common welfare of the people. Other regulations are law because they are considered by the people to have this relation as is shown by their reaction to violations.

Such a universality of regulations among men is to be expected if they form the given value judgments which we discussed above. Concomitant with men's master drive for self-realization, men, as we saw, inevitably judge that they ought to use whatever means necessary to attain this end, that the means which lead to this end are different from those which do not, and that they are distinguished by whether they lead to the end or not. In other words, all men co-naturally judge that there is a difference between what is right and what is wrong, and that there is a way or norm of telling the difference. Such being the case, it is only to be expected that wherever men are found they are concerned with having norms or rules according to which they can know the difference between what is right and what is wrong for them in their actions. [17] Hence, one of the most basic of men's value judgments is that regulations are good, desirable, and helpful, and not bad, undesirable, and harmful. [18]

Men also have a universal recognition, however vague, that they ought to obey rules and regulations because what the regulations require is for their own welfare. In other words, there is a universal recognition of obligation because of the means-end relationship involved.

[12] Alfred Kroeber, *Anthropology* (rev. ed., New York, 1948), pp. 311–312.

[13] Lists of universals (the order in which references are given in this footnote, and in subsequent footnotes in which references are similarly grouped, follows the order in which their materials are presented in the text): Clark Wissler, *Man and Culture* (New York, 1923), pp. 74, 97; David Bidney, *Theoretical Anthropology* (New York, 1953), p. 133; Alexander Goldenweiser, *Anthropology* (New York, 1937), p. 455; Stuart Chase, *The Proper Study of Man* (New York, 1956), p. 78; Ashley Montagu, *Man: His First Million Years* (Cleveland, 1957), pp. 111–112; Ralph Piddington, *An Introduction to Social Anthropology* (London, 1950). p. 248; James Feibleman, *The Theory of Human Culture* (New York, 1946), pp. 104–105; George Murdock, "The Common Denominator of Culture," Ralph Linton ed., *The Science of Man in the World Crisis* (New York, 1945), p. 124.

[14] "Absolute chaos is inconceivable. The notion of regularity, of what is called law, is inescapable. . . . And these ideas of law and capriciousness are probably everywhere connected somehow with the ideas of good and evil." Robert Redfield, *The Primitive World and Its Transformations* (Ithaca, 1953), p. 100.

[15] A. Irving Hallowell, "The Nature and Function of Property as a Social Institution," *Journal of Legal and Polit. Sociology* 1 (1943) : p. 134.

[16] "[T]he Barotse think that certain kinds of social institutions are necessarily common to all mankind, in all societies. All men, they say, must have laws enforcing respect for chiefs and elders, controlling marriage, tabooing sexual relations between certain kinds of kin though these may vary from tribe to tribe, ordaining respect to and avoidance of senior in-laws." Max Gluckman, "Natural Justice in Africa," *Natural Law Forum* 9 (1964) : pp. 38–39.

[17] Research on young children playing games shows that they have a natural interest in the rules of the game. They desire to know the right way to play the game. They want to know the rules so they can follow them. They respect the rules and try earnestly to play according to them. See Jean Piaget, *The Moral Judgment of the Child*, trans. by Marjorie Gabain (Glencoe, 1948), pp. 1–2.

[18] Only if a "state of nature" theory were held, in which man supposedly lived naturally without any common regulations, could it be possible to hold that regulations are evil. But, as we shall see, such a "state" is purely hypothetical and without any historical support.

The yearning which men have for regularity and order implies a realization that rules ought to be obeyed because of what they bring about.[19] This is undoubtedly the source of the feeling of satisfaction which men attest to when they have done what they know they ought to have done. This is summed up in the testimony that "It is always good to be good." [20] The people's attempt to get a deviator to obey regulations, by bringing pressure to bear on him, finds its rationale in the deviator's obligation to obey the regulations in the first place. Hence, obligation is recognized in custom as well as in written law.[21]

## III. NO SOCIETIES WITHOUT REGULATIONS WHICH ARE LAW

According to the model of law which we constructed above, law is a directive judgment of means necessary for the common needs of the people. With such an approach to the problem of the nature of law, no difficulty is encountered in locating such regulatory judgments among preliterate peoples. But when researchers took to the field looking for "law" which was a command of the sovereign which he was able to enforce with power, or for "law" which was what the courts decided it was, little anthropological mileage was made.[22] Researchers were unable to find any sovereign among many preliterates who issued commands, much less who

was able to enforce them if he gave them. Among many groups there were no visible courts who decided on what the law was. Hence, the conclusion reached by these researchers was that there were societies of preliterates which were "lawless."

The absence of legislators or judges was immediately interpreted as indicating that there was no law among some peoples. Researchers looked for some individual in these societies whom they could identify as a sovereign who made law. Lack of enforceable coercion by courts was also stated as an indication that these peoples had no law. As far as these investigators could see, there were plenty of customs which were backed up by sanctions, but there were no laws. Anything which even remotely resembled law in these societies was warily labeled "not quite law." In the face of clear evidence that these groups preserved order and had a concern for justice, these men continued to report that some societies of preliterates were "lawless." Rather than question whether their ideas of law were correct, they questioned whether these people had any law.

To other anthropologists and ethnologists it seemed incongruous to hold that these societies which maintained order and cared for justice were "lawless." It became obvious that the command theory and the court theory of law had to give way in the face of the facts. What became more and more evident was that these peoples had law. They themselves made law in their custom regulations which related to their common welfare. The essence of what was termed law in literate societies was present in the custom law of preliterate peoples.

As regards enforcement by coercion, it was gradually recognized that preliterates were employing more efficient ways of bringing about obedience to laws than physical punishment. Non-physical means such as public opinion, ridicule, and others which we shall see, were sufficient to keep the great majority of possible deviators in line. Coercion administered by politically organized agencies, such as were prevalent in Europe, was now understood to be only one of the many possible ways of bringing pressure to bear on the members of a society who might become violators of the custom law. Support for this concept of custom law came from the history of law which indicated that the earliest laws of mankind were not commands of superiors enforced by sanctions. They were custom laws which the people realized were necessary for their own common welfare. Even criminal law, wherein clear prohibitions seem so evident, had its origin not in the commands of superiors but in the people's custom law of retaliation as a means for their own common protection.

The court theory of law, as we said, also had to be abandoned. Evidence was at hand showing that members of preliterate societies kept order and peace well enough among themselves in spite of their lack of formalized courts. It was found that the court theory, just

---

[19] "[T]here wells up in the breast of most men an emotional yearning for regularity and system in the daily conduct of human affairs. The majority, far from cherishing selfish ideals and pursuing the path of chaos, love peace and order. They realize that the best policy of social insurance against anarchy is law, and are therefore prepared to obey it for that reason, if for no other." T. Olawale Elias, *The Nature of African Customary Law* (Manchester, 1956), p. 60.

[20] Paul Radin, *Primitive Man as Philosopher* (New York, 1927), p. 65.

[21] Regulations and obligation: Bronislaw Malinowski, "A New Instrument for the Interpretation of Law—Especially Primitive," *Yale Law Jour.* 51 (1942): p. 1240: this is a reprint of the article which originally appeared in *Lawyers Guild Rev.* 2 (1942): pp. 1–12; Gladys Reichard, "Social Life," in: Franz Boas, ed., *General Anthropology* (Boston, 1938), pp. 478-479; Mischa Titiev, *The Science of Man* (New York, 1954), pp. 340, 431; Edward Tylor, *Anthropology* (New York, 1916), p. 410; Robert MacIver, *The Web of Government* (New York, 1947), p. 22; Ashley Montagu, *Man: His First Million Years* (Cleveland, 1957), p. 169; Paul Radin, *Primitive Man as Philosopher* (New York, 1927), pp. 63–75; David Bidney, *Theoretical Anthropology* (New York, 1953), pp. 11, 154; Paul Vinogradoff, *Outlines of Historical Jurisprudence* (London, 1922), p. 152; Ralph Piddington, *An Introduction to Social Anthropology* (London, 1950), p. 227; William Mariner, *An Account of the Natives of the Tonga Islands* (2 v., London, 1817) 2: p. 141: quoted by H. Ian Hogbin, *Law and Order in Polynesia* (London, 1934), p. 283.

[22] "In the study of communities where law is neither codified nor administered before courts nor yet enforced by constabulary, certain problems arise which can be easily overlooked in a jurisprudence based on our own formal and crystallized systems." Bronislaw Malinowski, "A New Instrument for the Interpretation of Law—Especially Primitive," *Yale Law Jour.* 51 (1942): p. 1238.

as the command theory, broke down when applied to factual situations of preliterates living according to their custom laws.[23] The fairly efficient manner in which custom law operated among preliterates without courts was proof enough that the court theory was inadequate.[24]

The custom regulations of preliterates which have a bearing on their common welfare, then, are law. According to the data of psychology, value judgments, some universal and some otherwise, can be expected in the custom law areas of life, sex, knowledge and decision, mine and thine, and association in social living. It is into an examination of data relevant to these areas that we must now proceed.

## CHAPTER 4

## LIFE AND SEX

The value judgments of custom law which we will first examine are those pertaining to the existence of individual persons and the existence of the human race. It is on the continued existence of individuals and the race that all other development obviously depends.

### I. PRESERVING LIFE

The preservation of life is a primary necessity of all human living. That men have a basic drive to preserve

their lives is a point on which there is the greatest agreement.

### A. UNIVERSAL VALUE JUDGMENTS IN ALL SOCIETIES

All normal men form the given value judgment that self-preservation is good and not evil in itself, for reasons we have already seen. It is found, then, in all individuals and in all societies. "The history of life itself is predicated on the assumption that life, whether sweet or not, is desirable; desirable not merely for the individual but for the group of which he is a part."[1] It is impossible to conceive what life would be like or how there could even be life if men had the opposite drive for self-destruction.[2] The value judgment that the preservation of human life is good rather than evil is a postulate of all law.[3]

Besides this universal value judgment regarding the preservation of life, there are other value judgments which they make concerning life. Some of these value judgments are universal in all known societies of men. The others are less than universal in varying degrees. They manifest men's tendency, once past the given value judgments, to diverge in their evaluations of the means necessary for preserving human life. The plasticity of the basic drives here shows itself. There is no divergence in value-judging about the end of the drives or the elementary means of obtaining it. There is, however, variation in value-judging about the other means.

Although men have a basic drive to preserve their

---

[23] "When we attempt to apply this [Cardozo's] definition to certain primitive communities we discover that it will not work." Huntington Cairns, "Law and Authority," in: Victor Calverton, ed., *The Making of Man* (New York, 1931), p. 337.

[24] An approach demanding the existence of courts "vitiates the study of the unformalized law found among preliterates." Jane Richardson, "Law and Status Among the Kiowa Indians," *Amer. Ethnol. Soc.* 1 (1940): p. 2. "The absurdity of this [Gray's] view of the law is that while it recognizes precedents as a source of law it refuses that name to statutes and customs until both become precedents by being embodied in judicial decisions. The logical conclusion, then, is that precedents alone are law." T. Olawale Elias, *The Nature of African Customary Law* (Manchester, 1956), p. 39.

"Lawless societies:" Edward Evans-Pritchard, "The Nuer of the Southern Sudan," in: Meyer Fortes and Edw. Evans-Pritchard, eds., *African Political Systems* (London, 1940), p. 293; Barend Ter Haar, *Adat Law in Indonesia* (New York, 1948), p. 228; Arthur Diamond, *The Evolution of Law and Order* (London, 1951), p. 56; Alfred Radcliffe-Brown, "Primitive Law," *Encyc. of the Social Sciences* 9 (1933): p. 202; Robert Redfield, "Maine's Ancient Law in the Light of Primitive Societies," *Western Polit. Quart.* 3 (1950): p. 581; W. Seagle, "Primitive Law and Professor Malinowski," *Amer. Anthropologist* 39 (n.s., 1937): p. 280.

No "lawless societies:" Arthur Goodhart, "The Importance of a Definition of Law," *Jour. African Administration* (1951): p. 107; E. Sidney Hartland, *Primitive Law* (London, 1924), pp. 136, 137; E. Adamson Hoebel, "Fundamental Legal Concepts as Applied in the Study of Primitive Law," *Yale Law Jour.* 51 (1942): p. 952; Paul Vinogradoff, *Outlines of Historical Jurisprudence* (London, 1922), p. 359; Melville Herskovits, *Man and His Works* (New York, 1948), p. 345; Isaac Schapera, *Government and Politics in Tribal Societies* (London, 1956), p. 217; Paul Howell, *A Manual of Nuer Law* (London, 1954), p. 22; Richard Cherry, *Lectures in the Growth of Criminal Law in Ancient Communities* (London, 1890), pp. 7, 16.

[1] Walter Goldschmidt, *Man's Way* (Cleveland, 1959), p. 226. "Savages, no less than civilized mankind, practically regard a man's life as his highest good. Whatever opinions may be held about the existence after death, whatever blessings may be supposed to await the disembodied soul, nobody likes to be hurried into that existence by another's will." Edward Westermarck, *The Origin and Development of the Moral Ideas* (2 v., London, 1908-1912) 1: p. 372.

[2] "The so-called instinct of self-preservation . . . might better be regarded as the general goal which many of the [homeostatic] drives have in common. . . . On the basis of biological evolution, it is possible to understand why all existing species should have patterns of behavior directed to this end; if these patterns worked in the opposite direction, they would obviously result in the destruction of the individual and therefore of the species." Otto Klineberg, *Social Psychology* (rev. ed., New York, 1954), p. 119.

[3] Opinions regarding life, and in what it consists, have given rise to some peculiar practices among preliterates. "The belief underlying headhunting generally is that life is a material substance residing *par excellence* in the head, and that the abstraction of an enemy's head enables the life-substance in it to be carried off to the head-taker's home to replenish the stock there and increase the fertility of its inhabitants, its crops, and its livestock. Incidentally a surplus of life-substance is necessary to beget children, and hence comes the importance of head-taking as a preliminary to marriage. The tuft left on the head by Albanians, as by many Indian tribes and castes, by Chinese, American Indians and others, was probably left originally to shelter life-substance regarded as residing, as in the case of Samson, in the hair." Margaret Hasluck, *The Unwritten Law of the Albanian Mountains* (Cambridge, 1954), p. xii.

own lives, they do not have such a drive to preserve the lives of other men. But men do have a drive to distinguish mine from thine and they form the given value judgment that it is good to make such a distinction. I recognize that the life of another man is not "mine" but "thine." Hence, the drive to distinguish mine from thine is at work in the value-judging I do in regard to the taking of the lives of other men. The problem of taking the lives of other men could consistently be treated in the later chaper on "mine" and "thine." But it has seemed advisable for practical reasons to consider both kinds of killing—of myself and of others—under the one head of life and its preservation.

The universal value judgments which are found among all preliterate societies concern self-defense, regulations controlling the taking of life, and taking the lives of others without justification, that is, murder.

## 1. *Self-Defense*

Self-defense is an aspect of self-preservation. As such, it is universally judged to be good. In the reported cases regarding killing in self-defense, which we shall examine later, it is assumed that self-defense in itself is good although killing the assailant in self-defense may or may not be value-judged to be desirable. In all men there is a natural tendency to react against any kind of threatening attack. This reaction is not the result of any reasoning process but is the immediate and direct assertion of the basic drive for self-preservation.[4] The value judgment, therefore, that it is good to defend oneself against an attacker is universal in all individuals in all known societies. It is a postulate in all law.

## 2. *Regulations Regarding Title to Life*

The flexibility of the basic drives makes regulation of them possible. The drives are plastic regarding the means to their ends and even regarding their ends themselves in the sense already explained. It is only natural for men to desire guides in this process. This is an aspect of men's master drive. Men form the given value judgment that norms according to which they can tell right from wrong are good. This given value judgment manifests itself in regulations regarding killing.

It has long been known that there are no societies of which we have knowledge which are without regulations of the taking of life, whether their own or others. Men have never allowed killing to be haphazard.

Regulations regarding the killing of men are characteristic of all peoples. "[N]o known tribe, however low and ferocious, has ever held that men may kill one another indiscriminately for even the savage society of the desert or the jungle would collapse under such lawlessness. Thus all men acknowledge some law 'thou shall not kill,' but the question is how this law applies."[5] It is only obvious that if societies are to survive there must be regulations controlling killing.[6] Preliterates universally judge, then, that regulations controlling the taking of human life are good.

Regulation by custom law of the manner in which self-defense and war are to be conducted among preliterates is further evidence that they judge limitation on killing to be good. War, which we shall discuss shortly, is looked on as a necessary means of survival. It is a form of self-defense. It is usually thought of as an act of retaliation of one group which has suffered what it considers to be injury at the hands of another group. This retaliation must be controlled if it is not to be endless. Among the Australians, for instance, war is regulated by a recognized body of custom laws. These regulations have been likened to the international law of literate nations.[7]

## 3. *Failure to Respect Title to Life: Murder*

Although men do not have a drive to preserve the lives of others as they do their own, nonetheless they do judge universally that the lives of others cannot be taken without justifying reasons. In all societies of men of which we have knowledge there is found the value judgment that taking the life of another human being without a justifying reason is bad. Murder is wrong. "No society approves murder."[8] This value judgment implies a distinction between justified and unjustified killing. Such a distinction is universal in all societies of men. "[W]e may note . . . the existence of a category of murder—a type of killing that is different from all other killings, falling in specified ways within the circle of protected persons. The distinction may vary from one group to another . . . . But the categories of justified versus unjustified killing

---

[4] "There is a natural, inherited reaction, of defence against the attack of a stranger or enemy. . . . The reaction is not due to reflection, does not arise out of concepts of justice or right or property, and is not due to any antecedent feeling." Ellsworth Faris, "The Origin of Punishment," in: Albert Kocourek and John Wigmore, eds., *Primitive and Ancient Legal Institutions* (Boston, 1915), p. 157.

[5] Edward Tylor, *Anthropology* (New York, 1916), p. 412. "There is perhaps no tribe which has no definition of murder." Gladys Reichard, "Social Life," in: Boas, ed., *General Anthropology* (Boston, 1938), p. 481. "In every society—even where human life is, generally speaking, held in low estimation—custom prohibits homicide within a certain circle of men. But the radius of the circle varies greatly." Edward Westermarck, *The Origin and Development of the Moral Ideas* (2 v., London, 1908–1912) 1: p. 331.

[6] "Since no society likes to face extinction, it follows that there will always be laws to prevent the killing of people, especially if they are members of one's own group and capable of parenthood." Mischa Titiev, *Introduction to Cultural Anthropology* (New York, 1959), p. 300.

[7] Alfred Radcliffe-Brown, "Primitive Law," *Encyc. of the Social Sciences* 9 (1933): pp. 202–206.

[8] Ralph Linton, *The Study of Man* (New York, 1936), p. 433.

remain for all known societies." [9] "Murder and incest . . . are even now instances of negative moral values which are concrete ethnological universals, even though there is considerable disparity in the range of their application in different cultures." [10]

### B. LESS THAN UNIVERSAL VALUE JUDGMENTS

The remaining value judgments in regard to the taking of life, and they are the great majority, are less than universal. In ever widening divergence they exemplify the tendency of constructed value judgments to fan out from a central, given point of departure. This is the case with the value judgments in the areas we will now consider, namely, killing in self-defense, abortion, in-group versus out-group killing, suicide, infanticide, and senilicide. These range, as we will find, from general to common to occasional.

### 1. *General*

#### a. *Killing in Self-defense—War*

Preliterates generally value-judge that killing in self-defense is not wrong, although they do not always so judge. In the majority of cases, the killing is excused and the killer is not held responsible for the death of the attacker. Among the Nomadic tribes of Siberia, for instance, a killing which occurs during the course of necessary self-defense is not held to be punishable. With the Gikuyu, not only is killing in self-defense excused but it is looked on understandingly. If two men fight and one is killed, the killer has the respect of the community because he acted in self-defense as any man should. For this reason, he receives considerate treatment at his trial.

Although self-defense may excuse from punishment, it does not always relieve the killer from compensation. With the Nabaloi in Northern Luzon, if a man kills another man who was at fault because he began the attack, the killer is not subject to punishment but he must furnish everything for the funeral rite of the

deceased. If two men fight and both are at fault and one kills the other, the killer is executed by hanging. Among the Basoga, homicide is always considered to be wrong except in self-defense and war.

It appears to be general among preliterates, then, to consider killing done in self-defense justifiable and not liable to punishment. "[I]n the savage world self-defense and killing in self-defense are not infrequently justified by custom." [11] The value judgment, therefore, that it is good to defend oneself even to the point of killing an assailant seems to be general in preliterate societies.

Preliterates consider war to be a form of self-defense. It is necessary for their survival. War is very widespread. "There are exceedingly few human societies known to us in which there is not some form of warfare." [12] The open armed conflict of war is "found in nearly all existing human groups, however primitive." [13] Making war has been said to be "the most universal and probably the oldest of the tribe's functions." [14] No central authority is needed for this purpose as is the case with making and keeping peace. War has been claimed to be universal and present in all parts of the world wherever there have been men. All recorded languages, it is said, have a term corresponding to the word "war," the implication being that war is universal.[15]

But war does not appear to be universal. Data indicate that war was unknown during the Old Stone Age and in the earlier part of the New Stone Age in Europe and the Orient. Likewise, there is no evidence that organized warfare was known in aboriginal Australia nor in certain parts of the New World in the pre-European period. Among the Ashanti, for instance, war in its modern meaning is unknown. It is also said that the Vedda of Ceylon never knew war, that the oldest inhabitants of Umnak and Unalaska never engaged in war, and that the Greenlanders held that war was repulsive and had no word for it.[16]

In the absence of reported statements by preliterates regarding the goodness or badness of war, this value judgment will have to be inferred from its widespread

---

[9] Margaret Mead, "Some Anthropological Considerations Concerning Natural Law," *Natural Law Forum* **6** (1961): p. 52.

[10] David Bidney, *Theoretical Anthropology* (New York, 1953), p. 426. These statements concerning the universality of the value judgment about murder are apparently contradicted by certain other reports. The Kalinga, for instance, are reported as making no distinction between justifiable and unjustifiable killing. But it is immediately added that this attitude is modified by the judgment of the people and their custom law. Ralph Barton, *The Kalingas* (Chicago 1949), p. 231. All of which means that, practically speaking, the Kalinga make a distinction between justified and unjustified killing. The Bantu also are said to consider the killing of a human being to be the same offense regardless of the circumstances surrounding the killing. Provocation, self-defense, and intention are, it is reported, irrelevant. Charles Dundas, "Native Laws of Some Bantu Tribes of East Africa," *Jour. Royal Anthropol. Inst.* **51** (1921): p. 239. Rather than question the accuracy of the authorities already quoted, it seems more prudent to question the accuracy of this individual report.

[11] Edward Westermarck, *The Origin and Development of the Moral Ideas* (2 v., London, 1908–1912), p. 288.

[12] Alfred Radcliffe-Brown, "Preface," to Meyer Fortes and Edward Evans-Pritchard, eds., *African Political Systems* (Oxford, 1940), p. xix.

[13] Quincy Wright, *A Study of War* (2 v., Chicago, 1942) **1**: p. 36.

[14] Ralph Linton, *The Study of Man* (New York, 1936), p. 238.

[15] Maurice Davie, *The Evolution of War* (New Haven, 1929), p. 9; Clark Wissler, *Man and Culture* (New York, 1923), p. 79.

[16] Edward Westermarck, *The Origin and Development of the Moral Ideas* (London, 1908–1912), p. 334. These data do not support the assumption that men have a hostility instinct to which we referred above. "Facts now known do indicate that Freud's view [that all men have an aggressive instinct] was needlessly pessimistic, biased presumably by exclusive contemplation of recent centuries of European history." Clyde Kluckhohn, *Mirror for Man* (New York, 1949), p. 55.

occurrence. It is true that the widespread occurrence of an action is no indication of how widespread the approval of the action may be, as already noted. But in the case of war among preliterates, such an inference seems justified. There is no evidence that preliterates in general consider war to be an evil from which they must abstain at all costs. Preliterates are not reported to be pacifists and conscientious objectors concerning war. They appear to judge that, although it entails physical evils and hardships, war is not in itself a moral evil from which they must refrain. In this sense, then, preliterates appear to judge that war is good and not evil. Since, according to the reported data, war appears to be general among preliterates, the value judgment that war is good and not evil seems to be general among preliterates.

Some of the values over which preliterates go to war may be noted. Homicide is one of the principal ones. Other values are: women and sexual offenses; disputes over the possession of personal property, even trifles; sacrilege and violation of taboos; common assaults; witchcraft; quarrels arising out of personal abuse. With some preliterates, such as the Nyakyusa, marriage is said to be by far the most frequent cause of disputes and quarrels. A common value over which wars are fought is land. Land, as the source from which means of subsistence is drawn, has a prime value for the growth and development of any people.[17]

### b. Abortion

The practice of abortion or feticide among preliterates appears to be rare among some groups and frequent among others. Most preliterates welcome children. Their hope is that their wives will be fertile. Among the Nuer who value children highly, abortion is said to be very rare and practiced only by unmarried girls. The Bantu also prize children highly and intentional abortion is reportedly uncommon, although it does occur among some tribes. Among the Naskapi, it is said that birth control and abortion are not practiced. The Nabaloi say they never have heard of a woman who killed her child before it was born.

But among other preliterates abortion appears to be frequent. Of the Tswana it is said that abortion is practiced fairly extensively, especially by unmarried women. As a matter of fact, it has been stated that abortion is an absolutely universal phenomenon with the claim being made that the reports on abortion among preliterates are unreliable. One report, it is said, will state that abortion is not practiced by a certain group, while another report will give detailed accounts of abortionist practices among the same group.[18]

The motives or values for which abortions are induced among preliteraes are many. A girl's lover in Tswana may put pressure on her to abort her child. He may do this because he fears he may have to pay damages to her father or because he is afraid he will lose some responsible position he already holds. The girl's mother may persuade her to have the abortion, hoping that sometime later she may make a better match. The girl herself may resort to feticide for the same reason. The girl may also desire an abortion because custom demands it. Among the Gunantuna, bastards and incestuously conceived children are expected to be disposed of.

Another reported motive for abortion is cannibalism. Some Central Australian women abort in order to feed the fetus to their starving children. It is also related that in the same region small children are killed and fed to their older siblings. Among the Tupinamba, local girls are given to prisoners as bedfellows or wives. Their offspring are eaten because by this action they can hurt the feelings of the father's kin to whom the child belongs. It is said that sometimes the wife of the prisoner does not want to have her child eaten and aborts it so that it will not suffer this fate.

The value judgment made by the great majority of preliterates concerning abortion is one of disapproval. There are some relatively few groups, however, which reportedly approve abortion. The Choroti approve of the abortion of premarital pregnancies. The Pima justify the abortion of a lactating woman, saying that it is in the interest of the baby already born and that the mother loves the child she can see more than the one she cannot see. Among the Samoans, the Mitchell Islanders and the Dakota it has been said that abortion procured by artificial means is not held to be objectionable.

But the greater part of preliterates consider abortion simply to be wrong. "Although abortion is extensively and rather openly practised in many societies, few groups give it unqualified approval." [19] The Alorese disapprove of it. In Yap it is considered shameful. In Truk it arouses the anger of relatives. The Ojibwa and Orang-Laut deem it a horror and an abomination.

---

[17] Self-defense—war: Valintin Riasanovsky, *Customary Law of the Nomadic Tribes of Siberia* (Tsiensin, 1938), p. 118; Jomo Kenyatta, *Facing Mount Kenya* (London, 1953), p. 227; Claude Moss, "Nabaloi Law and Ritual," *Amer. Archaeology and Ethnology* 15 (1920): p. 257; Paul Bohannon, *African Homicide and Suicide* (Princeton, 1960), p. 71; Clyde Kluckhohn, *Mirror for Man* (New York, 1949), p. 55; K. A. Busia, *The Position of the Chief in the Modern Political System of Ashanti* (London, 1951), p. 65; Leonard Hobhouse, *The Material Culture and Social Institutions of the Simpler Peoples* (London, 1915), *passim;* Robert Rattray, *Ashanti Law and Constitution* (London, 1929), p. 6; Godfrey Wilson, "Introduction to Nyakyusa Law," *Africa* 10 (1937): p. 29.

[18] "Abortion is generally suspected when a girl who was known to be pregnant suddenly recovers her normal physical appearance, without anybody knowing when and where she had given birth. Or, when a foetus is found lying about, all the unmarried women of the vicinity are called and examined. . . . The one whose breasts are found to contain milk will be regarded as guilty." Isaac Schapera, *A Handbook of Tswana Law and Custom* (London, 1938), p. 262.

[19] George Devereux, "A Typological Study of Abortion in 350 Primitive, Ancient, and Pre-Industrial Societies," in: Harold Rosen, ed., *Therapeutic Abortion* (New York, 1954), p. 141.

The Cherokee call it outright murder. Among the Flatheads the words meaning abortion have as their root the word meaning "murder." The Navaho think that if a girl has an abortion she must have had sexual relations that were bestial or incestuous. In Annam, if it is known that a girl is about to induce an abortion, attempt is made to stop her. In Bali, abortion is considered to be criminal and related to black magic. The Kgatla disapprove of abortion and say that, even though the child is a bastard, "the knot of the cradle-skin is a flower." [20] The natives of Tenimber and Timor-Laut are said to punish abortions with heavy fines. The Kafir, although widely practicing abortion, judge it to be a great crime. The value judgment, then, that abortion is wrong appears to be general among preliterates.

It is worth noting that the value judgment that abortion is wrong may or may not be followed by physical punishment, as is the case with other offenses. In Ponape abortion is not punished but it is deemed improper. In other places, such as among the Wabunga, Banyika, Wakitusika, and Wasove, abortion is said not to be punished. The Wanyamwesi are said not to punish abortion physically but the woman who is guilty of the offense is driven out of the land. [21]

### c. In-group versus Out-group Killing

The distinction between in-group and out-group activities is one which runs deep in all human thinking, literate as well as preliterate. Much of men's distinguishing between right and wrong has always taken place on this basis. The tendency to look upon those outside of our group as even radically different from those inside our group has too often been the questionable grounds for racism, nationalism, and other forms of discrimination. The man outside the group is the stranger, even the enemy. [22]

Not only does this distinction lead to the view that all foreigners are enemies but it also at times has fostered the notion that those outside the group were not complete men. The giving of bemeaning and debasing names to foreigners is an indication of this tendency to underevaluate those outside the group. But within an individual's own group, his activities are well regulated by rules concerning the rights of others in the group and by a subordination of his own interests to those of the group. As time has gone on and awareness of intertribal and international living has developed, however, the rights of out-group people have been increasingly recognized.

Out-group killing is ofttimes looked on as a noble act. To kill a stranger is a good action. "Killing a tribesman of another kin would be exactly like killing an enemy." [23] Out-group killing many times takes on the aspect of war, and killing in war is good. "To kill a foreign warrior is a praiseworthy action." [24] One of the chief virtues of a man is to be successful in war and to kill many enemies. Conversely, to kill a member of one's own group is for most preliterates a serious wrong. All people have regulations concerning this type of killing. "Homicide within the society is, under one set of conditions or another, legally prohibited everywhere." [25]

The punishments inflicted for in-group killings are manifestations of underlying value judgments. They can take the form of vengeance or compensation. Among some preliterates, vengeance is the only sanction employed when the murderer and the victim belong to different groups. Such is the situation among the Bushmen and Hottentots of South Africa. With other peoples, the injured group may have a choice between vengeance and compensation. Vengeance may be exercised only if the murderer is caught soon after the act. If he is not, compensation must be accepted. Such are the Nandi, the Gikuyu, the Vugusu of Kenya Colony, and the Mesakin of the Nuba Hills in Kordofan. Among still other groups, only compensation is allowed and vengeance is not permitted for homicide. This is the situation among the Northeastern Sotho and the Southern Sotho of South Africa. Here, if the injured parties attempt to take the law into their own hands and inflict vengeance, it is an offense and they are liable to punishment.

Sometimes a distinction is made in in-group homicide between killing a clansman and killing a near

[20] George Devereux, "A Typological Study of Abortion in 350 Primitive, Ancient, and Pre-Industrial Societies," in: Harold Rosen, ed., *Therapeutic Abortion* (New York, 1954), pp. 141–142.

[21] Abortion: Edward Evans-Pritchard, *Kinship and Marriage Among the Nuer* (Oxford, 1951), pp. 136–137; Charles Dundas, "Native Laws of Some Bantu Tribes of East Africa," *Jour. Royal Anthropol. Inst.* (1921): p. 247; Julius Lips, "Naskapi Law," *Trans. Amer. Philos. Soc.* 37 (1947): p. 415; Claude Moss, "Nabaloi Law and Ritual," *Amer. Archaeology and Ethnology* 15 (1920): p. 261; Isaac Schapera, *A Handbook of Tswana Law and Custom* (London, 1938), p. 262; George Devereux, "A Typological Study of Abortion in 350 Primitive, Ancient, and Pre-Industrial Societies," in: Harold Rosen, ed., *Therapeutic Abortion* (New York, 1954), pp. 115, 140–142; Edward Westermarck, *The Origin and Development of the Moral Ideas* (2 v., London, 1908–1912) 1: p. 414.

[22] "The old state of things is well illustrated in the Latin word *hostis*, meaning originally stranger, passed quite naturally into the sense of enemy. Not only is slaying an enemy in open war looked on as righteous, but ancient law goes on the doctrine that slaying one's own tribesman and slaying a foreigner are crimes of quite different order, while killing a slave is but a destruction of property." Edward Tylor, *Anthropology* (New York, 1916), p. 413.

[23] Robert Lowie, *An Introduction to Cultural Anthropology* (2nd ed., New York, 1940), p. 287.

[24] J. G. Peristiany, "Law," in: Edward Evans-Pritchard and others, *The Institutions of Primitive Society* (Glencoe, 1956), p. 49.

[25] E. Adamson Hoebel, *The Law of Primitive Man* (Cambridge, Mass., 1954), p. 286. "The killing of a fellow-clansman was, in fact, unthinkable. . . . The killing of a fellow tribesman was always a serious crime and punishment inexorably exacted." Paul Radin, *The World of Primitive Man* (New York, 1953), pp. 250–251.

relative. Among the Albanian mountaineers, if a man murdered his son, father, brother, paternal uncle, paternal uncle's son, brother's son, the verdict usually was that in killing such a near relative the murderer had "killed himself." Since the victim's blood was lost, no one tried to avenge him. It was his misfortune to have died in this manner. Among the Arabs, a man who kills one of his own kin is dealt with severely. He may be either put to death by his own people or he may be outlawed and forced to take refuge in an alien group. The controlling idea is that he has committed an "inexpiable offense" for which no compensation can be taken. Death or exile is necessary to obviate the anger of the deity and to keep it from resting on the whole kin. Among the Mesakin, if a man kills a clansman nothing is done to the killer except to demand his ritual purification. But if a man kills his own brother, ceremonial purification is of no help and exile must be his fate. Although fratricide is judged as peculiarly bad in almost all societies, the consequences for the killer vary with the customs of the group within which it occurs.

In some places, sanctions for in-group killing are not enforced or else settlement is made for greatly reduced compensation. This is the case among the Bushmen, Hottentots, Nandi, Gikuyu, and Vugusu. The reason for this procedure is that, although vengeance for homicide is a sacred duty, in cases of fratricide the parents may forgive the killer in order to prevent further bloodshed and the possible loss of another son. Out-group killings, although not evaluated as wrong in themselves, were punished by some peoples because of their potential in the situation for starting wars. Among the Tlingit, murder committed outside the clan was punishable by death. Among the Tiv, if a man kills a man of another lineage, a general war is the usual consequence.

We have some reports, then, on the value judgments preliterates make concerning in-group versus out-group killing and on the punishments inflicted for such killings. On this basis the statement can be ventured that the value judgment that out-group killing is good and in-group killing is bad is general among preliterates.[26]

## 2. Common: Suicide

Men have a basic drive to preserve their lives and form without a reasoning process the value judgment that it is good to do so. This is a postulate of all law regarding human life. The intentional taking of one's life implies, on the other hand, the value judgment that it is better to take one's life than to preserve it. On this over-balancing of one value judgment by the other, we have already remarked above.

By the very fact that we are considering suicide as the intentional death of the victim brought about by an act which he knew would have a deadly effect, we are also assuming that suicides are not necessarily insane. In view of current psychiatric opinion, it seems extreme and without confirming evidence to hold that all suicides are *eo ipso* insane.[27] Among preliterates, as we shall see later, a distinction is made between sanes and insanes. There is no evidence that preliterates consider all suicides to be insane.

Suicide among preliterates appears to be common. The values on account of which it occurs, as they are alleged by either the suicide himself or his survivors, are varied.[28] The Comanche are reported to take their own lives because of a sense of shame for something which has occurred. Shame and ridicule are also among the reasons given why the Ashanti commit suicide. Cases are on record where men and women have taken their own lives because of the disgrace ensuing upon such actions as uncontrolled flatulence in public. Among the Nandi, reasons for suicide have been neglect of old people by their children, cruel treatment of wives by their husbands, being the victim of a curse, being accused of witchcraft, failure of warriors in raids, disappointment of boys in love, girls nagged by their mothers regarding love affairs, sons accused by their fathers of neglecting their work.

Among the values on account of which suicide is committed among the Melanesians of Buka Passage is that a man's wife was angry and insulted him, a woman was beaten by her husband, a man's ceremonial currency was stolen, a man was angry with another man.

[26] In-group v. out-group killing: Gladys Reichard, "Social Life," in: Franz Boas, ed., *General Anthropology* (Boston, 1938), p. 479; Boas, "Culture," *Encyc. of the Social Sciences* (1930): p. 97; Boas, *Anthropology and Modern Life* (New York, 1928), p. 228; Edward Westermarck, *The Origin and Development of the Moral Ideas* (2 v., London, 1908–1912) 1: p. 331; Isaac Schapera, *The Khoisan Peoples of South Africa* (London, 1930), pp. 153–154, 345–346; George Huntingford, *The Nandi of Kenya* (London, 1953), p. 111 ff.; John Middleton, *The Kikuyu and Kamba of Kenya* (London, 1953), pp. 44–45; Gunter Wagner, *The Bantu of North Kavirondo* (London, 1949), pp. 222–223; Siegfried Nadel, *The Nuba* (London, 1947) p. 302 ff.; Edmund Ashton, *The Basuto* (London, 1952), p. 255; Margaret Hasluck, *The Unwritten Law of the Albanian Mountains* (Cambridge, 1954), p. 210; W. Robertson Smith, *Kinship and Marriage in Early Arabia* (2nd ed., London, 1907), p. 25; W. R. Smith, *The Religion of the Semites* (3rd ed., London, 1927), p. 419 ff.; F. E. Williams, "Group Sentiment and Primi-

tive Justice," *Amer. Anthropologist* **43** (1941): p. 530; Paul Bohannon, *Justice and Judgment Among the Tiv* (London, 1957), p. 148; Isaac Schapera, "The Sin of Cain," *Jour. Royal Anthropol. Inst.* **85** (1955): pp. 33–43; W. J. Burchell, *Travels in the Interior of Southern Africa* (2 v., London, 1953) 1: p. 319; Kalervo Oberg, "Crime and Punishment in Tlingit Society," *Amer. Anthropologist* **36** (1934): p. 146.

[27] Edwin Schneidman and Norman Farberow, "Some Facts About Suicide," *U. S. Department of Health, Education and Welfare,* Publication 852, Series 101 (1961): p. 5; Emile Durkheim, *Suicide: A Study in Sociology,* trans. by J. A. Spaulding and G. Simpson (Glencoe, 1951), p. 67; Louis Dublin and Bessie Bunzel, *To Be or Not To Be: A Study of Suicide* (New York, 1933), pp. 307–308.

[28] "We must not confuse 'motive' which means psychic aetiology with either intent or folk explanation. In order to avoid confusion, we shall talk of 'folk explanations' of suicide or homicide instead of 'motive'." Paul Bohannon, *African Homicide and Suicide* (Princeton, 1960), pp. 26–27.

The Kamchadal of Siberia are said to commit suicide at the slightest sign of danger on the theory that the next life is happier than this one. A Cherokee Indian is reported to have committed suicide because smallpox had disfigured his face. Capture or disappointment was a reason for an Ojibwa to kill himself. The death of a loved one or jealousy could be the cause of suicide among the Navaho.

On the other hand, there are groups of preliterates among whom it is reported that suicide does not occur. The Naskapi are reported to have said that suicide "is not practised among our Indians." It is also said that no cases of suicide have been reported among the Yahgans of Tierra del Fuego, the Andaman Islanders, the natives of western and central Australia, and the Auni of New Mexico. Other groups of preliterates have been listed who do not have suicide among them.

The value judgments preliterates make concerning suicide vary. Among the Yoruba, if a man commits suicide because he finds life difficult or burdensome, he is "given credit and honour." Among the Ashanti it was considered honorable to kill oneself in war rather than fall into the hands of the enemy or return home to tell of a defeat. It was "acclaimed as praiseworthy" to take one's own life in order to accompany a loved one to the land of the spirits, or to end one's existence as a way of wiping out the dishonor which the ridicule of companions has brought on. With the Tlingit, if it could be shown that a man committed suicide because of the foul treatment of his wife, his wife's clan had to produce a man who could be killed in retaliation. A beneficial consequence of this custom law, it is reported, is that Tlingit women were very careful how they treated their husbands.

But on the other hand, reports show that preliterates also form other value judgments regarding suicide. The Basoga judge that suicide is always wrong. In some Nigerian tribes, a suicide was considered an "abominable offense." The suicide's relatives would be defiled if they touched the body and it was buried in "the bush of evil." Among the Yoruba which we mentioned, if a man commits suicide out of shame, his body is considered "abominable and cast into the bush unburied." With the Ashanti, suicide was considered wrong when it was done to avoid the consequences of some injurious act. It was also thought wrong when no motive could be ascribed for it, in which case it was presumed that there had been some kind of evil influence at work on the suicide. The Nabaloi hold that the soul of the person who kills himself goes to a different place from where the souls of others including murderers go. The souls of murderers go to a definite place, but the souls of suicides are condemned to wander.

On the basis of these reports it is difficult to determine what the prevalence of value judgments of preliterates is concerning suicide. Some groups apparently approve of suicide if there are justifying reasons.

Other groups seem not to approve of suicide under any conditions. Hence, the estimate may be ventured that the value judgments among preliterates that suicide is wrong unless there are justifying conditions is common, and that the value judgment that suicide is wrong under any conditions is also common.[29]

It has been said that there are two motives in preliterate suicides. One is that there has been some action which has infringed upon the suicide's rights or he is trying to escape from some obligation. The other is that the suicide is protesting against having been put in such an unbearable situation. In a word, underlying suicide among preliterates is a rupture of the individual's integration with the group of which he has been a part. This fact correlates with the finding that suicide is related to the segregation of an individual from the group to which he desires to belong.[30] Preliterate suicides further appear to belong to the "anomic" type of suicide. They are not "egoistic" and marked by apathy and disillusionment nor are they "altruistic" and distinguished by energy of will and a calm feeling of duty.[31] Rather they are characterized by irritation and recriminations against life in general because of the way things have gone. It has also been found that among literates there are fewer suicides where there are conditions of poverty. Unfulfilled needs and desires are at the bottom of all suicides. Poverty tends to limit the desires which a man effectively hopes to fulfill. It would be valuable to know to what extent this finding holds for preliterates.

The function of integration-segregation in suicide also bears on our understanding of the relation between the conditions of suicide among preliterates and their motives for committing the act. Most suicides among preliterates reportedly occur among men who are old and sick, among women who have lost their husbands, and among followers of a chief who has died. But the reasons why these people kill themselves is not simply because the men are old and sick, or the women without their husbands, or followers without their chief. The reason why they take their own lives is that the condition in which they find themselves is looked on by

---

[29] "[I]t seems fair to say that the only tenable position in the present state of the literature is that the suicide situation in various primitive societies is open to investigation but has not been investigated. Therefore, we do not know what the suicide situation is in 'primitive society.'" Paul Bohannon, *African Homicide and Suicide* (Princeton, 1960), p. 24.

[30] "So we reach the general conclusion: suicide varies inversely with the degree of integration of the social groups of which the individual forms a part." Emile Durkheim, *Suicide: A Study in Sociology*, trans. by J. A. Spaulding and G. Simpson (Glencoe, 1951), pp. 208, 209.

[31] "Egoistic suicide results from man's no longer finding a basis for existence in life; altruistic suicide, because this basis for existence appears to man situated beyond life itself. The third sort of suicide . . . results from man's activities lacking regulation and his consequent sufferings. By virtue of its origin we shall assign this last variety the name of *anomic suicide*." (Durkheim, *ibid.*, p. 258).

others as a state which separates them from the rest of the group who should go on living. These men and women are expected by their society to take their own lives and they are considered to have a duty to do so. If they fail to fulfill this duty, they lose public respect.[32]

### 3. *Occasional: Infanticide and Senilicide*

The killing of infants and the killing of the aged are met with occasionally among preliterates. "A small percentage of tribes allow infanticide or permit the killing of the very aged or the hopelessly sick, but most societies regret the loss of a member under any circumstances."[33]

The motivating values for infanticide are varied. Among the Eskimo, infanticide is looked on as an institution necessary for the protection of the group. The proportion of infants to adults in each group cannot be allowed to rise too high. Eskimo female children are the most frequent victims of infanticide because the male is the main food-getter. Shortage of food is also given as the motive for infanticide among other peoples. The Bushmen practice infanticide for this reason. In Australia, shortage of food is one of the reasons for killing and eating children. Among the Maori, children were killed and eaten during times of famine. Parents exchanged children so that they would not have to eat their own children. Other reasons given for infanticide are that a mother finds it too hard to carry a child over long distances and keep up with the group, that the child is weak and cries too much, that the first or second child should be killed because it will not grow up to be strong.

Still other values are given as motivation for infanticide. With the Ibo, twin children are killed, for they are thought to be abominable inasmuch as a woman cannot nurse two children at the same time. It is also thought to be an abomination for the same reason if a woman becomes pregnant before her last child has been weaned. When the child is born, it is thrown away. Children are also killed who are born crippled, born with teeth, born feet first, and who do not cry soon after birth. Likewise, children who cut the upper teeth before the lower, or who begin to walk before they have cut any teeth, are destroyed or handed to slave traders.

It would appear, then, that the great majority of preliterates do neither practice infanticide nor consider it good or right. In other words, the value judgment that infanticide is good seems to be only occasional among preliterates.[34] Preliterates who practice feticide are horrified at the thought of infanticide.[35]

The killing of old people is perhaps not as widespread as infanticide but it is occasionally encountered among preliterates. The main value consideration appears to be the practical one of non-contribution to the well-being of the community. The Eskimo are a prime example of this. Senilicide, as well as infanticide, invalidicide, and suicide, are all said to be responses to the basic demand of Eskimo society that only those who are able to contribute actively to the economic welfare of the community may survive. The Bushmen are also cited as a group among whom senilicide is practiced because of an insufficient supply of food.

It is the practice among some preliterate peoples for elderly persons, whose physical and mental capacities have deteriorated, to ask their sons to kill them. Some believe, such as the Chukchee, that everyone continues to live in the next life as he did in this. Hence, to die and enter the next life before one becomes too feeble and decrepit is assurance of a better status in that life. In some groups, it is loss of respect consequent upon becoming aged, as well as a burden to the community, that causes old people to desire to die. Loss of physical strength and loss of memory are matters of which the elderly are ashamed. Among the Assiniboine, this

---

[32] Suicide: E. Adamson Hoebel, "The Political Organization and Law-ways of the Comanche Indians," *Mem. Amer. Anthropol. Assoc.* **54** (1940): p. 112; Robert Rattray, *Ashanti Law and Constitution* (London, 1929), pp. 299, 372–373; Geoffrey Snell, *Nandi Customary Law* (London, 1954), p. 73; Beatrice Blackwood, *Both Sides of Buka Passage* (London, 1935), *passim;* Otto Klineberg, *Social Psychology* (rev. ed., New York, 1954), p. 120; Julius Lips, "Naskapi Law," *Trans. Amer. Philos. Soc.* **37** (1947): p. 415; Louis Dublin and Bessie Bunzel, *To Be or Not To Be: A Study of Suicide* (New York, 1933), *passim;* Edward Westermarck, *The Origin and Development of the Moral Ideas* (2 v., London, 1908–1912) 2: p. 229; A. J. Ajisafe, *Laws and Customs of the Yoruba People* (London, 1924), p. 32; Kalervo Oberg, "The Kingdom of Ankole in Uganda," in: Meyer Fortes and E. Evans-Pritchard, *African Political Systems* (Oxford, 1940), p. 150; Paul Bohannon, *African Homicide and Suicide* (Princeton, 1960), p. 71; C. K. Meek, *Law and Authority in a Nigerian Tribe* (London, 1937), p. 213; Claude Moss, "Nabaloi Law and Ritual," *Amer. Archaeology and Ethnology* **15** (1920): pp. 261, 283; Bronislaw Malinowski, *Crime and Custom in Savage Society* (New York, 1951), p. 97; Malinowski, "The Forces of Law and Order in a Primitive Community," *Proc. Royal Inst. Great Britain* **24** (1925): p. 539; Emile Durkheim, *Suicide: A Study in Sociology,* trans. by J. A. Spaulding and G. Simpson (Glencoe, 1951), pp. 219, 242–246, 254, 293.

[33] Mischa Titiev, *Introduction to Cultural Anthropology* (New York, 1959), p. 300. See also Titiev, *The Science of Man* (New York, 1954), p. 390. Among the Tswana, cases of infanticide "are still met with occasionally." Isaac Schapera, *A Handbook of Tswana Law and Custom* (London, 1938), p. 262.

[34] "Though infanticide is thus regarded as allowable, or even obligatory, among many of the lower races, we must not suppose that they universally look upon it in this light. . . . [E]ven peoples among whom infanticide is habitual seem now and then to have a feeling that the act is not quite correct. . . . Where infanticide is not sanctioned by custom, the occasional commission of it has a tendency to call forth disapproval or excite horror." Edward Westermarck, *The Origin and Development of the Moral Ideas* (2 v., London, 1908–1912) 1: pp. 402, 404.

[35] "It should be stressed that even people who practice abortion may condemn infanticide. The Kafir . . . of Central Asia practice abortion, but call infanticide murder. The Macusi . . . practice abortion and . . . contraception but not infanticide, and those who heard of infanticide among the Pirara were horrified." George Devereux, "A Typological Study of Abortion in 350 Primitive, Ancient, and Pre-Industrial Societies," in: Harold Rosen, *Therapeutic Abortion* (New York, 1954), p. 143.

shame was so keenly felt that the aged sought death by permitting themselves to be abandoned on the plains. As we have noted above when treating of suicide, one of the reasons why the aged sometimes desire to die is not so much a dissatisfaction with their own declining condition as it is the realization that the rest of the community expect them to do away with themselves.[36]

The value judgment which preliterates make concerning senilicide appears to be much the same as that regarding infanticide. Hence, it seems to be a fair estimate of the available data to say that the value judgment that senilicide is good is only occasional among preliterates.

## II. UNITING SEXUALLY

Men have a drive to unite sexually. Sexual union is basic to the continued existence of the human race. It is fundamental both to the marital and to the familial union.

### A. UNIVERSAL VALUE JUDGMENTS

The evidence will show that there are value judgments regarding sexual union which are universal in all known societies of men. All normal men form the given value judgment that sexual union is in itself good rather than evil, as we have seen. This is the postulate of all laws regarding sex. If sex were evil in itself, there should be laws to stamp it out. Starting from this focal point of departure, other value judgments regarding sex are constructed. Some of these are universal. Others are almost universal. The remaining value judgments are less than universal and will be seen to be general or common in preliterate societies.

### 1. *In All Societies*

The universal value judgments concerning sexual union which we shall treat relate to regulations controlling sexual relation, selectivity and permanence in sexual matters, marriage and the family.

#### a. *Regulations Regarding Title to Sexual Union*

The plasticity of men's basic drive for sexual union again makes possible the regulation of how it will be

exercised.[37] Men universally recognize the necessity and value of regulating sexual activities. "No society fails to have some restrictions on sexual behavior."[38] "[C]ultural anthropologists have never found a group whose way of life permitted completely unregulated relations between the sexes."[39] "[I]n all cultures we find social mechanism for the satisfaction and restriction of the sexual impulse."[40]

That there are two sexes is a given biological fact about which men have no choice. That this difference necessarily entails certain values is also a given about which men have no decision. The regulations, for instance, of the sexual union of two persons of differing sex could not possibly be the same as the regulations of the sexual union of two persons of the same sex. The impossibility of children in the one union and the possibility of them in the other is, among many other reasons, a basis for different regulations. This fact throws into clear relief some given values which are necessarily in law.[41]

#### b. *Selectivity and Permanence*

Promiscuity and transience are not the ideal in human mating. Discrimination and permanence, to some degree at least, are what is desired. Sex relations of men and women are marked by discerning choice. Selectivity is a graphic example of the pliability of the drive for sexual union being molded by the influence of ideas, appraisals, and preferences.[42] All societies of men consider selectivity to be good and not evil. "[No] people regard all women as possible mates."[43] "Promiscuity . . . occurs nowhere . . . . Societies differ in the restrictions they impose, but all of them somehow limit choice of mates."[44] "In every community known to us there are certain restrictions on

[36] Infanticide and senilicide: Walter Goldschmidt, *Man's Way* (Cleveland, 1959), p. 227; E. Adamson Hoebel, "Lawways of the Primitive Eskimos," *Jour. Criminology and Criminal Law* 31 (1941): pp. 670-671; Isaac Schapera, *Government and Politics in Tribal Societies* (London, 1956), p. 204; Eldon Best, *The Maori* (Wellington, 1924), p. 413; Arthur Diamond, *The Evolution of Law and Order* (London, 1951), p. 11; C. K. Meek, *Law and Authority in a Nigerian Tribe* (London, 1937) p. 224; Nathan Miller, *The Child in Primitive Society* (New York, 1928), *passim*; Gladys Reichard, "Social Life," in: Franz Boas, ed., *General Anthropology* (Boston, 1938), p. 481; David Rodnick, "Political Structure and Status Among the Assiniboine Indians," *Amer. Anthropologist* 39 (1937): p. 416.

[37] "Man is endowed with sexual tendencies but these have to be moulded in addition by systems of cultural rules which vary from one society to another." Bronislaw Malinowski, *Sex and Repression in Savage Society* (London, 1927), p. 200.

[38] Clyde Kluckhohn, *Mirror for Man* (New York, 1949), p. 3.

[39] Mischa Titiev, *Introduction to Cultural Anthropology* (New York, 1959), p. 262.

[40] Ralph Piddington, *An Introduction to Social Anthropology* (London, 1950), p. 255.

[41] Regulation of sexual union: Clark Wissler, *Man and Culture* (New York, 1923), p. 94; Ashley Montagu, *Man: His First Million Years* (Cleveland, 1957), p. 147; Clyde Kluckhohn, *Mirror for Man* (New York, 1949), p. 20; François Geny, *Science et Technique en Droit Privé Positif* (4 v., Paris, 1922-1927) 2: p. 372, my translation.

[42] "We can now formulate more precisely what we mean by the plasticity of instincts. The modes of behavior associated with sex interest are determined in man only as regards their ends; man must mate selectively, he cannot mate promiscuously." Bronislaw Malinowski, *Sex and Repression in Savage Society* (London, 1927), p. 197.

[43] Ruth Benedict, *Patterns of Culture*, (New York, 1934), p. 32.

[44] Robert Lowie, *An Introduction to Cultural Anthropology* (2nd ed., New York, 1940), p. 231.

the choice of the marriage partner." [45]   This selectivity is but an aspect of the exclusiveness which is characteristic of all marriage.   The value judgment that selectivity in sex is good and not evil is universal in all societies of men and is one of the postulates of all law regarding sex.

The theory that was prevalent at one time that in the primeval days of human living promiscuity prevailed regarding sex.   Men supposedly lived more or less like animals.   There was no marriage and sex relations were promiscuous.   Such a theory was attractive to those who wished to hold that a state of primeval promiscuity regarding sex, and property too, was men's natural state.   In the ensuing evolutionary process, so it was thought, other adverse factors were at work which resulted in the development of sex and property relations which were no longer common but individual.[46] The only thing approaching marriage at this time was, supposedly, the group marriage.   In this situation, it was assumed, groups of men formed for the purpose of acquiring bevies of females as sexual partners.

But more recent research data have shown that there never was a time when human living was characterized by promiscuous sex relations.   The idea of a promiscuous horde is totally unsupported by any evidence.   The hypothetical theories indulged in by earlier anthropologists show the necessity of reliable data according to which hypotheses can be checked.   The theory of group marriage, which has been called "the residuary legatee of the old theory of promiscuity," [47] likewise is now seen to be a fiction unsupported by any anthropological evidence.   All the reliable data now available indicate that from the earliest days there was marriage and the family.   Where some semblance of group marriage has been encountered, it turns out to be a grouping of men and women who are individually married, or transient affairs carried on in a group.

Permanence in sex activities, such as that found in what we call "marriage," is judged to be good and desirable by all societies of men.   "The ideal marriage is everywhere that in which the members remain together for life." [48]   "[N]o society appears to recognize in principle that marriage is not a permanent union . . . .   The ideal, probably universal in human societies [is] that marriage once contracted should be a permanent tie." [49]   "Marriage is the lasting union of the sexes." [50]   "Every community regards as superior a relatively permanent bond between permissible mates,

and this is marriage; on the other hand, it condemns other forms of relationship as vicious." [51]   Permanence can be absolute or relative, and the connotation that "permanent" has in marriage can vary according to the meaning given to it by different peoples.   But regardless of what meaning is given to it, permanence and not transitoriness is what is desired as good.   The value judgment that permanence, at least relative, is good and not evil is universal in all societies of men. It also is a postulate of all law regarding marriage.[52]

### c. Marriage and the Family

The result of exclusiveness and permanence in human mating is marriage.   Marriage is both a contract by which a marital union is created and it is the state resulting from this contract.   As a contract, title to sexual union is mutually exchanged between the spouses.   As a state, and as distinguished from mere sexual intercourse, marriage has always been recognized by preliterates as a lasting union.   Sexual relations among humans have more than the temporary, biological implications they have for animals.   The continuous duration of marriage has elementary value-meanings for all societies and cultures.   Because of its elements of exclusiveness and duration, marriage is always recognizable throughout the world in spite of its many variations.

Marriage is universal among all mankind.   "All societies recognize the existence of certain close-knit internally organized cooperative units intermediate between the individual and the total society of which he is a part." [53]   Marriage "is the most basic of all institutions, and is found among all peoples." [54]   "[I]n all probability there has been no stage in the social history of mankind where marriage has not existed." [55]   Marriage in its exclusiveness and permanence is a socially and legally sanctioned union for the mating of husband and wife and the procreating and raising of children. There may be economic overtones in some marriages,

[45] Otto Klineberg, Social Psychology (rev. ed., New York, 1954), p. 138; Jomo Kenyatta, "Facing Mount Kenya (London, 1953), p. 156.

[46] See chap. 6 on property.

[47] Edward Westermarck, The Origin and Development of the Moral Ideas (2 v., London, 1908–1912) 2 : p. 396.

[48] Ralph Linton, Study of Man (New York, 1936), p. 176.

[49] Ralph Beals and Harry Hoijer, An Introduction to Anthropology (New York, 1953), p. 118.

[50] Arthur Diamond, The Evolution of Law and Order (London, 1951), p. 220.

[51] Robert Lowie, An Introduction to Cultural Anthropology (2nd ed., New York, 1940), p. 231.

[52] On selectivity and permanence: Lewis Morgan, Ancient Society (Chicago, 1907), p. 507; John Layard, "The Family and Kinship," in: E. Evans-Pritchard and Others, The Institutions of Primitive Society (Glencoe, 1956), p. 50; Ashley Montagu, Man: His First Million Years (Cleveland, 1957), p. 158; Ralph Linton, The Study of Man, (New York, 1936), p. 147; E. A. Hoebel, Man in the Primitive World (New York, 1949), pp. 190–191, 235; E. Evans-Pritchard, Social Anthropology (Glencoe, 1951), p. 69; Wilhelm Koppers, Primitive Man and His World Picture, trans. by Edith Raybould (New York, 1952), p. 55; Bronislaw Malinowski, "Introduction," to H. Ian Hogbin, Law and Order in Polynesia (New York, 1934), p. xlvi; Ralph Piddington, An Introduction to Social Anthropology (London, 1950), p. 114.

[53] Ralph Linton, The Study of Man (New York, 1936), p. 152.

[54] Eliot Chapple and Carleton Coon, Principles of Anthropology (New York, 1942), p. 297.

[55] Edward Westermarck, The Origin and Development of the Moral Ideas (2 v., London, 1908–1912) 2 : p. 364.

and marriage may be one means of assuring male assistance to the woman and her children. But marriage in its essence is the one publicly recognized union of love and procreation in human living.

A great part of the regulations controlling sex activities are the regulations relating to marriage. Marriage regulations are universal. "Every society prescribes limits to the individual's freedom and regulates his conduct through established institutions, for example, the universality of marriage regulations." [56] These rules of marriage not only guide sex activities to the proper channels but also promote the propagation and rearing of children. In other words, sex activities are not dominated by physically more powerful males. They are controlled by regulations which consider the females and the children. These rules of custom law recognize the many values which underlie the union of marriage and endow them with legal status. The value judgment, then, that marriage is good rather than evil is universal in all preliterate law and is a postulate of that law.

The sexual union of husband and wife ordinarily results in children. Together these form the elementary society we term the "family." As the flowering of marriage, the society of husband, wife, and immature children is the basic society from which all other societies and cultures grow. Marriage is as extensive as is the human race. "The nuclear family is a universal human social grouping." [57] As far as our records show, the family has always existed. "There is no positive evidence to show that man ever existed without the family." [58] The value judgment that the family is good and not evil is universal in all societies of men and is also a postulate of all law.

The values attaching to the family are multifold. Among the many others, are the obvious sexual, economic, reproductive, and educational values. Although the family may have other functions and values, it is these which are at its core. This indicates that, although the sex drive is plastic and can be molded according to preferences and choices, this molding is not limitless. After the influence of original preferences, this drive runs to the definite patterns of marriage, family, and all that these unions entail. This focus on core values is noteworthy. "This coincidence of behavior is truly remarkable in view of the diversity of responses in other departments of culture." [59] These are values which must necessarily be in law. [60]

[56] David Bidney, *Theoretical Anthropology* (New York, 1953), p. 11.

[57] George Murdock, *Social Structure* (New York, 1949), p. 2.

[58] Gladys Reichard, "Social Life," in: Franz Boas, ed., *General Anthropology* (Boston, 1938), p. 424.

[59] George Murdock, "The Common Denominator of Culture," Ralph Linton ed., *The Science of Man in the World Crisis* (New York, 1945), p. 140. See Ashley Montagu, *Man: His First Million Years* (Cleveland, 1957), p. 159.

[60] Marriage and family: Arthur Diamond, *The Evolution of Law and Order* (London, 1951), p. 220; Robert Lowie, *An In-*

Value judgments which preliterates make regarding children deserve some note. The affection of preliterates for their children is well known. "There is almost a direct ratio between rudeness of culture and gentleness with children." [61] A preliterate father reportedly will ruin himself to indulge his sons. A preliterate mother is treated with deference because of her children for whom she is the provider of comforts. The physical punishing of children among some preliterate groups is said to be non-existent. [62] Very few data are available on the comparative study of value judgments made by preliterates and literates regarding children. Such a study could contribute to our understanding of constructed value judgments in this fundamental area of human living.

## 2. *In All Societies With Rare Exceptions*

There are certain value judgments regarding sex relations which are universal but with rare exceptions. They are almost universal. They relate to selectivity in sexual union. Some of these value judgments refer to sex relations of one wife with a number of husbands to the exclusion of all other men. Others of these value judgments regard the failure to respect the title to sexual union which is had only by husband and wife. Still other value judgments concern sex relations between parents only to the exclusion of intercourse between parents and children and between brothers and sisters. The most universal judgments we shall treat here, then, refer to polyandry, adultery, and incest.

### a. *Polyandry*

The type of marriage in which one woman has many husbands is polyandry. [63] This kind of marriage is very rare. "As an established institution polyandry is very

*troduction to Cultural Anthropology* (2nd ed., New York, 1940), p. 231; Paul Bohannon, *Social Anthropology* (New York, 1963), p. 74; Ashley Montagu, *Man: His First Million Years* (Cleveland, 1957), p. 149; Ralph Piddington, *An Introduction to Social Anthropology* (London, 1950), pp. 153, 227; Ralph Linton, *The Study of Man* (New York, 1936), p. 135; Huntington Cairns, "Law and Anthropology," in: Victor Calverton, ed., *The Making of Man* (New York, 1931), p. 354; John Layard, "The Family and Kinship," in: Edward Evans-Pritchard and others, *The Institutions of Primitive Society* (Glencoe, 1956), p. 50; Robert Lowie, *Primitive Society* (New York, 1920), pp. 66–67; James Feibleman, *The Theory of Human Culture* (New York, 1946), p. 105.

[61] Robert Lowie, *Are We Civilized?* (New York, 1929), p. 167.

[62] Charles Dundas, "The Organization and Laws of Some Bantu Tribes," *Jour. Royal Anthropol. Inst.* **45** (1915): p. 303; Edward Evans-Pritchard, *Kinship and Marriage Among the Nuer* (Oxford, 1951), p. 137.

[63] In its Greek origin, "polygamy" has the generic meaning of many marriages or mates as distinguished from monogamy meaning one marriage or mate. Polygamy refers to a marriage between two persons one of whom is already married to someone else, and to the resulting family and household. More specific in connotation are polyandry meaning many men, and polygyny meaning many women.

rare."[64] "Fewer than ten adequately authenticated instances are to be found in the literature."[65] Among the groups now reported as practicing polyandry are the Sinhalese in Ceylon, the Thandans and Kammalans of Kerala, the Walluvanad Taluk of South Malabar and North Cochin, the Toda of the Nilgiris in Madras in Southern India, the Lahul, Rupchu and Ladak of Western Tibet, and the U, Tsang and Kham of central Tibet. Among the Toda who are one of the best known groups practicing polyandry, several brothers who live together may be married to one woman. If the husbands are not related and live separately, the woman ordinarily spends a month or so with each of them.

Polyandry should be distinguished from wife-lending, concubinage, cicisbeism, or passing love affairs. Wife-lending, for instance, is a prevalent custom among the preliterates. Among the Wataveta of East Africa it is the practice for a man to lend his wives to his friends of the same age-rank as himself. Among the Bantu a similar custom prevails of men offering visitors one of their wives providing the visitor is about the same age as the host. With the Eskimo, likewise, wives are lent to friends. But what is to be noted is that the reason such practices are not looked on as adulterous is that the husband gives his consent. If one of his wives should have sexual relations with another man without his consent, it would be considered adultery with all its consequences.

The values which motivate polyandry are not easy to locate. One of the main reasons for polyandry is a supposed disproportionately larger number of men than women in some societies. But this does not seem to be the case. The proportion of men in excess of women in polyandrous societies is relatively small. Another reason given is that it is necessary for the solidarity of the family in some places. The Tibetans, for example, say that some one must stay at home and care for the household while the husband first married is away on business or other travels. Fraternal polyandry is considered the ideal solution. Should the wife become pregnant during this period, the child will be of the same blood as the first husband. Or, again, the Toda say that they practice polyandry because if there is only one woman instead of many there is no quarreling and there is peace in the home. Polyandry also keeps the men from jealous quarreling by teaching them solidarity and sharing of their most precious possession. But again, such reasons seem specious because similar problems are solved among non-polyandrous peoples by other means. Polynesian men, for instance, go on long maritime expeditions and they do not have recourse to polyandry as a solution to problems incidental to the husband's absence. Nor do most peoples turn to polyandry as a solution to the inevitable quarreling in domestic life.

The values which are the most convincing motives for polyandry are economic. Polyandry is usually found among groups that are economically poor and who live in a natural environment which is unfertile and unproductive. Many times this is a region cut off from the rest of the world of culture and commerce. For such peoples it is most desirable to retain undivided what holdings they have and pass them on to their children intact. This explanation receives backing from the fact that among some groups, such as the Tibetans, polyandry is found only among the poor while those who are better off are monogamous or even polygynous. Being poor, these families cannot afford to hire extra male help when it is needed. The practical solution is to take another husband into the household.[66]

The value judgment that polyandry is good is, therefore, rare among the societies of men. Or to put it the other way around, the value judgment that polyandry is wrong is almost universal in human societies. One of the grounds sometimes given for the value judgment that polyandry is wrong is that it contributes to the sterility of the woman. But the correlation between polyandrous sex and sterility has never been clearly established. In one polyandrous group at least, the Jaunsaris, the cause of female sterility has been declared to be venereal disease.[67]

---

[66] It has been hinted, without clarification, that there is a connection between polyandry and Buddhism. "It should be noted that two important polyandrous communities in the world today, the Tibetan and the Sinhalese, are Buddhist. Related to Ceylon by popular belief, are the Thandans (Tiyas), Kammalans and allied artisan castes of Kerala. The Todas, admittedly, do not appear to be so, but then their own contention that they are indigenous to the Nilgiris is open to question. From this, it may be suggested that the connection between polyandry and Buddhism is closer than it would seem at first, and that the Central Asian Cultural texture common to both is perhaps not entirely fortuitous." Prince Peter, *A Study of Polyandry* (The Hague, 1963), p. 574.

[67] "A theory has been advanced that the extremely low birth rate in Jaunsar-Bawar [in the Himalayas] may be attributed to polyandry. It has been suggested that excess of sex indulgence which is inevitable when a woman has to live with many husbands, leads to a kind of sexual atrophy which is responsible for the widespread prevalence of sterility among Jaunsari women. . . . [But] sixty to seventy percent of the population were suffering from venereal disease. . . . Sterility, therefore, is mainly due to this affliction among the Jaunsaris." R. N. Saksena, *Social Economy of a Polyandrous People* (rev. ed., New York, 1962), p. 18.

Polyandry: Prince Peter, *A Study of Polyandry* (The Hague, 1963), *passim;* Robert Lowie, *An Introduction to Cultural Anthropology* (2nd ed., New York, 1940), p. 245; Robert Hamilton, "East African Native Laws and Customs," *Jour. Comp. Legislation* 11 (1910): p. 187; Charles Dundas, "The Organization and Laws of Some Bantu Tribes," *Jour. Royal Anthropol. Inst.* 45 (1915): p. 271; E. Adamson Hoebel, *The Law of Primitive Man* (Cambridge, Mass., 1954), p. 83; Edward Westermarck, *The Origin and Development of the Moral Ideas* (2 v., London, 1908–1912) 2: p. 387; Ralph Linton, *The Study of Man* (New York, 1936), p. 183.

---

[64] Robert Lowie, *An Introduction to Cultural Anthropology* (2nd ed., New York, 1940), p. 244.

[65] Paul Bohannon, *Social Anthropology* (New York, 1963), p. 110.

*b. Failure to Respect Spouse's Title to Sexual Union: Adultery*

The exclusiveness of marriage expresses itself in the demand that sex activity be limited to intercourse between husband and wife. Sexual relations with anyone else are adulterous. The minimal meaning of adultery for all peoples has to do with intercourse with the recognized mate of another person. Beyond this, the meaning of adultery takes on variations. It may refer to such sex relations when there is question of the wife only, when these relations occur without the consent of the husband, when they are with someone within the same group, or when they are with someone not of the same age-grade.

Adultery, with whatever meaning is given to it, is considered wrong in all known societies of men with but rare exceptions. Older reports of groups in Mongolia in which adultery was said without qualification not to be wrong appear questionable. So also do older reports seem dubious which imply that adultery is not evaluated as wrong by some peoples such as the Rendile because they do not physically punish it. But because of the possibility that these reports may convey factual information, the value judgment regarding adultery has been located not with the universals but with the almost universals.

Almost universally do the societies of men judge that adultery, as they understand it, is wrong and not right. Among preliterates in general, it is reported, adultery is considered an offense only a degree less than manslaughter because manslaughter is the usual consequence of it. In Tsonga, sexual intercourse by a wife with any man other than her husband gives the husband a claim for damages from the adulterer.

Among other preliterate groups, adultery is judged to be wrong when it is a case of sexual intercourse with a married women without the consent of her husband. The Eskimo are a good example of a people who make this value judgment. In Kutubu a man who commits adultery is guilty of a wrong act because he has abused the husband's rights without his consent. In Polynesia, adultery is also looked on as an abuse of the sole rights of the husband. With the Dinka likewise adultery is committed only when the act is without the knowledge and consent of the husband. Among the Australian Dieri and the American Comanche it is the prerogative of the husband to give his wife to another man. If a wife presumes to do this on her own she is punishable for adultery. With the Wataveta, a man is liable to fine and compensation if he has sex relations with another's man wife without his consent. In Tswana, once the husband has told his wife of his intention to give her to another man, she has no right to object.

Another value which enters into preliterate judging regarding the wrongness of adultery is age-rank. Thus among the Kamba it is not wrong for a man of the husband's age group, or his brother, to have sexual relations with his wife. Among the Masai, sexual intercourse by a man with a woman of his own age-rank is not judged to be wrong. Nothing is said in these reports about the consent of the husband. It has been remarked concerning such reports that it would certainly be extraordinary if jealousy among these preliterates is in such abeyance that a husband would make no objection to his wife having sexual relations with one of her own age-rank without his consent.

Still another value found in preliterate thinking regarding adultery is the in-group versus out-group distinction. In Nigeria, adultery within the kinship group is judged to be an "abomination" and "an outrage on Ala" and is therefore considered a matter of public concern. But adultery outside the group is considered a private injury and not a matter of public interest. In the Schouten Islands in New Guinea, adultery within the clan is considered much more serious than when committed with the member of another village. The whole community shows disapproval but only the people from the area in which the parties live show great concern.

The punishments inflicted by preliterates for adultery are almost universal. "[I]t appears to be universal on the primitive level (and general on the civilized level) that the husband may kill the adulterous wife caught *in flagrante delicto*. For the wife to enjoy such a privilege-right is most rare." [68] In earlier times on the Orinoco all groups recognized adultery, especially when one of the partners was a married woman. The Carib, however, are reported as the only nation which had a fixed punishment for adulterers. The adulterer was put to death by all the people of the village in a public place.

The punishment of death for adulterers is an indication of value judgment of wrongness which preliterates place on adultery. In Africa, the Useguha, Ungoni, and Rombo recognize the right to kill an adulterer. With the Wasove, the adulterer caught in the act could be killed. Among the Wabunga, the husband had the right to kill his wife's paramour if compensation was withheld. In Unyamwesi and Ubena the man who had sexual relations with the chief's wife was put to death. With the Uhehe, the adulterer had his shin bones crushed between stones. Among the Nabaloi in Northern Luzon, a husband or wife who catches their mate in adulterous intercourse can kill their spouse and paramour with no penalty attached. If the killing takes place sometime later, the killer is hanged. Among some tribes in Nigeria, the husband can kill with impunity an adulterer caught in the act with his wife. He could, however, condone the wife's action and assault the paramour. The paramour might apologize to the husband or offer him a gift.

The custom law of preliterates reinforces the value judgment that adultery is wrong and not right. "Law

---

[68] E. Adamson Hoebel, *The Law of Primitive Man* (Cambridge, Mass., 1954), p. 286.

universally supports the principle of relative exclusiveness in marital rights. Adultery seems always to be punishable under the law, although just what constitutes adultery will be variable as marriage and kinship forms vary." [69] Some preliterates have been reported as having no laws against adultery. But the vicious reactions contrived against adulterous women by members of the community belie the accuracy of these reports.[70] The value judgment, therefore, that adultery is wrong is almost universal in preliterate custom law. This place of adultery in law has not always been recognized in written law, for instance the law of England.[71]

### c. Incest

The sexual relations of parents and their children, and of brothers and sisters, constitute incest in its strict sense. Some preliterate groups extend the concept of incest to sexual relations between members of the same clan or group. The rules of endogomy-exogamy are the result.

All societies have always had the minimal restriction that parents and their children, as well as brothers and sisters, may not have sex relations nor marry. "Incest regulations are an inevitable accompaniment of marriage and are found in all societies." [72] They are "universal among all peoples." [73] "[T]he incest taboo . . . appears to be a universal one." [74] These regulations are necessary because of the biological sex attraction which exists between members of the same family. In preventing sexual relations within the family, these regulations guide the attention of its young members to persons outside the family. Unless controlled, sex attraction within the family could destroy it. The proper and necessary function of the family would be impaired through sexual rivalry and contention. Incest has been said to be worse than murder. Murder destroys a man but not a society. Incest destroys the society of marriage inasmuch as it corrupts it from within.

The exceptions to the universality of incest regulations are the well-known cases where, for certain reasons, incest was allowed. These reasons had to do with the "nobility" who considered that only those of royal blood were fit to continue the royal line. On these grounds, brother-sister marriages were justified in Egypt, Hawaii, Peru, and on the Northwest Coast of America. These examples of brother-sister sexual relationships are undoubtedly the rare exception to the general rule found in all societies which prohibits such relations.

How widespread the practice of incest has been is difficult to determine. Among some peoples, according to the reports, incest is said never to occur. Thus among the Kalinga, incest even between first cousins is reported never to happen. On the other hand, in Nepal it is reported that, although it is not approved, the "frequency of the various forms of incest is striking." [75] But the frequency with which incest or any other action occurs, as we pointed out, has no direct relation to the value judgment that people make regarding it. Even those who practice incest may judge that it is wrong.

Among preliterates incest is considered to be "the most heinous of offences." [76] Incest with a sister is looked on as "an unspeakable, almost unthinkable crime." [77] Among the Polynesians, it is said that no one would think of accusing a man of having sexual relations with his sister unless he wished to start a fight. The seriousness of the offense of incest for preliterates can be gauged by the punishments they inflict on those guilty of it. "No matter to what primitive people one

---

[69] Ibid.

[70] J. Adair, History of the American Indians (London, 1775), pp. 145–146. This report gives an account of how upwards of fifty young men, who belonged to the family of the husband of an adulteress in a Cherokee village, reacted to her adulterous activities. They followed the woman into the woods and, having extended her hands and feet and tied them to stakes, had sexual relations with her. They said that since she loved a great many men instead of her husband, justice told them that they should gratify her desire for many men!

[71] Adultery: Nikolas Prejevalsky, Mongolia (London, 1876), pp. 70–71; W. Chandler, Through Jungle and Desert (New York, 1896), p. 317; Robert Marett, Anthropology (New York, 1911), p. 195; T. D. Ramsey, Tsonga Law in the Transvaal (Pretoria, 1941), p. 21; E. Adamson Hoebel, The Law of Primitive Man (Cambridge, Mass., 1954), pp. 83, 253; F. E. Williams, "Group Sentiment and Primitive Justice," Amer. Anthropologist 43 (1941): p. 533; H. Ian Hogbin, Law and Order in Polynesia (London, 1934), p. 226; Hugh O'Sullivan, Dinka Laws and Customs, Jour. Royal Anthropol. Inst. 40 (1910): p. 187; Isaac Schapera, A Handbook of Tswana Law and Custom (London, 1938), p. 156; Arthur Diamond, The Evolution of Law and Order (London, 1951), p. 114; Robert Hamilton, "East African Native Laws and Customs," Jour. Comp. Legislation (1910): p. 188; Lewis Tupper, "Customary and Other Law in the East Africa Protectorate," Jour. Soc. Comp. Legislation 8 (1908): p. 179; C. K. Meek, Law and Authority in a Nigerian Tribe (London, 1937), pp. 218, 220; H. Ian Hogbin, "Social Reactions to Crime," Jour. Royal Anthropol. Inst. 68 (1939): p. 244; John Gillin, "Crime and Punishment Among the Barama River Carib," Amer. Anthropologist 36 (1934): p. 336; Charles Dundas, "Native Laws of Some Bantu Tribes of East Africa," Jour. Royal Anthropol. Inst. 51 (1921): p. 244; Claude Moss, "Nabaloi Law and Ritual," Amer. Archaeology and Ethnology 15 (1920): p. 259.

[72] Ralph Beals and Harry Hoijer, An Introduction to Anthropology (New York, 1953), p. 440; Mischa Titiev, The Science of Man (New York, 1954), p. 368.

[73] E. Adamson Hoebel, Man in the Primitive World (New York, 1949), p. 191; Ashley Montagu, Man: His First Million Years (Cleveland, 1957), p. 149.

[74] Leslie Paul, Nature into History (London, 1957), p. 106. The term taboo is derived from the Oceanic word tapu or tabu. It refers to that type of prohibition whose violation is thought inevitably to bring undesirable consequences. See Ralph Piddington, An Introduction to Social Anthropology (London, 1950), p. 378.

[75] Leonhard Adam, "Criminal Law and Procedure in Nepal," Far Eastern Quart. 9 (1950): p. 164.

[76] Arthur Diamond, The Evolution of Law and Order (London, 1951), p. 50.

[77] Bronislaw Malinowski, "The Forces of Law and Order in a Primitive Community," Proc. Royal Inst. of Great Britain 24 (1925): p. 540.

turns, incest meets with horrified condemnation and is held to merit exile or death." [78] The Ashanti consider that both parties to incest be put to death. The Tlingit judge likewise with the execution being performed by clansmen. In Nigeria incest was punished either by killing or sale into slavery. In Upare incest is looked upon as a form of madness. The Wamakonda punish incest by payment of slaves. The Wanuamwesi and Wabunga are said to punish incest by death. Among the Bantu, although homicide and theft are compensable, incest and witchcraft were punished as crimes. With the Naskapi, incest is not physically punished but the sanction of public opinion and avoidance is so strong that the offender is forced to leave the community.

With some preliterates, the offense of incest has preternatural implications. In East Africa, "severe supernatural vengeance" can be wreaked upon the offenders, their progeny, and their whole group. In Yoruba, the offending parties are required to offer sacrifice to appease the anger of the gods of the family. With the Nuer, the word for incest is also the word for misfortune. Syphilis and certain forms of yaws, as well as any kind of misfortune which occurs, are thought to be punishments for incest. Some Nuer consider whiteness of skin to be a punishment by God for incest committed by an ancestor of the white man with his mother.

The value judgment that incest is wrong and not right is almost universal in the custom law of all societies of preliterates. Once again, this place of incest in law has not always been recognized among literates. Incest was never a crime at common law.

The value judgment that incest is wrong is a constructed value judgment. It is not given nor is it instinctive. This is generally admitted. Men's basic drive for sexual union does not of itself exclude sexual relations between brothers and sisters or parents and their children. There is no inherent aversion or psychological distaste for incestuous sex relations, as is shown by the prevalence of incest among certain peoples who even judge it to be wrong. The examples of incest among royalty also indicate that the horror of incest is not inborn. [79]

[78] Leslie Paul, *Nature into History* (London, 1957), p. 108.

[79] Incest: Robert Lowie, *An Introduction to Cultural Anthropology* (2nd ed., New York, 1940), pp. 232–233; Max Gluckman, "Political Institutions," in: Edward Evans-Pritchard and others, *The Institutions of Primitive Society* (Glencoe, 1956), p. 68; Alexander Goldenweiser, *Anthropology* (New York, 1937), p. 298; Robert Fortune, "Law and Force in Papuan Societies," *Amer. Anthropologist* 49 (1947): p. 244; Margaret Mead, "Some Anthropological Considerations Concerning Natural Law," *Natural Law Forum* 6 (1961): p. 52; John Layard, "The Family and Kinship," in: Edward Evans-Pritchard, *The Institutions of Primitive Society* (Glencoe, 1956), pp. 51, 52; Leslie Paul, *Nature into History* (London, 1957), pp. 103, 123–124; Gladys Reichard, "Social Life," in: Franz Boas, ed., *General Anthropology* (Boston, 1938), pp. 438, 480; E. Adamson Hoebel, *Man in the Primitive World* (New York, 1949), p. 191; Ralph Piddington, *An Introduction to Social Anthropology* (London, 1950), p. 131; Ralph Barton, *The Kalingas* (Chicago, 1949), p. 246; H. Ian Hogbin, *Law and Order in*

## B. LESS THAN UNIVERSAL VALUE JUDGMENTS

The value judgments about sex which we shall now consider are less than universal. They concern sexual intercourse and childbirth before marriage, exchanges of items at marriage, failure to respect title to sexual integrity in rape, divorce, polygyny, and monogamy. These value judgments will be general or common.

### 1. General

#### a. Premarital Intercourse and Premarital Childbirth

The value judgment formed by preliterates regarding sexual intercourse and childbirth before marriage varies. [80] Some, according to the reports, consider neither premarital sex relations nor premarital childbirth to be wrong. Premarital sexual relations were not thought to be wrong among the Nsukka. The Bagesu, a Bantu people, do not think it disgraceful if a girl becomes a mother before marriage. This does not prevent her from getting a husband. In fact it enhances her chances of doing so. The men in the group like to know whether a woman is capable of bearing a child.

Among some groups, such as the Bushongo, much the same notion is prevalent concerning premarital relations. When a girl, as a result of premarital sex relations, gives birth to a child no shame attaches to it. The child is left with her parents and she feels that she has proved she is capable of bearing a child. This also appears to be the thinking of the Bontoc Igorot of the Philippines. The Masai give evidence of having similar notions. All normal girls spend some time living with the warriors and when they become pregnant they return to the village to be married with no stigma upon them. Again, having borne a child enhances the girl's chances of obtaining a husband. Among some Bantu such as the Wabunga, premarital intercourse is looked upon as a prelude to marriage. It is understood that when a

*Polynesia* (London, 1934), p. 162; Robert Rattray, *Ashanti Law and Constitution* (Oxford, 1929), p. 304; Kalervo Oberg, "Crime and Punishment in Tlingit Society," *Amer. Anthropologist* 36 (1934): p. 147; C. K. Meek, *Law and Authority in a Nigerian Tribe* (London, 1937), pp. 223–224; Charles Dundas, "Native Laws of Some Bantu Tribes of East Africa," *Jour. Royal Anthropol. Inst.* 51 (1921): p. 248; T. Olawale Elias, *The Nature of African Customary Law* (Manchester, 1956), p. 113; Julius Lips, "Naskapi Law," *Trans. Amer. Philos. Soc.* 37 (1947): p. 471; A. K. Ajisafe, *Laws and Customs of the Yoruba People* (London, 1924), p. 28; Edward Evans-Pritchard, *Kinship and Marriage Among the Nuer* (Oxford, 1951), p. 30; Evans-Pritchard, *Nuer Religion* (Oxford, 1956), p. 6; Otto Klineberg, *Social Psychology* (rev. ed., New York, 1954), p. 147; Ralph Beals and Harry Hoijer, *An Introduction to Anthropology* (New York, 1953), p. 440.

[80] Pre-marital sex relation has been said to be a survival of the supposed state of sexual promiscuity mentioned above. The same criticism, however, made of this notion above applies here. "That promiscuous pre-nuptual unchastity is a survival of earlier general promiscuity is ... an assumption [for which] there is no justification whatever." Edward Westermarck, *The History of Human Marriage* (3 v., 5th ed., New York, 1922), p. 162.

couple have sexual intercourse they will subsequently marry.

On the other hand, there is evidence that many peoples form a different value judgment regarding premarital sexual intercourse. They judge it to be wrong. Among the Samoans, girls were supposed to be virgins. If a girl was of the chief's house, she had to undergo a public breaking of the hymen. If it was already broken, it was considered a disgrace. The Cheyenne Indians highly regarded premarital chastity as well as marital chastity. The chastity belt worn by Cheyenne girls was considered to be inviolable by custom law.[81] Self-control was held in the highest esteem. With the Gikuyu, a girl is also expected to be a virgin with an unperforated hymen. All premarital intercourse is forbidden and any man who causes a girl to become pregnant is severely punished. The girl also is punished.

The value which some preliterates put on chastity and virginity can also be seen in the dowry differential when the bride is not a virgin. In many such instances a certain amount is deducted from the dowry. Both the Wakitusika and the Waziguha pay more dowry for a virgin. In Sumbwa, where most marriageable girls are said not to be virgins, an amount is subtracted for loss of virginity. It is also said that premarital sexual intercourse is looked upon as a disgrace and a crime among the Vedda of Ceylon, the Igorot of Luzon, and some Australian tribes.

Regarding premarital childbirth, opinion regarding its rightness or wrongness appears to vary. For instance, it is reported that in Java no distinction is made in the kinship status of children born in or out of wedlock. The father assumed responsibility for his child born out of wedlock and the child's relationship to the father's kin is thereby regularized. But this does not seem to be the general opinion among preliterates. Among the Trobrianders, although unmarried girls are not censored for premarital affairs, they are disgraced by giving birth to a child in an unmarried state. It has further been claimed that such an unfavorable view of premarital childbirth is universal in all societies. All peoples, it is said, invariably look upon premarital pregnancy and childbirth as disgraceful.[82] The important implication

of this claim is that the unit composed of an unmarried woman and her offspring is not a complete sociological unit. The presence of the male is required for completion. This is especially true regarding the education of a male child.[83] The regulations requiring his presence are expressions of the demands of men's nature.

This claim for the universality of the value judgment that premarital childbirth is wrong appears to be at variance with the report just cited concerning the evaluation put on it by the Bantu Bagesu, the Bushongo, the Bantoc Igorot. There may be other such reports. This discrepancy may be due to inaccurate reporting. Or if the reporting is accurate, the value judgment that premarital childbirth is wrong is not universal but only general.

The number of preliterates who judge premarital sexual intercourse to be wrong appears to be greater than the number who judge it to be right. Hence, we shall venture the opinion that the value judgment that premarital sex relations are wrong is general among preliterates. Likewise, it seems certain that the number who evaluate premarital childbirth as wrong is far greater than the number who judge it to be right. We shall also estimate, therefore, that the value judgment that premarital childbirth is wrong is at least general, if not almost universal, among preliterates.[84]

### b. Exchange of Items at Marriage

The constructed value judgment placed on the exchange of items of value at marriage has implications regarding the evaluation made of women. They may be valued as things or property, or they may be valued as persons.

---

Bronislaw Malinowski, *Sex and Repression in Savage Society* (London, 1927), pp. 212, 213. What constitutes "illegitimacy" undoubtedly varies from one society to another. The word itself could beg the question. That a child is born of parents who are not married to each other is one thing. That this child is not recognized by law as having the same status as other children is entirely another thing.

[83] "[E]ducation is one of the family's universal functions and only a man is capable of training a male child in masculine cultural skills." C. K. Meek, *Law and Authority in a Nigerian Tribe* (London, 1937), p. 298. For the need of the father in the family task of educating the children, especially boys, see chap. 5.

[84] Premarital intercourse and premarital childbirth: C. K. Meek, *Law and Authority in a Nigerian Tribe* (London, 1937), p. 299; John Roscoe, *The Northern Bantu* (Cambridge, 1951), p. 171; Isaac Thomas, *Primitive Behavior* (New York, 1937), p. 271; Albert Jenks, *The Bantoc Igorot* (Manila, 1905), *passim*; Ralph Beals and Harry Hoijer, *An Introduction to Anthropology* (New York, 1953), p. 416; Charles Dundas, "Native Laws of Some Bantu Tribes of East Africa," *Jour. Royal Anthropol. Inst.* **51** (1921): p. 246; H. Ian Hogbin, *Law and Order in Polynesia* (London, 1934), p. 283; Jomo Kenyatta, *Facing Mount Kenya* (London, 1953), p. 160; Edward Westermarck, *The Origin and Development of the Moral Ideas* (2 v., London, 1908–1912) 2: pp. 424–425; Barend Ter Haar, *Adat Law in Indonesia* (New York, 1948), p. 154; Bronislaw Malinowski, *Sex and Repression in Savage Society* (London, 1951), pp. 9, 213.

---

[81] "Cheyenne girls wore a chastity belt which was assumed upon puberty. It consisted of a thin rope placed about the waist, knotted in front over the abdomen, with the free ends passing down between the thighs to the back, thence down around the legs to the knees. It was worn always at night, as well as during the day when away from the home lodge." Karl Llewellyn and E. Adamson Hoebel, *The Cheyenne Way* (Norman, 1941), p. 261.

[82] "In all human societies . . . there is universally found what might be called the rule of legitimacy. By this I mean that in all human societies a girl is bidden to be married before she becomes pregnant. Pregnancy and childbirth on the part of an unmarried young woman are invariably regarded as a disgrace. . . . I know of no single instance in anthropological literature of a community where illegitimate children, that is children of unmarried girls, would enjoy the same social treatment and have the same social status as legitimate ones."

Marriage is both a contract and the state resulting from this contract, as we have already noted. This idea of contractual agreement is present in all marriages. Ceremony of some kind usually accompanies the agreement, a part of which many times is the exchange or promise to exchange some item of worth. Preliterates are no exception. Some Africans, for instance, look on this exchange as a prerequisite to the marriage contract. This transfer is governed by set rules and unless it takes place there is no marriage. Among other Africans, such a payment of dowry is said to be of the essence of marriage. Without the dowry there is no marriage and any children born of such a union are considered to be illegitimate. If there is a divorce, the husband's dowry is returned to him and the wife goes back to her family with her children.

The question has arisen, however, of what the implications are in the exchange of items of worth at marriage. If it is a price paid for the bride, she is reduced to the status of a chattel or property. Not a few have maintained that such is the case among some preliterates. In Samoa it is said that marriage is an economic exchange of property. In East Africa, the women in a man's family are said to be considered property in the same manner as his cattle. Marriage is a matter of purchase. Among the Comanche, women reportedly have the status of a chattel such as horses do.

In Fiji wives are sold at pleasure and the usual price is a musket. Among the Shoshone, a man is the sole owner of his women and can dispose of them in any way he wishes. With the Wanika in East Africa, a woman is said to be a tool or slave and can be treated as an animal. Among the Kirgiz, the woman is thought of as the property of her husband with no relation to her family. With the Ho in West Africa, a proprietary title to the wife is said to be established by payments and services. It has also been said that "wife-purchase" was widely practiced in Europe by the Anglo-Saxons and the Teutons, and also by the Chinese, the Semites, the Arabs, the Greeks, and the Hindus. From the practice of wife-purchase supposedly came the practice of providing the wife with a dowry. The suggestion has been made that instead of using the prejudiced term "bride-price" another more non-committal term such as "bride-wealth" be employed. But a rejoinder has been made to this proposal. Economic terms are justified in this context if wives are transferred in a certain society in the same manner in which ordinary economic commodities are exchanged in this same society.

On the other hand, there are those who maintain that the transfer of items of worth at the time of marriage is not the purchase of a woman as a piece of property. Rather it is the acquisition of protectorship over her. What is purchased, according to this view, is what the Teutons called the *mund* or protectorship. The general view held today of the exchange of items of worth at marriage, it is claimed, is that marriage is actually the sale of this protectorship. Supporting this view is the fact that after marriage wives cannot be traded exactly as other chattels can be. A woman may have economic value to her husband, but she does not become property in the sense that he can dispose of her at will without reactions from herself or her family. A husband has duties to his wife that he does not have, say, to his cattle. If a husband kills his wife in some places, he has to compensate her family. This would not be the case if she were the husband's property in the sense of any other chattel.

Other explanations of the exchange of items of worth at marriage have also been forthcoming. It has been explained as a dowry paid in composition for wife-stealing or for the loss of a member of the family. But against this notion it is argued that some preliterates' services have no value. The exchange has also been said to be an earnest, the acceptance of which is a guarantee by the girl's family of the good conduct of their daughter. The higher the amount paid, the greater the guarantee. The girl knows that, if she leaves her husband, the amount paid will have to be returned by her family. The result of such an arrangement is stability in marriage. A woman fears to leave her husband because of the consequences to her family.

Another explanation of the exchange is that it is in the nature of "consideration" which, according to some, is essential to the contract of marriage. In this position, "marriage by consideration" would be opposed to "marriage by purchase." But in the opinion of many, consideration is not essential to a contract.[85] If the exchange is seen as external evidence of the internal intention to bind by contractual promise, the exchange will be recognized as a pre-condition to the contractual promise of marriage. That which makes a contract what it is, is not what is exchanged or the reason why the exchange is made. It is the promise itself. It is the consent to effect a change in relationships.[86]

From the prevalence of exchanges at marriage, it seems safe to say that the value judgment that the exchange of some item of worth at marriage is good is general among preliterates. From the data showing that wives generally cannot be freely disposed of as pieces of property without reactions of the wife, her family or others, it seems a fair estimate that the value judgment that women are valued more as persons than as property at marriage is also general among preliterates.[87]

[85] Thomas Davitt, *The Elements of Law* (Boston, 1959), pp. 277–290.

[86] Lord Wright, "Ought the Doctrine of Consideration Be Abolished from the Common Law?" *Harvard Law Rev.* **49** (1936): pp. 1225, 1229.

[87] Marriage exchanges: T. Olawale Elias, *The Nature of African Customary Law* (Manchester, 1956), pp. 146, 147; Jack Driberg, "Primitive Law in East Africa," *Africa* 1 (1928): p. 63; Margaret Mead, "The Role of the Individual in Samoan Culture," in: Alfred Kroeber and Thomas Waterman, eds., *Source Book in Anthropology* (New York, 1931), p. 553; Robert Hamilton, "East African Native Laws and Customs," *Jour. Comp. Legislation* **11** (1910): pp. 181, 185; E. Adamson

*c. Failure to Respect Title to Sexual Integrity: Rape*

The act of sexual intercoure with another person forcibly and without consent occurs in all societies. It is a violation of another person's claim to sexual integrity; that is, it is a failure to respect this person's title to sexual union with the partner of his or her free selection. The frequency with which rape occurs may at times be related to the cultural status of the people and to the availability of sex partners. Among the Comanche, for instance, sex relations were so free that rape was an infrequent occurrence. With the Samoans also the idea of forced sexual relations or sexual intercourse not freely entered into was foreign to their minds.

Some preliterates consider rape to be neither good nor bad. They think it is a matter of indifference. Thus the Tonga Islanders and the Pelew Islanders are reported to have looked on rape as of no moral significance, except when it was committed with a woman who was married or who was of a rank superior to that of the raper. A similar judgment was made, it is said, by the Rejang of Sumatra and the Assiniboine of the Sioux. If rape was punished, it was because it depreciated the price the woman could command for marriage and thereby lessened her chances of getting married. In doing this, rape also implied contempt for the kindred of the woman.

With other preliterates, however, rape was viewed as wrong. Among the Nandi, rape was regarded as an outrage against the female sex. It received punishment whether the offender be young or old. The Nabaloi likewise look on rape as wrong. When a man rapes a woman, he is compelled by the council to forfeit some of his holdings provided he is still alive and not already killed by the husband. If he has no property, he has to borrow some and work off the payments on it. If a young man raped a young woman, they were ordered to marry by the council. With the Bantu, accusation of rape by either a married or unmarried woman, raised

the presumption of guilt. The elders took action on very little proof.

But one of the best indications of the value judgment preliterates make of rape and how extensive it is, is the number of times rape appears on lists of punishable offenses. We shall examine some of these later. Based on such evidence, it seems that the value judgment that rape is wrong is general among preliterates.[88]

*d. Divorce*

The complete dissolution of the marriage union is not uncommon among preliterates. Among some groups, in Dobu and Manu for instance, divorce appears to be frequent. Barrenness is very widely accepted as a reason for divorcing a wife. Among the Eskimo in Greenland, divorce can occur for the slightest reason before the birth of children. After children are born, the parents are much less inclined to separate. A similar condition prevails among the Chukchi and the Crow. In Madagascar it is understood that, if the husband does not care well for the wife, she may be taken back by her family. Conversely, the husband may divorce the wife if she misbehaves.

But among other preliterate groups divorce is rare. With the Zuni, the great majority of marriages last for a lifetime, in spite of the fact that divorce is easy to obtain. Among the Andaman Islanders for married mates to stay together until death is not the exception but the rule. The Bantu discountenance divorce. Marriage is looked on as a very permanent union especially with regard to the first wife who can never be the wife of more than one man. There is also here a religious element to marriage which gives it a sacred meaning. Among the Kirghiz and the Kai, the high amount a man must pay to the family of the girl he wants to marry has the effect of keeping him more or less content with the wife he already has. With these peoples, consequently, divorce is not common.

The evaluation which preliterates put on divorce has to be distinguished. As an ideal, no preliterate society judges divorce to be good. "Although practically all societies recognize divorce, there is no society which approves it in principle. The ideal marriage is everywhere that in which the members remain together for

Hoebel, "The Political Organization and Law-ways of the Comanche Indians, *Mem. Amer. Anthropol. Assoc.* **54** (1940): p. 119; Ernest Beaglehole, *Property, A Study of Social Psychology* (New York, 1932), p. 158; Huntington Cairns, "Law and Anthropology," in: Victor Calverton, ed., *The Making of Man* (New York, 1931), p. 355; Edward Evans-Pritchard, "An Alternative Term for 'Bride-Price,'" *Man* **31** (1931): p. 36; Robert Gray, "Sonjo Bride-Price and the Question of African 'Wife-Purchase,'" *Amer. Anthropology* **62** (1960): p. 35; Charles Dundas, "The Organization and Laws of Some Bantu Tribes," *Jour. Royal Anthropol. Inst.* **45** (1915): pp. 290-291; E. Sidney Hartland, "Introduction," to Hugh O'Sullivan, "Dinka Laws and Customs," *Jour. Royal Anthropol. Inst.* (1910): pp. 171-172; Franz Boas, *Anthropology and Modern Life* (New York, 1928), p. 236; Dundas, "Native Laws of Some Bantu Tribes of East Africa," *Jour. Royal Anthropol. Inst.* **51** (1921): p. 256; C. L. Harries, *The Laws and Customs of the Bepedi and Cognate Tribes of the Transvaal,* (rev. ed., Johannesburg, 1929), p. 3; K. H. Crosby, "Polygamy in Mende Country," *Africa* **10** (1937): p. 250; Edward Westermarck, *The History of Human Marriage* (3 v., 5th ed., New York, 1922) **2**: p. 414.

[88] Rape: E. Adamson Hoebel, "The Political Organization and Law-ways of the Comanche Indians," *Mem. Amer. Anthropol. Assoc.* **54** (1940): p. 111; Margaret Mead, "The Role of the Individual in Samoan Culture," in: Alfred Kroeber and Thomas Waterman, eds., *Source Book in Anthropology* (New York, 1931), p. 552; Edward Westermarck, *The Origin and Development of the Moral Ideas* (2 v., London, 1908–1912) **2**: pp. 437–438; Geoffrey Snell, *Nandi Customary Law* (London, 1954), p. 33; Claude Moss, "Nabaloi Law and Ritual," *Amer. Archaeology and Ethnology* **15** (1920): p. 261; Charles Dundas, "The Organization and Laws of Some Bantu Tribes," *Jour. Royal Anthropol. Inst.* **45** (1915): p. 274; Ruth Benedict, *Patterns of Culture* (New York, 1934), p. 139.

life." [89]  "No society appears to recognize in principle that marriage is not a permanent union. . . . Even in divorce, then, we find support for the ideal, probably universal in human societies, that marriage once contracted should be a permanent tie." [90]  In divorce there is implicit recognition of the basic values which are explicitly expressed in marriage.  In practice and in spite of this ideal, however, divorce is allowed by preliterates as we have seen.  On the evidence available, it appears that the majority of preliterate groups judge that divorce is right if there is some semblance of a reason for it. If this is the case, the value judgment that divorce is good providing there are justifying reasons for it is general among preliterates. [91]

## 2. *Common*

### a. *Polygyny*

The marriage of one man to many women, on the first reading of reports, appears general among preliterates. [92] Among the Wakarra of Ukarra in Lake Victoria and among other Bantu, according to the reports it is the rule for one man to have many wives.  One wife is an indication of poverty.  Many wives are a sign of wealth.  Polygyny brings respect and esteem.  In some groups such as the Luo, to have many wives is the goal desired in marriage.  Among the Bapedi, polygyny is said to be practiced commonly.  There is no limitation placed on the number of wives a man may have be he chief, headman, or commoner. [93]  But other reports claim that the prevalence of polygynous marriages among preliterates is by no means general.  "An actual analysis of marriage in various societies shows that there are very few groups in which plurality of spouses

is the general condition.  Even when polygyny is the ideal, there are usually only a few men who can afford to have more than one wife." [94]

The values underlying polygyny are many.  Values which motivate the Bapedi are said to be the satisfaction of the husband's sexual desire for more than one woman, the favorable impression which the presence of many wives gives, and the possibility of more daughters and therefore of more profit from the marriages of these daughters when they marry.  Another motivating value among preliterates is the idea that a mother upon the birth of a child should devote full time to it and nurse it even up to three years.  In the meantime, the husband should not have sex relations with her for the good of both mother and child.

One of the reasons given formerly for polygyny was the supposed disproportion of the sexes.  The number of males killed in war and hunting, according to this theory, was so large that the males were greatly outnumbered by the females and polygynous marriages were the inevitable consequence.  As wars and death rates of men decreased, it was said, polygyny also decreased and the tendency to monogamy increased.  It was assumed that more advanced preliterates indulged in polygyny to a greater extent than less advanced groups.  Later research, however, has shown that this assumption is not supported by the facts.  There is no great disproportion between the number of males and females.  In some polygynous groups, as a matter of fact, there are more males than females.  The mortality rate of preliterate women giving birth to children, it is reported, is greater than has been recognized.

The values which appear to be the strongest motives for polygyny, however, are economic.  Such, as we saw, is also the case with polyandry.  In an agriculture economy, often the more wives a man has the more workers he has for his fields.  Frequently it is the first wife who asks that her husband acquire another wife so that the first wife will be relieved of some of her burdens.  Further, it is no mere happenstance that polygyny continues to flourish in societies in which it is possible for women to acquire property rights.  In many polygynous marriages the inheritance of rights to property, as we shall see, is in accordance with the rank of the wives.  To these motivating values for polygyny can be added those we have already mentioned.  In a word, polygyny can be looked on as a social system which is intimately bound up with property, labor, and the difference in status which exists between men and women.

The "first-wife" is a datum of first-rank value in polygynous marriages.  Almost invariably one of the wives enjoys a position of favor.  Among the Kamba, for instance, the first wife is entitled to give orders to the other wives.  With the Yoruba, the first wife is the mistress of the entire compound.  Among the Kirghiz and Mongol tribes there is a similar recognition of one of the wives as the chief mistress who is the keeper of

[89] Ralph Linton, *The Study of Man* (New York, 1936), p. 176.

[90] Ralph Beals and Harry Hoijer, *An Introduction to Anthropology* (New York, 1953), p. 118.

[91] "There is almost no documentation on the folk evaluation of the processes of divorce, or even the full examination of what divorce entails in various societies."  Paul Bohannon, *Social Anthropology* (New York, 1963), p. 114.
Divorce: Robert Lowie, *Primitive Society* (New York, 1920), pp. 19, 69, 75; Ralph Linton, *The Study of Man* (New York, 1936), pp. 175–176; Ruth Benedict, *Patterns of Culture* (New York, 1934), p. 75; Charles Dundas, "The Organization and Laws of Some Bantu Tribes," *Jour. Royal Anthropol. Inst.* **45** (1915) : p. 290.

[92] Human polygyny, sometimes designated by the broader term polygamy, has its counterpart in animal life.  "Bark-beetles, semi-domesticated pheasants (wild forms are monogamous), the Indian buffalo, deer, antelope, wild sheep and goats, elephants, and certain apes have organized groups of one male and many females which are intolerant of intrusion by other males.  Within the same families (bees, ants, and wasps) solitary species are found as well as highly social varieties." Gladys Reichard, "Social Life," in: Franz Boas, ed., *General Anthropology* (Boston, 1938), p. 411.

[93] As one preliterate put it regarding having only one wife: "To own one wife is as big a risk as to own only one belt for palm climbing.  If it breaks you are done for." Leo Simmons, *The Role of the Aged in Primitive Society* (New Haven, 1945), p. 180.

[94] Ralph Linton, *The Study of Man* (New York, 1936), p. 188.

the house. The other wives assume a subordinate position. The ranking of wives in polygynous marriages is not peculiar to preliterates. It occurs also in literate cultures. In China it was the first wife who had the most prestige and who controlled the other wives in the household.

The "first-wife" in the great majority of cases appears to be the first woman the husband marries, but this is not necessarily the case. In Tswana the first wife married is the "great wife." The next is the "second-wife" and so on. Among some Bantu tribes a similar situation obtains with the first woman married called the "big wife" who has charge of the other wives. Among other Bantu, however, the "first-wife" may not be the first one married but her position is clear and definite. In the Cape Nguni tribes, the first wife a man marries is his Great Wife who lives in the Great House. The second wife he marries is the Right-Hand wife who lives in the Right-Hand house. The third wife becomes a "supporter" of the Great House, the fourth a "supporter" of the Right-Hand house, and so forth.

The value of the "first-wife" position is not limited to mere domestic preference and domination of the household. It may extend to rights of inheritance. With the Ifugao, the children of the woman first married to the husband have the right of inheriting all the property their father had at the time he married the second wife. In Tsonga likewise it is the first wife's children who succeed to all the father's property. Succeeding wives and their children acquire rights in relation to the order in which they were married. Even chiefs cannot change this status of the wives, which derives from the order in which they were married. The ability of women to acquire property in this manner, as already noted, is undoubtedly one of the reasons why polygynous marriages continue to flourish in the cultures wherein they have already taken root. As has been said of the Ashanti, it is the position of women and their children that forms the heart of preliterate society.

Jealousy is an important value-factor in polygynous marriages. This is due principally to the inequality established by the formal ranking of wives, even though an attempt is made to treat them "equally." In some languages the word for co-wife is also the word for jealousy. Such is the case with the Luo and the Nuer. Among the Nuer, the first wife is said to have no special status, although as first married she is consulted by her husband more than the other wives. It has been noted that the possibility of jealousy is reduced where the wives are sisters. So also has it been said that the superiority accorded to the first wife by the other wives makes for harmony among them. In Siberia the second wife is practically the maid of the first wife. A similar condition prevails among the Kai in New Guinea and among the Masai. The first wife directs the others and receives from her husband a larger portion of cattle and gifts. True polygyny, it has been pointed out, is more than multiple monogamy. The key to smooth working of polygyny is the successful playing of the role of co-wife.

The most important value of the "first-wife" phenomenon lies perhaps in its significance in regard to monogamy. It has been interpreted as a manifestation of monogamous exclusiveness and the first stage in the process of evolution toward complete monogamy. The second stage is the placing of the secondary wives in the status of concubines, as was done at one time in China. The third stage is the denial of legal recognition of the status of concubines or the positive prohibition of such "wives," as also occurred in China. According to this interpretation, the polygynous marriages in Africa and elsewhere have within themselves, in the fact of the "first-wife," the seeds of evolution into monogamous unions.

The evidence seems to indicate that, regardless of how widespread polygyny actually is or is not among them, preliterates commonly form a value judgment regarding it. Hence, we shall say that the value judgment that it is good and desirable for a man to be married simultaneously to many wives appears to be common among preliterates. Within these polygynous marriages, the value judgment that it is good to recognize the superiority of one wife over the others seems general.[95]

### b. Monogamy

The marriage of one man to one woman is the only kind of marriage which is found in all the societies of men. "The only form of marriage which is recognized and permitted in all social systems is monogamy. It coexists with all the other forms, although it is the pre-

[95] Polygyny: Charles Dundas, "Native Laws of Some Bantu Tribes of East Africa," *Jour. Royal Anthropol. Inst.* **51** (1921): pp. 248–249; Paul Bohannon, *Social Anthropology* (New York, 1963), pp. 108–109; C. L. Harries, *The Laws and Customs of the Bapedi and Cognate Tribes of the Transvaal* (rev. ed., Johannesburg, 1929), p. 2; Arthur Diamond, *Primitive Law* (London, 1935), p. 220; Edward Westermarck, *The Origin and Development of the Moral Ideas* (2 .v., London, 1908–1912) **2**: p. 390; Robert Lowie, *An Introduction to Cultural Anthropology* (2nd ed., New York, 1940), p. 244; K. H. Crosby, "Polygamy in Mende Country," *Africa* **10** (1937): p. 249; D. J. Penwill, *Kamba Customary Law* (London, 1951), p. 10; A. K. Ajisafe, *Laws and Customs of the Yoruba People* (London, 1924), p. 3; Valintin Riasanovsky, *Customary Law of the Nomadic Tribes of Siberia* (Tsiensin, 1938), p. 136; Mischa Titiev, *The Science of Man* (New York, 1954), p. 383; Isaac Schapera, *A Handbook of Tswana Law and Custom* (London, 1938), p. 14; Schapera, *Government and Politics in Tribal Societies* (London, 1956), p. 50; S. M. Seymour, *Native Law in South Africa* (Capetown, 1953), p. 78; Ralph Barton, "Ifugao Law," *Amer. Archaeology and Ethnology* **15** (1919): p. 17; T. D. Ramsey, *Tsonga Law in the Transvaal* (Pretoria, 1941), p. 9; Meyer Fortes, "Time and Social Structure: An Ashanti Case Study," in: Fortes, ed., *Social Structure* (Oxford, 1949), p. 72; Paul Bohannon, *African Homicide and Suicide* (Princeton, 1960), p. 191; Edward Evans-Pritchard, *Kinship and Marriage Among the Nuer* (Oxford, 1951), pp. 134–135; Robert Lowie, *Primitive Society* (New York, 1920), pp. 44–45.

ferred form in a relatively small number of societies." [96] Older theories which maintained that there was an evolution from primeval promiscuity through group marriage, polyandry, polygyny to monogamy have had to be abandoned. All the evidence now indicates that monogamy was a prevalent form of marriage from the earliest days.

In some preliterate groups monogamy is the ideal and it is practiced as such. Among the Andaman Islanders single pairs are faithful to each other until death. The Zuni, the Hopi, and various groups of Pygmies are also reported as strictly monogamous. It has been noted that monogamy is more generally the rule in lower tribes, such as the Andamanese or the African Pygmies, than it is with more advanced groups.

Other groups of preliterates practice monogamy because of practical necessity, even though polygyny is the ideal. Most men cannot afford more than one wife, as we have mentioned. Among the Greenlanders, where polygyny is permitted, only one Eskimo in twenty is said to have more than one wife. The Ona for the most part also had only one wife, though prominent men might have several. More than one wife aroused unfavorable talk.[97] Similarly among the Kirghiz, the Kai, and the Gikuyu, although polygyny is allowed, few men have more than one wife. Such economically enforced monogamy, in relation to the ideal of polygyny, has been referred to as "maimed polygyny." [98]

But in all groups there are marital unions that are monogamous by preference, even though polygyny is the ideal and monogamy is a practical necessity. "Although economic factors are mainly responsible for this condition, all groups can also show certain unions which are monogamous by preference. When the partners find complete emotional satisfaction in each other, they prefer not to admit additional spouses even where there is social pressure for them to do so. Such unions seem to provide the maximum of happiness to the parties involved." [99]

Inasmuch as monogamy is found and permitted by custom law among all groups of preliterates even those in which polygyny is the ideal, the value judgment that it is good and desirable to be married to one wife, whether by preference or necessity, appears to be common among preliterates. But the value judgment that although monogamy is good polygyny is better when possible, is also probably common among preliterate societies.[100]

Contraception, prostitution, and homosexuality among preliterates are areas concerning which there are very little data. Prostitution has been reported to be disreputable among the Bantu.[101] Homosexuality is said to have been approved among various non-Pueblo tribes of the American Southwest.[102] But beyond these scattered reports, very little seems to be known about the extent of such activities among preliterates and about the value judgments they make concerning them.

## CHAPTER 5

## KNOWLEDGE AND DECISION

The value judgments which we shall next examine are those which especially make men's existence human. These are the value judgments regarding his knowledge and decisions. It is their knowledge and decisions which most distinguish men from animals. Of all of men's basic drives, the basic drive to know and to decide shows the greatest plasticity. This is evident in the vast number of objects about which men can have knowledge and make decisions. Their number is myriad.

### I. KNOWING

All normal men have a basic drive to know and to acquire knowledge. "All men by nature desire to know." [1]

[96] Ralph Linton, *The Study of Man* (New York, 1936), p. 187. "Monogamy appears to be by far the commonest accepted marriage form and the prevailing form even in societies which permit polygamous unions." Ralph Beals and Harry Hoijer, *An Introduction to Anthropology* (New York, 1953), p. 440. Monogamous unions among animals and birds are well known. "Monogamy, a form of marriage considered by many the peak of social achievement in the evolution of marriage types, is found among birds (penguins, herons, guineas, gulls, parrots, ravens, many pigeons, ducks, cormorants, and others) among rhinoceri, and among the higher apes. Monogamy among these animals is sometimes temporary, although there is good evidence that it is permanent for some ostriches, cranes, swans, and geese. Some of these animals may not live in pairs the entire year. The male lives alone for a part of it and returns to the same female in the mating season. Surely this array does not establish any kind of systematic sequence. The birds for which monogamy is most surely established are not by any means the highest biological forms, nor do they by any means belong to the same genera. Only a twisted evolutionary scheme would account for the rhinoceri between the birds and the apes." Gladys Reichard, "Social Life," in: Boas, ed., *General Anthropology* (Boston, 1938), p. 411.

[97] It has been said that in "the non-Christian civilizations such as those of India, China or Islam, the ratio is almost as low." Ralph Linton, *The Study of Man* (New York, 1936), p. 188.

[98] Paul Bohannon, *Social Anthropology* (New York, 1963), p. 108.

[99] Ralph Linton, *The Study of Man* (New York, 1936), p. 188.

[100] "As for the moral valuation of the various forms of marriage, it should be noticed that even among polygynous and polyandrous peoples monogamy is permitted by custom or law, although in some instances it is associated with poverty and considered mean, whereas polygyny, as associated with greatness, is thought praiseworthy." Edward Westermarck, *The Origin and Development of the Moral Ideas 2* (2 v., London, 1908–1912), p. 392.
Monogamy: Ralph Beals and Harry Hoijer, *An Introduction to Anthropology* (New York, 1953), p. 441; Robert Lowie, *Primitive Society* (New York, 1920), pp. 42, 167; Lowie, *An Introduction to Cultural Anthropology* (2nd ed., New York, 1940), pp. 243–244; Alexander Goldenweiser, *Anthropology* (New York, 1937), p. 298.

[101] Charles Dundas, "Native Laws of Some Bantu Tribes of East Africa," *Jour. Royal Anthropol. Inst.* **51** (1921) : p. 248.

[102] John Gillin, *The Ways of Men* (New York, 1948), p. 345.

[1] Aristotle, *Metaphysics*, Book I, chap. 1, 980ª22, trans. by W. D. Ross, Richard McKeon, ed., *The Basic Works of Aristotle* (New York, 1941), p. 689.

All men universally want to understand things and to learn what causes them to be what they are. Men are not satisfied with fulfilling the drives for self-preservation and sexual union. They want to cultivate and live the life of the mind.[2] This drive for knowing manifests itself in the incessant prying of children into the "why" of almost all things which come within their ken and in their incipient attempts to reason about them. This drive shows itself further in the insatiable curiosity with which men are obsessed throughout their lives.[3] The spirit of science springs from values related to this drive. Among these values are the "longing to know and to understand; questioning of all things; search for data and their meaning."[4] Science is the pursuit of knowledge which is factually verifiable. But such a quest is but an aspect of men's over-all drive to know.

Human knowledge is radically distinguished from the knowledge animals have in that men have the ability to deal in symbols and abstract concepts. All the data indicate that men alone have developed the use of symbols.[5] Man is by nature a symbol-using creature. Symbolic and abstract concepts are unique inasmuch as they contain no particular, material object. Their object is partially or wholly immaterial and to this degree they are universal in their application to a class.

Such concepts may have quantitative and qualitative aspects, or they may not. The symbol $H_2O$ refers to no particular water and is applicable to any water; but it does have both a qualitative limitation (hydrogen and oxygen only) and a quantitative one $(2 + 1)$. The concept "blue" applies to any blue object; it carries the connotation of quality (color is a sensation produced on the eye by light waves) but not of quantity (inasmuch as no number of blue objects is specified). The number 5 in mathematics is an abstract symbol which applies to any aggregate having this many units; it has a quantitative implication (number presupposes quantitative division) but not a qualitative one (no type of object is designated). Finally, a concept such as existence applies to all existing things; and it has no qualitative or quantitative limitations. Hence, $H_2O$, blue,

5, and existence are all examples of symbolic or abstract concepts.[6]

All preliterates give evidence of symbolic or abstract thinking. All can enumerate or count, which implies the ability to think in an abstract manner. The need for such thinking may vary. Among the Ona, the highest number is 5. To express the number 8, the digits of one hand are shown together with three fingers of the other and at the same time the words for 5 and 3 are uttered. This manner of counting with the hands, or with the feet, is said to be general among preliterates. Methods of counting are sometimes quite elaborate. The North Californians had measures marked on their hands so they could estimate the value of a chain of shells. Tribes of British Columbia counted by tens of thousands. The Pueblos determined the yearly cycles for the performance of their religious rites with a fair degree of accuracy. A knowledge of geometry is also shown by preliterates who apply it to such things as squaring boxes.

Preliterates also incorporate an abstract knowledge of geography into sailing charts. The charts of the Marshall Islanders and the Eskimo show this in marking the location of islands and noting the direction of swells, currents, and cross seas. Other preliterates, somewhat like the Stonehenge people of England, show an abstract knowledge of astronomy. Based on their knowledge of the movement of celestial bodies, they develop calendars which serve as a guide for their seasonal occupations.

The ability of preliterates to think abstractly is further shown in their application of the principles of what literate peoples call physical sciences to their making of tools and artifacts, which we shall consider more in detail shortly. Numerous examples are given of the application of such knowledge, for instance the flaking of an arrowpoint, the twirling of a fire-drill, the felling of a tree, the carrying of weights at the ends of a balancing pole, the boiling of water and the firing of pottery. The Maori are cited as an example of a people who apply the wedge and the lever. They also show an abstract knowledge of physics in treating of the inclined plane and the skid. They are also said to evince an abstract knowledge of chemistry in their cooking, as other preliterates do in their treating of hides.

Further evidence of preliterates' ability to deal in abstract thinking is their formulation of rules and regulaitons which must of necessity be abstract generaliza-

[2] "Feeding and breeding are dependent upon inquiring to furnish them with a purpose. Had we no objective in life but to secure food and a mate, life would seem empty, as indeed it does in those times when it is thought to be confined to such activities. . . . [I]nterest in ultimates remains." James Feibleman, *The Theory of Human Culture* (New York, 1946), p. 11.

[3] It is the drive to know, it has been said, that motivates gossip—a universal institution pretending to satisfy the need of knowing more about others. "Human nature being what it is, to know about people is to want to know more about them. Gossip is one of the universal institutions of mankind." Alexander Goldenweiser, *Anthropology* (New York, 1937), p. 297.

[4] D. Wolfle, "The Spirit of Science," *Science* 152 (1966): p. 1699. "In my view, the pursuit of science is motivated throughout by a passion to understand; and, in a more general sense, the craving to understand actuates the whole mental life of man." Michael Polanyi, *The Study of Man* (Chicago, 1959), p. 84.

[5] John Gillin. *The Ways of Men* (New York, 1948), p. 449.

[6] "[N]one but humans have algebraic mentalities," can "think up symbolic values," and are "capable of assigning arbitrary values to vocal utterances." Mischa Titiev, *The Science of Man* (New York, 1954), p. 441. Careful discernment is needed in interpreting the results of experiments with animals that supposedly involve abstract concepts. What is supposedly the result of immaterial "abstraction and symbolization," may in fact be merely the product of material color association. See Robert Faris, *Social Psychology* (New York, 1952), p. 174; quoting Harry Harlow and Margaret Harlow, "Learning to Think," *Scientific American* 181, 2 (1949): pp. 36–39.

tions admitting of concrete application. The Winnebago are cited as an example of preliterates whose abstractly formulated rules pertained in their application to a result which also was abstract. Thus, they said that if you invite a traveler to your table, "you will do good and it is always good to do good." [7]

One of the important implications of men's power to deal in abstract concepts, is their ability to reason. Reasoning is essentially a mental process by which conclusions are reached inductively or deductively. From the specific fact that a man accused of theft has unsuccessfully undergone an ordeal, preliterates conclude that he is guilty. And from the general principle that those guilty of theft should be punished, they conclude that he should be made to pay a penalty. The relationships between ordeal and guilt, between guilt and punishment, are abstract ideas. It is these that make reasoning possible. A simple example of reason among preliterates concerns the Barama River Carib. To indicate the direction an advance party is taking, a split sapling with a pointer on it is fixed in the ground. This obviates the need of leaving anyone behind to direct the group that is following. The abstract idea at work is obviously that the pointer did not just happen to be there but that someone caused it to be there for the purpose of indicating a direction.

This type of reasoning based on an abstract concept of the relation between effect and cause is, as far as the evidence goes, distinctively human. It is universal among all medically normal men. The whole problem of the cause and "why" of things, alien to all other earthly beings, is common to men. This unique ability of men to think abstractly and reason in a manner not limited to material objects, explains the most readily observable phenomenon, namely, that men are almost limitlessly creative of variety in their lives. The lives of animals, on the other hand, manifest a stereotyped and "programmed" sameness. Men can imagine new things because they can think in an abstract manner which gives them an almost endless range of creativeness. This creative power of men finds one of its most elementary expressions in human language and art. All of which again exhibits the great moldability of men's basic drive to know.[8]

A. UNIVERSAL VALUE JUDGMENTS IN ALL SOCIETIES

The value judgment that it is good and not evil to know is universal in all individuals and in all societies. It is given and is formed without any reasoning process. It is a postulate of all men's search for knowledge. It underlies all the efforts of preliterates to inquire, explore, and know. There are other value judgments which preliterates make regarding knowledge which are also universal in all of their societies. These relate to the communication of knowledge, to regulation of knowledge acquired by the young, and to knowledge about the nature and origin of man and the universe.

### 1. Regulations Concerning Title to Know

There is no society which leaves the acquiring of knowledge by its young to mere chance. Some effort is always made to communicate to the child the rudimentary knowledge needed for living in the society into which he has been born. "Every society has a set of ideals in accordance with which it trains its people to act." [9] Such knowledge is necessary for the continuation of these societies. "[S]ocieties are constantly perpetuating themselves socially by inculcating in each new generation time-tried ways of believing, feeling, thinking, and reacting." [10] Once this handing-on of knowledge stops, the disintegration of any society is not far off. "Destroy all knowledge, stop all education, and you will kill off the members of the tribe as by a deadly microbe." [11]

Preliterate societies are no exception to this universal practice of transmitting knowledge to new generations. What knowledge is to be handed on is regulated by custom. It is not a random happening. The knowledge imparted to preliterate children by their parents is patterned in this manner. More especially is this the case regarding knowledge inculcated through initiation rites. The value judgment, then, that regulation of the knowledge to be transmitted to children is good and not evil is universal among all societies of preliterates.

### 2. Failure to Respect Title to Know: Unjust Repression of Thought

Regulation of knowledge is justified, then, if it fulfills a common need. Regulations which go beyond this, however, represent a failure to respect the individual's title to know. They are an unjust repression of thought. It is an ever-recurring problem in all societies, of course, to determine the extent to which such regulation should go. Some areas of knowledge need to be regulated, as we have just seen. The regulation of all areas would be tyranny. Those areas which do not pertain to common needs should not be regulated. Implicit in the value judgment that the regulation of knowledge is good when it fulfills common needs is the value judgment that regulation is bad when it does not fulfill common needs. This value judgment is a postulate in all societies of men.

[7] Paul Radin, *Primitive Man as Philosopher* (New York, 1927), pp. 69–70.

[8] Knowing: Robert Lowie, *An Introduction to Cultural Anthropology* (2nd ed., New York, 1940), pp. 329–330; Franz Boas, "Culture," *Encyc. of the Social Sciences* 2 (1930): pp. 93–94; John Gillin, *The Ways of Men* (New York, 1948), p. 450; Boas, *The Mind of Primitive Man* (rev. ed., New York, 1938), pp. 163–164.

[9] Paul Bohannon, *Social Anthropology* (New York, 1963), p. 296.

[10] Clyde Kluckhohn, *Mirror for Man* (New York, 1949), p. 205.

[11] Bronislaw Malinowski, "Introduction," to H. Ian Hogbin, *Law and Order in Polynesia* (New York, 1934), p. xxxii.

## 3. Communicating

Men have a natural propensity to communicate with others, especially through the use of language. This is an aspect of men's basic drive to live in the society of others, as we shall see later. Without communication social living would be impossible. The early attempts at speech made by infants seem to be evidence of this tendency. Men universally form the value judgment that communication with others is good and not evil. This is also a postulate of all social living.

### a. Language

Men's communication with one another takes place through language. Language, therefore, has a special value for men. Language may employ vocal sounds, writings, gestures, or felt signals as in the case of the totally deaf, dumb, and blind. Language is the embodiment of symbolic and abstract thinking. "By far the most ubiquitous type of symbol system used by human beings is spoken language." [12] Language is found wherever there are men. "Language is absolutely universal in the human species and at the same time is extraordinarily diverse." [13]

Language is composed of signs which are neutral symbols capable of taking on any meaning. The different oral and written signs in various languages which have come to mean, say, "horse," is an example of this. The universality of the symbolic or the abstract in language pertains not only to words but also to grammar and syntax. Men everywhere use the same parts of speech, the same sentence structure, the same uses of metaphor and abstraction, the same use of general and particular. The function of language is to produce in the mind of the hearer or viewer what is in the mind of the speaker or writer. And because, as we have said, words are capable of conveying symbolic meanings, language by the use of these words can create the same abstract signification in the mind of one as were in the mind of another. The words on this page are an example of such creation in action. [14]

Gestures, which are a unique type of symbolic language, also manifest men's dealing in abstract concepts. Gesture has been described as an auxiliary language. It is found among all men. "Gesture is . . . a universal accompaniment of speech, where it plays a role of varying importance. Some gestures are very widely diffused among mankind." [15] Although some gestures of themselves are clearly descriptive of the idea they are designed to convey, as when one person beckons another to come to him, other gestures are in themselves neutral symbols which can take on the signification of any abstract idea. Thus the gesture of thumbing one's nose has no particular meaning in itself. It assumes the coarse meaning it has because the idea of disdain which it connotes is an abstract concept. Gestures are not imitations of the spoken word. They are expressions of ideas.

Men, through their ability to communicate symbolic and abstract ideas, have constructed a cultural world which is nonexistent outside of human living. Men alone have created the endless variety which has characterized their personal, familial, social, and political living. Animals communicate but they give no evidence of communicating symbolic or abstract culture-building ideas. It is the content of communication, and not the mere fact of communication, which distinguishes men from animals.

Language is judged by men, apparently without much reasoning, as a necessity in social living. The value judgment, then, that language is good and not evil is universal among all individuals and all societies of men. It is a postulate of all social living. [16]

### b. Art

Men communicate their concepts not only in language but also in materials which they form according to these concepts. In this sense, what men make is an expression of their ideas, as we shall see in regard to labor. This process of making, by which men give form and meaning to the materials on which they work, is, broadly speaking, art. And because art is an expression of ideas, it is a form of communication. In this lies its value. The results of men's creative abilities have been divided into useful and aesthetic, for want of better categories. We have, then, men creating usefully and aesthetically.

The useful artifacts are, in the main, tools. Whether because of necessity or curiosity, men have conceived of

[12] John Gillin, *The Ways of Men* (New York, 1948), p. 451.

[13] Robert Lowie, *An Introduction to Cultural Anthropology* (2nd ed., 1940), p. 343.

[14] Worth noting also is the fact that, although language never transmits the whole and complete image which is in the mind of the speaker or writer, nonetheless from what it does convey the mind of the hearer or reader can create the whole image. The part of the voice which is carried by the telephone, or the part of the incompletely scrawled word which is contained in a letter, are often sufficient for the mind of the hearer or reader to fill out from what it already knows whose voice it is, or what the word is and perhaps who wrote it. See Clark Wissler, *Man and Culture* (New York, 1923), p. 83.

[15] Clark Wissler, *Man and Culture* (New York, 1923), p. 85. The question has been raised whether men first spoke by gesture, then by the spoken word. All the evidence indicates that there never was a time when men did not speak orally. "There is no evidence that human language was ever preceded by a stage in which gestures alone were used for the purposes of communication." Ashley Montagu, *Man: His First Million Years* (Cleveland, 1957), p. 119.

[16] Language: John Gillin, *The Ways of Men* (New York, 1948), p. 451; Robert Lowie, *An Introduction to Cultural Anthropology* (2nd ed., New York, 1940), p. 343; Bronislaw Malinowski, "A New Instrument for the Interpretation of Law—Especially Primitive," *Yale Law Jour.* 51 (1942): pp. 1240–1241; Clark Wissler, *Man and Culture* (New York, 1923), pp. 83, 85; Ashley Montagu, *Man: His First Million Years* (Cleveland, 1957), p. 119; Melville Herskovits, *Man and His Works* (New York, 1948), p. 38; Eliot Chapple and Carleton Coon, *Principles of Anthropology* (New York, 1942), p. 575.

ways of improving their lot. After incorporating these concepts into material substances, they called the result a "tool." Tools are fundamentally extensions of the hand. The presence of tools among men is universal. Besides tools in the strict sense, human artifacts include many other products of human creativeness such as dwellings, weapons, means of transportation and locomotion and obtaining food. The basic techniques are found everywhere there are men. All men have known the preparation of food, the chipping of stone, the idea of the knife and the drill, the art of twisting string and making cord and weaving, and the use of fire.

Men's ingenuity is particularly shown in their use of fire, a technique completely unknown in animals. How men first came to use fire can only be speculated on. But regardless of the reasons that first caused men to use and preserve fire, its presence in human living is very ancient. There is evidence of the use of fire as early as Pre-Mousterian times. No one knows how much earlier it may have been discovered. It has been said that the use of fire and cooking in heated water are almost universal.

Another product of men's creative ability is methods of transportation. Various devices for conveyance are found among all men. Transportation may not be evidence of men's creative abilities at their highest, but it is nevertheless an example of men applying abstract principles to concrete needs. Men have walked and they have ridden on the backs of animals, but they have also built boats with oars and sails, and vehicles with wheels. Preliterate man's development of the wheel is a star example of his creative genius.

Men's unique ability to deal in abstract concepts, and to express them in various kinds of materials, reaches its apex in the aesthetic, the graphic, the fine arts. Drawing, painting, sculpture, ceramics, literature, music, drama, dancing, architecture, bodily adornment, are among these arts. It is here that men's creative genius goes beyond the useful and enters the realm of the beautiful. Men have an impulse to create beautiful things. Beauty is difficult, if not impossible to define. A description would be that it is a quality which a person or thing has—such as line, color, texture, form, proportion, rhythm, tone, behavior—that pleases and delights. Over the ages men have constantly shown a love of beauty. "The love of beauty is universal." [17] "The desire for beauty is a deep-seated human urge." [18] Children, once again, manifest this bent for creating. Without any instruction or urging, children will spontaneously create drawings with the materials at hand. Human endeavors to create beautiful things, then, are universal among all societies of preliterates.

The ceaseless craving for beauty has caused preliterates to tatoo and scarify their bodies and adorn their hair. "Everywhere men have taken trouble to embellish themselves and their implements." [19] Objects of all kinds are beautified by preliterates. Many of them also serve a useful purpose such as baskets, pots, and moccasins. The Eskimo engrave their needle cases. The Plains Indians painted their rawhide bags used for storing buffalo meat. The Bali in Kamerun molds a head on his clay pipe-bowl. The Azande of the Nile-Uelle watershed puts two spires on his hut and two bowls on his pipe because he considers twin effects to be beautiful.

Beautification of even useful objects goes back to the early days of the human race. Painting and sculpture were present in Paleolithic cultures. In the latter part of the Old Stone Age there is evidence of incised tools, ivory carvings, and animal paintings. In the earlier Old Stone Age fist-hatchets were being shaped more symmetrically and gracefully. The artistic techniques of these ancient artists are said to be as far advanced as those of today's artists. Caves in southern France and northern Spain contain animated pictures, polychrome paints, frieze reliefs, and animal sculptures which were executed with great skill during the Magdalenian period.

The art styles of some preliterates are reported that would seem to presignify certain "modern" trends. Not realism but conventionalized signs are the vehicle. Among the Indians of the Northwest Coast, animals are depicted as cut in two with the halves spread out on a flat surface. The preliterate artist, like any artist, composes his work for his own community whose members are part of the same environment and tradition that he is. He can therefore afford to communicate to them in conventionalized signs and symbols which will be more or less readily understood.

The dance and music are also examples of men's expression of abstract ideas through symbols. Dances and music, along with certain other art forms, are found among all peoples. Music stands at the vertex of the arts. In music, abstract concepts are expressed in sound waves which, in a sense, are less material than paint and marble. Through the sound waves these same concepts are recreated in the mind of the hearer. Birds produce agreeable sounds but only men grasp the relations between the sounds and hear them as a series with set intervals and thereby understand what is being communicated. Preliterates, such as the South Sea Islanders, have shown upon testing that they can understand such sets of sounds.

The evidence is preponderant that the preliterate artist deals in symbols and abstract concepts as well as does his literate colleague in any part of the world. Artistic creation however, whether useful as tools or aesthetic as beauty, has never been found among animals. Animals can learn through practice to adapt tools to their use which have already been made by men, but animals have never made tools. No examples of fine

[17] Robert Lowie, *Are We Civilized?* (New York, 1929), p. 187.

[18] Robert Lowie, *An Introduction to Cultural Anthropology* (2nd ed., New York, 1940), p. 177.

[19] *Ibid.*

art have ever been encountered which were produced by animals.[20] One explanation of this observable fact relates not only to the nature of men but also to their origin.[21]

The value judgment that it is good to create in the manner we have described, usefully and aesthetically, is universal among all societies of preliterates. The implications of this process of creation in regard to title to the thing created will be discussed later. The value judgment is also universal among all known societies of men that it is good to adorn the human body, to dance, and to make music as expressions of beauty.[22]

### 4. Learning

Men's desire to know is a desire to learn. Men can learn either on their own by conducting their own inquiries and developing their own insights, or they can learn from others by receiving from them their knowledge of discoveries and understandings. My learning from others is the counterpart of their communicating to me and teaching me.

[20] A gorilla, it is reported, was found tracing his own shadow. A child explained her drawing as drawing a line around her thought. The one has been likened to the other. Ashley Montagu, *Man: His First Million Years* (Cleveland, 1957), p. 215. But it should be noted that the shadow which the gorilla is reported to have traced is an external, physical datum caused by the relation of his body to the sun or some other source of light. The thought around which the little girl drew a line is an internal, abstract creation of her own mental and imaginatory power. See Ralph Beals and Harry Hoijer, *An Introduction to Anthropology* (New York, 1953), p. 567.

[21] "Man has been possessed by a creative urge since very ancient times. Forever impelled to experiment and explore, it is as if he senses something within him which he must extract and examine so that, seeing it, he will know something of his own personality. And so he starts to create, to express his inmost and most personal thoughts in a free and untrammelled manner. This is where the claim that God created man in His own image finds its truest and most profound fulfillment, for God and man are both creators, one in nature and the other in art. Eons ago, inspired by a God-given restlessness and desire for self-expression, man reached tentatively for materials and began to mold them to his ideas." Ivar Lissner, *Man, God and Magic*, trans. by J. M. Brownjohn (New York, 1961), p. 203.

[22] Bronislaw Malinowski, "A New Instrument for the Interpretation of Law—Especially Primitive," *Yale Law Jour.* **51** (1942) : p. 1240; Ralph Beals and Harry Hoijer, *An Introduction to Anthropology* (New York, 1953), pp. 3, 567; Clark Wissler, *Man and Culture* (New York, 1923), pp. 76–89; Franz Boas, "Culture," *Encyc. of the Social Sciences* 2 (1930) : p. 89; Boas, "Invention," in: Boas, ed., *General Anthropology* (Boston, 1938), p. 239; Wilhelm Koppers, *Primitive Man and His World Picture*, trans. by E. Raybould (New York, 1952), pp. 15–16; James Feibleman, *The Theory of Human Culture* (New York, 1946), p. 106; Ashley Montagu, *Man: His First Million Years* (Cleveland, 1957), p. 215; Ruth Bunzel, "Art," in: Franz Boas, ed., *General Anthropology* (Boston, 1938), p. 535; Robert Lowie, *An Introduction to Cultural Anthropology* (2nd ed., New York, 1940), pp. 177, 203; Ivar Lissner, *Man, God and Magic*, trans. by J. M. Brownjohn (New York, 1961), p. 214; John Gillin, *The Ways of Men* (New York, 1948), p. 578; Edmund Leach, "Aesthetics," in: Edward Evans-Pritchard and others, *The Institutions of Primitive Society* (Glencoe, 1956), p. 31.

### a. Oral Instruction

A main source of the child's learning is from the oral teaching of his parents and family. This is especially true of preliterates among whom, outside of initiation rites, there may be no formal education. Thus, among the Gikuyu in Kenya, parents are described as the custodians of truth and public representatives in teaching. In Tswana and among the Indians of western North America, it is the parents who first teach the children the difference between right and wrong. The Eskimo child, riding in his mother's parka and living intimately with his family in a one-room iglu, learns from observation much about domestic life. Skills of all kinds are taught him by his parents. In the Schouten Islands in New Guinea, parents first teach their children respect for things that belong to others and the evils that result from theft. Parents in Nigeria similarly instruct their young concerning theft and also regarding bad language and truthfulness.

The father is the natural educator of his son in many areas of human living. In contrast to many lower animals, the human father is always a member of the family. Only a man is capable of training a male child in the skills of a man. Thus, in Kenya, the father teaches his son what he should know about land and land tenure. Among the Fanti, the father instructs his son about custom law and correct conduct by taking the boy to a meeting of the local court. He also teaches him respect for the rights of others and correct forms of address. Preliterate mothers instruct their daughters. This is usually, as among the Nuer, about household tasks but it may also concern moral advice and wordly wisdom. In Nigeria, as a child progresses in age it is the mother's duty to teach it obedience, eating without assistance, hoeing and working on the farm.

Ideas about what is proper are in some places taught children by other children. Among the Amara of Ethiopia, for instance, younger children learn from older children with whom they play their games. The older children scold and penalize for improper behavior. Instruction to preliterate children is sometimes given in groups. Correct behavior, respect for elders, liberality and truthfulness are among the things taught. Among the Chippewa campfire talks were a means of teaching ethical standards. Many times the lessons taught were embodied in stories. Among the African Muganda, children are given general advice which includes dealings with relatives, payment of debt, avoidance of adultery and theft. A boy is counseled that when he grows up and marries, he should not listen to his wives telling tales of one another or he will be left alone. Among the Alorese, the commission of an offense is taken as an opportunity by the chief for an instruction in morals.

Etiquette, whatever its specific meaning in individual cases, is an area of human living which is a matter of concern to many preliterates. They are at pains to inculcate their own particular rules. Among the Muganda, children are taught the phrases of greeting and farewell as well as correct gestures in the presence of strangers. With the Gikuyu, learning etiquette is a means of attaining a proper station in life. Hence, they are taught the manners and deportment proper to their station in their group. In Tikopia children at an early age are taught that most important for them is quietness and self-effacement.[23]

Sexual matters are also the subject of instruction for the child. This may be done informally or, as we shall see shortly, formally in the rites of initiation. In Nigeria a mother warns her daughter not to let boys or men meddle with her and to report her first menstruation, which can be of ritual importance. The father warns his son to be careful about his relations with girls lest he contract a venereal disease. Among the Fanti, because the child observes sexual relations between his parents it is not necessary to instruct him in the details of sex. A father will impress on his son the necessity of abstaining from sexual relationships before marriage. If an unmarried boy engages in such conduct, the father of the girl may sue the father of the boy for compensation.

Some preliterates place a premium on a girl's virginity until marriage. Among the Kiwai Papuans, women instruct the girls in this regard. At the time of marriage, she is tested and if she is still a virgin a song of triumph is in order. The Fanti mother will instruct her daughter that she should abstain from sexual relations until she is married. It is a great shame for the parents if the girl becomes pregnant before marriage.

The instruction of preliterate youth, boys especially, reflects the type of economy prevailing in the group. In a hunting society, a youth must know the habits of the animals he pursues, the dodges the animal uses to avoid detection, and how to make snares and cages with which to capture prey. The goal of Naskapi education of boys is to make them good hunters. To this end, boys are instructed in the behavior and habits of the game animals, the making of necessary tools and implements, and the setting of traps. Fishing peoples train boys in the techniques of the art of fishing. The Fanti youth learns the moods of the sea, the changes in the weather, the kinds of fish and how they are caught, and the care of nets.

Another matter that preliterates stress in their education of youth is respect for elders. The Cheyenne taught the child early in life the importance of self-control and self-restraint in the presence of elders. Xosa children, when sitting around the fire at night to hear tales by grandparents, were taught never to question the words of an aged person according to the axiom that "the old men know best." For the Fanti, a basic principle of their culture is respect for elders. The training of the children in this regard is primarily the responsibility of the father. Both he and his sons are judged accordingly. The preliterate child learns respect not only for persons, it is reported, but also for property, animals, and places.

One feature of preliterate education of children deserves to be highlighted. Preliterates are sure of what they want the children to learn. This is true of the teaching of parents as well as of initiation rites. The Indian child of the Northwest Coast, for instance, is clearly taught the value of the potlatch or ceremonial feast at which gifts were exchanged, which we will discuss later. The child of the Plains Indians learns the unquestioned importance of counting coup at an early age. Counting coup was the claim a warrior made to a new feather in his bonnet for every blow he struck on a dangerous enemy in battle. There is no doubt in the mind of the one that potlatch-giving will be a great thing in his life, any more than there is in the mind of the other that becoming proficient in dealing blows to the enemy in battle will be important in his.[24]

## b. Example

Learning from example plays a great part in preliterate education of the young. It is a method as old as man himself. Children are not inclined to do what adults tell them to do as much as they are to do what

---

[23] It has often been reported that many preliterates do not use physical punishment on their children. The Bantu of the upper Congo, for instance, are said never to strike their children. Ellsworth Faris, "The Origin of Punishment," in: Albert Kocourek and John Wigmore, *Primitive and Ancient Legal Institutions* (3 v., Boston, 1915) 1: p. 153. Other preliterates, such as the Tonga, are said to use ridicule very effectively instead of physical punishment. William Mariner, *An Account of the Natives of the Tonga Islands*, (2 v., London, 1817) 2: p. 141; quoted by H. Ian Hogbin, *Law and Order in Polynesia* (London, 1934), p. 282. Thus the mocking and taunting of a child's mother or playmates is sufficient to lessen ill behavior. See also Jomo Kenyatta, *Facing Mount Kenya* (London, 1953), p. 106; Raymond Firth, *We, The Tikopia* (2nd ed., London, 1957), p. 150.

[24] Oral instruction: Jomo Kenyatta, *Facing Mount Kenya* (London, 1953), pp. 20, 112; Isaac Schapera, *A Handbook of Tswana Law and Custom* (London, 1938), p. 36; E. Adamson Hoebel, "Law-ways of the Primitive Eskimos," *Jour. of Criminology and Criminal Law* 31 (1941): p. 665; H. Ian Hogbin, *Law and Order in Polynesia* (London, 1934), p. 261; C. K. Meek, *Law and Authority in a Nigerian Tribe* (London, 1937), pp. 298–299; James Christensen, *Double Descent Among the Fanti* (New Haven, 1954), pp. 97–99; Edward Evans-Pritchard, *Kinship and Marriage Among the Nuer* (Oxford, 1951), p. 137; Simon Messing, *The Highland-Plateau Amara of Ethiopia* (Ann Arbor, 1957), pp. 435–438; Franz Boas, "Culture," *Encyc. of the Social Sciences* 2 (1930): p. 102; Inez Hilger, *A Social Study of One Hundred Fifty Chippewa Indian Families* (Washington, 1939), p. 100; Lucy Mair, *An African People in the Twentieth Century* (London, 1934), pp. 65–66; Cora DuBois, *The People of Alor* (Minneapolis, 1944), p. 62; Leo Simmons, *The Role of the Aged in Primitive Society* (New Haven, 1945), pp. 202–203; Julius Lips, "Naskapi Law," *Trans. Amer. Philos. Soc.* 37 (1947): p. 413; Karl Llewellyn and E. A. Hoebel, *The Cheyenne Way* (Norman, 1941), pp. 240–241; Carleton Coon, "Tribes of the Rif," *Harvard African Studies* 9 (1931): p. 114; Siegfried Nadel, *A Black Byzantium* (London, 1942), p. 378; Lawrence Frank, *Society as the Patient* (New Brunswick, 1948), p. 143; Gladys Reichard, "Social Life," in: Franz Boas, ed., *General Anthropology* (Boston, 1938), p. 470.

they see adults doing. The example of adults is a teaching which children learn to imitate. Children are naturally imitative. This imitation at times takes the form of play. In play, children learn and participate in social and cultural patterns.

In play, preliterate boys often imitate men's activities and girls imitate women's activities, as do boys and girls all over the world. In Nigeria, a boy follows the behavior patterns of his older brothers, his father and his uncles. A girl imitates the actions of her older sisters, her mother and her aunts. Likewise among the Ashanti, children are said to be constantly learning by imitation of their elders. Among the Bantu of Kavirondo, education of children through example and imitation occurs by bringing up the child in the family and helping it to adjust to its everyday surroundings. With the Mende, boys learn much about custom law by holding mock trials and enact the roles they have seen played by their elders. Preliterate girls learn in the same way of imitation. Bemba girls play at cooking as soon as they can stand, and learn house work by helping at it most of the day.

The advantage of preliterate learning from example and imitation is that the child is being educated for life by living it here and now. Under such conditions, education is not so much an imagined preparation for life as it is an actual, vital part of it. The child learns not only from his participation in all the ordinary activities of his early years, but also from his attempts to meet the needs from ever-arising new situations.[25]

### c. Initiation Rites

The value which preliterates put on initiation rites, as a means of teaching their children the patterned knowledge necessary for living in their societies, is high. Initiation rites are the closest thing to formal education some preliterate children receive. The central purpose of these educative practices is to fit the child for the life of an adult. "Every primitive society possesses a consistent body of mythical traditions, a 'conception of the world'; and it is this conception that is gradually revealed to the novice in the course of his initiation." [26] It is through the initiation rites that the preliterate child comes to know the image of himself as a man which his society conceives of him. These procedures teach not

only material but also spiritual values.[27] In fitting the child for adult life, severe hardships are sometimes imposed upon boys. Their endurance is thereby developed and tried. This prepares them for facing whatever difficulties living in the group will present. The ceremonies through which girls pass is coincidental with first menstruation and readies them for the life of wife and mother.

Among the Mende, boys are trained in the bush to symbolize their change in status. They are taught self-discipline and self-reliance. They learn how to work cooperatively with others and how to take orders from others. Initiation rites for the Nandi youth confer on him his age-grade, entitle him to take his father's name and to engage in war. With the Tswana, initiation ceremonies impress on the youth certain definite rules of behavior. These prepare him for his life as husband, father, kinsman, subject, fellow tribesman, worker, and owner of property.

Girls among the Mende are taught in the initiation ceremonies that they should be hard-working, modest in their behavior particularly towards older people, and that failure in these regards will be severely punished. The initiation of Bemba girls, it is said, teaches them not so much the detailed activities of the wife, mother, and housewife, as the proper attitude towards these positions. It teaches them also the necessity of being intelligent, socially competent, and well informed about etiquette.

Among some groups of preliterates, initiation rites and ceremonies were the means used to pass on to the new generation a general understanding of their whole way of life. The Iroquois, for instance, instilled into the youth a knowledge of the way Iroquois society was structured, and stimulated patriotic sentiments in this regard. By the use of legends, with which the children were already acquainted from infancy, knowledge about more profound things such as the origin of the world and the existence of suprahuman power and beings was inculcated.

Circumcision for some preliterates is an important part of the rites of initiation. The Gikuyu are an example of a group of preliterates for whom circumcision is the step that admits a boy or girl to full membership in the group. The trials of circumcision teach the boy how to bear pain, meet misfortune, and bear himself like a warrior. He is taught that he should not act impulsively. Girls are also taught how to act as wife and mother. Before circumcision a youth has limited rights. He cannot possess anything, build a home of

---

[25] Example: Franz Boas, "Culture," *Encyc. of the Social Sciences* **2** (1930): pp. 89, 102; C. K. Meek, *Law and Authority in a Nigerian Tribe* (London, 1937), p. 299; Robert Rattray, *Ashanti Law and Constitution* (Oxford, 1929), p. 11; Gunter Wagner, "The Political Organization of the Bantu Kavirondo," in: Meyer Fortes and Edward Evans-Pritchard, *African Political Systems* (London, 1940), p. 212; Kenneth Little, *The Mende of Sierra Leone* (London, 1951), p. 121; Audrey Richards, *Chisungu—A Girl's Initiation Ceremony Among the Bemba of Northern Rhodesia* (New York, 1956), p. 126; Raymond Firth, *We, the Tikopia* (2nd ed., London, 1957), p. 147.

[26] Mircea Eliade, *Rites and Symbols of Initiation*, trans. by W. R. Trask (New York, 1958), p. x.

[27] "[T]he various types of initiations can be classed in two categories: first, puberty rites, by virtue of which adolescents gain access to the sacred, to knowledge, and to sexuality—by which, in short, they become *human beings;* second, specialized initiations, which certain individuals undergo in order to transcend their human conditions and become protégés of the Supernatural Beings or even their equals." Mircea Eliade, *Rites and Symbols of Initiation*, trans. by W. R. Trask (New York, 1958), pp. 128–129.

his own, go to war, boast or brag, wear his hair long, have intercourse with circumcised girls or have a circumcised man as an intimate friend. After circumcision he is a warrior, a dancer, an eater of good food, eligible to own property and get married and put up his own homestead. He is now considered a man who knows the difference between right and wrong and is therefore punishable for his errors.

Noteworthy in the initiation ceremonies of some peoples, for instance the Bemba, is the use of pottery images, wall designs and songs to convey instructions concerning various aspects of daily life. Among these are the protection of fire, social obligations of husband and wife, obligations to in-laws, domestic duties, agricultural duties, maternal duties, obligations between mother and daughter, sex and fertility, the chief's power, and general ethical rules. Other obligations are also mimed in the initiation ceremony such as the submission of a girl to her husband, the distribution of food to the family, and the exchange of gifts. The lazy wife is depicted as a squat and unattractive figure.

There are some preliterates who have neither initiation rites nor circumcision. Such peoples usually demand of a youth some other sign that maturity has been reached. Among the Naskapi, the attainment of puberty is accepted as such a sign for the girls. For the boys, the killing of a bear is taken as an indication that the youth has passed the test of courage and he is henceforth regarded and treated as a man. Other preliterates are said not to allow a man to marry until he has cut off at least one human head.

Initiation rites, as such, no longer play a prominent part in the educational processes of literate societies. There is no ceremony in which the youth is made publicly conscious of the fact that he has reached not only physical but also political adulthood, as was the case when the Romans conferred the toga on young men when they attained a certain age. There are groups within literate societies, of course, which are the exception and still have similar rites. Such are certain ceremonies of various religions. But there are no formal procedures by which every youth is oriented regarding not only life but death as well. A most interesting comparison has been drawn between psychoanalysis and initiation rites. "From a certain point of view, psychoanalysis can be regarded as a secularized form of initiation, that is, an initiation accessible to a desacralized world."[28]

The value judgment, therefore, that learning is good —whether through oral instruction, example or initiation rites—is universal among all known preliterate societies. It is a postulate of all law.[29]

5. *Explanations of Life*

Men have always been preoccupied with explaining the meaning of life. This concern is but a manifestation of their basic drive to know. Attempts have always been made to know the nature of men, the possibility of a life after death, the possibility of beings who are of a higher intelligence than man. Men have always searched for knowledge about the origin of man and the universe, the existence of a supreme power, and the possible relationships which exist between men and this power. Such explanations are universal among all peoples.[30] All know societies put a high value on knowing the solutions to these basic problems.[31] Their value judgments, however, vary. Some are universal. Others are less than universal, being general or common.

a. *Life Principle*

The conviction that man is not only matter but also spirit, not only body but also soul, has always been universal among all peoples. "The belief in a soul or spiritual counterpart of some kind . . . is universal."[32] "Primitive man reflected and concluded that there are two parts to man: the bodily self of mortal flesh and the spiritual alter ego, the soul. The soul concept . . . is a universal concept."[33] "All peoples the world over believe in a kind of existence less material than that of solid bodies."[34] This insight, that whatever it is that

---

[28] Mircea Eliade, *Rites and Symbols of Initiation*, trans. by W. R. Trask (New York, 1958), p. 165, n. 57. "[T]he pattern is still recognizable: the descent into the depths of the psyche, peopled with monsters, is equivalent to a descent to the Underworld; the real danger implied by such a descent could be connected, for example, with the typical ordeals of traditional societies. The result of a successful analysis is the integration of the personality, a psychic process not without resemblance to the piritual transformation accomplished by genuine initiations." Eliade, p. 165, n. 57; see also Eliade, pp. 132–136.

[29] Initiation rites: Mircea Eliade, *Rites and Symbols of Initiation*, trans. by W. R. Trask (New York, 1958), *passim*; Franz Boas, "Culture," *Encyc. of the Social Sciences* 2 (1930): p. 102; Kenneth Little, *The Mende of Sierra Leone* (London, 1951), pp. 118, 120, 127; Geoffrey Snell, *Nandi Customary Law* (London, 1954), p. 68; Isaac Schapera, *A Handbook of Tswana Law and Custom* (London, 1938), p. 36; Audrey Richards, *Chisungu—A Girl's Initiation Ceremony Among the Bemba of Northern Rhodesia* (New York, 1956), pp. 125, 128–129, 140; John Noon, "Law and Government of the Grand River Iroquois," *Viking Fund Publ. in Anthropology* 12 (1949): p. 33; Jomo Kenyatta, *Facing Mount Kenya* (London, 1953), pp. 107–111; Julius Lips, "Naskapi Law," *Trans. Amer. Philos. Soc.* 37 (1947): p. 413; Edward Westermarck, *The Origin and Development of the Moral Ideas* (2 v., London, 1908–1912) 1: p. 333.

[30] Melville Herskovits, *Man and His Works* (New York, 1948), p. 347; Clyde Kluckhohn, *Mirror for Man* (New York, 1949), p. 18; David Bidney, *Theoretical Anthropology* (New York, 1953), pp. 5, 325; Robert Redfield, "The Primitive World View," *Proc. Amer. Philos. Soc.* 96 (1952): p. 33.

[31] It has been said that there are four "basic organizing concepts" to the "persistent tasks of life": the nature of the universe, man's place in the universe, man's relation to his group, and man's nature and conduct. Lawrence Frank, "Science and Culture," *Scientific Monthly* 50 (1940): p. 492.

[32] Clark Wissler, *Man and Culture* (New York, 1923), p. 77.

[33] E. Adamson Hoebel, *Man in the Primitive World* (New York, 1949), p. 406.

[34] Robert Lowie, *An Introduction to Cultural Anthropology* (2nd ed., New York, 1940), p. 306.

makes the body live must be different from the body which of itself may be dead, is as old as the reasoning of men. It is the bio-principle, the source of life of the body.[35]

What this life principle is in itself is as difficult for preliterates to describe as it is for anyone else. Being spiritual or immaterial, it cannot be depicted in material concepts. When attempts are made to do so, the soul is ofttimes spoken of as something like a shadow. Thus the Nuer associate the soul with shade or reflection. Their word for soul is closely related to their word for shade or shadow. The Nuer say that twins have their own independent life but they have a single soul and are therefore only one person. Polynesians hold that men have two spirits. One spirit is manifest in the shadow. It has no separate being apart from the living person and is vaguely protective of the person during his lifetime. This spirit ceases to exist soon after the person dies and is not in any way a principle of life. The other spirit does not die with the death of the person and is the only part of the person which survives after the person's body is buried in the grave. It grows old with the person of whom it is a part and appears to be subject to the ills which the person himself suffers.

The idea of a soul held by some preliterates, the Nuer for instance, closely resembles that held in certain well-known schools of philosophical thought, it has been pointed out. The soul in this conception is that part of life in which are rooted men's intellectual and volitional faculties. Hence, men's soul or life-principle is rational as distinct from the non-rational souls or life-principles of all other living beings.

The value judgment, then, that it is good and desirable to know about men's soul or life-principle is universal among all preliterate peoples.[36]

### b. Life after Death

In all preliterate societies is found the idea that the souls or life-principles of men continue to live on in another life. "All peoples the world over . . . credit men with a soul that survives his body."[37] "All primitive people without exception believe in another life."[38] "Some form or other of the belief in immortality is found in all primitive societies."[39] "The belief in a soul . . . that defies death, is universal."[40]

Preliterates' thinking about life after death is apparently related to their conviction that in sleep the soul goes wandering. If it does not return, death ensues. Some peoples, like the Nabaloi, have ceremonies to persuade a wandering soul to return to its living person. While the soul of the husband or the wife is wandering about, no children will be born to them. The Nuer are reported to believe that when a man dies, his soul departs from him and returns to God from whom it came.[41]

Although the idea of a life after death is found in all preliterate societies, preliterates are far from agreement as to what it is like. The Yamana say they do not know what it is like and that is the reason they are so sad when relatives die. The Semang and the Batwa of Ruanda say that all sins have been atoned for in this life, with no distinction being made between good and bad persons in the next life. The great part of preliterates, however, think that good persons will be distinguished from the bad in the next life.

For the Ashanti, a man's life in the next world will be much like what it was in this world. The deceased goes to join his kinsmen who have preceded him. Hence, it is the wish of every Ashanti that he be buried beside his ancestors. The Akan hold that death is a painful transition from an unhappy material world to an equally unhappy spiritual world. Here unhappiness is rendered tolerable, it is reported, by freedom of thought and power. But they appear to think that the inhabitants of the next world will be happy or unhappy according to whether their earthly lives were justified or unjustified in the eyes of the custom law.

Some preliterates think that immortality is relative both to persons and time. Only the souls of high rank may be immortal. Existence after death may not be perpetual but only temporary. Survival may take the form of reincarnation. In Polynesia when a man dies his spirit is thought to join the spirits of those who have preceded him and who have no special dwelling place. They live an airy existence which is quite understood. The Andaman Islanders, on the other hand, think that the souls of the departed live on in the sky and also land or sea.

For preliterates, the ties that bind them to relatives and friends are not severed with "death." The Ashanti

---

[35] Aristotle said the soul is "the first grade of actuality of a natural body having life potentially in it." Aristotle, *On the Soul*, Book II, chap. 1, 412ᵃ29–30, trans. by J. A. Smith, Richard McKeon, ed., *The Basic Works of Aristotle* (New York, 1941), p. 555.

[36] Life-principle: Edward Evans-Pritchard, *Nuer Religion* (Oxford, 1956), p. 155; H. Ian Hogbin, *Law and Order in Polynesia* (London, 1934), p. 143; E. Adamson Hoebel, *Man in the Primitive World* (New York, 1949), p. 407; Claude Moss, "Nabaloi Law and Ritual," *Amer. Archaeology and Ethnology* 15 (1920): p. 273.

[37] Robert Lowie, *An Introduction to Cultural Anthropology* (2nd ed., 1940), p. 306.

[38] Wilhelm Schmidt, *The Origin and Growth of Religion*, trans. by H. J. Rose (New York, 1931), p. 275.

[39] Ralph Piddington, *An Introduction to Social Anthropology* (London, 1950), p. 375.

[40] Clark Wissler, *Man and Culture* (New York, 1923), p. 77.

[41] If the reports on the universality of preliterate belief in the human soul and its immortality are accurate, other reports to the contrary are suspect. "There are, it is true, some savages who are reported to believe in the annihilation of the soul at the moment of death, or to have no notion whatever of a future state. But the accuracy of these statements is hardly beyond suspicion. We sometimes hear that the very people who are said to deny any belief in an after-life are afraid of ghosts." Edward Westermarck, *The Origin and Development of the Moral Ideas* (2 v., London, 1908–1912) 2: p. 515.

hold that the bond between the living relatives and their dead continues to persist. Polynesians think that departed spirits are able to observe the conduct of living persons, are aware of the most hidden motives, and can directly influence the destiny of their living relatives. No birth, illness, or death takes place without their influence. The Ibo hold that any departure from custom law incurs the displeasure and vengeance of ancestors. They are the guardians of morality and owners of the land. Because departed spirits remember the treatment they received in this life, old men are feared as potentially troublesome spirits. This adds to their authority, as occurs among the Bantu Kavirondo.

Because preliterates think that departed spirits can have a malevolent influence, they attempt to win their good will. The Ibo offer sacrifice at regular intervals to appease the spirits and ward off sickness which they can cause. The Nabaloi think that departed spirits can become hungry. Spirits appear in dreams or cause sickness as a reminder of their needs. The funeral rites of preliterates show their conviction of the continued life, influence, and need of the departed spirits. Like many other preliterates, the Ibo place food, in this case yams, alongside the body of the deceased. The dead person is addressed and told that the yams are being given to him for his use and he is asked to look favorably upon those he is leaving.

To the minds of some preliterates, there is no reason why the life of men should not continue on indefinitely. So when death was first encountered, they reasoned there must have been a special cause. The Margi of Nigeria explain that men sent a chameleon to God to find out the cause. God told the chameleon to tell men that if they threw baked porridge over a corpse it would be restored to life. The chameleon was slow in returning, however, and death was occurring everywhere among men. Hence, men sent a second messenger. This time it was a lizard. The lizard reached God soon after the chameleon had left. God was angered at the second message and told the lizard that men had to dig a hole in the earth and bury the corpses there. The lizard reached home before the chameleon. When the chameleon arrived, the corpses were already buried. So now the ghosts of the dead must hover around their graves until they are finally released to a place from which they may be reborn. Though couched in the familiar animistic imagery of preliterates, this account clearly expresses one fact: preliterates' belief in the unlimited continuance of life.

The value judgment, then, that it is good to know about a life after death is universal among all societies of preliterates.[42]

### c. Suprahuman Power

The conviction that there exists a suprahuman power is found in all preliterate societies. "All peoples have some concept of supernatural power, related in some fashion to man, and more or less subject to his influence and control."[43] "[T]he belief in supernaturalism . . . is absolutely universal among known peoples, past and present."[44] Men can know about the existence of a non-material, non-sensual suprahuman power because they have the mental ability to think and reason in abstract and symbolic concepts.[45]

The understanding of what this power is ranges from the less to the more concise. It is thought of as both impersonal and personal. When considered as impersonal, this power is vague in nature. It can be a wonderful power which works of itself. Whoever is touched by it enjoys extraordinary skills. A master craftsman is skillful in his craft because he possesses this power. The learned man excels in knowledge because he has this power. A warrior surpasses other warriors in killing the enemy in battle because he is endowed with this power. Any man who excels his fellows in his endeavors, may be doing so because he possesses this power. This impersonal, suprahuman power goes by different names. It may be called mana. Manitou, orenda, and wakan are also names by which this power is known.

This suprahuman power may also be thought of as intelligent and personal. Conviction regarding the existence of personal, suprahuman powers is "widespread."[46] This is shown especially in the idea that these powers or beings rule the universe and are dis-

---

[42] Life after death: E. Adamson Hoebel, *Man in the Primitive World* (New York, 1949), p. 406; Claude Moss, "Nabaloi Law and Ritual," *Amer. Archaeology and Ethnology* **15** (1920): p. 282; Edward Evans-Pritchard, *Nuer Religion* (Oxford, 1956), p. 154; K. A. Busia, *The Position of the Chief in the Modern Political System of Ashanti* (London, 1951), p. 23; Joseph Danquah, *Gold Coast: Akan Laws and Customs* (Lon-

don, 1938), p. 230; Ralph Piddington, *An Introduction to Social Anthropology* (London, 1950), p. 375; H. Ian Hogbin, *Law and Order in Polynesia* (London, 1934), p. 144; Arthur Diamond, *The Evolution of Law and Order* (London, 1951), pp. 84, 144; C. K. Meek, *Law and Authority in a Nigerian Tribe* (London, 1937), pp. 53, 61, 303; Gunter Wagner, "The Political Organization of the Bantu Kavirondo," in: Meyer Fortes and Edward Evans-Pritchard, eds., *African Political Systems* (London, 1940), p. 235.

[43] Ralph Beals and Harry Hoijer, *An Introduction to Anthropology* (New York, 1953), p. 503.

[44] Robert Lowie, *An Introduction to Cultural Anthropology* (2nd ed., New York, 1940), p. 298.

[45] "When we describe something as supernatural . . . we mean that it lies beyond the reach of the sense organs and that it can never be made manifest to human taste, touch, smell, sight, or hearing. . . . Beliefs of this kind . . . comprise the quintessence of algebraic mentality which can deal with abstract and symbolic concepts as readily as if they had objective reality." Mischa Titiev, *Introduction to Cultural Anthropology* (New York, 1959), p. 334. There is, however, another meaning of "supernatural." This meaning, which is theological, refers to what is added to the "natural." It is natural for a man to have a mind. But it is not natural for a man to have the insights into life which he gets from Revelation. This is "supernatural." The non-sensory, non-material meaning of "supernatural" mentioned in the quotation above would, in this theological context, be called "spiritual."

[46] Ralph Beals and Harry Hoijer, *An Introduction to Anthropology* (New York, 1953), p. 503.

pleased or pleased when men disobey or obey their rules. Thus the Nandi hold that Asis is the power behind the world. Asis is the source of all life and hence of fertility. He can be angered and the cessation of rain when crops are growing is a sign of his disapproval. With the Lamba, Lesa is the high god who is angered when men commit murder, theft, or adultery. He punishes them by sending smallpox and leprosy. The Nuer believe that Kwoth, who is the Spirit in the Sky, is a living person whose breath or life sustains man. He can be angry and he can love. He is the father of men. The supreme being which many preliterates believe in, as we shall see shortly, is also a personal power or being.

The evidence shows that preliterate conviction concerning the existence of a suprahuman power—impersonal or personal—is universal. Hence it can be asserted that in all preliterate societies the value judgment is formed that it is good to be convinced that there exists a suprahuman power.[47]

### d. Relationship with Suprahuman Power

Once a man is convinced that a suprahuman power exists, his relationship with this power becomes one of the most important things in his life. This importance increases as he conceives this power to be intelligent and personal. If he recognizes his relationship with this power to be one of dependence and he expressly acknowledges it, this is his "religion." "[R]eligion is everywhere an expression in one form or another of a sense of dependence on a power outside ourselves, a power which we may speak of as a spiritual or moral power."[48] The heart of a man's religion, then, is a suprahuman being who is greater than himself and in whom this relationship is centered.[49]

Religion is universal among all known societies of men. "No people of whom we have knowledge is without a religion."[50] "No age, no country, and no people seem to have lacked such experience altogether."[51] All peoples make a distinction between what is religious and what is non-religious. With strikingly little readjustment, this distinction is the same in all known societies. "No matter into how exotic a society the traveler has wandered, he still finds the distinction made and in comparatively familiar terms. And it is universal."[52] No religion, it has often been noted, has ever been found among animals.

Sacrifice is an integral part of the religion of preliterates. It has been said to be inseparable from all religion. Sacrifice is the central propitiatory act of religion. Sacrifice must be offered by someone. So sacred is this function considered to be that those only are allowed to perform it who have certain qualifications of character. Among the Bantu of Kavirondo, the members of the senior line of a lineage or any classificatory father or elder brother whose character is suitable may offer sacrifice. Suitable qualities of character are kindness and honesty, age past the time of sexual desire, care for the people, and in general an unblemished life. The elder of the clan who has these qualifications is known as "the great sacrificer" and among the Logoli he offers public sacrifice to the tribal ancestor and deity. The office is not based on heredity but on personal qualifications.

Among the Gikuyu, only those who are immune from sullying earthly contacts, that is, the old and the young, are qualified to offer sacrifice. These are the elders who no longer have worldly desires and are now concerned with only the common welfare. They are also women who, when they are allowed to sacrifice, must be "past the age of mischief" and childbearing and must be esteemed as mothers of the whole community. They are, finally, children who, when they sacrifice, must be in pairs, a male and a female, and not over eight years of age. Below this age they are considered with certainty still to be pure in mind, heart, and body.

Another qualification for offering sacrifice frequently encountered among preliterates is the abstinence, temporary or permanent, from sexual contacts. There are many examples of this and they have long since been noted. Thus among the Ibo in Nigeria, the priest as offerer of sacrifice must not sleep away from home, nor have sexual relations with a widow, nor allow a menstru-

---

[47] Suprahuman power: Herbert Rose, "The Wiro Sky-God," in: L. H. Dudley Buxton, ed., *Custom Is King* (London, 1936), p. 52; Ashley Montagu, *Man: His First Million Years* (Cleveland, 1957), p. 185; E. Adamson Hoebel, *Man in the Primitive World*, (New York, 1949), p. 407; Ruth Benedict, "Religion," in: Franz Boas, ed., *General Anthropology* (Boston, 1938), p. 629; Geoffrey Snell, *Nandi Customary Law* (London, 1954), pp. 1–2; Arthur Diamond, *The Evolution of Law and Order* (London, 1951), p. 230; Edward Tylor, *Anthropology* (New York, 1916), p. 359; Edward Evans-Pritchard, *Nuer Religion* (Oxford, 1956), pp. 1, 7.

[48] Alfred Radcliffe-Brown, *Structure and Function in Primitive Society* (Glencoe, 1956), p. 157. On definitions of religion see Theophile Meek, *Hebrew Origins* (rev. ed., New York, 1950), p. 83; Rudolph Otto, *The Idea of the Holy*, trans. by J. W. Harvey (New York, 1958), p. 176; Edgar Brightman, *A Philosophy of Religion* (New York, 1940), p. 415; Edward Westermarck, *The Origin and Development of the Moral Ideas* (2 v., London, 1908–1912) 2: p. 584.

[49] "[Religion] is, in one way or another, in the Jewish way, or the aboriginal way, or the Greek way, or the Persian way, or the Egyptian way, an institution deriving its authority from the greater than human, the greater than nature." Leslie Paul, *Nature into History* (London, 1957), p. 144.

[50] Ashley Montagu, *Man: His First Million Years* (Cleveland, 1957), p. 180.

[51] Joachim Wach, *Sociology of Religion* (Chicago, 1944), p. 376.

[52] See Ruth Benedict, "Religion," in: Franz Boas, ed., *General Anthropology* (Boston, 1938), p. 628; Robert Lowie, *Are We Civilized?* (New York, 1929), p. 214; Mischa Titiev, *Introduction to Cultural Anthropology* (New York, 1959), p. 334. "At all times and in all states of culture religion has been and is the means whereby human beings adjust themselves to their physical, social and spiritual environment and categories of thought." Edwin James, *The Nature and Function of Priesthood* (London, 1955), p. 13.

ating woman to enter his house.[53] Likewise in Kenya among the Gikuyu, the elders who offer sacrifice are not allowed to have sexual intercourse with their wives or sleep in their wives' huts during the six nights before the offering of the sacrifice when preparations are being made and the two nights after the sacrifice is offered.

The office of priest-sacrificer has been called the most comprehensive of all specifically religious activities. Through his delegated position as master of the sacrificial offering, the priest is depicted as exercising a transcendental power in maintaining a living bond between men and a higher being. The position of priesthood, therefore, is characterized as a steadying force in the group in which it functions. Its tendency, it is said, is to stabilize the religious and social structures of which it is a part. As the guardian of sacred tradition and learning, the priesthood fulfills an important cultural role. Inevitably, especially among preliterates all the aspects of whose lives are so closely interwoven, religion also has definite effects on their political activities.

There have been reports that some preliterate peoples had no religion. But, much as was the case regarding law which we mentioned above, the basis of this inaccurate reporting was the inadequate notion of religion which the field researchers themselves had. A distinction should have been drawn, for instance, between the fact that Australians did not believe in one all-powerful god and the fact that they did have some kind of religion. A differentiation should also have been made, for example, between the Crow Indian age-society ceremony which was not religious and their sun-dance rites which had a religious character. The concept which the field researcher had of religion, and also of law, was not necessarily the correct one as was later proved.

Reports on religion among preliterates have been interspersed with attempts to explain its origin. This fact in itself shows the value judgment which was operative in the minds of the reporters themselves, namely, that it is good to know the origin of religion. Along with factual reporting, there is much philosophical speculation. Some authors account for the origin of religion by describing how the idea of a supreme being originated, to which we shall refer later. Others, either taking the non-existence of a supreme being for granted or declaring the question to be irrelevant to the understanding of religion, simply explain how men acquire a sense of relatedness to something supposedly existing beyond themselves. They project beyond themselves the most intense aspects of social living and represent them symbolically. Other authors hold that religion originates in a "mystic" experience which a few endowed persons in every community have and which is then communicated to others. Still other authors say that religion is a subjective response to the felt psycho-

logical need of allaying dissatisfactions, anxieties, and fears.

Such speculation, included in supposedly factual reporting, would seem to justify a comment. It is obvious enough that when the origin of religion is accounted for by belief in a suprahuman power, the term of reference is ontological and objective. When this origin is explained in relation to anxiety complexes, this term is psychological and subjective. This subjective explanation of the origin of religion has been shown to entail circular reasoning. Any understanding of an inner experience of religion comes only through interpreting its objective expression. But an adequate interpretation of the objective expression can come only from a prior insight into the inner experience. In other words, the subjective explanation of the origin of religion is an account of a response without any reference to the stimulus.

The force of this criticism can be seen in relation to the manner in which anthropological data have been interpreted. How can the religion of preliterates be explained as a subjective reaction to psychological anxieties and fears when in the minds of the preliterates themselves they believe in the objective existence of a suprahuman power in whom their religious belief is anchored? To interpret the religion of preliterates as merely such a subjective reaction—when as a matter of recorded fact preliterates relate their belief to something objective—is not to explain *preliterate* religion. It is to impose on preliterate religion terms which are foreign to it—those of the interpreter himself.

The cultural value of religion is a matter of record. It has been called "the main bond which binds human beings together." [54] It is a maxim that "all culture depends on divine belief." [55] Nearly all the great social institutions "have been born in religion." [56] Religion is "the dominant institution within a culture." [57] Typical among preliterates is the part religion plays among the Gikuyu. It is integrated with the whole of their lives. Religion is for them an expression of belief which relates to all the things which are most significant in human life.

Religion and law are everywhere allied in preserving order. This is so because the general rules of law, unwritten or written, are usually coincidental with the broad prescriptions of religion or are actual expressions of them. In fact, one of the outstanding characteristics of religion is its formulations of guidelines for the behavior of its adherents. Among the Ibo, the relation of religion and custom law is so close that many of the law's most powerful sanctions are derived directly from religion.

[53] The English word "priest" comes from the Greek "presbyteros" and the Latin "presbyter" meaning "elder."

[54] Ashley Montagu, *Man: His First Million Years* (Cleveland, 1957), p. 180.

[55] Ivar Lissner, *Man, God and Magic*, trans. by J. M. Brownjohn (New York, 1961), p. 79.

[56] Emile Durkheim, *The Elementary Forms of the Religious Life,* trans. by J. W. Swain (Glencoe, 1947), p. 419.

[57] James Feibleman, *The Theory of Human Culture* (New York, 1946), pp. 115–116. See also Barend Ter Haar, *Adat Law in Indonesia* (New York, 1948), p. 50.

With the Basuto, custom law derives ultimately from God and the ethical beliefs of men. This is the basis of justice between man and man. Similarly, the Yap believe that their custom law came from suprahuman spirits long ago. It was the spirits who, for instance, originally forbade incest and who react to it when it occurs. The spirits are the ultimate source of authority. Among the Ifugao, the coincidence of religion and law appears in many practical matters. The Ifugao say that much of their custom law was given to them by Lidum who is a deity of the Skyworld and their great teacher. Included in these regulations are transferals of family property, ordeals, payments of larger fines, peacemaking, and certain taboos.

Consistent with this view is the conviction that observance of the rules of custom law brings good fortune. This idea that ill luck can be avoided by keeping the law is reportedly universal. Consequently, religion and law have had a controlling effect on the social and political life of peoples. Religion together with law has made it possible for people to live together in orderly social relationships. Offenses against law in preliterate societies, because of this coincidence of religion and law, are more often than not also offenses against religion. Thus the offenses we have seen against the custom law of life, sex, property, and so on, are usually offenses against religion. Conversely, offenses against religion are also offenses against custom law. Sacrilege, sorcery, witchcraft, and black magic are punishable according to custom law.[58]

The value judgment, then, that it is good to acknowledge a relationship of dependence on a supreme power is universal among all preliterate societies.[59]

---

[58] The effectiveness of religion and law working together can be seen in the Islamic world. "[T]he fact is that this system which seems so unworkable to us has an amazing record of accomplishment. Such was the cohesive and animating power of Muhammadanism that within a century of the Prophet's death his tribal people, who had no real organized state or standing army or common political ambitions, had overrun the African shores of the Mediterranean, had conquered Spain, and had threatened France until the victory of Charles Martel at Poitiers in 732. . . . Today the anxious countries of the West find in the Islamic world some of their most bold and uncompromising allies in resisting the drive for world supremacy by those whose Prophet is Marx." Robert Jackson, "Foreword," to Majid Khadduri and Herbert Liesbesny, *Law in the Middle East* (Washington, 1955), pp. vii, viii.

[59] Relationship with suprahuman power: Gerardus Van Der Leeuw, *La Religion* (Paris, 1948), p. 342; Gunter Wagner, "The Political Organization of the Bantu Kavirondo," in: Meyer Fortes and Edward Evans-Pritchard, eds., *African Political Systems* (London, 1940), pp. 233–234; Jomo Kenyatta, *Facing Mount Kenya* (London, 1953), pp. 244, 246, 316; Edward Westermarck, *The Origin and Development of the Moral Ideas* (2 v., London, 1908–1912) 2: pp. 405–421; C. K. Meek, *Law and Authority in a Nigerian Tribe* (London, 1937), pp. 20, 60; Joachim Wach, *Sociology of Religion* (Chicago, 1944), pp. 14, 361; Edwin James, *The Nature and Function of Priesthood* (London, 1955), pp. 13, 298; Ruth Benedict, "Religion," in: Franz Boas, ed., *General Anthropology* (Boston, 1938), p. 628; Evans-Pritchard, "Religion," in: Evans-Pritchard and others, *The Institutions of Primitive Society* (Glencoe, 1956),

## B. LESS THAN UNIVERSAL VALUE JUDGMENTS

There are other value judgments not universal which preliterates make regarding knowledge. Value judgments concerning the control of events appear to be general, and value judgments in regard to lying, above-human spirits, a personal supreme being, and creation seem to be common.

### 1. General: Control of Events

In their relationship with the supreme power, men attempt to influence the course of events in one of two ways. Either they acknowledge dependence on this power and seek a favorable reaction, or they do not acknowledge any dependence and attempt to bring about on their own what they desire. In the first instance, it is presupposed that the supreme power is not under the control of men but can be influenced by them. Prayer and petition are directed to the power in the hope of obtaining a favorable response. In the second case, it is assumed that this power is under the control of men and can be manipulated by them. A tested formula, if perfectly used, forces the power to respond as men desire. These two differing relationships with the supreme power have been given the names "religion" and "magic." The concept of "magic," however, was never implied in the traditional use of the word "religion." Because of the difficulty in distinguishing the difference between what is connoted by the two terms in many instances, it has been suggested that the term "magic" be dropped altogether.

"Magic" has been divided into positive magic or sorcery whose aim is to produce a desired event, and negative magic or taboo whose purpose is to avoid an undesirable event. Magic is used for good and evil purposes—white and black magic. Black magic can be the same as sorcery or witchcraft if it implies the use of evil supernatural powers. But if the supposed power at work in sorcery or witchcraft is the result of a compact with evil spirits and dependence upon them, the sorcery or witchcraft is more like perverted religion. Charms are carried by many preliterates as a protection against particular dangers. Such is the case among the

p. 1; Emile Durkheim, *The Elementary Forms of the Religious Life*, trans. by J. W. Swain (Glencoe, 1947), *passim*; L. Hauer, *Die Religionen* (Berlin, 1923), *passim*; Ralph Beals and Harry Hoijer, *An Introduction to Anthropology* (New York, 1953), p. 503; Ralph Piddington, *An Introduction to Social Anthropology* (London, 1950), p. 366; Anthony Allott, *Essays in African Law* (London, 1960), p. 67; David Schneider, "Political Organization, Supernatural Sanction and Punishment for Incest on Yap," *Amer. Anthropologist* 59 (1957): p. 797; Ralph Barton, "Ifugao Law," *Amer. Archaeology and Ethnology* 15 (1919): p. 14; Clark Wissler, *Man and Culture* (New York, 1923), p. 77; Alfred Radcliffe-Brown, *Structure and Function in Primitive Society* (Glencoe, 1956), p. 154.

On Peyote religion and its increasing importance as a potent form of Pan-Indianism in American Indian life, see David Aberle, *The Peyote Religion Among the Navaho* (Chicago, 1966), *passim*.

Gikuyu. This practice has been called a form of individual magic and its practice in the daily life of the community is looked on as a symbol of security.

A man or woman, who is sometimes called a shaman, can acquire magical power over spirits, especially those who bring sickness and death. This power is acquired by indoctrination and initiation. These empowered persons, it is said, can predict and control suprahuman events. Such predictions and control, however, have been explained in terms of psychic capacities to influence others. The relation between these practices and the results obtained are said to be subjective rather than objective. The relation is not one of cause and effect. It is one of psychological association.

Attempts to bring about certain events by controlling a suprahuman power is universal in all preliterate societies. "Magic is another universal feature of human culture." [60] "[T]hat the twin forces of white and black, of positive and negative [magic], exist everywhere is beyond doubt." [61] But, although such practices are universal, it does not follow that in all their forms they are approved by all preliterates. Hence, it seems a fair estimate of the data to say that the value judgment that it is good to attempt to bring about events by controlling a suprahuman power is general among preliterate societies. [62]

## 2. Common

### a. Lying

Knowledge and its communication are essential for all social life, as we have noted. Truthfulness in communication is necessary if the value of communication is to be realized. Untruthfulness or lying lessens the possibility of obtaining this value. Truthfulness is implied in men's drive to associate with others and to communicate with them.

The reports on the value-judging which preliterates do in regard to lying are not too plentiful. According to older reports, some preliterates judge that lying is good and others judge that lying is bad. Long lists are given as evidence of this. Some groups are said to have a great respect for truthfulness. The ancient Scandinavians, for instance, are said to have considered it a disgrace to tell a lie. Other groups of preliterates are said

to hold that lying is not bad. The Point Barrow Eskimo, for example, think that a detected lie is no more than a good joke. Deceit is commonly practised in trading and it is not considered to be wrong. For many preliterates, the successful lie is a matter of "popular admiration." [63]

From these most inadequate data, only a broad conjecture can be made regarding the value judgments which preliterates make about lying. Some seem to think it is good and some seem to think it is bad. Hence, the value judgment that lying is bad appears to be common among preliterates. The value judgment that lying is good also appears to be common among their societies.

### b. Other-than-human Spirits

Preliterates are convinced that there are, besides the disembodied spirits of those departed from this life, spirits who are of another nature than the nature which men have. The Nuer speak of spirits of the below or earth, in contrast to the spirits of the above or the sky. Those above are great spirits, while those below are lesser spirits who are not held in high esteem. These higher spirits are believed by some to be more powerful than human beings. The Navaho hold that, as distinguished from ordinary human beings who walk the earth's surface, there are divinities who possess special suprahuman power and are immortal. The Navaho word for "holy" is defined in terms of power which exceeds human effort.

The tendency of many preliterates to personify certain natural phenomena, such as the sun, thunder, and the like, could be related to their belief in the great spirits "in the sky." Similar to many other preliterates, the Andamanese personify the sun, moon, thunder, and lightning. The sun is the wife of the moon, and the stars are their children. Some, like the Nabaloi, identify the sun as a supreme ruler undoubtedly because of its physical prominence. They regard the heavenly bodies as objects of worship but not of sacrifice. The sun is regarded as the most powerful of the deities and is always appealed to in ordeals as the god of justice.

The extent of preliterate conviction concerning other-than-human spirits has been said to be fairly wide. [64] On this basis, it seems that the value judgment made in preliterate societies that it is good to believe in other-than-human spirits is probably common among them. [65]

[60] E. Adamson Hoebel, *Law of Primitive Man* (Cambridge, Mass., 1954), p. 267.

[61] Bronislaw Malinowski, *Magic, Science and Religion* (Boston, 1948), pp. 66, 70.

[62] Control of events: Hoebel, *Man in the Primitive World* (New York, 1949), p. 408; Edward Westermarck, *The Origin and Development of the Moral Ideas* (2 v., London, 1908–1912) 2: p. 584; Edwin James, *The Nature and Function of Priesthood* (London, 1955), pp. 13–14; James Frazer, *The Golden Bough* (abridged ed., New York, 1927), p. 19; Jomo Kenyatta, *Facing Mount Kenya* (London, 1953), p. 281; Walter Goldschmidt, *Man's Way* (Cleveland, 1959), pp. 176–177; Adolf Jensen, *Myth and Cult Among Primitive Peoples,* trans. by M. Choldin and W. Weissleder (Chicago, 1963), pp. 326–327; Paul Bohannon, *Social Anthropology* (New York, 1963), p. 313.

[63] Edward Westermarck, *The Origin and Development of the Moral Ideas* (2 v., London, 1908–1912) 2: pp. 72–86, 96, 109–110, 125.

[64] "Widespread are beliefs in personalized supernaturals, such as gods, spirits, and the ghosts of the dead." Ralph Beals and Harry Hoijer, *An Introduction to Anthropology* (New York, 1953), p. 503.

[65] Other-than-human spirits: Edward Evans-Pritchard, *Nuer Religion* (Oxford, 1956), p. 63; John Ladd, *The Structure of a Moral Code* (Cambridge, Mass., 1957), p. 217; Arthur Diamond, *The Evolution of Law and Order* (London, 1951), p. 84; Claude Moss, "Nabaloi Law and Ritual," *Amer. Archaeology and Ethnology* 15 (1920): p. 281.

## c. Supreme Being

Preliterates not only have convictions concerning a suprahuman power or powers, being or beings, but they also have convictions in regard to one supreme being. Exactly what this supreme being is considered to be varies with preliterate groups. The Gikuyu believe in one god, Ngai, who is the creator of all things. He has no companion of any kind and lives in solitude. He loves and hates people according to their behavior. The Mende of Sierra Leone hold that Leve is the Supreme God. All life, both material and non-material, comes from him. He is the source of the non-material power which pervades the universe. Little is known of Leve, the Mende say, because no one has ever seen him. The Nuer believe in Kwoth, as we mentioned. Inasmuch as he is creative spirit he is their supreme being.

It has been said that a "vast number" of preliterate religions include a belief in a supreme being.[66] It has also been stated that belief in a supreme being, with the various connotations it may have, is found among "two thirds to three quarters or perhaps even more" of the preliterate peoples.[67] On the basis of these estimates, it can be said that the value judgment in preliterate societies that it is good to know there is a supreme being appears to be common.[68]

There is also a value judgment made regarding a supreme being which is similar to the one made concerning religion. This is the value judgment that it is good to know the origin of the idea of a supreme being and belief in this being. This value judgment is made by anthropologists and ethnologists themselves. Much ink has been spilled by them over this question and it is this value judgment which urges them to seek an answer. Their efforts to find a solution to this problem is a good example of the reasoning which can be related to a constructed value judgment which is inspired by the drive to know. In the main, these reasonings go in two directions: one holds that the belief in a supreme being originated in the evolution of preliterates' own subjective thinking, the other maintains that this belief had its beginning in an objective, manifestive event on the part of this actually existing being which occurred sometime in the historical past.

During the latter part of the last century it was axiomatic among most anthropologists that the idea of a supreme being and belief in it were the product of a long period of evolutionistic development. Anthropologists of the day attempted to determine how they would have reached such beliefs if they were preliterates. Some reasoned that preliterates, from the idea that they had souls which left the body during dreams and survived it after death, evolved the idea that spirits which had been powerful in this life attained positions of deity in the next life. Even the power of creation was ascribed to these ancestor-deities.[69]

Other anthropologists, representative of the time, reasoned that belief in superior beings or a superior being originated in preliterates' realization that, their magic having failed to alter the course of natural events, superior beings must be directing these events and should be prevailed upon to act in men's favor. Thinking in this manner, the anthropologists reasoned, preliterates came to believe in supreme beings and thus hit upon the basis of religion. The transition was thus made, it was claimed, from magic to religion.[70]

The advances made by anthropology in the intervening years, however, have caused other anthropologists to observe that these theories are pure speculation. They are not held by any anthropologist today. But these theories were so widely accepted as common coin of the anthropological realm that evidence pointing in the opposite direction got but a scant hearing for some time after it was first adduced. The burden of this new evidence was that belief in a supreme being by no means evolved but rather is found among the earliest peoples of which we have records.[71]

According to this explanation, whatever evolution took place was a degeneration from the idea of one supreme being to the notion of a thousand new gods. The extent of the belief in a supreme being was at one time, it is said, well-nigh universal. If this is true, it would mean that belief in a supreme being goes back to the very beginning of time before the races were separated. That this belief was not the result of the mere imaginings of these early peoples, it is said, is shown by its universality and consistent continuity among all early groups.[72]

The clear implication of this is that there was one objective source from which men learned to know of God and to believe in him and this was God's own revelation of himself in the very act of creation. Primitive mono-

[66] Arthur Diamond, *The Evolution of Law and Order* (London, 1951), p. 86.

[67] Albert Muntsch, *Cultural Anthropology* (Milwaukee, 1934), pp. 268–269.

[68] The extent of the belief in a Supreme Being or God among literates is a matter of conjecture. According to one estimate, regarding a section of the United States such as New York City, out of a hundred people about twenty believe in the existence of a supreme being, ten to twenty in his nonexistence, and the balance of sixty to seventy sometimes do and sometimes do not believe or are always in a state of doubt. Arnold Brecht, *Political Theory* (Princeton, 1959), p. 467. Another surmisal regarding western Europeans says that approximately one-half believe in God who is the Christian Creator of all things. Ignace Lepp, *Atheism In Our Time*, trans. by B. Murchland (New York, 1963), p. 190.

[69] Edward Tylor, *Anthropology* (New York, 1916), p. 358.

[70] James Frazer, *The Golden Bough* (abridged ed., New York, 1927), pp. 57–58.

[71] Edward Evans-Pritchard, "Religion," in: Evans-Pritchard and others, *The Institutions of Primitive Society* (Glencoe, 1956), pp. 2–3, 10.

[72] Wilhelm Schmidt, *Origin and Growth of Religion*, trans. by H. J. Rose (New York, 1931), pp. 261–267, 289; Wilhelm Schmidt, *Ursprung der Gottesidee* (6 v., Munster, 1926–1935) 6: p. 485; Wilhelm Koppers, *Primitive Man and His World Picture*, trans. by E. Raybould (New York, 1952), p. 131; Ivar Lissner, *Man, God and Magic*, trans. by J. M. Brownjohn (New York, 1961), p. 219.

theism can be explained, it is stressed, only by the fact of God's having revealed himself to man at the beginning of time. In other words, creation of men by God is the focal point of this explanation of the origin of men's early belief in a supreme being.[73]

The evidence for primordial monotheism has received various evaluations. A large number of anthropologists today agree that the evidence indicates that there was an early belief in a supreme being. As a consequence, the notion of an evolutionary development of belief in a supreme being has been gradually rejected, as we have noted. The beliefs of certain contemporary preliterates themselves indicate the inadequacy of the evolutionistic approach. The religion of the Nuer, which is undoubtedly little changed from what it has been in the past, reflects a sensitivity, refinement, intelligence, and complexity which is hardly congruent with a theory of evolutionistic development.

Not all anthropologists and ethnologists, however, have accepted primordial monotheism as an historical fact. Some have suggested that the alternatives are not limited to animistic evolution or primordial revelation. There could be, it is said, a plurality of centers of origin of belief and religious expression. Others maintain that there are instances of ancient peoples whose belief in a high god gives every evidence of not having begun with a clear idea of deity but of having been the result of gradual advance. Others hold that the case for primordial monotheism starts from a preconceived position and ends up by not proving a true monotheism. The kind of god proved by the proponents of early monotheism, this criticism says, is the vague and uncertain deity of the proverbial common man. It is not the clear-cut idea of God had by Jesus and the Prophets.

Others, maintaining that the evidence is too fragmentary to warrant anything like a definitive statement of the origin of religion, hold that historically the concept of a "Dema-deity" is to be recognized along with that of a "Highest Being." It is suggested that, instead of attempting to locate the origin of religion, emphasis should be placed on the problems with which religion is concerned and on the solutions it offers—solutions which can be found nowhere else. Others have contended that the introduction of a "religious dogma"— primitive revelation—into anthropological-ethnological discussions is unscientific and turns such discussions into theology.

Still others, looking upon anthropology as history rather than as science, maintain that the question of God is one for the philosopher, not the historian. Finally, there are those who make the point that it does not pertain at all to the anthropologist or ethnologist, either as scientist or historian, to attempt to explain the origin of belief in a supreme being and of religion. Their task is not to explain religion but to show its relation to social life. The historian and the scientist as such are limited to interpretations of their data within the ambit of their fields of history and science.[74]

### d. Origin of Man and World

Most concepts of a supreme being relate him to the origin of man and the world.[75] Ngai, the one God of the Gikuyu, is the creator and giver of all things. Leve, the supreme being of the Mende, created the world and everything in it. Asis, the supreme power of the Nandi, is the source of all life. Likewise, the Great Spirit of the Nuer is a creative spirit. Preliterate accounts of the origin of things include the universe and its various aspects, fire, food, animals, and plants, the beginnings of death or illness, the beginnings of societies of men, and the sources of ceremonies and rituals.

Most noteworthy in these accounts of origins is the symbolism of light and the value implicitly placed on it. Over and over light is the central symbol. It is the symbol of human consciousness coming into being from darkness or nothingness. Along with light, the sun or the moon play the part of the conquering hero who annihilates the monster of darkness. The dawn of light and the advent of "creation" are interwoven in preliterate thinking regarding the origin of themselves and the world. The idea of light has greatly influenced accounts of origins.

Reports of preliterate accounts of the origin of man and the world, much like the reports on the origin of religion and the idea of a supreme being, are often interlaced with an appraisal according to the reporter's own value judgments. To some, these accounts are novelistic and fictitious. They are "myths" in the strict sense of the word. To others, the accounts can be taken as historical. They are "myth" only in an accommodated sense. But this double use of the word "myth" has given rise to great ambiguity and confusion. An account given by preliterates of their ideas about the

---

[73] Wilhelm Koppers, *Primitive Man and His World Picture*, trans. by E. Raybould (New York, 1952), pp. 194, 232; Ivar ᴊ .ssner, *Man, God and Magic*, trans. by E. Raybould (New ʸᴼ rk, 1952), pp. 194, 232.

[74] Supreme Being: Jomo Kenyatta, *Facing Mount Kenya* (London, 1953), pp. 233–234; Kenneth Little, *The Mende of Sierra Leone* (London, 1951), pp. 217–218; Edward Evans-Pritchard, *Nuer Religion* (Oxford, 1956), pp. 1, 7, 49, 311; David Bidney, "The Ethnology of Religion and the Problem of Human Evolution," *Amer. Anthropologist* **56** (1954), pp. 5, 16; Herbert Rose, "The Wiro Sky-God," in: Buxton, ed., *Custom is King* (London, 1936), p. 53; Gerardus Van Der Leeuw, *La Religion* (Paris, 1948), pp. 158, 159, 163–165; Adolf Jensen, *Myth and Cult Among Primitive Peoples,* trans. by M. Choldin and W. Weissleder (Chicago, 1963), pp. 8, 9, 325; Edward Evans-Pritchard, "Religion," in: Evans-Pritchard and others, *The Institutions of Primitive Society* (Glencoe, 1956), p. 6.

[75] It is perhaps better to discuss preliterate ideas of the beginnings of man and the world as "origins" rather than as "creation." The word "creation" can have two meanings. It can refer to the supreme being taking something which pre-existed and giving it form and order. Such seems to be the idea which most preliterates have when they speak of the way the supreme being "created" man and the world. "Creation" can also relate to the action of the supreme being by which he, taking nothing which pre-exists because nothing does pre-exist, creates in the strict sense all things whatsoever which exist.

origin of man and the world becomes "myth" only when the reporter himself questions its objective and historical validity according to his own standards. The poetry of Dante becomes "myth" when one questions the convictions which Dante brought to the writing of the *Divine Comedy*. Preliterates use analogies such as sun : light : : creator : creation. But this does not imply that they identify the sun with the creator. It is only when the reporter himself identifies sun and creator that the credibility of such accounts arises. Allegories and metaphorical settings have their place in the communication of facts. They should not, however, be taken as literally identical with the facts they are intended to communicate.

Some anthropologists say it is unfortunate that the word "myth" carries the connotation of untruth. The important point to keep in mind is "who is trying to prove what when he repeats a myth or writes a memoir?"[76] If the word "myth" is so unsatisfactory, perhaps it would be more accurate to speak of preliterates' accounts of origins of man and the world. This could lessen the possibility of reporters' values being superimposed on the facts he reports.

Some preliterate accounts of the origin of man are couched in terms that may appear somewhat fanciful. Underlying the imagery in which it is stated, however, is the clear idea that men were made by powers that were above the human. The gods came to the earth long ago, say the Nabaloi, but there were no people. The gods said it would be good if there were people, so they took some earth and made two people and stood them up. On the principle that they would live if they laughed, the gods caused one of the people to laugh by making a chicken jump. He became a man. The other, hearing the first laugh, laughed also and became a woman. The beliefs of other preliterates are more definite regarding the origin of man and the universe. The Nuer, for instance, say that all things were made by the creative spirit, God. He made the heavens, the earth, the seas, beasts, birds, reptiles, and fish. He is also the source of custom and custom law.

The prevalence of preliterates' value judgment regarding the origin of man and the world appears to be coextensive with their judgment concerning a supreme being. Hence, the value judgment it is good to know that men and the world have their origin in the supreme being seems to be common among preliterate societies.[77]

## II. DECIDING

A man's basic drive to decide is an aspect of his drive to know. The mind's ability to know alternative facts or modes of actions is meaningless as far as action goes unless a man has the power of deciding between these alternatives. Such a power of self-determination is a postulate of all psychology. "[T]he psychologist in the field of personality research either explicitly or implicitly assumes that the human being is the . . . chooser or producer . . . of his activity."[78] "Every school of therapy, even those based on positivism, assumes that the goal of treatment is to lead the patient to a relatively greater freedom of decision than his disorder originally allowed."[79]

This freedom of determination or choice is a unique type of freedom, and should be distinguished from other types of freedom. It is not my freedom of spontaneous action, which means I am under no external force or physical restraint. Nor is it my freedom of independence, which means that I am under no obligation or law. It is rather my freedom of decision, which means that I am under no determination by alternative modes of action which present themselves to me when I cognize them as good and desirable.[80] It is *I* who make the decision between conflicting values.[81] There are, of course, varying degrees of this freedom which I exercise at different times. But to the extent that there is some degree of freedom present, the decision is mine and I am responsible for it.[82]

The drive for decision-making, as is the case with other basic drives, shows itself early in the life of the child. His refusals to follow the directions of others is

*Social Sciences* **2** (1930) : pp. 95–96; Ashley Montagu, *Man: His First Million Years* (Cleveland, 1957), p. 190; David Bidney, *Theoretical Anthropology* (New York, 1953), p. 313; Godfrey Leinhardt, "Modes of Thought," in: Edward Evans-Pritchard and others, *The Institutions of Primitive Society* (Glencoe, 1956), pp. 106–107; Claude Moss, "Kankaney Ceremonies," *Amer. Archaeology and Ethnology* **15** (1919–1922) : p. 384.

[78] Magda Arnold, "Basic Assumptions in Psychology," in: M. Arnold and J. Gleason, eds., *The Human Person* (New York, 1954), p. 47.

[79] Gordon Allport, *Pattern and Growth in Personality* (New York, 1961), pp. 562–563.

[80] "All choices are caused but they are caused by the chooser. All choices are motivated (in fact, where there are alternatives there is a plethora of motives) but the motives are the alternatives as they are apprehended as suitable or unsuitable, desirable or undesirable." Magda Arnold, "Basic Assumptions in Psychology," in: M. Arnold and J. Gleason, eds., *The Human Person* (New York, 1954), p. 40.

[81] "Psychologists, on the basis of both common experience and controlled observation, can recognize in self-determination the ability we have to settle the issue betwen conflicting motives by the active interposition of the ego." Magda Arnold, "Basic Assumptions in Psychology," in: M. Arnold and J. Gleason, eds., *The Human Person* (New York, 1954), pp. 38–39.

[82] Gordon Allport, *Pattern and Growth in Personality* (New York, 1961), p. 563.

[76] Paul Bohannon, *Social Anthropology* (New York, 1963), p. 329.

[77] Origin of man and world: Jomo Kenyatta, *Facing Mount Kenya* (London, 1953), pp. 233–234; Kenneth Little, *The Mende of Sierra Leone* (London, 1951), pp. 217–218; Geoffrey Snell, *Nandi Customary Law* (London, 1954), pp. 1–2; Edward Evans-Pritchard, *Nuer Religion* (Oxford, 1956), pp. 1, 6; Ralph Beals and Harry Hoijer, *An Introduction to Anthropology* (New York, 1953), p. 567; Leslie Paul, *Nature into History* (London, 1957), p. 193; Gerardus Van Der Leeuw, *Religion in Essence and Manifestation*, trans. by J. E. Turner (London, 1938), p. 579; Franz Boas, "Culture," *Encyc. of the*

a manifestation of his desire to make his own decisions.[83] It is through responsible decision-making that every human being grows and develops. When decisions are made for a person too often by others, the effect on the person cannot but be one of enfeeblement.[84] For it is by his decision-making that a man molds his plastic drives according to whatever ideal he has set for himself in his pursuit of his self-actualization and happiness. The image he has chosen for himself, of what he wants to be, controls his future decisions.[85] The plasticity of the drives takes its final meaning from the shape given them by knowledge and free decision. It is this flexibility, as we noted above, which makes many cultures possible.[86]

### A.  UNIVERSAL VALUE JUDGMENTS IN ALL SOCIETIES

Self-determination is a postulate of all culture and law. Hence the value judgment that freedom of decision is good and desirable is universal in all individuals and in all societies. Even those who would deny that there is such a thing as free decision admittedly must act as if they had free decision. There are certain constructed value judgments which all preliterate societies make in regard to deciding. These judgments concern the regulations which guide their decisions, their responsibility for making decisions, the observance and violations of regulations and the consequences of observing or violating regulations.

### 1. *Regulations Concerning Title to Decide*

The regulations which guide the decisions of preliterates, regarding what is necessary in the fulfillment of their common needs, are their custom laws. These, as

---

[83] It is "contrary to human nature to accept any constraint as a matter of course." Bronislaw Malinowski, *Crime and Custom in Savage Society* (New York, 1951), p. 10. See also Melville Herskovits, *Man and His Works* (New York, 1948), pp. 40–41.

[84] Abraham Maslow, *Toward a Psychology of Being* (New York, 1962), pp. 47, 50. "What one sees, what one observes, is inevitably what one selects from a near infinitude of potential percepts. Perceptual selection depends not only upon the 'primary determinants of attention' but is also a servant of one's interests, needs, and values." Leo Postman, Jerome Bruner and Elliot McGinnies, "Personal Values as Selective Factors in Perception," in: Richard Teevan and Robert Birney, eds., *Readings for Introductory Psychology* (New York, 1965), p. 162.

[85] Gordon Allport, *Pattern and Growth in Personality* (New York, 1961), pp. 563–564.

[86] "The dual nature of man, his determinate, psychobiological structure and functions, on the one hand, and his indeterminate, historically acquired cultural personality, on the other, presupposes a certain measure of human freedom, or self-determination. Man is a cultural problem to himself because he is capable of choosing between alternatives and to envisage new forms of expression which he may realize, any given culture or mode of life thus represents an original choice on the part of its adherents taken collectively, since other 'designs for living' are equally compatible with human nature." David Bidney, *Theoretical Anthropology* (New York, 1953), p. 9. See Franz Boas, *Anthropology and Modern Life* (New York, 1928), p. 226.

we saw, are universal among all known preliterate societies. All preliterate societies form the value judgment that it is good to have such guiding regulations. These guides for decision-making are but patterns of action which help in the molding of the drives as they express themselves in everyday living.

### 2. *Failure to Respect Title to Decide: Unjust Repression of Action*

The regulation of decision by law is obviously necessary for the fulfillment of common needs. But again, as was the case with knowledge, regulation of decisions which do not relate to common needs is a failure to respect the individual person's basic title to decide. It is an unjust repression of action. Some regulation of action is obviously a common need. Undisciplined freedom is license. Irresponsible permissiveness is mob rule. To talk of my rights without at the same time stressing my responsibilities, is to speak of my claims on others to respect my titles to things without at the same time recognizing that I have an obligation to respect the titles to things which others also have. The regulation of decisions which do not relate to common needs, however, is dictatorship. In the value judgment that regulation of decisions is good when it fulfils common needs is also implict the value judgment that regulation is evil when it does not fulfill common needs. This value judgment is likewise a postulate in all societies of men.

### 3. *Individual Responsibility for Decisions*

Responsibility follows upon deciding. In making a decision, a person becomes the cause of the decision and of what follows upon the decision. The decision creates a causal relation between the decider and what he does as the result of his decision. Preliterates are no exception to the universal tendency to relate an action, and responsibility for it, to the one who performs the action. This is primary. Whether the responsibility will be later scaled downwards because of certain mitigating factors affecting the freedom in deciding, is secondary. It will be the intention, anger, or negligence of the one who performed the act, and no one else's, which will be in question. The value judgment that it is good and desirable to relate responsibility to the doer of an action is universal in all preliterate societies. It is a postulate of all social living and of all law.

The further value judgment which preliterates make concerning the part these extenuating circumstances play in assessing responsibility is not universal. Preliterates are said to have fixed responsibility originally without taking into account the premeditation or bad intention, the consciousness or unconsciousness of the performer of an action. The very fact that the deed was done was sufficient grounds for imputing responsibility to the doer. On this basis, responsibility was attached to minors, madmen, and even animals. It has usually been said that in preliterate law the ground of responsibility for wrong done, whether to man or animal, is causation and not culpability.

A shift in the grounds of responsibility has gradually taken place, it is said. This change is from *causa* to *culpa,* from cause to fault. Instead of the norm of responsibility being the objective damage caused, it is the subjective state of the doer's mind and intention. Wrongs which were not the result of bad intention or negligence came to be regarded more and more as accidental and not the responsibility of anyone. There is evidence, however, that no such clean-cut shift from causation to culpability took place. From the earliest days, it appears, wrongs were excused on the grounds of self-defense, inevitable accident, mistake, necessity, negligence, and the like. In preliterate law, as we shall see presently, the evidence shows that such excusing factors were recognized generally.[87]

#### 4. *Decision to Violate Regulations—Reactions*

Decisions to keep custom laws or to break them entail values. These values relate to the common needs of the people. For this reason the people react to offenses against custom law and inflict punishment or exact compensation from violators, as we shall see more in detail later. These sanctions are indications of the value judgments the people make concerning decisions to observe or to violate their laws. All preliterate societies value-judge that the observance of custom law is good and that the violation of it is bad. They also value-judge that the punishment which is inflicted, or the compensation which is exacted, is good and desirable.

#### B.   LESS THAN UNIVERSAL VALUE JUDGMENTS

The remaining value judgments regarding deciding and responsibility, which we shall consider, are less than universal. Value judgments concerning actions performed intentionally or accidentally, with malice aforethought or without it, appear to be general among preliterates. So also do value judgments concerning common responsibility appear to be general. Value judgments regarding actions performed by the insane and inebriates, killings done in self-defense, and injuries resulting from negligence, seem to be common.

#### 1. *General*

##### a. *Intention versus Accident*

It has been maintained that preliterates are incapable of distinguishing between intention and accident. It has been asserted, for instance, that preliterates' belief in

suprahuman powers precluded their understanding of an "accidental" occurrence. Because of their belief in witchcraft and possession they are inclined to interpret any incident that occurs as having been directed by spirits. Thus, it is said, if a tree falls upon a man's head, the preliterate says a spirit guided it. If a man who is cutting a branch from a tree drops his axe on another's head, it is because he is temporarily possessed by the soul of another. To the preliterate mentality, it is claimed, there are either incidents which have behind them a suprahuman cause, or there are offenses which are freely intended by the offender who can be easily identified. Thus, among the Carib, when a man kills or poisons another by accident, he is merely acting unconsciously as an agent of some spiritual power. No personal animosity is involved, the solidity of the group is unimpaired, and no compensation is in order. When, however, a man commits an offense of his own free intent and decision, that he is the cause of this act can easily be determined and compensation called for.

The result of preliterates not making a distinction between intention and accident, it is said, is that intentional and accidental harms are treated in the same way. Among the Bapedi, no distinction is made between culpable and purely accidental homicide. Both offenses are treated in the same manner. Compensation for injuries likewise is the same among many peoples whether the injuries were done intentionally or accidentally. With the Bantu, there is no difference in general between the compensation paid for offenses done intentionally and those done accidentally. The Gikuyu near Mount Kenya demand the same compensation for a death caused by accident or design—one hundred goats for a man and thirty for a woman.

With the Dinka, a man who kills another whether by mistake or accident, or on purpose in anger, is liable to the death fine in force in the district. In Yurok custom law, it is reported, the intention of the offender is completely irrelevant. Injury occurred and must be paid for, whether it happened on account of malice, chance, or ignorance. In Kamba custom law, no distinction is made between murder, manslaughter, or accidental death. Blood-price is payable in each case. In an instance such as when a man shoots an arrow at an animal and hits a man beyond, whom he did not know was there, he is considered fully liable.

But there are reports showing that preliterates do make a distinction between intentional and accidental offenses. The evidence for this is widespread. "It is seriously argued here that motive, accident, intention, etc., largely enter into nearly every considered judgment from which the incautious observer would apparently regard them to be absent."[88] The Kavirondo Bantu punish wrongs which are intentional by imposing twice the compensation that is ordinarily imposed for unin-

---

[87] Individual responsibility: Valintin Riasanovsky, *Customary Law of the Nomadic Tribes of Siberia* (Tsiensin, 1938), p. 146; T. Olawale Elias, *The Nature of African Customary Law* (Manchester, 1956), p. 159; Percy Winfield, "The Myth of Absolute Liability," *Law Quart. Rev.* **42** (1926): pp. 37–51; Percy Winfield, "The History of Negligence in the Laws of Torts," *Law Quart. Rev.* **42** (1926): pp. 184–201.

[88] T. Olawale Elias, *The Nature of African Customary Law* (Manchester, 1956), p. 143.

tentional wrongs. The Baluba also distinguish between voluntary and involuntary homicide. In Tswana, acts done through negligence ordinarily involve liability for the harms inflicted. Acts done accidentally, on the other hand, are almost invariably excused or less severely punished. An unsuccessful attempt to do wrong entails less liability than one which has succeeded. The Nuer make a distinction between killings that are intentional and killings that are accidental. The Ashanti likewise discriminate clearly between murder and accidental homicide. Most of their accidental killings are the result of hunting accidents. If it is proved that the killing was not intended, the killer is declared liable only for damages. The Barama River Carib believe that killing is justified and without liability in only two cases, adultery and when the killing is accidental.

A similar view prevails among the Bapedi. When an accidental death occurs among them, the chief investigates to determine whether there was intent to kill. If no intent is found, the killer is free of the capital charge. He must, however, settle the claims the relatives have against him. This compensation supplies the means of raising seed to the deceased if a male, or of compensating the parents for their loss if a female. With the Waboni, if a person kills someone by accident, he is bound merely to produce another person to take the place of the person he killed. The Wateita also distinguish between accidental and other homicide. Other peoples do not even demand compensation when the killing is accidental, though they feel that certain offenses are always intentional. The Barama River Carib do not demand satisfaction for clear cases of accidental killing and accidental poisoning. But it is reported impossible for the mind of the Carib to conceive how sorcery, theft, and adultery can be committed without evil intent.

With the Ifugao, intent is said probably to be the largest factor in determining responsibility. An offense which is committed without carelessness and evil intent is excused. If a bolo flies out of a man's hand and puts out the eye of another, there is no liability involved. A number of men are said to be injured each year, and some even killed, in scuffles which take place over sacrificed carabaos. But even in cases where death occurs, no damages are assessed. Although compensation is not demanded, the offender sometimes shows his regret that he had a part in the accident. A case is given of a not uncommon acident which occurs when many men are engaged in chasing a wild boar. When the boar charges one of the men, the man leaps backward and draws back his spear to throw it at the boar. In doing so, he stabs a fellow-hunter behind him with the shod end of the spear handle. Upon the testimony of the witnesses that the killing was accidental, no damage is levied. The killer, however, as a gesture of his sorrow over the affair usually assists in the funeral feast.[89]

Some preliterates make a distinction between accidental killing and accidental injury to property. Underlying the distinction would seem to be a certain relating of life to the welfare of the community, and property to the welfare of the individual. The Southeastern Bantu, for example, hold that all homicide is a crime because it deprives the chief of a subject. Compensation, therefore, is due to the chief regardless of whether there was evil intent or not. On the other hand, harm done to another's fields or possessions is considered a tort. If the harm was inflicted without intent, the offended is not liable for damages.[90]

When compensation follows an offense regardless of how it was committed, this fact cannot be taken as evidence that no distinction is being made between what is done intentionally and what is done accidently. A distinction regarding intention may not be made as far as compensation goes, but it may be implied concerning punishment. Thus, concerning in-group and out-group killing among the Kapauku, if a man accidentally kills another from the same sib or political unit, he is not punished by execution but he is required to pay blood money to the nearest kin of the dead man. The reason given for this lenient attitude is that the offender did not intend to kill. The killing of a man from another political unit is the equivalent of murder.

It should also be borne in mind that compensation may be demanded for an offense, regardless of whether it was perpetrated intentionally or accidentally, as a means of heading off a continuing blood feud. As among the Yurok, compensation is accepted for the killing or injuring of a person because it is a useful way of obviating an otherwise endless blood feud. But some preliterate groups consider blood retaliation to be a matter of such sacred duty that it cannot be compensated for by any kind of money payment.

The use of compensation for either intentional or accidental killings to avoid blood vengeance is further shown by the difference drawn by some peoples between in-group and out-group killings. With the Nandi, the clan of a man who was killed, whether deliberately or accidentally, had to be paid blood money by the clan of the killer. Blood-money was not payable, therefore, if the person killed was of the same clan as the killer. In such a situation, a reduced compensation of two or three cattle would be payable depending on the circumstances of the case. Sometimes the manner in which compensation is made indicates that a distinction is recognized between intentional and accidental homicide. Throughout the Machakos District of Kenya, for instance, homicide is compensable by the blood-money payment of eleven cows, the first cow of which is called the "cow of the accident." This arrangement, it has been said,

---

[89] In Islamic law, as in other written law, the difference between intentional and accidental homicide is recognized. See,

James Anderson, *Islamic Law in Africa* (London, 1954), p. 358. In Chinese law, killings that were accidental have been punished the same as if they were intentional. See Leonard Hobhouse, *Morals in Evolution* (New York, 1906), p. 87.

[90] Crimes and torts will be explained later.

shows that the greater part of the homicides which occur in this area are deemed to be accidents and without evil intent.

The existence of places of refuge among a people indicates that they make a distinction between offenses that are intentional and offenses that are unintentional or accidental. Otherwise such sanctuary lacks a meaningful rationale. If the killing is intentional, the offender should be punished. If it is accidental, he should be protected until the anger of the blood avengers has subsided or been placated by compensation. References to cities of refuge are very old. The code of the Hebrews specifies that there shall be such places of sanctuary where those who have killed unintentionally may take refuge until they are safe.[91] Places of refuge exist among preliterates. In Samoa, a killer could seek asylum with any 'talking chief.' Whether the chief could give him protection depends on the amount of authority the chief had in the village. There were places which were commonly respected as places of refuge.

With both the Nandi and Masai, a killer will hide himself for a time in order to protect himself from the avenging brothers, sons, and cousins of the deceased. Among the Nandi, the killer may take refuge under a tree or by a river. It is reported that no Nandi will kill a man who has taken refuge in this manner. A Nuer may take refuge in the hut of the leopard-skin chief. The chief supposedly is sufficiently respected and revered to keep anyone from spilling blood in his presence. Places of refuge among preliterates are, then, but another indication of their realization of the difference between intentional and accidental offenses.

The value judgment, then, that it is good to distinguish between actions which are performed intentionally and those which occur accidentally appears to be general in preliterate societies.[92]

### b. Hot Blood versus Cold Blood

Preliterates distinguish between actions done in hot blood and actions done in cold blood. Among the Cheyenne, for instance, a killing done without forethought and intention lessened responsibility. In fact, it lessened it several degrees. With the Wadigo, a cold-blooded murder demands a compensation four times the number of persons demanded by a killing in hot blood.

Among the Akamba, offenses committed during anger or rage may be excused. If a rapist is killed in the act, the killer is not liable for compensation. In Tswana, if the killer was provoked to do what he did, this provocation is looked on as excusing from guilt and rendering the act justifiable. Among Nandi, also, provocation was considered to excuse from responsibility for a killing especially if it occurred immediately upon the provocation. With the Gikuyu, unless a man is a foreign enemy, it is considered a crime against all the people to strike and murder him without warning. The man who kills another in cold blood is shown the greatest contempt because he has disgraced himself and his age-group.

In whatever reports are available, preliterates are seen making the distinction between actions performed in hot and cold blood. Hence, the opinion may be ventured that the value judgment preliterates make that it is good to distinguish between premeditated and unpremeditated actions is general in preliterate societies.[93]

### c. Collective Responsibility for Decisions

Among most preliterates, the actions of the individual person, especially the harmful ones, reverberate concentrically to the group of which he is a member. This is inevitable in kinship living. The individual is so merged into his group that the group is often considered collectively responsible for his offenses against those outside the group. With preliterates, besides individual responsibility there is also collective responsibility.

Generally, the group is responsible for the individual's offenses against the whole community and pays compensation for the harms done to other individuals. Thus, with the Ifugao, the kin of an individual are responsible for his actions to a degree only slightly less

[91] Numbers 35: 11–12; Deuteronomy 19: 4–6.

[92] Intention v. accident: Leonard Hobhouse, *Morals in Evolution* (New York, 1906), p. 84; John Gillin, "Crime and Punishment Among the Barama River Carib," *Amer. Anthropologist* 36 (1934): pp. 334, 337; C. L. Harries, *The Laws and Customs of the Bapedi and Cognate Tribes of the Transvaal* (rev. ed., Johannesburg, 1929), pp. 101, 103; Charles Dundas, "The Organization and Laws of Some Bantu Tribes," *Jour. Royal Anthropol. Inst.* 45 (1915): p. 272; Lewis Tupper, "Customary and Other Law in the East Africa Protectorate," *Jour. Soc. Comp. Legislation* 8 (1908): pp. 175–176; Hugh O'Sullivan, "Dinka Laws and Customs," *Jour. Royal Anthropol. Inst.* 40 (1910): p. 189; Robert Lowie, *An Introduction to Cultural Anthropology* (2nd ed., New York, 1940), p. 286; Isaac Schapera, *A Handbook of Tswana Law and Custom* (London, 1938), p. 51; D. J. Penwill, *Kamba Customary Law* (London, 1951), p. 81; Paul Howell, *A Manual of Nuer Law* (London, 1954), p. 223; Robert Rattray, *Ashanti Law and Constitution* (Oxford, 1929), p. 296; Ralph Barton, "Ifugao Law," *Amer. Archaeology and Ethnology* 15 (1919): pp. 65–66; Robert Lowie, *Primitive Society* (New York, 1920), p. 401; Leopold Pospisil, *Kapauku Papuans and Their Law* (New Haven, 1958), pp. 149–150; Geoffrey Snell, *Nandi Customary Law* (London, 1954), p. 63; T. Olawale Elias, *The Nature of African Customary Law* (Manchester, 1956), p. 142; Richard Cherry, *Lectures in the*

*Growth of Criminal Law in Ancient Communities* (London, 1890), p. 46; Julius Lips, "Government," in: Franz Boas, ed., *General Anthropology* (Boston, 1938), p. 525; Arthur Diamond. *The Evolution of Law and Order* (London, 1951), p. 108.

[93] Hot blood v. cold blood: Karl Llewellyn and E. Adamson Hoebel, *The Cheyenne Way* (Norman, 1941), p. 138; Robert Hamilton, "East African Native Laws and Customs," *Jour. Comp. Legislation* 11 (1910): p. 183; Lewis Tupper, "Customary and Other Law in the East Africa Protectorate," *Jour. Soc. Comp. Legislation* 8 (1908): p. 176; Isaac Schapera, *A Handbook of Tswana Law and Custom* (London, 1938), p. 51; Geoffrey Snell, *Nandi Customary Law* (London, 1954), pp. 83–84; Jomo Kenyatta, *Facing Mount Kenya* (London, 1953), p. 227.

than his and in proportion to the nearness of their kinship. This holds both for his torts and his crimes. Among the Nuer, collective responsibility is operative to the point where there is rarely an isolated individual wrong. The extent of the wrong is related to the relationship of the related kin.

A man's responsibility for the actions of his wives and children can touch his nearest clan relatives. With the Nandi, if a man is unable to pay compensation for the offenses of his wives and children, as well as his own, his near clan relatives are bound to come to his aid. With the Kalinga, the responsibility for an offender's torts is usually centered on himself or his nearest kin. A man's fields will be seized first, if he has any. If not, the fields of his brothers or sisters will be taken. Failing this, the fields of his first cousin will be possessed. But the responsibility for an offender's crimes may be inflicted on any member of the offender's group, male or female and sometimes even a third cousin. Because the retaliating group is ready to pay compensations, they will pick a victim who has the fewest near relatives.

The collective responsibility of the family and the clan extends also to the actions of the insane. With the Kamba, a madman's family and clan are held responsible for his actions. They are supposed to care for him properly. In a case where a madman killed another man with his arrow, his clan was held responsible on the grounds that they were responsible even though he was not. The age at which children begin to participate in the collective responsibility of the group varies among preliterates. With the Kalinga, it is said to be somewhere around eleven to thirteen years of age. The group's responsibility for the child begins much sooner, but demands are lessened according to various circumstances.

The idea of collective responsibility is, of course, not limited to preliterates. It has been prevalent in the ancient East, in ancient Persia, and in many countries of medieval Europe. It has been in the Far East, China, Korea, Japan, and France until the time of the Revolution. In the early law of the Hebrews, collective responsibility prevailed. In the course of time, however, there was a shift to individual responsibility.[94]

In collective responsibility motive, intention, accident, and negligence on the part of the individual offender become more or less immaterial. Causation, and not culpability, is predominant. An injury has been caused, regardless of the circumstances, and retaliation or compensation are called for. Someone has been killed and the family of the deceased must have some satisfaction out of the killer and his family. The part played here by any attenuating circumstances is minimal.

The value judgment that it is good for the group to be collectively responsible for the offenses of its individual members appears to be general among preliterate societies.[95]

## 2. Common

### a. Insanes and Inebriates

Persons incapable of some degree of knowledge and free decision are not responsible for their actions. The question of whether those deemed insane or drunk have this minimal requirement of knowledge and freedom, and to what degree, is a good example of divergently constructed judgments.

Preliterates recognize that certain persons among them are incapable of conduct and judgment which is regarded by the group as normal and rational. These individuals are judged to be mentally deficient. Among the Tiv, for instance, a case is reported in which a madman killed a woman who was married to a man from a neighboring lineage. A girl from the killer's lineage was given to the victim's husband as a replacement. The elders said this unusual procedure was allowed in this particular instance because they had erred in letting the killer go free. They knew he was mad but thought it was only "the small madness." [96]

Symptoms considered by the Alor as indicative of insanity are such actions as spending the night in the fields rather than returning to the house, shouting and singing the whole night on the trail, destructive attacks on animals and crops, attacking people indiscriminately with stones, clubs, and arrows, grabbing up children and running off with them, and eating refuse with animals. Violence, obscenity, and scatologic behavior are consistently reported as symptomatic of insanity.

The manner in which those considered insane are treated also confirms the fact that preliterates recognize insanity among themselves. In Indonesia, the insane are permitted to roam at large if they are not dangerous. If they become violent, they are tied up but they are not killed. In Kamba a dangerous madman would have his hands and feet chained. Again, it is said that the clan would not kill him because of the trouble he had caused. Among the Nandi, insanity was not socially ridiculed but was considered to be a sickness. A violently mad man was tied in a hut by himself and fed by his relatives. His children were placed in the hands of

---

[94] Leonard Hobhouse, *Morals and Evolution* (New York, 1906), pp. 87–88; Ezekiel 18: 2; Jeremiah 31: 29; Deuteronomy 24: 16.

[95] Collective responsibility: Ralph Barton, "Ifugao Law," *Amer. Archaeology and Ethnology* 15 (1919): p. 14; Paul Howell, *A Manual of Nuer Law* (London, 1954), p. 23; Geoffrey Snell, *Nandi Customary Law* (London, 1954), p. 83; Ralph Barton, *The Kalingas* (Chicago, 1949), pp. 218–219; D. J. Penwill, *Kamba Customary Law* (London, 1951), p. 102.

[96] Paul Bohannon, *Justice and Judgment Among the Tiv* (London, 1957), p. 148. The words "insane" or "mad" carry for us here only the broad meaning that preliterates give them, namely, the inability to think and act as others in the group do who are considered normal. How psychiatrists would diagnose these conditions and under what classification of mental defect or deficiency they would put them is immaterial to the fact that preliterates do make a distinction between the sane and the insane.

those who would have charge of them if the man died. If he should recover, he could claim them back. Anticipating the possibility of recovery, a man's property was not distributed until he had died.

Among some preliterates the insane are not held responsible for their actions. In places in Africa, the family were held responsible for his offenses. The reasoning behind this judgment was that his family should have given him the necessary care. Or they should have kept him in confinement so that he would not be free to hurt people. The family is responsible for any offense the man commits while at large. Among the Nomadic tribes of Siberia, insane men were not punished. A similar situation prevailed among the Nandi.

At one time among the Ashanti, madness in a killer was a reason for not executing him. He was tied to a tree and left to die, unless food was brought to him by his relatives. It is said that one of the reasons why the Ashanti did not execute mad killers was that they were superstitiously reluctant to kill a man with such an affliction. There were suspicions, however, that although a man may be abnormal there may be some degree of mental capacity still remaining in him. The Ashanti King Osai Yao questioned the justice of excusing a killer because of madness. He set up a test. He put a drunkard and a madman in a house together. The house was then set on fire. The madman soon began to scream that he was being burned and ran outside the house. The drunkard remained still and was burned to death.[97]

Among other preliterates, the Ifugao for instance, insanity is not at all an alleviating circumstance in cases of murder, although it is in other offenses. With the Kamba, if a madman kills someone either he or his clan are expected to pay blood-money. If he burns down a house, he or his clan must pay compensation. If he steals repeatedly, he is executed in the normal fashion. If he murdered several people, he would pay the blood-money for each but would not be put to death.[98]

Drunkenness is also considered by some preliterates as excusing from responsibility. Others look on it as non-excusing. In some African law, drunkenness produced by ordinary intoxication is said to be no defense against any kind of charge. The reasoning back of this position is that a man is responsible for getting himself

drunk and should therefore be responsible for whatever offenses he commits while in this condition. Among the Nabaloi, if two men got into a fight while they were drunk and one killed the other, the killer was hung.

On the other hand, drunkenness is considered by some preliterates as diminishing responsibility. Among the Ifugao, being drunk lessens responsibility and punishment, provided there is no evidence that the inebriate became intoxicated with the intention of committing the offense and that he sincerely is sorry when he is sober. Among some Africans, killings which result from unpremeditated drunken brawls are looked on as manslaughter and not murder. Inebriates, it is reasoned, are incapable of forming any intention, much less a guilty one. If a man is made drunk by others and in this state he commits an offense, those who made him drunk are responsible for the offense and not he. With the Basonge, drunkenness lessens responsibility.

From these few samples of reporting, one gets the impression that the value judgment is common among preliterates that it is good to consider that insanity and inebriety lessen responsibility. The impression is also formed that the value judgment is common among preliterate societies that it is good to consider that insanity and inebriety do not lessen responsibility.[99]

### b. Negligence

From the reports available on negligence, it appears that preliterates commonly differentiate between harms done accidentally and harms done intentionally and negligently. The Ifugao are cited as an example of the people who carefully discriminate between voluntary and involuntary actions, and between actions which are purely accidental and those which result from carelessness. If a knife flies out of a man's hand and puts another man's eye out, it is considered accidental and no damages will be assessed. If a man is throwing spears at a target and kills a child who runs in the way, he is considered negligent in not taking proper precautions and must pay half the fine for manslaughter. If a man kills a neighbor whom he mistakes for an enemy, a heavy fine is imposed on the grounds of negligence aggravated by intent to kill.

In Tswana a man who commits an offense through negligence is considered responsible for the act and is liable for any resulting damage. Among the Nandi,

---

[97] Worthy of some consideration is whether such preliterate judicial wisdom in these matters is consonant with the well-known *M'Naghten* rules in criminal law for assessing the mental condition of an accused or with the rule of the more recent *Durham* decision which calls the adequacy of the former rules into question.

[98] The manner in which preliterates sometimes explain the etiology of insanity is irrelevant to the fact that they recognize insanity as an abnormal state. In some places what would be "described as a nervous or psychological derangement may be regarded in primitive societies as possession by a spirit or demon." Godfrey Leinhardt, "Modes of Thought," in: Edward Evans-Pritchard and others, *The Institutions of Primitive Society* (Glencoe, 1956), p. 103.

[99] Insanes and inebriates: Cora DuBois, *The People of Alor* (Minneapolis, 1944), pp. 157–158; Barend Ter Haar, *Adat Law in Indonesia* (New York, 1948), p. 149; D. J. Penwill, *Kamba Customary Law* (London, 1951), p. 102; Geoffrey Snell, *Nandi Customary Law* (London, 1954), p. 84; T. Olawale Elias, *The Nature of African Customary Law* (Manchester, 1956), pp. 141, 143–144; Valintin Riasanovsky, *Customary Law of the Nomadic Tribes of Siberia* (Tsiensin, 1938), p. 117; Ralph Barton, "Ifugao Law," *Amer. Archaeology and Ethnology* 15 (1919) : p. 65; D. J. Penwill, *Kamba Customary Law* (London, 1951), p. 102; C. R. Moss, "Nabaloi Law and Ritual," *Amer. Archaeology and Ethnology* 15 (1920) : p. 257; Robert Rattray, *Ashanti Law and Constitution* (Oxford, 1929), pp. 133, 296–303.

harms which occur accidentally, except to persons, are not punishable, but harms which occur because of negligence are compensable. With the Ankole in Uganda, compensation demanded for harms from negligence can be talionic. When a man is injured or killed accidentally while hunting with members of another clan, this clan has to compensate the injured or dead man's clan by payment of goods. But when a man of very high rank is killed and it can be shown that his death was due to the negligence of his hosts, the deceased's clan can demand that a man of the hosts' clan be killed. In South Africa injuries done to property by accident carry no liability, but those inflicted negligently or intentionally must be compensated for. In cases where a man's animals have caused damage, he is held liable on the basis of his own negligence. Negligence or carelessness is looked on as indifference to the common welfare for which a person is responsible.[100]

From the reports available, it would appear that preliterate societies commonly value-judge that it is good to hold persons responsible for harms done on account of negligence.[101]

CHAPTER 6

MINE AND THINE

The value judgments we shall now consider contribute further to the humaneness of men's existence. They relate to justice and its basis in the distinction between mine and thine. The foundations of this chapter have already been set out above. Justice is the constant disposition of one's will to give others what is due to them.[1] What is due to me, as we have seen, is respect on the part of others for the unique relations of title which obtain between some thing and myself. But to distinguish between what is due to me and what is not is to distinguish between what is mine and what is thine. Or, to put it another way, the distinction between mine and thine is the basis of justice. This distinction underlies the identity of value judgments themselves. It is only in the light of this distinction that I can speak of my ideas, my judgments, my decisions, my responsibility, my wrongs and my guilt. "At the very basis of

primitive morality stands the distinction between Mine and Thine." [2]

The distinction between me and thee, between mine and thine, is elementary to other concepts of persons and things as found in all cultures. Fundamental in every man's thinking is the fact that he distinguishes himself from all else. The self is the axis of every man's world view. Preliterates make this distinction as well as literates. The concept of inviolability depends on the distinction between me and thee, mine and thine. Respect for the inviolability of persons, things, and animals and even for certain kinds of situations, is taught all children. Part of this attitude is respect for others' relations of title. But, again, this concept presupposes the distinction between me and thee, mine and thine.

## I. UNIVERSAL VALUE JUDGMENTS

The value judgments which are universal in this area concern the distinction itself between mine and thine, respect for titles to things, failure to show this respect, and ways of establishing titles to things. In other words, we shall be dealing with the preliterate custom law of property, with theft, and with the procedures by which titles to property are acquired. The value judgment which is almost universal in this area regards occupation as a way of establishing title.

### A. IN ALL SOCIETIES

The value judgment that it is good to distinguish mine from thine is universal in all individuals and in all societies. It undergirds the universal value judgment that it is desirable to give every man what is due to him. All men manifest this desire to some extent. The term "justice," or its approximate equivalent, exists everywhere as a separate category of thought. There is everywhere a desire to see equal justice done. There is the daily experience of recognizing injustice when we see unequal treatment handed out to different people for no apparent reason.[3] All men living in human society have some notion about the rules of justice.[4]

[100] On "strict" or "absolute" liability, in which negligence is *eo ipso* immaterial, see Thomas Davitt, *The Elements of Law* (Boston, 1959), pp. 224–243.

[101] Negligence: Robert Lowie, *Primitive Society* (New York, 1920), p. 401; Ralph Barton, "Ifugao Law," *Amer. Archaeology and Ethnology* 15 (1919): p. 66; Isaac Schapera, *A Handbook of Tswana Law and Custom* (London, 1938), p. 51; Geoffrey Snell, *Nandi Customary Law* (London, 1954), p. 84; Kalervo Oberg, "Crime and Punishment in Tlingit Society," *Amer. Anthropologist* 36 (1934): p. 150; S. M. Seymour, *Native Law in South Africa* (Capetown, 1953), pp. 187, 189.

[1] "We see that all men mean by justice that kind of state of character which makes people disposed to do what is just and makes them act justly and wish for what is just; and similarly by injustice that state which makes them act unjustly and wish for what is unjust." Aristotle, *Nicomachean Ethics*, Book V, chap. 1, 1129*7-10, trans. by W. D. Ross, in: Richard McKeon, ed., *The Basic Works of Aristotle* (New York, 1941), p. 1002.

[2] F. E. Williams, "Group Sentiment and Primitive Justice," *Amer. Anthropologist* 43 (1941): p. 532. The drive to distinguish mine from thine is not the same as either the so-called "acquisitive drive" or the "aggressive drive." It is most basic and is presupposed by both.

[3] Arnold Brecht, *Political Theory* (Princeton, 1959), p. 389. It has been shown that the idea of justice develops early in the mind of the child and by no means merely as the result of instruction by adults. "We find that the notions of justice and solidarity develop correlatively and as a function of the mental age of the child." Jean Piaget, *The Moral Judgment of the Child,* trans. by M. Gabain (Glencoe, 1948), p. 312.

[4] "I think that our studies of African law demonstrate that all men, because they live in society, have some theory of rules of justice which they believe arise from reason itself; and my own evidence on the Barotse—the only evidence we have—suggests that Africans may well have formulated, in embryonic form at least, a theory of natural justice coming from human kindness itself." Max Gluckman, "Natural Justice in Africa," *Natural Law Forum* 9 (1964): p. 44.

### 1. *Regulations Regarding Title to Things*

Universally there are regulations concerning the exchange of relations of title and the failure to respect them. All societies of men regulate the transfer of property and they regulate theft. "Property will here be understood in the sense explained above, that is, as a web of relations which exists between persons in regard to some thing. "Perhaps the most widespread of all legal regulations are those concerned with the sanctity of property rights and of human life." [5] "Although all societies recognize the existence of individual property, all of them also place certain limits on its acquisition." [6] "[A] sense of property is a social necessity, and . . . if men are to live together, a curb on their desires is essential." [7] The value judgment that it is good to regulate property relations is universal among all societies of preliterates.

### 2. *Failure to Respect Title to Things: Theft*

When the respect due to others' relations of title is not given, the result is a failure in justice. Violation of these "property" claims is theft. All societies of men disapprove theft. "[T]hat all of them disapprove of it [theft] may be inferred from the universal custom of subjecting a detected thief to punishment or revenge, or, at the very least, of compelling him to restore the stolen property to its owner." [8]

The universal disapproval of theft or robbery indicates that property claims exist among all known societies of men. The abstract term "property" may not be used. But phrases are used which express much more clearly the unique relations of title which exist between individual persons and things. Such phrases as "This is mine," "This is his," "I owe him," "He owes me," "The house belongs to me," "This is my ground" communicate the relational aspect of property much better than the word "property" itself.

There can be no question but that the idea of property relation between individual persons and things is universal in all societies of men. "[T]here is no known culture without some institution of private property." [9] "[P]roperty as an institution is a unique as well as a ubiquitous human institution." [10] "Private property is

nowhere absent." [11] "A review of the relevant facts leaves no room for doubt that property as an historic phenomenon is indeed co-extensive with man as we know him." [12] "We do not know a single tribe that does not recognize individual property." [13] "[T]here is no society in which there is a complete communal ownership or property. A man's trousers, or their local equivalent, always belong to him." [14] "All legal systems give cognizance to the existence of rights to private property in some goods." [15]

It should be understood, of course, that when the claims of preliterates to individual property are spoken of, these claims are not completely absolute any more than are the claims of literates to "private property." The absolute dominion of one person over one thing is not the rule but the exception. Even in reports which relate that the individual has absolute dominion over his property to the exclusion of possible intrusion by public authority, it is added that the family or clan always has a claim to control over the property of its members.

Regarding failure to respect relations of title, most noteworthy is where preliterates put the emphasis in the triadic concept of "right" as analyzed above. When my relations are disrespected, preliterates put the accent not on my claims but on others' obligation. It is not my claims on others to do what they are obliged to do which is stressed. It is others' obligation in justice to respect my relations which is of primary importance. Thus among the Tiv, "their emphasis is on means of making others carry out their obligation. They discuss social acts by comparing them with what one 'ought' to do or to have done. Both the jir [court] and the institutions of self-help are used for the same purpose, that of making people carry out their obligations towards one." [16] The instincts of preliterate peoples are surer in this matter than those of many literate peoples. For preliterates, the fight is not for having civil rights enforced but for having civil obligations fulfilled.

The value judgment, therefore, that it is good and

[5] Mischa Titiev, *Introduction to Cultural Anthropology* (New York, 1959), p. 299.

[6] Ralph Linton, *The Study of Man* (New York, 1936), p. 142. "The methods for doing this are highly variable, suggesting that the acquisitive tendencies of individuals are fairly easy to inhibit or direct as soon as physical needs have been provided for." Linton, *ibid.*

[7] H. Ian Hogbin, "Social Reactions to Crime: Law and Morals in the Schouten Islands," *Jour. Royal Anthropol. Inst.* 68 (1939): p. 261.

[8] Edward Westermarck, *The Origin and Development of the Moral Ideas* (2 v., London, 1908–1912) 2: p. 3.

[9] Margaret Mead, "Some Anthropological Considerations Concerning Natural Law," *Natural Law Forum* 6 (1961): p. 53.

[10] A. Irving Hallowell, "The Nature and Function of Property as a Social Institution," *Jour. Legal and Polit. Sociology* 1 (1943): p. 135.

[11] Robert Lowie, *An Introduction to Cultural Anthropology* (2nd ed., New York, 1940), p. 283.

[12] Alexander Goldenweiser, *Anthropology* (New York, 1937), p. 146.

[13] Franz Boas, *Anthropology and Modern Life* (New York, 1928), p. 237.

[14] Ralph Linton, *The Study of Man* (New York, 1936), p. 142. "A destooled Chief [among the Ashanti] was always permitted to take away the cloths which he was actually wearing when destooled, an interesting indication of the possible identification of a person with his clothes." Robert Rattray, *Ashanti Law and Constitution* (Oxford, 1929), p. 332.

[15] E. Adamson Hoebel, *The Law of Primitive Man* (Cambridge, Mass., 1954), p. 286.

[16] Paul Bohannon, *Justice and Judgment Among the Tiv* (London, 1957), p. 131. On the relation between preliterates' emphasis on obligation and the dominance of status in various aspects of their custom law, see Max Gluckman, *The Ideas in Barotse Jurisprudence* (New Haven, 1965), *passim.*

desirable for individuals to have unique relations of title to things is universal among all known societies of men. All men judge that individual property is good and not evil.

A parenthetical note is called for here. It has been held by some that there was a time in the early existence of mankind when all things were either unrelated to any particular individual or were related to all the individuals in one clan-group—with few minor and inconsequential exceptions. Men supposedly went through the stages of barbarism, savagery, and civilization. In the original state, all things were supposed to be communal. This included sex as we saw above. In succeeding stages, it is said, the relationship of things to individuals gradually made inroads into the relationships of things to all the members of the clan. This was an after-development which sprang not from men's nature but from a passion of greed that gradually crept into human living. Whatever things were originally related to individuals were trifling and inconsequential. All property, besides scanty clothing, a few ornaments and a few utensils, were held in common by all the people of a community.

But there is no supporting anthropological data for such a theory of communal property. A universal clan system is essential to the theory and there is no evidence that such a system ever existed. The assumption that land was not uniquely related to individuals and families in the hunting state of men's history is without a factual basis. Further, certain practices were misinterpreted as indicating that no things were owned by individuals. The destruction of an individual's personal possessions at death and the attachment of camping sites and hunting territories to large groups led some to think that no property was held by individuals.

The main inspiration of the theory of original communal ownership appears to have been simplistic, straight-line evolution. The simple, which is "lower," must chronologically precede the complex, which is "higher." Evolution in the last century, as physics in the present century, became the "shibboleth" which solved all problems. The denial of landownership by hunters and pastoralists has been linked with the evolutionary theories of the nineteenth century. Communal ownership was one of the "ad hoc concoctions of the evolutionists" who were seeking something less definite and specific than individual ownership.[17]

The theory of primordial, communal ownership was warmly embraced by proponents of Marxism. It was used by Engels in his development of Marx's social history.[18] Here was anthropological evidence, it was thought, which sustained the ideological position that the ownership of the means of production by individuals

was the root of all economic and social evil and that it should be eradicated from the cultures of men. The theory of communal ownership gave historical dimension to Marx's economic ideas. But, as has been pointed out, it would be equally or more credible to hold that originally there was primordial individualism, all individualistic behavior was a survival of this, and that all communal activities were the result of gradually encroaching social control over the individual person.[19]

### 3. *Ways of Establishing Relations of Title*

Preliterate custom law recognizes specific ways of establishing relations of title between things and persons. Men do not promiscuously appropriate for themselves whatever strikes their fancy. Everywhere men have rules demanding respect for these relations and prohibiting disrespect for them. In other words, all societies recognize certain ways of acquiring title relations and theft is not one of them.

There are basic relations of title established by men's basic drives. All normal men form accordingly certain given value judgments, as we have seen. Men also fashion other relations of title and in all societies form other value judgments regarding them. These relations of title are brought into existence either by, what we may designate as, my own creative actions or by my own enterprising activities.

#### a. Labor

The most prevalent way relations of title are established between a thing and an individual person is by the person's creative actions. This is labor or art in its broadest sense. It is the process by which human beings bring things into existence. This may be by actions which approach the purely creative, as when I think of a new idea. Or it may be by actions which create new aspects of things already existing, as when I give to a piece of ivory the form of a figurine. It is

[17] Alexander Goldenweiser, *Anthropology* (New York, 1937), p. 147.

[18] Friederich Engels, *The Origin of the Family, Private Property and the State in the Light of the Researches of Lewis H. Morgan* (London, 1884), *passim*.

[19] Theft: Robert Redfield, "The Primitive World View," *Proc. Amer. Philos. Soc.* **96** (1952): p. 30; Ralph Barton, *The Half-Way Sun* (New York, 1930), p. 40; Lawrence Frank, *Society As The Patient* (New Brunswick, 1948), p. 143; Edmund Cahn, *The Sense of Injustice* (New York, 1949), *passim*. Julius Lips, "Naskapi Law," *Trans. Amer. Philos. Soc.* **37** (1947): p. 427; Julius Lips, "Government," in: Franz Boas, ed., *General Anthropology* (Boston, 1938), p. 494; Charles Dundas, "The Organization and Laws of Some Bantu Tribes," *Jour. Royal Anthropol. Inst.* **45** (1915): p. 291; Lewis Morgan, *Ancient Society* (Chicago, 1907), p. 537; E. Sidney Hartland, *Primitive Law* (London, 1924), p. 85; William Rivers, *Social Organization* (New York, 1924), pp. 106–107; E. Adamson Hoebel, "Anthropology of Inheritance," *Social Meaning of Legal Concepts* **1** (1948): p. 24; Robert Lowie, "Incorporeal Property in Primitive Society," *Yale Law Jour.* **37** (1928): p. 551; Margaret Mead, "Some Anthropological Considerations Concerning Natural Law," *Natural Law Forum* **6** (1961): p. 53; Huntington Cairns, "Law and Anthropology," in: Victor Calverton, ed., *The Making of Man* (New York, 1931), p. 333; A. Irving Hallowell, "The Nature and Function of Property as a Social Institution," *Jour. Legal and Polit. Sociology* **1** (1943): p. 127; Ralph Piddington, *An Introduction to Social Anthropology* (London, 1950), p. 315.

to the products of my creative actions, the new idea of the figurine, that I have a unique relation of title.

The unique relation which exists between the product of a man's creative efforts and himself is universally recognized in all preliterate societies. "By and large, what an individual makes, wears, or uses as a tool or weapon, is owned by him. This applies both to men and women. In this sense, individual property is universal among primitives." [20] "There is to some extent a psychological identity between an artisan and his creation. Primitive societies do in some degree recognize the artifact as 'an extension of personality,' and they do establish property relations in recognition thereof. Special identification of the individual with a particular good is the foundation of personal property and of inheritance." [21] "[F]rom the beginning, things identified as products of a man's labour are recognized as his. Even among the rudest peoples there is property in weapons, implements, dress, decorations, and other things in which the value given by labour bears a specially large proportion to the value of the raw material." [22]

The things to which preliterates consider they establish title by their creative efforts are both intangible and tangible. Thus, such intangibles as songs, stories, magical rites and formulae, and individual names are looked upon as individual property because of the basic creative effort which has gone into them. These things have exchange value as much as does "good will" among literates. Among the Central Eskimo, magical formulae used by hunters are intangibles to which individuals may have title. With the Greenland Eskimo spells are individually owned. The Carib consider their sorcerers and medicine men to have individual title to their knowledge and techniques.

Among the Andaman Islanders, the singing of certain songs is a matter of individual title. This is also the case among the Greenlanders. Among the North American Indians and the inhabitants of the Eastern Torres Straits Islands the recounting of legends is a thing to which only certain individuals have title. With the natives of British Columbia certain names and magical formulae are individual "property." The Carib likewise consider their personal names, which are secret, as individually owned. To prevent misuse, they guard the name closely and reveal it only to intimates.

With the Plains Indians, the songs and mystic power connected with shields were intangibles which were singularly related to individuals. Among other Indians,

such as the Crow in Montana, certain designs which might be painted on the cheeks were individually owned intangibles. In places where land is not owned by anyone in particular, the claim to hunting-use of the land by individuals is an example of an intangible individually owned. This was the situation among the Lango. Any encroachment by hunters on individually claimed hunting territory was looked on as wrong.

Tangibles also are things to which preliterates consider they acquire individual relations of title. The tools which a person makes are regarded as his as long as he uses them. Household utensils, dress, ornaments, and weapons are the individual property of the individual who makes them. Among the Andamanese bows and pots are individually owned by their maker. With the Tlingit, the canoes, tools, traps, weapons, masks, and dancing shirts which a person makes are his. Among the Ifugao, the one who makes the knife, spear, dish, basket, pot, house, blanket is its individual owner. With the Carib, all things are said to be owned individually. These include a man's house, hunting and fishing equipment, his canoes, ornaments and tools. For the women, individual ownership embraces the implements she uses in the field and the house, the pottery she makes, her clothing and ornaments.

Dances are regarded by preliterates as the individual property of the original inventor. Among the Trobrianders, only the one who has invented a dance can perform it in his village. Saddles made for themselves by Comanche Indian women were held by them as their own property. With the Semang, it is the builder of a hut who is its owner. Among the Nabaloi, the man who first digs a ditch is its owner. If someone makes a ditch above the first one constructed, the elders will give the water to the one who made the first ditch.

The labor which is expended on the cultivation of land is considered by preliterates as establishing a relation of title to the land. Among the Nabaloi, land becomes the property of the one who works it first. In Ukamba, a man acquired a relation of title to a piece of land when he cultivated it. This relation of title continues in existence whether the man makes further use of the land or not. Also among the Ukamba, when a man builds a village on virgin soil he establishes a relation of title to this land and no one may cultivate it or settle on it without his permission. With the Ashanti, women were considered to have a relation of title to the product of their work. A woman might, therefore, own the crops she has raised such as ground-nuts. Any help which the husband gave by way of clearing the farm or felling heavy trees, would thereby make the husband the owner of the crops. With the Pima, wild products on the land could be gathered by anyone, on the principle that they matured without the work of any one individual. This applied, however, only to the products and not to the trees or bushes. Only the owner of the land could rightly cut down a tree, cactus, or bush that grew on his land.

[20] Alexander Goldenweiser, *Anthropology* (New York, 1937), p. 148.

[21] E. Adamson Hoebel, "Anthropology of Inheritance," *Social Meaning of Legal Concepts* 1 (1948) : p. 16.

[22] Edward Westermarck, *The Origin and Development of the Moral Ideas* (2 v., London, 1908–1912) 2 : p. 42. Written laws have recognized that labor creates a unique relation between the laborer and his product. "In the old Hindu law-books, the performance of labor is specified as one of the lawful modes of acquiring property." Westermarck, *ibid.*

Preliterates also consider that the game which a man catches is his. This is the view of the Barama River Carib. Among the Ammassalik of East Greenland, the game taken by individual effort belongs to the one who makes possible the kill. The man who chops a seal hole in the ice has claim on the seal caught. With the Naskapi, the bear, moose, caribou, or other meat-supplying animal is the individual property of the hunter who killed it.

Instances have been cited which supposedly are exceptions to the universal judgment among preliterates that what is the product of a man's effort, belongs to that man as his own. Some of these examples relate to hunting. Thus, it is said that among some preliterates, the result of the hunt does not belong to the one who did the killing. Among the Kiangang Indians of Brazil the hunter who kills an animal is not allowed to keep it for himself but must give it to a close relative who butchers it and gives some to the hunter, some to other members of the group, and keeps the greater part for himself. With the Arapesh, the hunter gives most of his kill to his mother's brother, his cousin, or to his father-in-law. With the Siberian tribes and the Eskimo the seal or whale which is killed by an individual is divided up with the other members of the community.

But even within these instances, which are cited as exceptions to the universal recognition of a relation of title between the doer and the thing done, there is evidence of such a recognition. The Kiangang Indian who fells an animal gives the animal to *his* relative and some of the meat is returned to *him* the killer. The Arapesh hunter gives most of his kill to *his* mother's brother, *his* cousin or *his* father-in-law. The Siberians and Eskimo share the kill with others because of economic necessity, but even in this sharing there is a recognition of the unique relation of killer to killed. The Baffin Islanders hold that the first man who strikes a walrus receives the tusks and one of the forequarters; the first one who assists him gets the other forequarter; the next man receives the head and neck, and so on. Among the Australian tribes, the custom law clearly prescribes that when a kangaroo is killed by a hunter, one hind leg goes to the father of the hunter, the other to his paternal uncle, the tail is given to his sister, the shoulder to his brother and he keeps the liver for himself. With the Ngarigo, the hunter who kills a wombat keeps the head and distributes the other parts both to his own family and to others.

Another example which used to be cited as an exception to the universal recognition of the relation between the maker and his product relates to fishing. The Trobrianders are a fishing people among whom canoes are essential. Although the canoes are made by individuals, they are used communally and to all intents and purposes are owned communally. If this is the case, the maker of the canoe does not own the canoe and it is an exception to the rule of maker-owner.

Further research among the Trobrianders, however, has shown that this case is not an exception to the maker-owner rule. Within each canoe is one man who is recognized as its rightful owner. The rest act as crew. Each gets his fair share in the distribution of the catch according to his defined position among the crew and the work he does. The position of owner is recognized and rewarded accordingly.

There are examples of preliterates confiscating things which are owned by individuals and allowing others to use them. Thus among the Samoans, a ring or a dance skirt or a fishing-rod which was made by an individual can be taken as an obligatory loan to a relative or seized by one of the elders at any time. This does not mean that the thing made by the individual was not recognized as uniquely related to him and his. This is shown by the fact that it could be taken as an obligatory loan to one of *his* relatives.

The value judgment, then, that it is good to consider things made by a man's labor as uniquely related to him is universal among all preliterate societies.[23]

[23] Labor: Alexander Goldenweiser, *Anthropology* (New York, 1937), p. 14; A. Irving Hallowell, "The Nature and Function of Property as a Social Institution," *Jour. Legal and Polit. Sociology* 1 (1943): p. 129; Huntington Cairns, "Law and Anthropology," in: Victor Calverton, *The Making of Man* (New York, 1931), p. 348; John Gillin, "Crime and Punishment Among the Barama River Carib," *Amer. Anthropologist* 36 (1934): p. 335; Robert Lowie, *An Introduction to Cultural Anthropology* (2nd ed., New York, 1940), p. 28; E. Adamson Hoebel, "Fundamental Legal Concepts as Applied in the Study of Primitive Law," *Yale Law Jour.* 51 (1942): p. 964; Robert Lowie, "Property Rights and Coercive Powers of Plains Indian Military Societies," *Jour. Legal and Polit. Sociology* 1 (1943): p. 62; Lowie, "Incorporeal Property in Primitive Society," *Yale Law Jour.* 37 (1928): pp. 553, 561, 563; Ralph Beals and Harry Hoijer, *An Introduction to Anthropology* (New York, 1953), p. 374; Julius Lips, "Government," in: Franz Boas, ed., *General Anthropology* (Boston, 1938), p. 495; Robert Redfield, "Maine's Ancient Law in the Light of Primitive Societies, *Western Polit. Quart.* 3 (1950): p. 581; Kalervo Oberg, "Crime and Punishment in Tlingit Society," *Amer. Anthropologist* 36 (1934): p. 151; Ralph Barton, "Ifugao Law," *Amer. Archaeology and Ethnology* 15 (1919): p. 41; E. Adamson Hoebel, "The Political Organization and Law-ways of the Comanche," *Mem. Amer. Anthropol. Assoc.* 54 (1940): p. 120; C. R. Moss, "Nabaloi Law and Ritual," *Amer. Archaeology and Ethnology* 15 (1920): pp. 249, 251. Charles Dundas, "Native Laws of Some Bantu Tribes of East Africa," *Jour. Royal Anthropol. Inst.* 51 (1921): pp. 273, 296; Robert Rattray, *Ashanti Law and Constitution* (Oxford, 1929), p. 336; Willard Hill, "Notes on Pima Land Law and Tenure," *Amer. Anthropologist* 38 (1936): pp. 586–587; E. Adamson Hoebel, *The Law of Primitive Man* (Cambridge, Mass., 1954), p. 80. Julius Lips, "Naskapi Law," *Trans. Amer. Philos. Soc.* 37 (1947): p. 435; Otto Klineberg, *Social Psychology* (2nd ed., New York, 1954), p. 104; Franz Boas, "The Eskimo of Baffinland and Hudson Bay," *Amer. Museum Natural History* 15 (1907): p. 116; Julius Lips, "Government," in: Franz Boas, ed., *General Anthropology* (Boston, 1938), p. 494; Williams Rivers, *The History of Melanesian Society* (Cambridge, 1914), *passim;* Bronislaw Malinowski, *Crime and Custom in Savage Society* (New York, 1951), p. 18; Ralph Piddington, *An Introduction to Social Anthropology* (London, 1950), p. 283; Margaret Mead "The Role of the Individual in Samoan Culture," in: Alfred Kroeber and Thomas Waterman, eds., *Source Book in Anthropology* (New York, 1931), p. 552.

## b. Exchange Agreements

Certain enterprising activities which men engage in also establish relations of title between a thing and a person. These activities are exchange agreements, gifts, occupation, inheritance, adverse possession, and accession. Value judgments regarding exchange agreements and gift-giving among preliterate societies are universal. The value judgment regarding occupation is almost universal. In regard to inheritance, the value judgment appears to be frequent. There is practically no reporting on adverse possession and accession among preliterate associations.

Exchange agreement is a way in which a man's unique relation of title to a thing may be mutually exchanged for another's relation of title to another thing. It is the agreement to exchange the relations pertaining to an object, not the object itself, which constitutes a transfer of "property." Among all preliterates there is found the practice of exchanging relations of title to things or services for relations of title to other items of value. These items of value may be a medium of exchange or they may be objects such as are used in direct barter. There is "a certain propensity in human nature . . . to truck, barter, and exchange one thing for another."[24] This universal value judgment found among all preliterate societies, that it is good to agree to exchange relations of title, is a constructed value judgment based on the given value judgment that it is good to distinguish mine from thine.

In some places, preliterates enter into exchange agreements by mere oral utterance and confirmation by a handshake. Thus among the Naskapi, oral agreements are usual and their confirmation by handshake is occasional. Witnesses are not necessary for a binding agreement. In other places, more is required for a binding agreement. With the Yoruba, all agreements concerning land are questionable without the giving and receiving of kola nuts, regardless of whatever cash or goods may otherwise have been given. In Africa the exchange of promises by the parties of a marriage is not sufficient. It is the fixing of the amount the prospective husband will pay and the handing over of the girl which seals the agreement.

In still other places, there has been and reportedly still is the remarkable institution known as "silent trade." Usually occurring between peoples of differing cultural levels, this form of agreement is consummated without either party formally seeing, addressing, or hearing the other. At night the pygmies of the Congo will place an animal they have killed near the entrance to a village. The next night they come to take the price which they expect to find in the same place where they have placed the animal. It is said that no villager would dare to take the meat without paying what it is worth. "[U]nseen by him, he is watched by the little men, and should

he defraud them he is sure to be found dead a few days later with a tiny poisoned arrow in his side."[25] "Silent trade" is also practiced by the Negritos in the Lowlands of Northern Luzon.[26]

## c. Gift-giving

Relations of title can be transferred not only by exchange agreements but also by gift-giving. A gift, in the strict sense, is a voluntary giving of the relation of title to a thing without the expectation of an equivalent return. Gift-giving among preliterates may take the form of bestowing particular things on friends. Or it may take the turn of being generous towards the needy and showing hospitality towards visitors. But gift-giving among preliterates carries with it its own particular overtone. Gift-giving in preliterate societies implies a reciprocity. Sometime in the future the receiver of the gift is expected to make a return gift to the original giver. This reciprocity, which is considered obligatory, becomes a prominent characteristic of the economy. The rule and obligation of give and afterwards receive are universal characteristics of preliterate trade.

Gift-giving has been called the primary form of exchange, with its emphasis on the personal, rather than on the economic, relationship. Barter is second to gift-giving as a form of exchange. In gift-giving among preliterates, reciprocity and equivalence are underlying ideas. But the equivalence is not of the value of the thing given but of the generosity involved in the giving. The milieu of gift-giving is not the market of traders. It is rather the circle of friends.

Examples of gift-giving are numerous among preliterates. They involve the obligation of reciprocity, as just noted, and imply that the giver has a unique relation of title to the thing he is giving as a gift. Among the Yamana, gifts of food, necklaces, slings, spears, and implements are common. With the Trobianders, generosity shown in gift-giving is the highest virtue and the possession of the means to engage in it assure advance in influence and rank. Food, which is often the object of gift-giving, is stored in houses that are better made and better ornamented than are the houses used for dwelling.

The importance of gift-giving, real or apparent, in preliterate living is well exemplified in the ingenious role it interplays between Melanesian subjects and chiefs. Workers put some of the yams they grow into the storehouses of the chief. The community takes pride in the store of yams in the storehouse. The yams are looked on as belonging to the chief. But he is not free to consume them or to sell them. At the proper time, for

---

[24] Adam Smith, An Inquiry into the Nature and Causes of the Wealth of Nations (2 v., Oxford, 1869) 1: p. 14.

[25] Frank Schechter, "The Law and Morals of Primitive Trade," in: Max Radin and A. M. Kidd, eds., Legal Essays (Berkeley, 1935), p. 577.

[26] Exchange agreements: Julius Lips "Naskapi Law," Trans. Amer. Philos. Soc. 37 (1947): p. 438; A. K. Ajisafe, Laws and Customs of the Yoruba People (London, 1924), p. 75; T. Olawale Elias, The Nature of African Customary Law (Manchester, 1956), p. 154.

instance on festive occasions, he is expected to distribute them to the people of his own and other communities.

The economic overtones and values, however, of much of preliterate gift-giving cannot be missed. The potlatch of the northwest American Indians is a good example. Ostensibly this was a gift-giving ceremonial feast in which the lavish giver manifested his generosity and thereby acquired great prestige. But as a matter of fact it was much more than this. By giving away his possessions, the giver both paid his debts and made provision for the future. The insurance aspect of the potlatch is an important one. It was understood that the recipients of gifts would in due course return them either to the giver himself or, in case of his death, to his children. In this manner, either he as elderly or his children as orphans were provided for.

The principle of reciprocity is the dynamic of such gift-giving. The person to whom a gift is offered cannot refuse it and by accepting the gift he becomes obliged to repay it with interest in due time. If the recipient should die, his family are obliged to repay the gift. And, as explained, if the giver should die, his children will receive the repayment. Another important result of such extensive and reciprocal gift-giving is the prevention of the accumulation and concentration of wealth in the hands of one or few individuals. It has been pointed out that this leveling process, which occurs among the Naskapi, masses of arctic peoples and the northwest American Indians, is not limited to geographical locations and climate. The irrevocability of the transfer of relations of title by gift among preliterates, however, appears to be as uncertain as it is in the case of exchange agreements which we shall see. Among the Nabaloi, for instance, the giver of a gift may, after the elapse of some time, demand its return and receive it back.

The value judgment is universal in all preliterate societies that it is good to transfer relations of title to things by gift-giving.[27]

### B.  IN ALL SOCIETIES WITH RARE EXCEPTIONS: TITLE BY OCCUPATION

Taking possession of a thing not uniquely related to anyone else with the intention of using or developing it is recognized by preliterates as a way of establishing relations of title between the thing possessed and the

person possessing it. Occupation of a piece of land is necessary before a man can cultivate it and, conversely, it is with a view to such cultivation that the land is occupied. Such occupation makes the thing "mine." The recognition of occupation as a way of establishing relations of title between things and persons has been said to be universal in all preliterate associations.

With the Mende of Sierra Leone, for instance, the man who opens up virgin country is considered to have established relations of title to this land. Among the Tikopians, occupation is looked on as establishing a special and enduring kind of relation between certain areas of ground and the persons or groups of persons who occupy them. With the Akan along the Gold Coast, occupation of land with the intention of cultivating it sets up unique relations of title to the land. It was on this basis that relations of title were established to large parts of the land surface of the earth. So-called first occupiers claimed the land, by the "twig-in-turf" procedure, in their own name or in the name of those they represented.

The Andamans hold that a tree belongs to the first man who notices it as suitable for making a canoe and makes this fact known. Certain fruit trees belong to the first man who finds them. A pig is the property of the first man who hits it with an arrow. In some places, physical contact between a thing and a person is deemed a necessary part of occupation. In South Africa, the person who finds and touches a drinking cup considers it to be his. Natives of Baffin Bay and Eastern Eskimo run their tongue over things which they find and thereby make them "theirs." The idea that physical contact is necessary in occupation, it has been suggested, is related to the realization that "mine" connotes an extension of my own personality.[28]

But there are rare exceptions to the custom law that first occupancy results in the establishment of unique relations of title between the thing occupied and the person occupying it. This is the situation among some food-gatherers and hunters who regulate the distribution of food. The Bushmen, the Botocudo and the Vedda, for instance, consider certain things when found to pertain to the common needs of the whole community. The honey combs of rock bees are looked on by the Vedda as food for everyone. They are equally distributed, regardless of who finds them.

The value judgment, therefore, that it is good to recognize occupation as a way of establishing unique relations of title between the thing occupied and the

[27] Gift-giving: Edward Westermarck, *The Origin and Development of the Moral Ideas* (2 v., London, 1908–1912), p. 549; Frank Schechter, "The Laws and Morals of Primitive Trade," in: Max Radin and A. M. Kidd, eds., *Legal Essays* (Berkeley, 1935), pp. 567–568, 571; Robert Redfield "Maine's Ancient Law in the Light of Primitive Societies," *Western Polit. Quart.* **3** (1950): pp. 587–588; Robert Lowie, "Incorporeal Property in Primitive Society," *Yale Law Jour.* **37** (1928): p. 533; Bronislaw Malinowski, *Crime and Custom in Savage Society* (New York, 1951), p. 29; Franz Boas, "Tribes of Canada," *Report* **68** (1898): pp. 681–682; Julius Lips, "Naskapi Law," *Trans. Amer. Philos. Soc.* **37** (1947): p. 486; C. R. Moss, "Nabaloi Law and Ritual," *Amer. Archaeology and Ethnology* **15** (1920): p. 255.

[28] "In early German law it was necessary, in order to reclaim cattle found in the possession of another, to place the right hand above a relic, a fetish, and the left hand on the left ear of the animal. . . . It is an easy step from the idea that the thing possessed is connected with the body to the idea that it is necessary that there should be a physical contact of the donee with the thing transferred before the transfer is actually complete." Huntington Cairns, "Law and Anthropology," in: Victor Calverton, ed., *The Making of Man* (New York, 1931), p. 345.

person occupying it is almost universal in preliterate societies.[29]

## II.　LESS THAN UNIVERSAL VALUE JUDGMENTS

The remaining value judgments concerning mine and thine, which we will consider, are less than universal. They will be found to be general or common.

### A.　GENERAL

The value judgments which appear to be general among preliterate societies relate to the keeping of promises, inheritance, and in-group versus out-group taking of things belonging to others. These value judgments are formed by the majority of preliterate groups.

### 1.　*Keeping Agreements*

It is one thing for preliterates to value-judge that it is good to enter into exchange agreements. It is another thing for them to judge that they should keep such agreements. The evidence weighs in favor of preliterates judging that agreements should be kept. For some preliterates there is a clear obligation to keep agreements. For Africans, respect for one's given word is important. That agreements should not be broken at will is shown in their attitude toward the marriage contract, the traditional borrowing and leasing of land, and cooperative labor and economic units. Because of their conviction that agreements should be kept, some preliterates hold that there is no limit on the time an agreement or debt may run. The Ashanti, on account of their belief in the sanctity of agreements, hold that a debt "never rots" and may be collected to the third or fourth generation. Many groups consider it as disgraceful to break a promise as to lie. The ancient Scandinavians, as we remarked, put the breaking of agreements and lying in the class of treacherous acts.

But there is evidence also that not all preliterates have the same conviction regarding the permanent keeping of agreements. A man may agree to exchange an item of value for something of value which another man has and go through with the transfer. But after the transfer has taken place, he may demand a re-exchange. Thus among the Wakamba, a Bantu tribe of East Africa, a man who agrees to sell an animal to another man fully realizes that the agreement should be kept and that the sale implies a transfer of ownership. But after the exchange has occurred, he may want the animal back and

insist on refunding the purchase price. This procedure will find so much support from the people that, it has been suggested, there may be here a trace of some original custom regarding claims to property. Hence, the value judgment that it is good to keep promises, at least in this qualified sense, appears to be general in preliterate societies.[30]

### 2.　*Title by Inheritance*

Inheritance is another way in which relations of title can be established by transfer. There are few societies, it would seem, in which this manner of conveying relations of title is not important. The items which may be passed on by parents to their children depend upon the custom regulations of the society in which they live. The transfer of relations of title to things, it has been claimed, is either implicitly or explicitly recognized in all societies. The inheritance of movables and intangibles is said to occur on all levels of culture.[31]

The extent of inheritance among preliterates is limited by the fact that among some groups material things cannot be inherited because they are destroyed at the death of the owner. This custom is said to be widespread among preliterates. It was the practice, for instance, among the tribes of California. Where the custom prevails, although relations of title to tangible things cannot be inherited because they are destroyed, relations of title to such things as fields or fishing grounds can be inherited and passed on according to the rules of custom law. An important aspect of inheritance is land. Normally among preliterates, a man's male children inherit all his land. Thus, among Nigerian tribes, a man owns the portion of land which was given to him by his father. With the Bantu, every piece of land is inherited. Among the Ifugao of the Philippines, land is handed down from generation to generation.

The written laws of many peoples take a similar position regarding inheritance. In Islamic law, whatever a father owns during his lifetime reverts to his family upon his death. The reason for this is, principally, that the family is looked on as an extension of the father's life. Family benefits, brought about by family cooperation, should be shared mutually. As a consequence, cases of inheritance seldom come to court. Instead, everything is settled within the family according to custom law. The senior member of the family, for instance, succeeds to all the property except the clothing. This

[29] Title by occupation: Edward Westermarck, *The Origin and Development of the Moral Ideas* (2 v., London, 1908-1912) 2: p. 35; Kenneth Little, *The Mende of Sierra Leone* (London, 1951), p. 176; Raymond Firth, *We, The Tikopia* (2nd ed., London, 1957) p. 399; Joseph Danquah, *Gold Coast: Akan Laws and Customs* (London, 1938), p. 205; Alfred Radcliffe-Brown, *The Andaman Islanders* (Cambridge, Mass., 1933), p. 41; Huntington Cairns, "Laws and Anthropology," in: Victor Calverton, ed., *The Making of Man* (New York, 1931) p. 345; Julius Lips, "Government," in: Franz Boas, ed., *General Anthropology* (Boston, 1938), p. 494.

[30] Keeping agreements: T. Olawale Elias, *The Nature of African Customary Law* (Manchester, 1956), p. 145, 153, 296; Frank Schechter, "The Law and Morals of Primitive Trade," in: Max Radin and A. M. Kidd, eds., *Legal Essays* (Berkeley, 1935), p. 583; Edward Westermarck, *The Origin and Development of the Moral Ideas* (2 v., London, 1908-1912) 2: pp. 72, 96; Charles Dundas, "Native Laws of Some Bantu Tribes of East Africa, *Jour. Royal Anthropol. Inst.* 51 (1921): p. 275.

[31] Gladys Reichard, "Social Life," in: Franz Boas, ed., *General Anthropology* (Boston, 1938), p. 423; E. Adamson Hoebel, "Anthropology of Inheritance," *Social Meaning of Legal Concepts* 1 (1948): p. 24.

usually goes to the children. Wives stay in the custody of the brothers of their deceased husbands. If they want to marry them, a new marriage contract is required. The only bequests known are those giving a daughter in marriage.

The inheritance of property is claimed by some not to be a pristine feature of human culture. It is rather a "convention" developed during the course of history. The Comanche seem to be an example of a people who appear to have gone through an evolution concerning the disposition of a man's possessions upon his death. At first they were accustomed to destroy all a man's possessions at his death. These were limited to his clothing, and a few weapons and utensils. No great economic loss to the group was thereby sustained. But after the Comanche broke away from the Plateau tribes and took on the Plains culture, they acquired horses. Some individual men owned as many as 2,000 animals. To slaughter this number of horses, especially when others of the tribe depended on such herds for their mounts, would involve not only a great economic loss but would pose a definite threat to their hunting and war-making abilities. Hence, the custom developed of killing only a man's favorite horse and distributing the rest of the herd among the surviving relatives. This was done both by wills, which was a new custom for the Comanche, and by rules governing the rights of certain relatives to exercise their choice according to a fixed order.

But such examples of the development of inheritance of tangibles does not necessarily mean that there was not present in the course of history the idea of inheritance of intangibles. The criticism has been made that "inheritance is a mechanism of greater significance in early and simple primitive societies than most writers on legal history have been prone to allow." [32]

The transfer of relations of title by oral will is recognized by some preliterates, by others it is not. Among the Ifugao there are no wills or oral testaments. If a man wishes to make a disposition of his possessions that does not follow the rules of custom law, he has to do it before his death. In Bansang wills of any kind are unknown in some districts. Among other preliterates, however, the disposition of possessions by oral will is said to be general. Among the Tugunse, wills are looked on as supplementary to custom law. According to custom law, the closest relatives were brothers, children, grandchildren, great grandchildren, and other descendants. In Buriat law, wills were also considered as a supplement to custom law. With the Nabaloi, inheritance according to custom law is controlling and a will made contrary to this will not be enforced. If a man wills his possessions to only one of his children, the elders will see to it that his other children get their share.

Whether inheritance by the regulations of custom law or by oral will is the older and more basic process by which relations of title were transferred has been the matter of some controversy. It has been claimed that inheritance as governed by the custom law of intestate succession is the more fundamental. If this opinion is correct, it was a later development when individuals took it upon themselves to determine by testament how they wanted to dispose of their possessions upon their death, rather than follow the consensus of the people as expressed from time immemorial in the custom law.

The evidence being considered, it seems that the value judgment among preliterate societies that it is good to transfer title to tangibles or intangibles by inheritance is general. [33]

### 3. In-Group versus Out-Group Taking of Things

Theft is disapproved in all preliterate societies. What is considered to be theft, however, varies. The distinction between in-group and out-group activities runs throughout preliterate living, as noted above. Applied to taking things belonging to others, this distinction means that a different value judgment is made regarding things taken inside the group and things taken outside the group. Preliterates generally value-judge that taking things which belong to others inside the group is theft, while taking things which belong to others outside the group is not theft. The Wonevaro and Wogeo in Polynesia, for example, strongly condemn stealing within their villages and feel indignation about it. But they do not feel this way when things are taken from people outside their village. Among the Tallensi of the Northern Territories of the Gold Coast in West Africa, a thief caught in the act is severely beaten if he is a fellow-clansmen, but if he is an outsider his eyes may be put out or he may be otherwise maimed.

With the Ahats of British Columbia, prohibitions against stealing apply to taking things from tribesmen but not taking things from strangers. Theft of the possessions of other tribes or white men is prevalent. Among the Germanic tribes, robberies committed outside the group were not thought to be wrong. They were

---

[32] E. Adamson Hoebel, "Anthropology of Inheritance," *Social Meaning of Legal Concepts* 1 (1948) : p. 26.

[33] Title by inheritance: Robert Lowie, *An Introduction to Cultural Anthropology* (2nd ed., New York, 1940), p. 282; Gladys Reichard, "Social Life," in: Franz Boas, ed., *General Anthropology* (Boston, 1938), pp. 423–424; E. Adamson Hoebel, "Anthropology of Inheritance," *Social Meaning of Legal Concepts* 1 (1948) : pp. 12, 18; C. K. Meek, *Law and Authority in a Nigerian Tribe* (London, 1937), p. 110; Charles Dundas, "Native Law of Some Bantu Tribes of East Africa," *Jour. Royal Anthropol. Inst.* 51 (1921): p. 271; Ralph Barton, "Ifugao Law," *Amer. Archaeology and Ethnology* (1919) : pp. 39, 55; Majid Khadduri and Herbert Liebesny, *Law in the Middle East* (Washington, 1955), p. 160; James Anderson, *Islamic Law in Africa* (London, 1954), pp. 246, 265; Alexander Goldenweiser, *Anthropology* (New York, 1937), p. 150; Ralph Linton, *The Study of Man* (New York, 1936), pp. 297–298; Valintin Riasanovsky, *Customary Law of the Nomadic Tribes of Siberia* (Tsiensin, 1938), p. 77; Claude Moss, "Nabaloi Law and Ritual," *Amer. Archaeology and Ethnology* 15 (1920): p. 253; Henry Maine, *Ancient Law* (New York, 1879), pp. 171–172, 189–190.

looked on as a means of keeping the young men occupied. Idleness was thereby cut down and the youth received some discipline.[34] The Ossete are said to have considered robbery and theft which was perpetrated inside the village to be much more serious than that committed outside. It was an operative principle with them that whatever a man found on the highway was a gift of God.

In some places, however, it must be noted that taking things inside and outside the group is interpreted differently from the cases just cited. Among the Ashanti, for instance, taking things within the group is known as "pilfering," while taking things outside the group is called "stealing." Besides making the distinction between taking things inside and outside the group, preliterates also consider other circumstances. The Ibo in Nigeria, for example, in making their evaluations look at the kind of thing taken and whether the thief had stolen previously.

It has been reported that in some societies theft does not exist. Among the Comanche for instance, theft was said to be very exceptional. No provision was made for its punishment in their custom law. With the Tlingit it is said that theft does not exist, at least theoretically. But practically there is evidence that theft does exist among them. When a man takes something which belongs to a member of his own clan, he is made to return it. When a man of low rank is caught stealing from another clan, the clan can kill him. If he is of high rank, his own clan must make compensation.

The value judgment, therefore, that taking things belonging to others who are outside one's group is good appears to be general among preliterate societies.[35]

### B. COMMON: LAND

Land among preliterates is considered to be related to individuals, to families or groups of individuals, and to

[34] Julius Caesar, *De Bello Gallico*, (Renatus Du Pontet, ed., Oxford, 1900), Book VI, chap. 23, lines 6–7, my translation. Aquinas cites this passage from Caesar as evidence that there were peoples who had no idea that theft or robbery were wrong and therefore as an objection against his position on "natural law." "[A]mong the Germans at one time robbery was not considered wrong, as Julius Caesar relates, although it is expressly contrary to natural law." Thomas Aquinas, *Summa Theologiae*, Part 1–2, Question 94, Article 4 (Ottawa ed., Ottawa, 1941), p. 1228, my translation. Why Aquinas failed to see the distinction between in-group versus out-group taking of things which Caesar faithfully incorporates into his report can only be a matter of speculation.
[35] In-group v. out-group taking of things: H. Ian Hogbin, *Law and Order in Polynesia* (London, 1934), p. 261; Arthur Diamond, *The Evolution of Law and Order* (London, 1951), pp. 230–231; Edward Tylor, *Anthropology* (New York, 1916), p. 421; Edward Westermarck, *The Origin and Development of the Moral Ideas* (2 v., London, 1908–1912) 2: p. 16; Robert Rattray, *Ashanti Law and Constitution* (Oxford, 1929), p. 323; C. K. Meek, *Law and Authority in a Nigerian Tribe* (London, 1937), pp. 213–214; E. Adamson Hoebel, "The Political Organization and Law-ways of the Comanche Indians," *Mem. Amer. Anthropol. Assoc.* 54 (1940): p. 111; Kalervo Oberg, "Crime and Punishment in Tlingit Society," *Amer. Anthropologist* 36 (1934): p. 149.

no individual at all. Among the Ibo of Nigeria, land is looked on as being related to individual persons. Such personally owned land can also be inherited, as we shall see. The Vedda hold that land may be owned by individual males within group holdings. The Bantu are reported as holding that every piece of land is privately owned. The Australians are said to have vague ideas on the relation of land to individuals. Their rule of thumb seems to be one of first occupancy: whoever has been using land has title to its use.

Preliterates also hold that land is related to families. In Africa land is owned by families with all individual members of the family who are able to work having well-defined portions and specific assignments. Among the Bantu Wakarra, all land is owned by families. Relatives are consulted before the land is sold. The Akamba of East Africa recognize not individual claims to land but only family claims of occupation. With the Ifugao, land is also held by families. It is thought impossible for land to be uniquely related to individual persons.

Among many preliterates, then, land is uniquely related to individual persons or to individual families. It is not communally owned. Exceptions are certain pieces of land which are communally used. Sacred groves, market places and as yet unallocated forest land are communally owned in some places in Africa. This is the situation among the Kamba where encroachment by individuals is not allowed on sacred groves and market places. Likewise in Kenya, grazing lands, salt-licks, sacred groves, and meeting and dancing places, roads and paths which everyone uses are looked on as belonging to the whole community. Among the Bantu, individually owned land is considered to become related to the community when it is impossible to discern its boundaries. When the grass is cut, boundary lines disappear and cattle are allowed to graze where they will.

On the other hand there is evidence that among other preliterates there is no notion of land being especially related to any individual persons. The Kubu and Sakai, the Negritos of Malaya, the Andamanese and the Alacaluf are said to have no concept of ownership in land. The Wadigo feel that all land belongs to God and that selling it amounts to stealing. It has been stated that this view of "land communism prevails among most primitive peoples." The Eskimo are said to have no concept of land as property either individual or communal. The Comanche likewise are reported as having no idea of land value. They merely occupied the land communally.

It would be a mistake to say simply that some preliterates consider land of no value, without a qualification. Although some preliterates may not conceive of themselves as having a title to land in the sense of ownership, they do think of themselves as having a title to land in the sense of territorial exclusiveness. Hunters and fishermen may not think they have title to the land or water itself, but they certainly conceive of themselves as having title to hunting and fishing on the land or in the water. This is shown by reactions to intruders. The Comanche killed those of another society or tribe who trespassed upon "their" land. Preliterate groups, with the exception of true nomads, are usually attached to a specific geographical area. Anyone who is not a member of the group who attempts to utilize this area is an intruder and is treated accordingly. Such was the case with the Algonquin hunters of North America. They consider that title to hunt in certain areas was related to them and to no one else, probably because of previous title of occupation. "Land tenure" among such hunters, as well as among pastoralists, has been shown to exist among preliterates in many parts of the world.

Preliterates, then, consider the relation of land to themselves in various ways. Some think of the land as being uniquely related to them as individual persons or individual families. Others hold that the land can be related only to all the people of a society or group, the full connotation of which appears only when outsiders intrude upon the territory. For in such a situation, it becomes evident that the land is actually considered to be related to one individual society *vis-à-vis* another individual society.[36] Hence, the value judgment would appear to be common in preliterate societies that it is good and desirable for individual persons or individual families to have title to the land. The value judgment would also seem common that it is good for only the people as a whole to have title to the land.[37]

Before proceeding to the next chapter, it may be well to recall that the web of relations which exists between persons in regard to things, which we call "property," existed before man-made law. The distinction between mine and thine has a value which is presupposed by justice. Justice has a value which is postulated by man-made law. Both these values exist before they are necessarily incorporated into man-made law. It is unrealistic, therefore, to maintain that property is the creation of law. It is likewise illusory to hold that property and law are created together. Such statements are the expression of "an amazingly myopic point of view." What they fail to realize is that the distinction between mine and thine, as well as relations of title and relations of respect due to them, are prelegal facts. It is because of these facts that law exists and is what it is. This is borne out in preliterate custom law. Before custom law was formed by the peoples' value judgments, respect due to relations of title was first recognized by individual persons. It was because this respect was recognized by individuals, that it gradually became woven into what we call the custom law of preliterate peoples.[38]

## CHAPTER 7

## ASSOCIATION FOR PROTECTION AND SECURITY

The remaining value judgments which we shall examine concern our associating together for the purpose of fulfilling needs which are common to us all. The need of a matrix within which our basic drives and titles to life, sex, knowledge, decision, and property can function is common to all of us. We all need the protection and security which will assure this functioning. When this is had, order and peace result. Within this context we can pursue our own self-development. It is only in the milieu of these socio-political values that our eventual self-realization can take place.

All normal men have a basic drive to associate with each other, as we saw. This desire to live in the society of other men is universal among all men. "One of the most important of . . . universal reactions is the individual's need for company and his desire for emotional response from other individuals."[1] The "feeling of neighborliness . . . has been found a universal trait of human society."[2] "Man is naturally a social animal, for

---

[36] Value judgments regarding the permanency of the land, in contrast to the transiency of the life of men, have also been made by preliterates. "Land does not enter into the philosophy and sentiment of the Tikopia in the way in which it does in Maori society. No Tikopia ever wept over his soil or died in battle in defence of the sanctity of his orchards. And yet the natives have a feeling for the permanency of the land as opposed to the fleeting presence of man who draws his sustenance from it. If two people fight over the possession of an orchard, the chief may send a message to them, 'Do not go and fight. Each man go and plant food for himself. The land is laughing at us.' As it is said, 'the land stands, but man dies; he weakens and is buried down below. We dwell for but a little while, but the land stands in its abiding-place.' In other words, 'How futile are the struggles of men compared with the permanency of the soil.'" Raymond Firth, "Function," in: William Thomas, ed., *Current Anthropology* (Chicago, 1956), p. 374.

[37] Land: C. K. Meek, *Law and Authority in a Nigerian Tribe* (London, 1937), p. 110; Charles Dundas, "Native Laws of Some Tribes of East Africa," *Jour. Royal Anthropol. Inst.* **51** (1921): pp. 271–274; Arthur Diamond, *The Evolution of Law and Order* (London, 1951), p. 19; T. Olawale Elias, *The Nature of African Customary Law* (Manchester, 1956), pp. 83, 173; Lewis Tupper, "Customary and Other Law in the East Africa Protectorate," *Jour. Soc. Comp. Legislation* **8** (1908): p. 180; Ralph Barton, "Ifugao Law," *Amer. Archaeology and Ethnology* **15** (1919): p. 39; D. J. Penwill, *Kamba Customary Law* (London, 1951), p. 54; Jomo Kenyatta, *Facing Mount Kenya* (London, 1953), p. 36; E. Adamson Hoebel, "Anthropology of Inheritance," *Social Meaning of Legal Concepts* **1** (1948): p. 24; Hoebel, "Law-ways of the Primitive Eskimos," *Jour. Criminology and Criminal Law* **31** (1941): p. 666; Hoebel, "The Political Organization and Law-ways of the Comanche Indians," *Mem. Amer. Anthropol. Assoc.* **54** (1940): p. 118; Franz Boas, *Anthropology and Modern Life* (New

York, 1928), p. 237; A. Irving Hallowell, "The Nature and Function of Property as a Social Institution," *Jour. Legal and Polit. Sociology* **1** (1943): p. 127.

[38] Robert MacIver, "Government and Property," *Jour. Legal and Polit. Sociology* **4** (1946): p. 5; Jeremy Bentham, *The Theory of Legislation* (Ogden, ed., New York, 1931), p. 113; E. Adamson Hoebel, *Man in the Primitive World* (New York, 1949), p. 331. Hoebel's reference is to MacIver, "Government and Property," *Jour. Polit. and Legal Sociology* **4** (1946): p. 5.

[1] Ralph Linton, *The Study of Man* (New York, 1936), p. 141.

[2] Robert Lowie, *The Origin of the State* (New York, 1927), pp. 116–117.

he is not sufficient by himself to provide for his own life."[3] "He who is unable to live in society, or who has not need because he is sufficient for himself, must be either a beast or a god."[4]

Men's mental capacity especially can develop only by association with other men. The widening and deepening of the human mind has occurred not in the life of any one individual man but only in the course of the history of human living-together. Conversely, when men are deprived of the association of other men, a loneliness sets in which can be more keenly felt than economic deprivation. Solitude, if long lasting, can lead to insanity.[5]

But the very fact of men living together inevitably gives rise to needs which are common to them. The need arises for protection and security against failures to respect titles to life, sex, knowledge, decisions, and property which come from both inside and outside the group. Men living together need conditions of order and peace if they are to progress, not conditions of chaos and strife. These common needs demand common efforts to fulfill them. Men must unite in working together in satisfying these needs. Political association is such a union.[6] The fulfillment of these common needs are political values.[7]

These common values are unique inasmuch as they are communicable to all the members associated in political union.[8] All can participate in them. It is

within this political value-matrix, as just noted, that all other non-political associations exist and function—marital, economic, social, recreational, and religious. In fact, protection, security, order, and peace are the indispensable means of furthering these other individual and personal ends.

The evidence indicates that political living is universal. "Nowhere have we found a single family of parents and children living on its own."[9] "Every society exhibits this desire of human beings to live together in peace and creative harmony."[10] Living together inevitably gives rise to common needs which can only be fulfilled by common actions. Such needs are not acquired. They are innate to social living. Social living cannot be conceived without them. The basic drive to associate, then, is a drive to associate politically. "[M]an is by nature a political animal. . . . [A] social instinct is implanted in all men by nature."[11] This is evidenced in societies which have no personal leaders or chiefs, where cohesion and political functioning is maintained among composing groups "by an innate instinct for a practical, democratic ideal of orderly existence."[12]

There is an interrelation, if not identity, between men's basic drive to live with others and their drive to communicate with others, as we saw. One is meaningless without the other. Only men have the power of speech which is capable of communicating what is right and what is wrong, what is just and what is unjust. For, only men have the mental power of thinking abstractly and value-judging good and evil, justice and injustice. The association of human beings who thus communicate, constitutes not only the family but also political association.[13]

Before proceeding to examine the value judgments preliterates make regarding association for the attainment of common values, the question of the innateness or acquiredness of the drive to associate should be briefly noted, as well as the question of the universality of political association. Universality does not indicate innateness. Acquired drives, like constructed value judgments, can also be universal. If political association is not universal, however, it could hardly be said to be the object of a basic drive.

---

[3] Thomas Aquinas, *Summa Theologiae* (Ottawa, 1941), Part 2-2, Ques. 6, Art. 1. My translation.

[4] Aristotle, *Politics*, Book I, chap. 2, 1253ᵃ2, 27–29, trans. by B. Jowett, Richard McKeon, ed., *The Basic Works of Aristotle* (New York, 1941), pp. 1129–1130.

[5] David Bidney, "The Concept of Value in Modern Anthropology," in: Sol Tax, ed., *Anthropology Today* (Chicago, 1962), p. 446. See also Wilfred Trotter, *Instincts of the Herd in Peace and War* (London, 1916), p. 47; Ralph Linton, *The Study of Man* (New York, 1936), p. 141.

[6] "[I]f men were to hunt, herd, and to cultivate, they had to feel secure against incessant attack. . . . This security was achieved by many devices, and hence all the various ties of friendship linking one small group with another have political functions and are political institutions." Max Gluckman, "Political Institutions," in: Edward Evans-Pritchard and others, *The Institutions of Primitive Society* (Glencoe, 1956), pp. 67–68. "The political structure [consists]of the system of political institutions which maintain the unit as an entity, protecting it against disintegration from within as well as against dangers threatening from without." Gunter Wagner, "The Political Organization of the Bantu Kavirondo," in: Meyer Fortes and Edward Evans-Pritchard, *African Political Systems* (London, 1940), p. 199.

[7] Important thinkers in the East, as well as in the West, have seen and recognized the natural necessity for united effort in fulfilling common needs. "Human society having been achieved . . . then arises the need for restraining each man from another owing to his animal propensities for aggression and opposition. . . . There must exist accordingly a restraining force. . . . This is what is implied in the term . . . sovereignty or statehood which exists by nature in man and is necessary for his existence." Ibn Khaldun, *Al-Muqaddima* (Quatremere, 1858), passim.

[8] On this communicability, see Thomas Davitt, *The Elements of Law* (Boston, 1959), p. 18.

[9] Max Gluckman, "Political Institutions," in: Edward Evans-Pritchard and others, *The Institutions of Primitive Society* (Glencoe, 1956), p. 67.

[10] Ashley Montagu, *Man: His First Million Years* (Cleveland, 1957), pp. 113, 115.

[11] Aristotle, *Politics*, Book I, chap. 2, 1253ᵃ29–30, trans. by B. Jowett, Richard McKeon, ed., *The Basic Works of Aristotle* (New York, 1941), p. 1130.

[12] T. Olawale Elias, *The Nature of African Customary Law* (Manchester, 1956), p. 22.

[13] Aristotle, *Politics*, Book I, chap. 2, 1253ᵃ7–18, trans. by B. Jowett, Richard McKeon, ed., *The Basic Works of Aristotle* (New York, 1941), p. 1129. On the radical difference between human and animal association, see Gladys Reichard, "Social Life," in: Franz Boas, ed., *General Anthropology* (Boston, 1938), p. 410.

*Drive is innate.* It has been maintained by some observers that the drive to live in association with others is not innate but acquired. This drive, it is said, is but an extension of the sense of dependence learned in family life. From the first day of the infant's life, he learns that he must depend on his parents for the satisfaction of all his needs. It is not any "herd instinct" that men inherited from their animal ancestors that accounts for men's desire to live with other men. It is simply a prolongation of what the individual has learned in his family, namely, that he is totally unable to live by himself. Supporting reasons for this position are said to be found in the fact that men show no tendency to carry out in common such important acts as food-gathering, propagation, and religious ceremonies. If anything was inherited from animal ancestors, it was not a gregarious instinct but merely a "diffused gregariousness." [14]

Furthermore, the drive to live in society is said to be the result of social evolution. Man is not innately social. If the stages of evolution are retraced, it is said, less and less perfect types of association are found. From this it can be inferred that in the unknown past the degree of association approaches zero. Vestiges of such loose and scattered association can be seen among the Australian natives and the African Bushmen and Pygmies. In fact, it is claimed there are examples of such "atomistic" living even today. Many tribes in the Sahara and in Madagascar and the Jibaro Indians of Ecuador live in "practical isolation." The African Pygmies are reportedly very anti-social towards members of even their own group. Among the Indian tribes of Brazil, each family is said to live by itself. [15]

But these explanations of why the drive in society is acquired and not innate lack supporting evidence. If the drive to live in society is but an extension of the sense of dependence learned in family living, there should be anthropological evidence of a time when families lived in such a state. This would be the "state of nature" assumed by Hobbes, Locke, Montesquieu, Rousseau and others. [16] There is, however, no such evidence available.

[T]here is no foundation for the belief of the seventeenth- and eighteenth-century philosophers in a precultural 'state of nature' followed by a politically instituted cultural state. . . . They failed to realize, in spite of acquaintance with the cultures of native societies through contemporary travelers' tales, that there are no precultural peoples living in "a state of nature." [17]

The data indicate, as we shall see in a moment, that not only did men always live to some extent in association with one another but that they also always lived to this degree in political association with each other. Hence, the assumption that a retracing of evolutionary stages will show less and less association of men in society is unwarranted by the evidence. [18] Such an assumption has no relevance to the innateness or acquiredness of the drive to associate with others in socio-political living.

Indeed, when it is stated that men have no drive to gather food, procreate, or hold religious ceremonies in common, what is ignored is that there is no record of men ever carrying on these activities who were not at the same time members of some sort of political association. The drive is not to perform such acts in common. It is to live in a society which is political, so that such acts may be carried on individually within the matrix of common life. Besides, if it can be said that there is no gregarious instinct in men because there is none in animals from whom it would have to be inherited, it could logically be said that there is no power of abstract symbolizing in men because none can be located in animals from whom it would have to be inherited. But the evidence of symbolization is more obvious than that of socialization and cannot be so easily denied.

The examples usually adduced in support of the contention that some peoples are asocial, carry within themselves the refutation of this contention. Of the Teda or Tubu, for instance, a tribe of the Sahara who are supposedly asocial, it is reported that the tribe is united when there is common danger from without. [19] Overlooked in the interpretation of these data, assuming the report to be accurate, is that the united and organized action of a people for such a common end as protection from attack is a form of political action. For whatever duration these peoples are thus engaged in the common pursuit of such a common value, for this period at least they are associated in what is essentially political activity. So also is it with the other groups which are said to live in "practical isolation." There is no evidence that any of them live in absolute isolation, that is, having no

---

[14] Alfred Radcliffe-Brown, *Structure and Function in Primitive Society* (Glencoe, 1956), p. 176; Bronislaw Malinowski, *Sex and Repression in Savage Society* (London, 1927), pp. 185, 187–188.

[15] William Sumner and A. G. Keller, *The Science of Society* (4 v., New Haven, 1927) 1: pp. 11, 16; Otto Klineberg, *Social Psychology* (rev. ed., New York, 1954), p. 158.

[16] There is evidence that these men had in mind an actual historical state of human living. Hobbes, in discussing the general condition of warfare in the "state of nature," refers to America as a place where "they live so now . . . [with] no government at all." Thomas Hobbes, *Leviathan*, Part I, chap. 13, William Molesworth, ed., *The English Works of Sir Thomas Hobbes of Malmesbury* (11 v., London, 1839) 3: p. 114. Locke likewise mentions the Indians of America as an example of men living in this "state of nature" where "truth and keeping of faith belongs to men as men, and not as members of society." John Locke, *Two Treatises on Government*, Second Treatise, chap. 2, no. 14, Thomas Cook, ed. (New York, 1947), p. 128.

[17] David Bidney, *Theoretical Anthropology* (New York, 1953), pp. 67, 144.

[18] "The social-contract explanation left the tracks at the start when it assumed a 'state of nature' in which men had no social ties, so that they had to come together and agree to set up, under government, a social order. It was necessary to go back to the rejected insight of Aristotle, that man is a social animal." Robert MacIver, *The Web of Government* (New York, 1947), p. 20. See Aristotle, *Politics*, Book I, chap. 2, 1253$^a$1–2, trans. by B. Jowett, Richard McKeon, ed., *The Basic Works of Aristotle* (New York, 1941), p. 1129.

[19] William Sumner and A. G. Keller, *The Science of Society* (New Haven, 1927), p. 17.

relations of any kind with others in the pursuit of one single common value.

Among some peoples there may be periods during which their political unity is not evident. But this is no indication that it is not there latently. Upon the appearance of a common cause, this latent political unity shows itself actively.[20] The fact that a people will react so readily to a common cause, is evidence of this latent union. We shall see this more in detail immediately. The point has been made that conclusive evidence of the universality of political association is had in a people's immediate reaction when common values have been spurned. "[T]he universal recognition of some deeds as crimes—though the definition of the offenses may vary from tribe to tribe—is a decisive proof of the omnipresence of the state." [21]

*Political association is universal.* Some reports also have been worded in such a way that they appear to deny that political association is a universal mode of human living. It has been reported that some peoples live with "no political organization," "no political institutions," "no government," and that they live "without the state," and are "stateless societies." [22]

---

[20] "[T]he germs of all possible political developments are latent but demonstrable in the ruder cultures and . . . a specific turn in communal experience—say, contact with a weaker or stronger neighbor—may produce an efflorescence of novel institutions." Robert Lowie, *Origin of the State* (New York, 1927), pp. 112–113.

[21] Robert Lowie, *Origin of the State* (New York, 1927), pp. 114–115. It is not a crime for an Australian to maim his wife, but it is a crime, formerly punishable with death, to marry within the forbidden degrees of relationship. So a Plains Indian may not be liable for abduction of a married woman, but he is beaten and deprived of his possessions if he disobeys the police during a tribal hunt. (Lowie, *ibid.*) "The ethnographer frequently witnesses a group of natives discussing alternative projects—whether to go fishing or hunting, when or where to hold a religious ceremony. The discussion proceeds, various opinions are expressed, and suddenly the group will break up, having decided upon a specific line of conduct without any orders having been given. . . . Yet principles of organization exist, as is proved by the fact that subsequent activities are carried out in a systematic and efficient way, each individual playing a traditionally defined part. Too often the existence of this type of diffused authority has been obscured in the study of primitive communities by such negative statements as that 'no form of leadership or authority exists.'" Ralph Piddington, *An Introduction to Social Anthropology* (London, 1950), pp. 230–231.

[22] The word "state" ill serves the cause of clarity in this context. Its pristine political usage was embodied in the phrase "state of political union." But according to a relatively recent (from the historical point of view) meaning given the word by political theorists, the essential characteristic of the "state" is physical coercion and centralized authority. "The state is distinguished from all other associations by its exclusive investment with the final power of coercion." Robert MacIver and Charles Page, *Society* (New York, 1949), p. 456. "The state is thus a society of individuals submitted, if necessary, by compulsion, to a certain way of life." Harold Laski, *Introduction to Politics* (London, 1931), pp. 12, 13. If the word "state" is to have a viable meaning it must refer to the political association of the people for the attainment of their common values. Thomas Davitt, *The Elements of Law* (Boston, 1959), pp. 324–328.

It has been said that in most preliterate societies political institutions are few and simple or even entirely absent. Among the Australian Bushmen, it is reported, political groupings are absent. With the Andaman Islanders there is no organized government. The aboriginal Eskimo have no government in the formal sense. Their society is fundamentally anarchical because no one is compelled to submit to direction. Peoples such as the Tallensi, Nuer, and Bantu Kavirondo are stateless societies which have no formal government. The Nuer have no politically organized society.

Similarly, the Ifugao are said to live in a state of anarchy with no political organization or government whatever. The only organization, political or social, that the Ifugao has is the family, it is reported. Among the Kalinga, it is reported that no tribe even remotely approaches tribal organization or government. The Yurok have no political organization. They live in a society actually existing without the state, that is, without government or political organization. The Dobuans also are said to have no political organization.

The evidence indicates, however, that these various peoples do not live in a condition of lawless and orderless anarchy. What is implied by such statements is that these preliterates do not have the type of political organization the observer has known elsewhere. They do not have the institutional organizations and formalized government that direct and maintain order in other parts of the world.[23] The word "anarchy," unless it is to be used in a purely arbitrary and therefore uncommunicating fashion, means at the very least a state of orderless confusion. But complete chaos is non-existent in these preliterate societies where custom law prevails, embodying as it does value judgments of good and evil.[24]

Regulation of human activity in some form is, as we saw, a universal invariant among human beings. Ordered relations are essential to any society and this ordering must be done according to established norms or rules. Men's basic drives cannot be allowed to operate promiscuously. They need rational control.[25] Such regulation when it relates to the common good of the

---

[23] Reporters "do not intend to imply that the peoples to whom they refer live in a condition of anarchy; they mean merely that such peoples lack institutional organizations, of the kind found in the modern Western state, for maintaining law and order and directing public life generally." Isaac Schapera, *Government and Politics in Tribal Societies* (London, 1956), p. 39.

[24] "Absolute chaos is inconceivable. The notion of regularity, of what is called law, is inescapable. . . . And these ideas of law and capriciousness are probably everywhere connected somehow with ideas of good and evil." Robert Redfield, *The Primitive World and Its Transformations* (Ithaca, 1953), p. 100.

[25] "Regulation is a universal aspect of society. Society means a system of ordered relations. The system may be informal, folk-sustained, uncentralized, and without specific agencies, or it may be highly organized. But social regulation is always present, for no society can exist without some control over the native impulses of human beings." Robert MacIver, *Web of Government* (New York, 1947), p. 22.

people is political in nature. Any action, therefore, by the people themselves or by their leaders which is promotive of this common welfare—be it by way of establishing custom law, of settling disputes, of changing custom by new edicts or of punishing by ridicule and exile—is political and implies to some degree political union and political organization.

The very peoples mentioned above, concerning whom it was said that they had "no political organization," give evidence of actions that are of the essence of political effort. The Bushmen recognize rights, settle disputes, punish by collective attack those who have become public menaces, make decisions usually through the elders, follow their chief in hunting and warfare. Hence, the Bushmen cannot be said to live in a state of anarchy. There is also political activity among the Andaman Islanders. The affairs of the community are regulated entirely by the older men and women. Each local group has one man who by his influence controls and directs the others. The Eskimo, whose society has been said to be fundamentally anarchical, have leaders who function in a socio-political manner when their leadership relates to the common welfare of the group. They determine the movements of the tribe. The Eskimo headman is tacitly recognized as a first among equals. The shaman also assumes the profile of a political leader when religious rules, in the absence of custom law regulations, direct the Eskimo in social and economic life.

The Nuer and Tallensi live a political life to no small extent. They are not anarchistic and stateless as they have been depicted. They have chiefs who have political power. Their leopard-skin chief is the center of political cohesion. His functioning at times has a definite political connotation. The Ifugao, in spite of misleading statements to the contrary, also have political organization in varying degrees. There is an organized system of justice—which is political action of its very nature. The functions of go-betweens among the Ifugao are admittedly political in nature. Legal matters are conducted by and between families in what has been called the embryo of political organization.

Similarly among the Kalinga, the actions of pact-holders, pangats, and go-betweens are definitely of a political nature. Such are the publicly approved efforts of the pangats to interpret the custom law and of go-betweens to keep compensations in line. The enforcement by go-betweens of the custom law against mediation proceedings being interrupted by violence is clearly an act of political enforcement. Among the Yurok too, although they have no formal government, there is a whole web of personal relationships that are embodied in custom law. As far as the Dobuans go, it is said that nothing could be further from the truth than to see there a condition of anarchy. Dobuan societies are organized in concentric circles within each of which specified forms of warfare are allowed. No individual can take matters into his own hands. All action is taken by the war unit.

Sometimes the presence of political organization among a people appears in clear outline only during certain recurring events which demand united efforts in promoting the common welfare. Such was the case of the Teda noted above. This socio-political phenomenon occurs among the Australian aborigines and the African Tallensi when many clans are assembled for the celebration of religious rites. But more striking instances of the activation of latent political union when necessity demands were the politically controlled hunts of the American Plains Indians. Although they were in general averse to centralized political control, strict police regulations were enforced on the tribe. Disorganized, individual hunting would have endangered the food supply of the whole tribe. Any premature startling of the herd was punished by the tribal police. The Omaha special hunt police punished offenses against good order during the hunt.

There are other examples among the American Indians of the police controlling not only the hunt but also the safe conduct back to the village of the results of the hunt, protection against the exploitation of crops, safeguarding villages and punishing seducers of women. The Winnebago and Menomini police forestalled any premature exploitation of wild rice which was a main source of food supply. The Sauk and Fox war chiefs directed not only the hunt but also the homeward journey from it. Their purpose was to ward off hostile attacks on single families and the pillaging of corn. The Winnebago, Sauk, and Fox police, besides the functions mentioned, also regulated travel, guarded villages continuously, and whipped the seducers of women. There can be no doubt of the socio-political nature of the union effected among the people by such common endeavors as the hunt. The unchallenged supremacy of the police unified the entire people into a political whole that was superior to any individual person. After accomplishing the above mentioned contributions to the common welfare of the group during the hunt, this active political union with its governmental police lapsed back into a state of latency until the next year's hunt.

In other words, although researchers have at times reported that some preliterates have "no political association," what they meant was that they found no formal political society, institutions and agencies of the kind with which they were familiar in other parts of the world. For, upon examination of the data not only is it evident that some of the reported activities of preliterates are political in nature but the reporters themselves eventually identify some of them as such.[26]

[26] Political association is universal: Robert Redfield, *The Primitive World and Its Transformations* (Ithaca, 1953), p. 14; Bronislaw Malinowski, *A Scientific Theory of Culture and other Essays* (Chapel Hill, 1944), pp. 61, 165; Alfred Radcliffe-Brown, *The Andaman Islanders* (Cambridge, 1933), p. 44; E. Adamson Hoebel, "Law-ways of the Primitive Eskimos," *Jour. Criminology and Criminal Law* 31 (1941): pp. 667–668; Hoebel, *The Law of Primitive Man* (Cambridge, Mass., 1954), p. 81; Franz Boas, *Anthropology and Modern Life* (New York,

The case for the universality of political association is, then, well made. So also is the case well founded for the innateness of the drive to live in association with other men which of necessity is political association.

## I. UNIVERSAL VALUE JUDGMENTS

All normal men have a basic drive to associate with other men in the pursuit of common values. Hence, all individual men form the value judgment without a reasoning process that it is good to unite with other men in political association. This value judgment is given and is a postulate of all political living.[27] The other universal value judgments regarding political living are constructed. Some of these are universal in all societies of preliterates without exception. Others are universal but with rare exceptions.

### A. IN ALL SOCIETIES

The constructed value judgments in this area which are universal in all preliterate societies regard first the common needs of protection and security, order and peace, whose fulfillment is the rationale of living in political association. Among these needs are also the directive regulations of custom law and the cooperative efforts of all the people which are necessary if these needs are to be completely satisfied.

1928), pp. 23, 231–232; Paul Howell, *A Manual of Nuer Law* (London, 1954), pp. 29, 223; Ralph Barton, *The Half-Way Sun* (New York, 1930), pp. 29, 63, 94; Ralph Barton, "Ifugao Law," *Amer. Archaeology and Ethnology* **15** (1919): pp. 9, 11, 63, 67; Alfred Radcliffe-Brown, "Primitive Law," *Encyc. of the Social Sciences* **9** (1933): pp. 204, 205; Ruth Benedict, *Patterns of Culture* (New York, 1934), p. 131; Isaac Schapera, *Government and Politics in Tribal Societies* (London, 1956), pp. 119–120; Hoebel, "Three Studies in African Law," *Stanford Law Rev.* **13** (1961): p. 427; Meyer Fortes, "The Political System of the Tallensi of the Northern Territories of the Gold Coast," in: Evans-Pritchard, *Nuer Religion* (Oxford, 1956), p. 299; Ralph Barton, *The Kalingas* (Chicago, 1949), pp. 138, 146, 254; Hoebel, "Fundamental Legal Concepts as Applied in the Study of Primitive Law," *Yale Law Jour.* **51** (1942): p. 958; Radcliffe-Brown, "Preface," to Meyer Fortes and Edward Evans-Pritchard, eds., *African Political Systems* (Oxford, 1940), p. xix; Robert Lowie, *An Introduction to Cultural Anthropology* (2nd ed., New York, 1940), p. 285; Arthur Diamond, *The Evolution of Law and Order* (London, 1951), p. 62; R. Lowie, "Property Rights and Coercive Powers of Plains Indian Military Societies," *Jour. Legal and Polit. Sociology* **1** (1943): p. 66; R. Lowie, *The Origin of the State* (New York, 1927), pp. 103–105.

[27] There may be those from preliterate, as well as literate, societies who value-judge that it is good to live outside political association with others. This action does not imply that they do not form the value judgment, as all normal men do, that it is good to live in political association. It means at most that they value-judge it better to live outside society for specific reasons. Armed forces duty in isolated areas, with extra pay added as compensatory inducement, is such an example. Or a man may simply judge that, although it is good for other men to live in political association, it is better for him to live alone whatever his reason may be. It is only when there is no apparent reason why a man wants to be completely alone, that the possibility of psychiatric abnormality arises as we noted above. The normal man value-judges that it is better for him to live alone for definite reasons.

## 1. *Protection and Security*

Political association is the union by consent, expressed or implied, of individual persons for the purpose of attaining their mutual protection and security. Once attained, these conditions flower into order and peace. Only political association can fulfill these common needs of men and thereby produce these common values. The agreement of each member to work for these common ends is the bond which unites the members into a political union. Because of this agreement, each member can expect the cooperative effort of all the members in regard to these common ends, and he can expect to participate in these common values once they are realized. In this sense, each member has a title to the cooperative efforts of all the other members, and he has a title to the resulting protection and security. Each member owes it to the others to cooperate in fulfilling these common needs, and the other members owe it to him to share in these common values.

In other words, men have titles to proper values such as life, sex, knowledge, decision, and property. But they also have titles to common values such as the contributive efforts of all the members of their political community and the sharing in the common results. Put in terms of justice, respect is due to titles to proper values in commutative or exchange justice. It is due to titles to common values in contributive or distributive justice.

All societies value-judge that protection and security, order and peace are good and not evil. This is a postulate of all political living. That all peoples do form this value judgment is shown by their reaction to offenses which menace these common values. These values are threatened when injuries are done either to individuals or to the whole community. This is a breakdown in justice.[28] There has been a failure to respect others' relations of title. Called for immediately are measures to repair this failure and to restore protection and security. Sanctions may be required.[29] Respect for others' relations of title must be reinstated. This is brought about, to some degree at least, by the infliction of punishment or the payment of compensation or both.[30] The justifying rationale for punishment and compensation lies in the restoration of respect for

[28] "Traditional law can tolerate no rebels: equilibrium and non-conformity are incompatible." Jack Driberg, "Primitive Law in East Africa," *Africa* **1** (1928): p. 67.

[29] "A sanction is a social force which tends to produce in the actions of an actual or a would-be non-conformist conformity with social custom. Godfrey Wilson, "Introduction to Nyakyusa Law," *Africa* **10** (1937): p. 18.

[30] "The various types of punishment in both civil and criminal procedure are merely ways of conditioning the individual to the required behavior or of removing him and of indicating what the results will be for others who fail to act in the way defined by law. ... Anyone acting in such a way as to disturb this equilibrium must be taught not to do so again." Eliot Chapple and Carleton Coon, *Principles of Anthropology* (New York, 1942), p. 657.

others' relation of title which is due in justice.[31] Conditions of protection and security, order and peace are thereby reestablished.

The value judgment made by all people regarding these common values is further shown by the fact that deprivation of them has always been feared as one of the severest of punishments for offenses. Banishment, exile, and outlawry are such a punishment. To be deprived of the protection and security of one's homeland, of the orderly and peaceful existence with family and friends, is a deprivation which for some is tantamount to being deprived of life itself. This was realized early in the history of human punishments. Outlawry was a declaration that the offending individual would no longer be allowed to enjoy the benefits of living in association with other men. It was principally the deprivation of the common values provided by association which made outlawry such a harsh penalty. The excluded man was a stranger or enemy whom anyone could kill with impunity. No one could associate with him or give him food or lodging.

This deprivation is so elemental that it appears to be the first punishment imposed by peoples against those who refused to respect others' relations of title to things. Association with others in fulfilling common needs was valued so highly by the people that its deprivation was the first punishment which occurred to them in their reaction against offenders. It is said that the older a law is, the more detailed are its provisions concerning outlawry.

The value judgment, therefore, that protection and security, order and peace, are good and desirable as fulfilling common needs is universal in all preliterate societies. This judgment is another postulate of political living and custom law.[32]

### 2. Cooperative Effort

The necessity of fulfilling the common needs of protection, security, order, and peace faces every man living in political association. For, the achievement of these common values is the rationale, as we said, for being in such a society. Preliterates realize this fact of political life as well as do their literate brothers. The need of presenting a solid front against outsiders, for instance, is everywhere recognized. The spirit of cooperation animates preliterate living.

This spirit of cooperation may be based purely on self-interest. It is worth the individual's effort to pro-

mote common values because he has everything to gain by doing so. This recognition that the actions of every individual in the community have consequences for the whole group, tends to engender a sense of cooperative responsibility. Thus, reciprocity of cooperative effort is recognized as one of the strongest inducements for keeping the custom law and promoting common values. As a motive for obeying custom law, it has been said to be as important as punitive sanctions.

The necessity of cooperative effort is so great that it is not left merely in the hands of the individual. In all societies cooperative groupings are formed. These are organized efforts at achieving common values. Such are the family, the village or town, kin and clan, age-grades and occupational teams. These are universals. Cooperative efforts also take the form of representation through councils, leadership, and claims to political direction. It is their common needs and interests, as well as the necessity of working together for the achievement of these common values, which unites these individuals and groups into a political union. It is sometimes said that organized cooperative efforts imply a "central authority" which "administers" these efforts. If such a statement is intended to mean that among preliterates there is always a clearly identifiable person or group which sees to it that the custom law is observed, it is not accurate. For, as we shall see later regarding leaders, there are some groups in which it would be impossible to locate such a "central authority."

In realizing the necessity of working together for common values, preliterates are recognizing their obligation to obey their custom law which directs to this same end. For, as we saw, obligation is the necessity of employing the means necessary for a desired end. "A community of interests implies a common attitude, common obligations, and common rights as between all members of the community."[33] This recognition of the necessity of cooperative effort in satisfying common needs, then, is universal in all known preliterate societies. The value judgment that it is good to do what is necessary for the fulfillment of common needs is universal in all preliterate societies. To put it another way, all preliterate societies perceive their obligation to obey custom law.[34]

[31] "The general right to punish may be derived from the right of society to protect itself." Leonard Hobhouse, *Morals in Evolution* (New York, 1906), p. 125. On punishment as restorative rather than as revenge, see Thomas Davitt, "Criminal Responsibility and Punishment," *Nomos* 3 (1960): pp. 143–151.

[32] Protection and security: Paul Vinogradoff, *Outlines of Historical Jurisprudence* (London, 1922), p. 360; Leonard Hobhouse, *Morals in Evolution* (New York, 1906), p. 102; Henry Maine, *Early Law and Custom* (New York, 1883), pp. 170–171; Richard Cherry, *Lectures in the Growth of Criminal Law in Ancient Communities* (London, 1890), p. 13.

[33] Jack Driberg, "Primitive Law in East Africa," *Africa* 1 (1928): pp. 66–67.

[34] Cooperative effort: Julius Lips, "Government," in Franz Boas, ed., *General Anthropology* (Boston, 1938), p. 497; Anthony Allott, *Essays in African Law* (London, 1960), pp. 69–70; H. Ian Hogbin, *Law and Order in Polynesia* (London, 1934), p. 83; Ashley Montagu, *Man: His First Million Years* (Cleveland, 1957), p. 170; Bronislaw Malinowski, "The Forces of Law and Order in a Primitive Community," *Proc. Royal Inst. of Great Britain* 24 (1925): p. 533; Malinowski, "Introduction," to H. Ian Hogbin, *Law and Order in Polynesia* (New York, 1934), pp. xxxvi; George Murdock, "The Common Denominator of Culture," in Ralph Linton, ed., *The Science of Man in the World Crisis* (New York, 1945), p. 134; Malinowski, "A New Instrument for the Interpretation of Law—Especially Primitive," *Yale Law Jour.* 51 (1942): p. 1240; Alexander

### 3. *Regulative Judging*

One of the principal means of assuring protection and security are regulations which direct the people in the fulfilling of these common needs. Such directive judgments are necessary if cooperative action is to be effective. The basic drives of everyone must be molded, patterned, and directed not only to values which are proper to individual persons but also to values which are common to all persons in the community. These directive regulations, when observed, protect and secure the respect due to men's various relations of title. Preliterates universally judge that the regulations of their custom law which direct them in their protection and security are good and not evil. Such a value judgment has an obvious relation to the value judgments concerning self-defense and self-preservation.

The claim to make directive judgments in political living lies basically with all the people. It derives, as we have seen, from men's basic drive for self-realization. Such directive judging is government and the claim to judge directively is authority. The people may exercise this authority themselves directly, or they may exercise it indirectly through those they choose to do the judging for them. Preliterates universally recognize that the primary claim to political direction belongs to all the people. They give evidence of this by governing themselves in many instances without leaders of any kind. Evidence is also had in their ready assumption that they have a right to criticize leaders, to disapprove of them, to oppose them, to rebel against them, and to remove them completely if they do not work to fulfill the common needs of all the people.

The value judgments which preliterates make concerning government through councils and chiefs are not universal. They are, as we shall see, either general or common.

#### a. Self-government

All societies of preliterates manifest the tendency of the people to make judgments regarding what pertains to the fulfillment of their common needs. The vast majority of indigenous African societies are said to show a constant pre-occupation with the ideas of democracy in popular government. The self-government of the Albanian mountaineers is reported to be, in its elementary way, a government of the people, by the people, and for the people. The government of the Nsukka of Nigeria is the business of the whole community. Its basis is the family organization, and authority is widely distributed. Among the Ashanti, there is no such thing as government apart from the people. This political participation has been identified as one of their basic principles.

In some groups which are "acephalous" and without centralized government, political activities are carried on by the people themselves. Thus, the Nuer, the Tiv, the Bedouin Arabs and others which we shall mention later, govern themselves by kinship groups composed of families which function as small-scale political societies. The instrumentality employed, in an economy of hunting and gathering, is that of a balance of power and opposition. The preliterates of New Guinea and the Bismarck Archipelago also lack political organization and sanctions capable of uniting more than a few hundred persons in a cooperating society. Yet, even without a council of elders, they govern themselves by means of reciprocal sanctions—I'll help you if you help me—and certain individuals or groups are charged with keeping the unsteady peace.

The people's participation in political affairs is also shown by the part they play in public discussions on community topics and on the adjustment of custom law to the needs of daily life, as occurs in many places in Africa. At these public assemblies anyone who has something worth while to say may say it. Final decisions are reached not so much by formal vote as by the weight of the opinions expressed by the people. In Nyakyusa court cases are heard in public and anyone may speak and give his opinion of the case. The decision of the judges is swayed by the opinions the people have expressed. One reason for this is that if one of the parties refuses to accept the judges' decision, the judges can compel him to accept it only in so far as they have the general support of the people.[35]

The political power of the people is sometimes shown in public meetings where they may overrule the wishes of the chief. Among the Ngwato in Bechuanaland, the people are summoned to a public assembly to debate issues of interest to the tribe as a whole. Tribal disputes, wrangles between the chief and his relatives, new taxes, new public works, new decrees by the chief, and the relations between the people and his government are among the topics discussed. Any one may speak. Grievances are thus aired by the people and the chief and his advisers have an opportunity to find out the feelings of the people. Although ordinarily the people do not overrule the desires of the chief, it is not unknown that they do so. They are unafraid to speak openly and may even admonish the chief.

Goldenweiser, *Anthropology* (New York, 1937), p. 296; Anthony Allott, *Essays in African Law* (London, 1960), p. 69; Ralph Piddington, *An Introduction to Social Anthropology* (London, 1950), p. 231; Edward Westermarck, *The Origin and Development of the Moral Ideas* (2 v., London, 1908–1912), pp. 133, 135; Malinowski, *A Scientific Theory of Culture and other Essays* (Chapel Hill, 1944), pp. 61, 165; Meyer Fortes and Edward Evans-Pritchard, eds., *African Political Systems* (Oxford, 1940), p. 5; Eliot Chapple and Carleton Coon, *Principles of Anthropology* (New York, 1942), p. 656; T. Olawale Elias, *The Nature of African Customary Law* (Manchester, 1956), p. 45; Leopold Pospisil, *Kapauku Papuans and Their Law* (New Haven, 1958), p. 279.

[35] The similarity of these preliterate peoples' assemblies to the English county meeting, the American town meeting, and the Swiss canton meeting, is obvious.

Even in making decisions, the chief in many places will take into consideration the opinion of the people. In Samoa the government of the village is in the hands of the people who meet in the village place. Again, not a majority vote but the preponderance of public opinion is controlling. Because of this fact, the chief or his subordinates try to guide the thinking of the people in the direction they desire. Sometimes, as among the Ashanti, councils are subject to the people. They are composed of representatives of the people who attempt to present the opinions of their people at the councils. If a representative does not do so, he is changed. Councils and representatives are thus under the control of the people.[36]

### b. Making Custom Law

The prime example of the people exercising their basic governing authority is the making of custom law. Custom law is by and large the end result of generations of trial-and-error experiments. Many ways were probably tried, for instance, of how to declare and indicate that a couple were married. Most of these ways were judged to be unworkable and unsatisfactory. A few of them were eventually found to be acceptable and desirable. These are the ways which are now embodied in custom law. Such areas of custom laws have a quasi-scientific aspect about them inasmuch as they represent the result of centuries of this trial-and-error experimentation and test. In these areas, constant readjustment and adaptation to needs is the prevailing condition of custom law.

In other aspects, however, it is doubtful that this process of trial and error in custom law was a prolonged one or even one of some length at all. It is highly questionable that lengthy experiments were necessary with murder, rape, incest, adultery, theft, and robbery before men were able to evaluate them and judge whether they were right or wrong. Nor was an amount of time required for men to judge whether self-preservation, sexual union, knowing and deciding, distinguishing mine from thine and doing what is just, and living in association with others for common ends were desirable or undesirable. For these value judgments are given. The other value judgments are con-

structs and they give every indication of being formed without too much difficulty.

The end product of the custom law made by some preliterate peoples is a series of unwritten regulations which rivals written codes in definiteness and effectiveness. The Trobrianders, for instance, have developed a consistent and coherent body of custom law. What this law demands is clearly defined. The Yurok of northwestern California and the Ifugao of the Philippines have an intricate system of custom law. It has been developed by the people themselves in the absence of any centralized lawmaking authority. The Albanian mountaineers, too, have evolved by themselves their custom law that covers every aspect of their daily life—aspects which we would designate as social, administrative, and pastoral.[37]

### c. Removal of Leaders

The basic claim of the people to govern themselves is especially shown among preliterates by their removal of unsatisfactory leaders. Among the Tswana, a chief is chief by the approval of his tribe. With the Naskapi, the power of the chief is controlled and regulated by the opinion of the people. If he loses their backing, his orders are no longer obeyed and he finds himself bypassed. Among the Ngwato, if a chief is not satisfactory, the people may begin to plot his overthrow. A chief may be overthrown for various reasons. In Tswana, if a chief among other things ignores his advisers, neglects his tribal duties, assaults people and destroys their property, is partial in his judgments and punishments, wastes funds and leads a shocking life, the leading men counsel together and warn him to mend his ways. If the chief fails to heed such warning, the people will withdraw their support and plot against him. A civil war may be incited in the hope that he may be overthrown or secretly killed.

Among the Tswana a chief is warned at his installation that the people will not follow him if he does not treat them well. They will support one of his rivals or leave the tribe and go elsewhere. Among the Gikuyu, revolt was resorted to by the people when a tyrannical chief would not let them cultivate lands, settle down and obtain sufficient food. In desperation they rebelled against him. A whole group of the Maoto, because the chief attacked them and killed one of their men for failing to attend a meeting concerning which they had not been notified, broke away from the Kwena and attached themselves to the Ngwaketse. The

---

[36] Self-government: T. Olawale Elias, *The Nature of African Customary Law* (Manchester, 1956), pp. 21, 199; Margaret Hasluck, *The Unwritten Law of the Albanian Mountains* (Cambridge, 1954), p. 11; C. K. Meek, *Law and Authority in a Nigerian Tribe* (London, 1937), p. 164; Robert Rattray, *Ashanti Law and Constitution* (Oxford, 1928), p. 407; Paul Bohannon, *Social Anthropology* (New York, 1963), p. 364; Margaret Mead, "Some Anthropological Considerations Concerning Natural Law," *Natural Law Forum* 6 (1961): p. 55; Godfrey Wilson, "Introduction to Nyakyusa Law," *Africa* 10 (1937): pp. 34–35; Isaac Schapera, "The Political Organization of the Ngwato of the Bechuanaland Protectorate," in: Myer Fortes and Edward Evans-Pritchard, *African Political Systems* (Oxford, 1940), p. 72; Julius Lips, "Government," in Franz Boas ed., *General Anthropology* (Boston, 1938), p. 524; K. A. Busia, *The Position of the Chief in the Modern Political System of Ashanti* (London, 1951), p. 64.

[37] Making custom law: Charles Dundas, "The Organization and Laws of Some Bantu Tribes," *Jour. Royal Anthropol. Inst.* 45 (1915): p. 305; Robert Redfield, "Maine's Ancient Law in the Light of Primitive Societies," *Western Polit. Quart.* 3 (1950): pp. 580–581; Bronislaw Malinowski, "The Forces of Law and Order in a Primitive Community," *Proc. Royal Inst. of Great Britain* 24 (1925): pp. 537, 545; Robert Lowie, *An Introduction to Cultural Anthropology* (2nd ed., New York, 1940), p. 286; Margaret Hasluck, *The Unwritten Law of the Albanian Mountains* (Cambridge, 1954), p. 9.

chief of the Tlokwa became so unacceptable to his people, because as they said he fed his dogs but not them, that they deserted him in battle and he was killed.[38]

Further evidence of the peoples' prime position in preliterate political government is had in their power to destool or dethrone a chief formally which is, in fact, the complement of their authority to enstool him. Among the Ashanti, the people had the claim to destool a chief. He could be destooled for, among other things, not following the advice of his elders, for being a drunk and glutton, for his insulting remarks, for dealing in charms and harmful medicines, and for excessive cruelty. He could also be destooled if he became blind, impotent, mad, epileptic, or contracted leprosy. Although the actual act of destooling may be performed by members of the Council, the fact that they are representatives of the people makes the destooling an act of the people.[39] With the Akan, all sections of the community were represented on the Council which emphasized their elemental claim to self-determination.

Preliterates universally recognize that all the people have a claim to judge what is necessary for the fulfillment of their common needs. The value judgment, therefore, that it is good to participate in such directive judging is universal in all preliterate societies.[40]

### 4. Sanctions

In all societies of men there are failures to respect others' relations of title. If these failures have a bearing on the protection and security of the whole community, there will be a common reaction. The members of the community have been injured and wronged. The individual person who decided to violate the regulations of the community, and thereby harm it, is primarily responsible for his decision, as we have seen. The people will react against him who has committed the offense. Offenses against the common good are universal in all preliterate societies and so are the sanctions which are imposed because of them.[41] All societies of preliterates value-judge that such offenses are bad. This is shown, to repeat, by their reaction in imposing sanctions which are in turn value-judged to be good. Sanctions are a means of promoting the order and peace which is needed by all the members of the community.

The sanctions of law have to do with the rewards and punishments which follow the observance or violation of law. "To put it simply, rules of conduct are safeguarded not merely by penalties. They are invariably baited with inducements."[42] Sanctions relate to offenses directly against the whole community (which we shall later call "crimes") or directly against individuals and thereby indirectly against the whole community (which we shall later call "torts"). Sanctions may be intrinsic or extrinsic to a law. When laws regarding killing others are kept, the intrinsic reward is a condition of security in which there is respect for others' title to life. When these laws are not kept, the intrinsic sanction is a condition of insecurity in which the respect for others' title to life is lessened. Intrinsic reward or punishment, then, relates to the very purpose of law and the basis of obligation. Sanctions may also be extrinsic to the law itself. The extrinsic reward of carrying out laws which promise bounties for the killing of unwanted animals or men is the reception of the reward. The extrinsic punishment for violating laws prohibiting murder can be imprisonment or execution. Sanctions work prospectively by promising rewards and by threatening punishments. They also work retrospectively by distributing rewards or by imposing penalties and compensations.

A point to be noted here is the place of intrinsic and extrinsic sanctions in law, including preliterate law. Intrinsic sanctions are necessarily present in the working of law. This is inevitable from the very nature of law itself. This is not true, however, of extrinsic sanctions. They may be added to a law or they may not. It is not essential to law that there be extrinsic sanctions added to it. The Constitution of the United States of America, which is the basic law of the land, does not have sanctions affixed to it.[43] Neither do

---

[38] "There is a peculiar custom amongst the natives of Yoruba, called kirikiri. When a king or chief or a powerful or notable man of the country is no more wanted by the people, i.e., when they are tired of him because of his evil ways and his mischievous and tyrannical actions, a mob parades through the country or town, singing vituperative songs and loudly abusing the man, and when they get to his quarters they throw sand and stones into his palace or house, to show that he is no more wanted in the country. Such a parade usually takes place in the night and may continue for three successive months. Within the expiration of three months the man concerned must try to reconcile or vacate the country, or commit suicide, when he is given a decent and honourable burial according to his rank and title. Should he ignore or slight kirikiri (by depending upon his power and might for the defence of his body and property) a select body of masked and powerful men shall suddenly rush into his house one night and kill him." A. K. Ajisafe, *Law and Customs of the Yoruba People* (London, 1924), p. 36.

[39] "[T]he actual act of displacement [consists in] taking the Chief's sandals off his feet, and withdrawing the stool from under him." Joseph Danquah, *Gold Coast: Akan Laws and Customs* (London, 1938), p. 117.

[40] Removal of leaders: Isaac Schapera, *A Handbook of Tswana Law and Custom* (London, 1938), pp. 84, 85; Julius Lips, "Naskapi Law, *Trans. Amer. Philos. Soc.* 37 (1947): p. 486; Schapera, "The Political Organization of the Ngwato of Bechuanaland Protectorate," in Meyer Fortes and Edward Evans-Pritchard, *African Political Systems* (Oxford, 1940), p. 80; Joseph Danquah, *Gold Coast: Akan Laws and Customs* (London, 1938), p. 117; Schapera, *Government and Politics in Tribal Societies* (London, 1956), pp. 153–155; Jomo Kenyatta, *Facing Mount Kenya* (London, 1953), p. 186; K. A. Busia, *The Position of the Chief in the Modern Political System of Ashanti* (London, 1951), pp. 21–22.

[41] Godfrey Wilson, "Introduction to Nyakyusa Law," *Africa* 10 (1937): p. 25.

[42] Bronislaw Malinowski, "Introduction," to H. Ian Hogbin, *Law and Order in Polynesia* (New York, 1934), p. lxv.

[43] See United States v. Sabella, 272 F. 2d 206 (2d Cir. 1959); People v. Merolla, 18 Misc. 2d 383, 181 N.Y.S. 2d 476 (1958); State v. Fairlawn Service Center, 20 N.J. 468, 120 A. 2d 233

certain statutes have sanctions added to them, a fact of which courts have taken cognizance. Preliterate custom law also may be without extrinsically added sanctions. Thus among the Akan of the Gold Coast "the penalty attaching to the violation of a law is regulated according to the nature and extent of the offense involved. In most cases there is no definite penalty attached to the breaking of a law." [44]

Punishment consists in the deprivation of some valued object. [45] With preliterates these deprivations may be physical or non-physical. A man may be deprived of his property through confiscation or compensation, of his bodily well-being through flogging or mutilation, of his family and friends through exile, or of his life by execution. Or he may be deprived of his good name and reputation by adverse public opinion, ridicule, and disgrace. The severity of the punishment is related to the gravity of the offense. Preliterates universally judge, as we just saw, that offenses in general are bad and sanctions in general are good. Their value judgments regarding specific offenses and sanctions are less than universal. The value judgment that it is good to distinguish between offenses which bear on the common welfare and those which do not is almost universal. Other value judgments concerning various punishments and compensations are general, common, frequent or occasional, as we shall see. [46]

### 5. Judging Cases

Judging the innocence or guilt of an accused, the right and wrong in a dispute, is done among preliterates either by the people themselves or their councils and chiefs. These also judge the punishment to be inflicted on the guilty and the amount of compensation to be exacted from one found liable in a dispute. Men's drive to distinguish between what is due to a man and what is not is the inspiration of these proceedings of justice.

Preliterates look upon offenses as disruptive of the union which should prevail in their cooperative effort to pursue their own common good. Offenses cut "the cord that binds humanity." [47] The purpose of judging cases is not only to see that justice is done but to keep the peace and avoid feuding. In some places, Africa for instance, every effort is made to restore friendships and remove the cause of tension. Only when the offense is seriously damaging to the common values of the community will there be recourse to banishment, or death by impalement, shooting, or hanging. Among the Tiv, as with other preliterates, the main purpose of judging cases is not so much to reach decisions as to make suggestions for settlement. The parties in interest must agree to the final determination. The ideal is that all parties leave the proceedings feeling that a good solution has been reached. Ordinarily, family disputes about private matters are settled within the family by its head or elders.

The judging of cases among preliterates is done primarily by the people. "In the simplest societies the judges are the people." [48] In many places, the judging of cases clearly shows that decisions are made by the consent of the people. Among the Gikuyu and Kamba of Kenya who are without chiefs, it is the community as a whole which makes up a communal court. It punishes offenses against the common good and represses offenders who disturb the peace of the community. Among the Kiowa Indians, the people sometimes inflicted the death penalty on serious offenders. With the Comanche, the people themselves judged sorcerers. When their resentment had reached a certain point, they took immediate action and lynched the sorcerer. This procedure represented not mob hatred but public judgment and public policy. In Samoa, for such offenses as ridiculing a chief, theft on second conviction, and incest, the village community imposed sanctions of fines, slave labor, destruction of property, banishment, exposure to the sun and hanging.

The people's primary authority in decision-making is shown in the manner in which they choose certain individuals to do the judging for them. The "commoner" judges among some peoples attest to this influence of the people. Among the Nyakyusa, a man may become prominent because of a reputation for defensive witchcraft or because he has character or wealth. His house is a center of gatherings and his opinion is sought and often accepted in small quarrels. If, in the estimation of the people, he judges well, more cases are submitted to him for adjudication. The people begin to refer to him as the "commoner." He is then accepted by the "great commoner" of the whole village and recognized as an auxiliary judge in the judging of cases. In his position as co-judge with the great commoner, the commoner plays an integral part in the decision-making of the chief. For the chief does not make any important decisions without first consulting his great commoners. Among the Kalinga, the selection of "pangats" shows the same basic influence of the people. These men are "The Peacemakers" or "The Right-Determiners."

---

(1956); Horak. v. State, 95 Tex. Cr. R. 474, 255 S.W. 191 (1923); City of New Orleans v. Stein, 137 La. 652, 69 So. 43 (1915); Ex parte Ellsworth, 165 Cal. 677, 133 Pac. 272 (1913); Jenkins v. State, 13 Ga. App. 79 S.E. 861 (1913).

[44] Joseph Danquah, *Gold Coast: Akan Laws and Customs* (London, 1938), p. 63.

[45] On punishment as deprivation, see Thomas Davitt, *The Elements of Law* (Boston, 1959), pp. 136–139. Davitt, "Criminal Responsibility and Punishment," *Nomos* 3 (1960): pp. 143–151.

[46] "So far as I am aware, there is no modern cross-cultural study of punishment. It is becoming obvious that, although legal anthropology has made a good beginning, there are vast unexplored areas in this universal of human behavior." Paul Bohannon, *Social Anthropology* (New York, 1963), p. 296.

[47] A. K. Ajisafe, *Law and Customs of the Yoruba People* (London, 1924), p. 43.

[48] Ashley Montagu, *Man: His First Million Years* (Cleveland, 1957), p. 177.

They are chosen after a long informal process of testing. After they have shown power and influence, the people gradually give them recognition of "pangat."

The position of elders in judging cases also reflects the basic authority of the people in decision-making. Elders are the people grown old and wise. Councils of elders are general among preliterate peoples, as we shall see later. In many places they sit in judgment on cases. Among the food-gathering tribes of Australia, it was the old men "seasoned in life and in the tribal laws" who settled disputes and instructed the younger men on the rules of custom law. With the Nabaloi, disputes were settled by the council which was composed of the wisest and most respected men. All rich men were members of the council and poor men too if they were wise and old.

Among the Naskapi, the judging of cases was done by the chief together with the oldest and most highly respected men. Among the Akan, the head of the family, tribe, or nation was looked on as the one who determined rights, redressed wrongs and dispensed mercy. But when it came to the actual judging of cases, he always sat with the wise old men of the tribe and together they reached judicial decisions. With some tribes, where a council of elders can be assembled, a court of judges is constituted. Thus, the councils of the Australian aborigines and of an American Indian pueblo function as judges of cases.

One of the values of having elders as judges is their knowledge of custom law and of the background of cases. An instance is related regarding litigation over a cow where the elders traced the progeny of the cow over three generations, knew how it was acquired, and how the rights in its progeny had been conveyed. It is the older men who are reported as knowing the proverbs and maxims embodying custom law. Although it is probably true that at times the quoting of proverbs by elders is no more than an oratorical trick to sway the judges, nevertheless the quoting of proverbs is said to rank with legal precedents in importance in some courts. In Africa proverbs are quoted as the embodiment of custom law.

It is said that among some peoples the chief is the supreme judge. This is the situation among the Bantu and the Hottentot. Among other peoples, however, it is reported that whatever judging the chief does in inflicting punishments and awarding compensations faithfully reflects the value judgments of the community. These value judgments may not be expressed in words but they are the underlying value assumptions and judgments of the whole community. Further evidence of the influence of the people on the judging of the chief is had, as we have mentioned, in those instances where bystanders join in and express their judgments on the case. Such participation is accepted as part of the ordinary judicial procedure.

The value judgment, therefore, that it is good to seek what is just and what is unjust by judging cases is universal in all preliterate societies.[49]

## B. IN ALL SOCIETIES WITH RARE EXCEPTIONS

There are value judgments which preliterates make concerning political association which are universal but with rare exceptions. These relate to the distinction between offenses directly and indirectly relating to the common needs of the community, and to respect for elders.

### 1. Distinguishing Offenses Directly and Indirectly against Common Values

All of the actions of the members of a political association probably have some relation to common values. But some of these actions, for instance the manner in which food is eaten, are so remotely related that they are not of enough concern to the people to elicit a reaction and be a matter of their custom law. Other actions, however, relate more proximately to the fulfillment of common needs. Some of these actions, such as damaging a neighbor's crops, relate indirectly to the good of the whole community inasmuch as the order and peace are to this extent disturbed. Such actions will cause a repercussion from the injured neighbor and in some cases perhaps from the community also. Other actions, for instance setting fire to the neighbor's house, relate directly to the common needs of the whole community in so far as other dwellings are thereby endangered. This type of offense is certain to cause a reaction on the part of the community.[50]

---

[49] Judging cases: Leonard Hobhouse, *Morals in Evolution* (New York, 1906), pp. 100, 114; T. Olawale Elias, *The Nature of African Customary Law* (Manchester, 1956), pp. 160, 298; E. Adamson Hoebel, "Three Studies in African Law," *Stanford Law Rev.* **13** (1961): p. 430; Anthony Allott, *Essays in African Law* (London, 1960), pp. 69, 117; Jane Richardson, "Law and Status Among the Kiowa Indians," *Monograph Amer. Ethnol. Soc.* **1** (1940): p. 130; Hoebel, "The Political Organization of Law-ways of the Comanche Indians," *Mem. Amer. Anthropol. Assoc.* **54** (1940): pp. 77–78; Julius Lips, "Government," in Franz Boas, *General Anthropology* (Boston, 1938), pp. 496, 525; Godfrey Wilson, "Introduction to Nyakyusa Law," *Africa* **10** (1937): p. 22; Ralph Barton, *The Kalingas* (Chicago, 1949), p. 147; Claude Moss, "Nabaloi Law and Ritual," *Amer. Archaeology and Ethnology* **15** (1920): p. 237; Lips, "Naskapi Law," *Trans. Amer. Philos. Soc.* **37** (1947): p. 475; Joseph Danquah, *Gold Coast: Akan Laws and Customs* (London, 1938), p. 66; Ashley Montagu, *Man: His First Million Years* (Cleveland, 1957), p. 177; J. G. Peristiany, "Law," in: Edward Evans-Pritchard and others, *The Institutions of Primitive Society* (Glencoe, 1956), p. 42; Ralph Beals and Harry Hoijer, *An Introduction to Anthropology* (New York, 1953), p. 567; Isaac Schapera, *Government and Politics in Tribal Societies* (London, 1956), p. 92.

[50] Offenses have been distinguished by some on the basis of the punishment inflicted and not on the nature of the offense. But the rationale of punishment itself and its varying kinds can be nothing else but the nature of the offense committed and its relation to the common welfare. See Thomas Davitt, "Criminal Responsibility and Punishment," *Nomos* **3** (1960): pp. 143–151. "[A] very general definition of crime [would be] a

### a. "Crimes" and "Torts"

In written laws offenses which relate directly and indirectly to the common welfare are designated by various sets of terms. In English-speaking countries, those offenses which relate directly to the common needs of the people are called "crimes." Those which relate directly to the needs of individuals but indirectly to the common needs of all are termed "torts." [51] On this basis, offenses may be said to pertain to criminal and to civil law. These terms appear in the reports of field observers. But because of the many shades of meaning they have acquired in the written legal systems in which they are used, they will be accepted and used here only with a qualification. They will be employed here, when they are used, as shorthand expressions denoting offenses of preliterates which directly or indirectly relate to the common needs of the people and which cause reactions among the people accordingly.

Preliterates distinguish between offenses that call for no adverse reaction and those that do. Breaches of the rules of etiquette do not necessarily call for punishment. They also differentiate between offenses that call for a reaction either from individuals solely or from all the people together. Thus, among the Gikuyu, most offenses are of the kind that draw a response solely from the injured individual who may seek redress on a self-help basis. Other offenses, however, though not great in number demand a reaction on the part of the whole community. Killing by poisoning or witchcraft were such offenses and the penalty inflicted by the whole community was death by burning. The Akan make a clear distinction in the way they try criminal and civil cases. Offenses which have harmed the whole community are tried with court proceedings different from those offenses which have harmed only individuals.

Among some preliterates, the Caribou Eskimo for instance, theft and murder are not necessarily crimes.

But witchcraft, antisocial behavior, and eating seal and caribou at the same meal thereby endangering the food supply, are crimes. Among the Plains Indians, murder was only a tort against the victim's relations, but the premature frightening of a buffalo herd and consequent endangering of the tribe's food supply was a crime punishable by the tribal police. In some places in South Africa, theft is a tort which calls for individual indemnification, while hurting or killing a subject of the chief is a crime for which compensation went to the chief and not to the victim or his family. Among the Papuans, almost all offenses such as theft, murder, rape, and the like, are torts and call for individual redress. Offenses which could be classified as crimes and punishable by the community as a whole are said to be rare.

The evidence indicates, then, that most offenses among preliterates are regarded as torts and not crimes. These offenses relate only indirectly to the common welfare of the people and evoke a reaction only from the injured individual. To be sure, such offenses as murder even when looked on by preliterates as a tort inevitably had consequences that affect all the people, especially if a long blood feud ensued. The idea that such offenses actually did have a relation to the common good was not completely absent from preliterate thinking, as exemplified in the case just mentioned of the chief being indemnified for the killing of one of his subjects. But there does not seem to be justification for holding that such thinking was prevalent among preliterates. [52]

The custom of making compensation for private wrongs, thereby forestalling self-redress by the injured party, antedated the practice of paying a penalty for offenses which affected the whole group. There were no criminal offenses in ancient law, it is said, only penal offenses. The word "crime" originated in relatively recent modern Roman law and implied some kind of judicial procedure resulting in a condemnation, such as outlawry, by all the people. [53] According to this

---

wrong that affects the political community as a whole. . . . [T]he general classification of crime according to the nature of the offense [is] adopted in most modern treatises on criminal law." George Calhoun, *The Growth of Criminal Law in Ancient Greece* (Berkeley, 1927), pp. 120–136.
Wrongs have also been distinguished on the ground that some actions (for instance, murder, theft, unnatural sex acts) are "evil in themselves" and have been universally condemned as such; other actions (for instance, gambling) are only "evil because prohibited" and are considered wrong merely in relation to specific social needs. This distinction between *mala in se* and *mala quia prohibita*, though ancient and widely accepted, is open to criticism. It is impossible to find evil in the actions of killing another human being or taking things that belong to another person *"in se"* and without relating these actions to factors outside the actions themselves. Likewise, it cannot be said that playing a game of chance is evil merely *"quia prohibita"* without at the same time considering its relations to other factors on account of which it was necessary to prohibit it. Thomas Davitt, *The Elements of Law* (Boston, 1959), pp. 178–187.

[51] "Perhaps no single topic so cries out for cross-cultural comparison as does the whole problem of crime." Paul Bohannon, *Social Anthropology* (New York, 1963), p. 296.

[52] The tendency of preliterates to consider most offenses as torts, rather than as crimes, is also found among such widely separated groups as the Greeks, the Romans and the Scandinavians. If a thief was caught red-handed, it was taken for granted that he fell immediately into the power of his captor. Only if he had taken to flight and it was necessary to track him did the community take action. But even then, the aggrieved party retained the claim to search in person the house of the suspect. This was done, however, according to procedure and ceremonies set by custom law. Such ceremonies are indicated by the word "ransack," which is compounded of *ran*—loot, and *sōkia*—to seek. To "ransack" for something is, then, traceable back to the custom of searching for things which were stolen. Paul Vinogradoff, *Outlines of Historical Jurisprudence* (London, 1922), p. 356.

[53] The earliest laws which punished certain offenses against individual persons as also offenses against the people of the whole society were several centuries B.C. As political thinking advanced, it was seen that some offenses committed directly against individuals were also offenses indirectly against the common welfare of all. From this realization it was but a step to the recognition that offenses against all the people were

analysis, it would appear that the element of payment or penalty is older in custom law than that of crime.[54]

## b. Lists of Offenses

The lists of offenses compiled by field researchers show considerable variation in what preliterates consider to be offenses that indirectly or directly relate to the common welfare. Among the Ifugao in the Kiangan-Nagakaran-Maggok area, the major crimes in the order of their frequency are reported to be sorcery, adultery, theft, murder, kidnaping of women and children, making an innocent person appear to be an accessory to a crime, manslaughter, rape of a married woman, arson, and incest. The minor crimes are reported to be insult, slander, false accusation, and the rape of an unmarried woman. The Nguni are reported as considering witchcraft, treason, incest, bestiality and other sexual perversions as criminal offenses. With the Carib, homicide, poisoning, sorcery, theft, and adultery are the most serious offenses.

The Bapedi are reported to regard as among the more important crimes murder, incest, rape, seduction, abduction, concealment of birth, adultery, treason, theft, assault, and malicious damage to property. In Nandi custom law incest, rape, contempt of elders, and witchcraft are looked on as crimes. Adultery, assault, homicide, and theft are considered to be in the nature of torts. The Ashanti likewise distinguish between offenses that concern the chief and central authority and those that do not. Those offenses which in their minds relate to central authority and the whole community are murder, suicide, certain sexual offenses, certain forms of abuse, certain kinds of assault, certain kinds of stealing, invoking a curse upon a chief, treason and cowardice, witchcraft, violating any other recognized taboo, and breaking a law enjoined by the swearing of an oath. The offenses which do not have a relation to central authority are theft which in Ashanti included adultery and certain sexual acts, certain kinds of abuse including slander, certain kinds of assault, cases involving property, pawning, loans, suretyship, and recovery of debts.

In Tswana a distinction is made between those offenses which harm social life in general and are therefore deserving of punishment, and those offenses which merely injure individual persons. The crimes include homicide, grievous bodily assault, sorcery, incest and other unnatural acts, all offenses against tribal authorities acting in official capacity, and breaches of the laws decreed by the Chief. The torts comprise failure to keep agreements, seduction, adultery, trespass, damage, theft, defamation, and slander. For the Kapauku Papuans, offenses against society are disobedience of orders during a war, causing a war or avoiding participation in one, allying with an enemy, and being ungenerous with wealth. Offenses against individual persons are murder, attempted suicide, lying, incest, adultery and theft. Lying, if it injures anyone, is punishable with a stick-beating given by the offended person. Among the Eskimo, sorcery, chronic lying, and homicidal recidivism are considered offenses against the common welfare of all the people. The sorcerer who is a killer, and the liar who is a common danger, are both liable to execution at the command of the people. In Nepal an unnatural act with a cow is thought to be a crime and punishable capitally. Among the aboriginal Australians, homicide, wounding, adultery, wife-stealing, and theft were thought to be torts and not threats to the common welfare.

A summary listing of the offenses that occur among preliterates in general has it that among the offenses considered matters of community interest are incest, sorcery, repeated breaches of tribal custom, and sacrilege. Among the offenses deemed to be directly against the individual are killing, wounding, theft, adultery, and failure to pay debts. It is noted, however, that, although these latter offenses are thought of primarily as injurious to the aggrieved person, they nevertheless are seen as affecting the whole community and are therefore reprovable as antisocial actions. From the reports we quote, offenses against the community would appear in general to comprise killing by poison or magic; incest, abortion, rape, and adultery; robbery, theft, and arson; sorcery and witchcraft; treason and insult. Offenses which are primarily against the individual are homicide and wounding; adultery and wife-stealing; theft and non-payment of debts. As is evident, killing, adultery, and theft appear as offenses either directly against the whole community or directly against the individual person and thereby indirectly against the whole community.

The value judgment, then, that it is good and desirable to distinguish between actions which are directly and those which are indirectly offensive to the whole community is almost universal among all preliterate societies.[55]

---

offenses against the person representing the people. The result of this was an increase in the severity of punishments for offenses against the people and their representative. See Richard Cherry, *Lectures in the Growth of Criminal Law in Ancient Communities* (London, 1890), pp. 56–58; Robert Marett, *Anthropology* (New York, 1911), p. 194.

[54] "Crimes" and "torts": Jomo Kenyatta, *Facing Mount Kenya* (London, 1953), p. 228; T. Olawale Elias, *The Nature of African Customary Law* (Manchester, 1956), pp. 222–223; Robert Lowie, *An Introduction to Cultural Anthropology* (2nd ed., New York, 1940), p. 285; F. E. Williams, "Group Sentiment and Primitive Justice," *Amer. Anthropologist* **43** (1941): p. 531; Lewis Tupper, "Customary and Other Law in the East Africa Protectorate," *Jour. Soc. Comp. Legislation* **8** (1908): p. 175; Paul Vinogradoff, *Outlines of Historical Jurisprudence* (London, 1922), p. 361; Richard Cherry, *Lectures in the Growth of Criminal Law in Ancient Communities* (London, 1890), p. 14.

[55] Lists of offenses: Ralph Barton "Ifugao Law," *Amer. Archaeology and Ethnology* **15** (1919): p. 69; Arthur Diamond, *The Evolution of Law and Order* (London, 1951), pp. 22, 153; John Gillin, "Crime and Punishment Among the Barama River

## 2. *Respect for the Elderly*

The other value judgment regarding political living which is almost universal is respect for the aged. "Perhaps the most striking fact about respect for old age is its widespread occurrence. Some degree of prestige for the aged seems to have been practically universal in all known societies." [56] This does not mean that there are no exceptions to this value judgment or that respect automatically increases in relation to age alone. Usually there are circumstances when an optimum time of advanced years is reached by the individual when prestige is attained. On the other hand, under other circumstances renown may never be attained in old age by the individual, or if it is attained it may be lost. But the value judgment that it is good to show respect to the aged is almost universal in all known societies.

Different values underlie respect for elders. Some of them we have already seen when discussing the judging of cases. Older men have more knowledge. But one of the most important values of elders concerns their knowledge of the law. Elders with the best memories are revered as the custodians of custom law. This has special significance for preliterates. An aged person may be the possessor of more knowledge of custom law than any other source available. For this reason he may hold a controlling position in court proceedings, as we saw. The elders are the rolls, records and archives of preliterates. They are the living substitute for printed statutes and reported cases. This means that the elders perform the indispensable function of providing continuity for custom law. This knowledge of custom law and its precedents has given to elders a definite position of honor.

Among the Bantu, the elders are generally considered to be the most likely prospects for political leadership. It is the oldest member of the group whose judgment carries the greatest weight with the other members. Elders are the ones best qualified to sit on councils and courts. With the Albanians, the elders were obeyed more willingly than others because of the deference shown them. In Australia the aged constitute a group of recognized authority.

Respect for elders, it is said, is also due in part to the fact that children observe older people participating in religious rites, and to the early training the children receive in behavior with their elders, as we have already seen. In Nigeria children are impressed when very young by the importance of age when they observe religious rites, especially the cult of ancestors, being conducted by the older members of the group. This impression is reinforced by the education given the children in the use of proper terms when addressing older people. At what age men are "elders," "old," or "aged," depends on the point of view of the particular society of which they are members. With the Assiniboine, men are "old" when they reach the age of forty. They are no longer able to engage to any great extent in warfare. After this age they become members of the most influential body of men in the band. They are respected not so much because they are old but because of their past or present achievements. [57]

The question is sometimes raised whether the almost universal respect for old age is the result of a tendency in human beings that is innate. The better opinion would seem to be that respect for the elderly is acquired. There are practical reasons for esteeming those advanced in years, many of which have been enumerated above. Not the least of these reasons among preliterates is the fact that the aged will relatively soon join the ranks of departed ancestors who have the power of retaliating for mistreatment received in this life. It is cultural circumstances, as we said, which determine how the aged will be treated. When the circumstances do not demand that the aged be shown respect, they will not be respected. When the circumstances do demand that the aged be respected, they will be respected. [58]

## II  LESS THAN UNIVERSAL VALUE JUDGMENTS

The remaining value judgments regarding living in political association are less than universal. They are general, common, frequent, or occasional.

### A.  GENERAL

The value judgments which are general concern councils, obtaining evidence through witnesses and ordeals, and punishing by ridicule and shame and by death. They also relate to compensation and the enforcement of decisions.

Carib," *Amer. Anthropologist* 36 (1934) : p. 334 ; C. L. Harries, *The Laws and Customs of the Bapedi and Cognate Tribes of the Transvaal* (rev. ed., Johannesburg, 1929), p. 101 ; Geoffrey Snell, *Nandi Customary Law* (London, 1954), pp. 33, 78 ; K. A. Busia, *The Position of the Chief in the Modern Political System of Ashanti* (London, 1951), pp. 65–66 ; quoting Robert Rattray, *Ashanti Law and Constitution* (Oxford, 1929), chaps. 26–30 ; Isaac Schapera, *A Handbook of Tswana Law and Custom* (London, 1938), p 46 ; Leopold Pospisil, *Kapauku Papuans and Their Law* (New Haven, 1958), pp. 146–246 ; E. Adamson Hoebel, "Law-ways of the Primitive Eskimos," *Jour. Criminology and Criminal Law* 31 (1941) : p. 677 ; Leonhard Adam, "Criminal Law and Procedure in Nepal," *Far Eastern Quart.* 9 (1950) : p. 164 ; Alfred Radcliffe-Brown, "Primitive Law," *Encyc. of the Social Sciences* 9 (1933) : pp. 202–203.

[56] Leo Simmons, *The Role of the Aged in Primitive Society* (New Haven, 1945), p. 79.

[57] In this context it has been remarked that when "there is respect for the aged, the mores are safe!" Karl Llewellyn and E. Adamson Hoebel, *The Cheyenne Way* (Norman, 1941), p. 241. See also David Rodnick, "Political Structure and Status Among the Assiniboine Indians," *Amer. Anthropologist* 39 (1937) : p. 416.

[58] Respect for the elderly: Leo Simmons, *The Role of the Aged in Primitive Society* (New Haven, 1945), pp. 50, 79, 131 ; Gunter Wagner, "The Political Organization of the Bantu Kavirondo," in Meyer Fortes and Edward Evans-Pritchard, eds., *African Political Systems* (London, 1940), p. 235 ; Margaret Hasluck, *The Unwritten Law of the Albanian Mountains* (Cambridge, 1954), p. 34 ; Franz Boas, *Anthropology and Modern Life* (New York, 1928), p. 230 ; C. K. Meek, *Law and Authority in a Nigerian Tribe* (London, 1937), p. 299.

## 1. *Councils*

The presence of some kind of council representing the people, even where there are chiefs and headmen, is widespread. "Certain features, practices, and attitudes are well-nigh universal, [for instance] the principle of representation and government through councils."[59] They may be either advisory or governing. Typical examples are numerous. Among some peoples, like the Albanian mountaineers, it is said that it is impossible to understand the custom law of the people without understanding the various rankings of elders and their responsibilities. Among the Shona, the headman is assisted by the elders of the village and family heads. They make up an informal council which meets irregularly whenever there are matters of village or family interest to discuss. With the Nandi, the governing body of each group was its council. In fact, the word for neighborhood was also the word for the council and the place where it met.

Membership in a council of elders usually is not the result of appointment but of emergence as a respected leader, much as we saw elders emerging as the judges of cases. The source of their power is in influencing the opinion of the people. They attempt to reconcile conflicting interests and reaffirm the values long embodied in custom law. In South Africa, councilors are more than advisers to the chief. They are representatives of the people. A man becomes a councilor not by being formally appointed but by the influence he acquires because of his accomplishments. These may include his courage and exploits in war, his wealth, his oratorical skill, his knowledge of custom law in cases brought before the judges, and his over-all personality which qualifies him to be a public man. With the Nandi, membership in the council is acquired by seniority and personality. Decisions are made within the council by a relatively small number of elders who have the authority because of their natural leadership powers. A senior elder is the head of the council but he is actually considered to be only first among equals

Among some groups of preliterates, there is a carefully graded process of advancement through the stages of eldership. With the Gikuyu, among the first prerequisites is that a man has had a child circumcised and ready for marriage. He then becomes an elder of the lowest rank and gives one sheep to the head of his district. He is then an assistant at the elders' courts but cannot judge a case as yet. He can listen to cases as part of his legal training. After a certain period of time and after offering two sheep or goats to the oldest elder of his rank, he becomes an elder of the Gikuyu Court of Elders. The elders of this grade have a staff of a particular tree and a cluster of leaves to designate their office. These elders have authority over others in so far as they have the prerogative of administering Gikuyu

custom law and judging cases. Of these elders, the oldest are called the dignified elders who form the inner circle of the court and judge difficult points of custom law. They wear special brass earrings and carry a cluster of ceremonial leaves as a symbol of their position. They decide the dates of certain ceremonial feasts when an older generation of rulers gives place to a new one.

Councils of elders make laws if the necessity arises. Among some Ibo in Nigeria, the council of elders may pass a law that will meet some existing need. Thus, if it was obvious that fighting in the market place was becoming more frequent and likely to lead to murder and intra-kindred fighting, the assembly of elders might meet and decide that any fighting in the market place would be heavily fined. The lawmaking activities of the council of elders may also extend to changing custom law, which we shall discuss later.

In places of South Africa, the chief would not attempt to make any decisions of any great tribal importance without having first presented the matter to the council for discussion. If a chief did try to change a custom law without asking the advice of his councilors and allowing public discussion, the dissatisfied part of the tribe would possibly withdraw its allegiance to him and transfer it to some lesser chief in the same clan. From these instances and others like it, it is clear that the council of elders is important as a representative instrument of the people. The value judgment that it is good and desirable to have councils of elders appears to be general among preliterate peoples.[60]

## 2. *Witnesses and Ordeals*

Preliterates have the same problem as their literate brothers of obtaining evidence acceptable to judges regarding offenses committed. The testimony of witnesses is the principal source of evidence which is admissable in preliterate courts. Among the Tswana, eyewitnesses are favored over circumstantial and hearsay evidence. Accounts of court proceedings always emphasize the importance of witnesses. In practically all African societies, witnesses are called to testify both for the plaintiff and the defendant.

Some courts make it clear that their decision is based on the evidence furnished by witnesses. With the Akan, a court linguist addresses the accused and informs him of the court's verdict. He stresses the point that the court has heard witnesses and has accordingly attempted to reach an impartial decision. One of the reasons why witnesses are so important in preliterate court proceed-

---

[59] Anthony Allott, *Essays in African Law* (London, 1960), p. 60.

[60] Councils: Margaret Hasluck, *The Unwritten Law of the Albanian Mountains* (Cambridge, 1954), p. 130; J. F. Holleman, *Shona Customary Law* (London, 1952), p. 9; Geoffrey Snell, *Nandi Customary Law* (London, 1954), p. 10; J. G. Peristiany, "Law," in: Edward-Pritchard and others, *The Institutions of Primitive Society* (Glencoe, 1956), p. 42; G. M. B. Whitfield, *South African Law* (Capetown, 1948), p. 3; Jomo Kenyatta, *Facing Mount Kenya* (London, 1953), pp. 108–109; C. K. Meek, *Law and Authority in a Nigerian Tribe* (London, 1937), p. 247.

ings is that they may be the only means of obtaining evidence. Among the Albanian mountaineers, many cases were decided on the testimony of a single informant who was sworn in before he was allowed to testify. His testimony had to be based on personal observation. In secret offenses, this was the only way the offender could be discovered.

The desire of preliterate judges to get at the truth of the situation is shown by their willingness to hear the testimony of even passing strangers, as we have already noted. Among most African peoples any member of the audience who knows anything pertinent to a case may speak before the court. With these peoples also, passing strangers who may be able to contribute something of pertinence may speak as witnesses. Among the Bapedi in the Transvaal, strangers may not only testify but they may also participate in the ensuing debate on the case. Because of the nature of this kind of testimony, hearsay and irrelevant evidence may have to be admitted. The preliterate witness, who must tell his story in his own way, may testify to much that is hearsay and immaterial.

The value of a witness' testimony depends on how well his character shows under extensive questioning. If he is found to be deliberately lying, he is liable to punishment. Among the Bantu, a man's witness against his brother is considered to be worth while; but if in his brother's favor, it is taken to be worthless because it is probably biased. Loyalty is said to be more weighty than truthfulness in these courts. Truth is considered to be spoken by the accused more often than by witnesses. Hence, unless the witnesses are completely disinterested parties, more attention is paid to what the contending parties say than to what their witnesses testify.

Among some peoples the number of witnesses available has relevancy. With the Nabaloi, if there are witnesses to a quarrel between two men, the man with the most witnesses wins. If the number of witnesses is equal in a quarrel about property, the property is sometimes divided equally. When there are witnesses for one side of a dispute and none for the other, the party without witnesses sometimes asks for trial by ordeal. In Northern Nigeria, which is under the influence of Islamic law, a minimum number of witnesses—four— is required in cases of illicit sex relations. In many places, however, this required number has been reduced to two or one depending on the custom.

Witnesses can also be important among preliterates regarding the occurrence of a legal transaction. In Nyakyusa in a case involving the return of marriage-cattle, the plaintiff claimed six head and was able to describe each minutely. But because he could produce witnesses for the transfer of only three head, he was allowed only three head of cattle as a settlement. Witnesses are also employed in determining what the custom law is in certain matters, as we have already seen concerning the witness of elders. When particular patterns

of actions have been proved to be of custom law, courts take judicial notice of them.[61]

The value judgment among preliterate societies, then, that it is good to obtain evidence through the testimony of witnesses seems to be general.

Ordeals are still another means frequently employed by preliterates in determining the facts of a case, especially in the absence of confession or witnesses. They are a further indication of the extremes to which preliterates go to establish the truth in a case and to see that justice is done, although the practical purpose of getting cases expeditiously settled may also be present.

An ordeal is a trial in which the accused is exposed to physical danger the safe endurance of which is a sign of suprahuman intervention indicating that the accused is innocent. It is sometimes administered to the accuser as well as to the accused. The idea that an accused should prove his innocence by accepting an ordeal, is said to be prevalent among preliterates. "This conception of justice, common to all peoples in a primitive stage of development, [is] that an accused person must clear himself of the charge, and may do so by accepting an ordeal."[62] The advantage of the ordeal over the oath, especially a false oath, is that the results of the ordeal are more immediate and apparent. No institution, it is said, has been more frequent at certain stages of human development than the testing of the truth or falsity of a case by the process of ordeal.

Failure to accept a challenge to undergo an ordeal usually means an adverse decision for the refuser, as is the case in oath-taking. With the Ifugao, ordeals are resorted to in cases of offenses which affect the whole community, and in situations where there are disputes over property and boundary lines. Either the accuser or the accused may issue the challenge. Refusal to accept a challenge is the equivalent of losing the case and the challenger proceeds as if he had undergone the ordeal and successfully passed it. If the accused is vindicated by the ordeal, he has a claim to compensation from the accuser for false accusation. If two persons mutually accuse each other, they must both submit to an ordeal. If both are harmed by it, they must both compensate the injured person. If only one is harmed, he must compensate the injured person and also pay a fine for false accusation to the men he has accused.

The kinds of ordeals are many. Licking a hot knife blade is one of the most prevalent. The Ukamba lick both sides of a knife that has been brought to a great heat. Reports have it that no signs of fear are shown because of the pain inflicted. Only a slight scorching results but this is sufficient to indicate the guilty party. Immersion in water is another ordeal employed in some places. In Nepal two servants, each of whom represents one of the litigants in a case, immerse themselves in a

[61] Angu v. Attah, (1916) Privy Council 44; quoted by Anthony Allott, *Essays in African Law* (London, 1960), pp. 76–77.

[62] Robert Hamilton, "East African Native Laws and Customs," *Jour. Comp. Legislation* 11 (1910): p. 195.

tank of water at the same instant. The party whose servant is able to remain submerged for the longer time is considered to be the winner. The interpretation put on the outcome is that the gods, to whom all inward thoughts are known, have done justice between the litigants.

Several ordeals are used by the Nabaloi. One consists in putting the hands into boiling water up to the wrists. The sun is invoked to protect the one who is not at fault. The man who is scalded the more, loses the case. Another ordeal is a trial in which one of the elders positions the sharp point of an iron rod alternately on top of the heads of the two contending parties, hitting the iron with his hand. The sun is invoked to cause the blood to come from the head of the man who is at fault. The man whose head bleeds the more, loses. This ordeal is always allowed by the council when it is demanded. The chewing of rice is another ordeal also employed. The contending parties are each given the same amount of rice to chew. They all invoke the sun to help them chew the rice well because they are not at fault. They chew for the same length of time. The rice is then put on a plant leaf and examined by the council. The one who does not chew well, loses the case. If one of the parties had no teeth, he was subjected to the water ordeal. The rice-chewing ordeal is likewise used by the Kalinga.[63]

The explanation of how the ordeals, especially licking a hot iron, can be undergone without injury has been the subject of much discussion. It has been explained, apparently without satisfaction, that rinsing the mouth with water before licking the hot iron prevented burning. The tongue would show a scalding some hours after the event, whereas a burn would show immediately. Examination of the tongue of an accused two days after the trial shows no trace of scalds or burns. The shortcoming of this explanation, however, is that it does not account for the fact that by the same trial some are found guilty and others are found innocent.

Another explanation is that the mouth of the guilty man is dry and parched and therefore more likely to show burns. Among the Arabs, there is an implicit faith in the ability of the sheikh to discover the truth by means of the ordeal of licking a hot knife or spoon. The guilty man, then, is convinced that the truth will eventually be known and may confess before the ordeal. If he tries to bluff his way through, he is almost certain to face the hot spoon with a dry tongue and a parched throat because of his terror that the trial will go against him. The innocent man, on the other hand, faces the ordeal with confidence because he is innocent and because he believes the sheikh cannot give a wrong decision.

Still another explanation of this phenomenon is that a powder which acts as an insulator is applied to the tongue of the one undergoing the ordeal. Among the Bantu, who employ the ordeal of licking a hot knife, a medicine man applies a white powder to the man's tongue, hands, and nose. It has been conjectured that this powder is diatomite. Because of the obvious ability of the medicine man to control the effectiveness of the ordeal in this manner, the elders have expressed doubts as to its reliability and do not accept its outcome as conclusive. It is nearly always accompanied by an oath calling on higher powers to destroy the man who is in the wrong.

The value judgment, then, that it is good to obtain evidence by the use of ordeals is general among preliterate societies.[64]

### 3. Ridicule and Shame

Sanctions are not only physical but also non-physical, as we noted above. The non-physical sanction of public opinion shows itself in ridicule, insult, and shame and is one of the most powerful forces for preventing offenses and for punishing them when they occur. Indeed, in many preliterate groups no other means exists of keeping the people in line with custom law. The sanction of public opinion is peculiarly effective in certain types of living. Such is the association of preliterates. The life of the individual is closely dependent on the cooperative efforts of others. What others think of him is controlling in regard to the fulfilling of his needs. He cannot easily leave the group and join another. Hence, the man is rare who cares absolutely nothing about what others think of him. For this reason alone, public opinion is

---

[63] "Other tests or ordeals practiced on the body of the person are piercing the cheek or ear-lobe: If the needle passes through without causing bleeding the person is innocent in Usiguha, but guilty in Upare. In Uzigua another common ordeal is the smearing of a medicine under the eye: if the person is guilty the medicine penetrates the eye and smarts severely." Charles Dundas, "Native Laws of Some Bantu Tribes of East Africa," *Jour. Royal Anthropol. Inst.* **51** (1921): p. 228.

[64] Witnesses: Isaac Schapera, *Government and Politics in Tribal Societies* (London, 1956), pp. 80–81; T. Olawale Elias, *The Nature of African Customary Law* (Manchester, 1956), p. 244; Joseph Danquah, *Gold Coast: Akan Laws and Customs* (London, 1938), pp. 102–103; Margaret Hasluck, *The Unwritten Law of the Albanian Mountains* (Cambridge, 1954), p. 197; Julius Lewin, *Studies in African Native Law* (Philadelphia, 1948), p. 89; C. L. Harries, *The Laws and Customs of the Bapedi and Cognate Tribes of the Transvaal* (rev. ed., Johannesburg, 1929), pp. 99, 101; Charles Dundas, "Native Laws of Some Bantu Tribes of East Africa," *Jour. Royal Anthropol. Inst.* **51** (1921): pp. 226–227; Claude Moss, "Nabaloi Law and Ritual," *Amer. Archaeology and Ethnology* **15** (1920): pp. 267, 269; James Anderson, *Islamic Law in Africa* (London, 1954), p. 194; Godfrey Wilson, "Introduction to Nyakyusa Law," *Africa* **10** (1937): p. 30.

Ordeals: Leonard Hobhouse, *Morals in Evolution* (New York, 1906), pp. 116–117; Ralph Barton, "Ifugao Law," *Amer. Archaeology and Ethnology* **15** (1919): p. 96; Charles Dundas, "The Organization and Laws of Some Bantu Tribes," *Jour. Royal Anthropol. Inst.* **45** (1915): pp. 251–252; Leonhard Adam, "Criminal Law and Procedure in Nepal," *Far Eastern Quart.* **9** (1950): p. 161; Ralph Barton, *The Kalingas* (Chicago, 1949), p. 230; Austin Kennett, *Bedouin Justice* (Cambridge, 1925), pp. 112–113.

the strongest factor in bringing about observance of custom law among food-gatherers and hunters.[65]

In preliterate societies, then, non-material sanctions serve the same purpose as material sanctions. As a matter of fact, they may be much more effective than the material sanctions of literate societies.[66] In Polynesia, it is public opinion which checks the potential offender because he craves praise and hates to lose face. "The powerful urges of sex, acquisitiveness, and self-preservation are constantly repressed by the still more powerful wish to be appreciated by one's fellows." [67] Among the Naskapi, public opinion is the only practical sanction for preserving peace and order. With the Ifugao, the censure of public opinion is the only punishment for offenders against common values. Among Nigerian tribes, a man's good name is everything. To take away a man's good name is the equivalent of taking away his life. Swift steps are taken, therefore, to punish false accusers. With the Tiv, it is public opinion which makes a man concur in a punishment. Elders will threaten to withdraw their protection from witchcraft as a means of making a man concur in a decision which was agreed upon by all but himself. In the Trobriand Islands, men commit suicide after they have been publicly ridiculed for marrying within the clan.

Public opinion likewise is the effective force among the Nandi in preserving order and peace. Obedience to the regulations of custom law are insured by the desire to stand well in the opinion of others and by the fear that others would condemn the action or would deny their help in time of need. It was also guaranteed by the fear that the ancestors would take a hostile attitude. The Eskimo have long been known for their respect for public opinion. To a thief the Eskimo will do nothing physical. But they will laugh whenever his name is mentioned. The one thing most disturbing to the mind of the Eskimo is, reportedly, the possibility of standing alone against the rest of the community. This sanction

is so powerful that physical force is not needed and is negligible as a sanction.

Ridicule is used as punishment in Nyakyusa. It is employed as a sanction in cases of theft among the Tiv. With the Samoyeds, a nomadic tribe of Siberia, ridicule through public reprimand is an added punishment for fraud. Among many Indian tribes, custom law was obeyed only because of what the rest of the tribe would think. Among the Cheyenne, ridicule and shaming were said to be constantly at work. For instance, members of the tribe were ridiculed, especially by the women, for leaving an enfeebled person on the prairie to die. The Yurok have no policemen or public enforcers of judgments handed down. Public opinion is the principal support for any decisions reached.

The Kiowa used various forms of public ridicule. These ranged from informal scoldings within the family to formalized calling of names throughout the camp at night and composing and singing songs of ridicule. The Crow Indians also shamed offenders in a formalized procedure. Each individual's "joking relatives" had the privilege of mocking him for any offense before all the people. Fear of such ridicule is said to have been a sufficient safeguard against breaches of custom law. Among the Tlingit ridicule also had many forms. The most effective was the dissemination of songs and stories about an offender which made a laughing stock of him. Another form was the making of ludicrous wooden likenesses of the offender and putting them in prominent locations. Elaborate totem poles are said to have been carved sometimes with such ridicule in mind. Another form of ridicule was mimicry. Still another way of ridiculing was to call an offender a white man—which was considered to be the height of public insult.

Adverse public opinion shows itself in different ways among preliterates. Among the Ashanti, a person stealing yams or fowl might have them hung around his neck and be made to parade through the village street to the accompaniment of derisive shouts. For a second offense, the punishment was to be led around the town naked. A third offense brought on the punishment of anyone calling him "thief" in public and on any occasion. If caught on a farm he could be flogged on the spot. These punishments were the strongest inducement to observe the rules of custom law. The Kapauku consider shaming by public reprimand to be the worst possible punishment except execution. This shaming sometimes lasts many days. In the Sundra Islands a unique method of ridiculing chronic liars was used. Passersby heaped twigs on the spot where the lie or dishonesty had occurred. As other twigs were added and the pile grew, so the offender's shame increased.

Ridicule and shame are general, then, among preliterates. "Praise and ridicule are widespread among preliterate people as a potent means of encouraging both young and adult to behave properly." [68] The value

---

[65] Ridicule and shame have been distinguished by some writers from legal sanctions. Godfrey Wilson, "Introduction to Nyakyusa Law," *Africa* 10 (1937): p. 33. It has also been implied that such "non-legal" sanctions are "moral" sanctions. A. Irving Hallowell, "The Nature and Function of Property as a Social Institution," *Jour. Legal and Polit. Sociology* 1 (1943): p. 133. But it should be remembered that, unless one is going to hold the outmoded and unworkable Austinian notion that law is essentially court-inflicted physical sanction, sanctions are not necessarily physical and they can be brought to bear publicly on offenders by the people themselves who are at bottom custom lawmakers. To intimate also that such sanctions as public ridicule and shame are merely "moral" sanctions and not fully legal sanctions, is to imply that the physical carries no moral connotation and that the moral is merely the non-physical.

[66] "To become the laughing-stock of his daily associates for minor misdemeanours and to be completely ostracised for graver offences are terrible punishments for the native, and they have a deterrent force of which the infliction of penalties in our sense is often quite devoid." Robert Lowie, *Primitive Society* (New York, 1920), p. 384.

[67] Robert Lowie, *An Introduction to Cultural Anthropology* (2nd ed., New York, 1940), p. 284.

[68] Ralph Beals and Harry Hoijer, *An Introduction to Anthropology* (New York, 1953), p. 585.

judgment, therefore, that it is good to use ridicule and shame as punishments seems general among preliterate societies. Implied in this value judgment, of course, is the more elementary value judgment that a favorable repute is good and should be protected.[69]

### 4. Death

One of the punishments regularly inflicted by preliterates for serious offenses has been death. Among these offenses are murder, theft and robbery, treason, abortion, arson, sorcery and witchcraft, adultery, and the non-payments of debts.

Many peoples inflict the death penalty for murder. The Bantu punish acts of blood revenge and other forms of homicide by death. Likewise the Ifugao with little hesitation kill those who have murdered. Many African tribes impose as punishment for murder, death by shooting, spearing, hanging, drowning, and impalement. The nomadic tribes of Siberia also inflict the death penalty for murder. The mountaineers of Albania consider murder to be especially harmful to social cohesion and punish it by death.

Theft and robbery are also punished by death among many preliterate peoples. The Wapare put robbers to death. Among the Wabena, if robbers and thieves are caught in the act and killed or pursued and killed, the killing is subsequently sanctioned by the chief. The Wanyamwezi punish thefts, especially of slave women, with death. In Ukumba, Gikuyu, and Theraka a thief caught stealing honey hives in the forest is killed. The nomadic tribes of Siberia punish robbery-murder by death. The Albanian mountaineers punish theft by

[69] Ridicule and shame: Isaac Schapera, *A Handbook of Tswana Law and Custom* (London, 1938), pp. 36–37; Julius Lips, "Government," in: Franz Boas, ed., *General Anthropology* (Boston, 1938), p. 496; Lips, "Naskapi Law," *Trans. Amer. Philos. Soc.* 37 (1947): p. 471; Ralph Barton, "Ifugao Law," *Amer. Archaeology and Ethnology* 15 (1919): p. 14; C. K. Meek, *Law and Authority in a Nigerian Tribe* (London, 1937), p. 230; Paul Bohannon, *Justice and Judgment Among the Tiv* (London, 1957), p. 68; Robert Lowie, *An Introduction to Cultural Anthropology* (2nd ed., New York, 1940), p. 284; Geoffrey Snell, *Nandi Customary Law* (London, 1954), pp. 84–85; Ralph Linton, *The Study of Man* (New York, 1936), p. 141; Kaj Birket-Smith, *The Eskimos* (New York, 1936), pp. 54–55; Ellsworth Faris, "The Origin of Punishment," in: Albert Kocourek and John Wigmore, *Primitive and Ancient Legal Institutions* (3 v., Boston, 1915) 1: p. 156; Godfrey Wilson, "Introduction to Nyakyusa Law," *Africa* 10 (1937): p. 18; Valintin Riasanovsky, *Customary Law of the Nomadic Tribes of Siberia* (Tsiensin, 1938), p. 35; Karl Llewellyn and E. Adamson Hoebel, *The Cheyenne Way* (Norman, 1941), pp. 260, 265–266; Franz Boas, "Culture," *Encyc. of the Social Sciences* 2 (1930): p. 89; Robert Redfield, "Maine's Ancient Law in the Light of Primitive Societies," *Western Polit. Quart.* 3 (1950): pp. 583–584; Jane Richardson, "Law and Status Among the Kiowa Indians," *Monograph Amer. Ethnol. Soc.* 1 (1940): p. 16; Kalervo Oberg, "Crime and Punishment in Tlingit Society," *Amer. Anthropologist* 36 (1934): pp. 152, 153; Robert Rattray, *Ashanti Law and Constitution* (Oxford, 1929), pp. 324–325, 372; Leopold Pospisil, *Kapauku Papuans and Their Law* (New Haven, 1958), p. 268.

death if it becomes habitual, the reasoning being that the habitual thief is a social menace from whom no one is safe. Thieves are also frequently killed as a punishment by the Soga, Tiv, Alur, Gisu, and Luyia.

Treason and some types of political offenses are punished by execution by some African tribes. Among the Wapare, a traitor is looked on as the equivalent of an enemy and therefore has no rights and should be killed. Abortion is punishable by death among some groups. Thus in Sumbwa the woman who causes herself to abort may be put to death, along with anyone who helps her induce the abortion. The Ifugao hold that arson deserves the death penalty, but it is so rare an occurrence that its punishment by death can hardly be said to be a practice. The Wanyamwezi and Wamakonde punish incendiarism with death. If the arsonist is caught in the act, he is hurled into the flaming house.

Witchcraft and sorcery are offenses whose punishment is death among many preliterate peoples. Among the Ifugao, they are punishable by killing provided the kin of the slain be daring enough to execute it. Many African groups punish witchcraft and sorcery by death. The Luo, the Alurese, the Gisu and the Nyoro punish these offenses by death. The Eskimo also punish witchcraft by death. Execution is considered not so much a punishment for the practice of witchcraft as it is the removal of an undesirable person such as would be an incorrigible or an aged or sick person.

Adultery is likewise punishable by death among some preliterates. The Ifugao punish adultery by death, providing the offender is not a kinsman or person closely related by marriage. Blood revenge for adultery is a custom among some hill tribes in Nepal, such as the Parbatiyas, including the Brahmans, Khas, Gerung, and Magar. Other tribes such as the Newar, Nurmi, the Rai and the Bhote, however, do not have this practice. In Africa the Gisu, Alurese and Luyia punish adultery by death. The Ifugao also punish by death refusal to pay fines for which demand has been made in correct form, and refusal to pay debts when there is ability to do so and many and repeated demands have been made in the proper manner. Some tribes in Nepal also punish incest by death.

The distinction between in-group and out-group activities, which we have seen in relation to the presence and gravity of offenses, is also sometimes made regarding the kinds and severity of punishments to be inflicted. Among the Tlingit, death is inflicted within the group only for those offenses which entail dishonor to the whole group. Thus there is no punishment within the clan for murder, adultery, or theft. But the penalty of death is imposed for incest, witchcraft, marriage with a slave, and prostitution. Adultery, like murder, is not punishable within the clan. But when it occurs between a woman and a man who is not of the husband's clan, the killing of both guilty persons by the husband is the penalty. If the husband is fond of his wife, he may forgive her, but the wife's family has to pay him compensation to save his honor. With the Ifugao, death is more likely to be inflicted on an offender who is not a member of the village than it is on one who is a member. If a man from a foreign village is caught in the act of stealing or other serious offenses, he is almost sure to be killed. If a man commits an offense in a foreign village, if he is not killed he is caught and tied and held prisoner until he is ransomed.[70]

The value judgment that it is good to use death as a punishment for certain offenses appears general among preliterate societies.[71]

### 5. *Compensation*

Payment made to an individual who has been harmed, or to his relatives, has long been recognized as an effective means of stopping a possible chain reaction of physical or other retaliations. This has been fully appreciated by preliterates. Much cruelty has been avoided by the process of compensation, which can be every bit as effective and more so than punishment. Punishment, especially among preliterates, can easily be forgotten. It is of limited duration. But compensation is lasting. As one Bantu remarked, as long as a man lives and even after his death "his children will see his cattle increasing in the village of another." [72]

The importance of compensation as obviating blood retaliation can be seen especially in cases of murder. Murder affects not only the victim and the killer, but also the families or clans of both. The family is weakened by the loss of a member and this loss is felt beyond the immediate group. For this reason, murder is looked on as different from other offenses and blood-money in lieu of revenge is paid by families to families. Some tribes insist on blood vengeance as a sacred duty that cannot be satisfied by compensation. The Caribou

Eskimo exempt from guilt the man who has punished a murderer by killing him. But most preliterates provide for payment in the place of blood. The Yurok are typical among whom killing and injury are compensable by payment.

Adultery can also be compensated for in many places but sometimes with the understanding that the injured husband will not profit by the damages. With the Ashanti, the injured husband who has been awarded damages cannot use the money for his own personal advantage. It is considered dishonorable for a husband to profit by the adulterous actions of his wife. The money is distributed among friends and relatives. In South Africa the husband of an adulterous wife may accept compensation because of the custom law regarding divorce. When a husband refuses to condone his wife's adultery and accordingly divorces his wife, he forfeits the dowry because adultery is not considered a cause for divorce. Hence, a husband will condone his wife's adulterous action and claim the compensation from the adulterer. In custom law here the fine for adultery is imposed not only to compensate the husband but also to deter the adulterer. Incest can also be punished in some places by compensation. In East Africa incest with a daughter is punished by the elders pulling down the offender's kraal and confiscating his cattle.

Many peoples, however, make murder, adultery, and other grave actions exceptions to those offenses for which compensation can be had. The Ifugao, value-judging much like the Africans just noted, say that to accept compensation in instances of adultery would be to profit by the pollution of the wife's body and to give suspicion of conspiracy on the part of the husband and his wife to promote the adultery so that they could profit by it. Similarly in the matter of murder, no self-respecting family would accept payment for the life of a kinsman except as a way of avoiding a blood feud. German tribes made similar exceptions. Most offenses could be compounded by fine, but the penalty for murder and rape was blood revenge. Many African tribes also allow compensation for offenses but with certain exceptions. Among the Kimdunba, the exceptions are sorcery and treason; with the Barolong, rebellion; among the Kaffir, treason, sorcery, and sometimes murder.[73]

[70] It has been said that there is "abundant reason for questioning whether any one inside the primitive group was ever punished, at least by those within his own tribe. In an instinctive way the members of the group are bound together and in the most homogeneous groups they do not punish each other." Ellsworth Faris, '"The Origin of Punishment," in: Albert Kocourek and John Wigmore, eds., *Primitive and Ancient Legal Institutions* (3 v., Boston, 1915) 1: p. 152. On balance, the evidence we have examined indicates otherwise. See also Ralph Barton, "Ifugao Law," *Amer. Archaeology and Ethnology* 15 (1919): p. 66.

[71] Death: Charles Dundas, "Native Laws of Some Bantu Tribes of East Africa," *Jour. Royal Anthropol. Inst.* 51 (1921): pp. 232–233; Ralph Barton, "Ifugao Law," *Amer. Archaeology and Ethnology* 15 (1919): pp. 99–100; T. Olawale Elias, *The Nature of African Customary Law* (Manchester, 1956), p. 261; Valintin Riasanovsky, *Customary Law of the Nomadic Tribes of Siberia* (Tsiensin, 1938), p. 35; Margaret Hasluck, *The Unwritten Law of the Albanian Mountains* (Cambridge, 1954), pp. 10, 233; Paul Bohannon, *African Homicide and Suicide* (Princeton, 1960), pp. 233–234; Kai Birket-Smith, *The Eskimos* (New York, 1936), p. 151; Leonhard Adam, "Criminal Law and Procedure in Nepal," *Far Eastern Quart.* 9 (1950): pp. 166, 168; Kalervo Oberg, "Crime and Punishment in Tlingit Society," *Amer. Anthropologist* 36 (1934): pp. 146, 148.

[72] Charles Dundas, "The Organization and Laws of Some Bantu Tribes," *Jour. Royal Anthropol. Inst.* 45 (1915): p. 262.

[73] The word "bootless" is said to derive from those offenses for which no bot payment was acceptable. "Our *Leges Henrici* still distinguish emendable offences, in which sacrilege and wilful homicide without treachery are included, from unemendable offences such as housebreaking, arson, open theft, aggravated homicide, treason against one's lord, and breach of the church's or the king's peace. These are crimes which in the Anglo-Saxon term had no bot—or money payment atoned for them—they were bot-less, boot-less. Even when the bot was payable it stood at first at the discretion of the injured family to accept or reject it, and we find the Germanic codes in the early Middle Ages setting themselves to insist on its acceptance as a means of keeping the peace. If the fine is not forthcoming, of course the feud holds." Leonard Hobhouse, *Morals in Evolution* (New York, 1906), p. 76.

The in-group, out-group distinction likewise applies to the matter of compensation in some places. Among the Tlingit, if a dog injures a person belonging to another clan, the owner of the dog compensates the injury by a payment of goods to the injured person. Harm caused to members of another clan, as distinguished from harm done to members of one's own clan, could have wide ramifications and compensation was always made by payment. With the Ifugao, such offenses as insult were compensable by the same amount of fine for a foreigner as for a co-villager, but less effort would be made to settle the matter peaceably. If the fine demanded of the foreigner was not paid quickly, the offender could be kidnaped and killed.

The gradation of compensations by preliterates is evidence of their constant concern with justice in the process of restoring the relations of justice that should obtain both between the offender and his victim, and between the offender and the whole of the community. In assessing the amounts to be paid in compensation for various offenses, however, the satisfaction of the victim and his family is many times as much a consideration as the culpability and future deterrence of the offender, as we have mentioned. If the peace is to be kept, the size of the remedy offered has to be sufficient to induce the injured party not to proceed on his own and inflict his own retaliation.

Schedules of specific items and amounts to be paid for offenses under varying circumstances are prevalent among preliterates. For adultery, for instance, the Bantu demand detailed numbers of cows, goats, bulls, oxen, slave girls, and hoes, depending on the circumstances of the act. The Ifugao list amounts of blankets, kettles, irons, and ceremonial clouts as compensation for adultery. Other groups, such as the Akamba, itemize the number of cows, bulls, and goats that must be paid as compensation for adultery, homicide, injuries, rape, and theft.

The determining of the grades of compensation sometimes takes into account the importance or difference of the persons involved. With the Ifugao, rank and position in the community is said probably to be the greatest single factor in determining the severity of punishment. In the Kiangan-Maggok area, there are three grades of fines—the highest for the punishment of offenses of one rich man against another, the medium for offenses of the middle class against each other, and the lowest for offenses of the poverty-stricken against each other. Each lower grade of fine is a little more than half of the next higher fine. In other areas there are four and five grades. In the Kababuyan area, there are five grades—grades for the very rich, the fairly rich, the middle class, the poor, and the poverty-stricken. In Sapao and in Asin there are four grades. As long as the offender and the offended are of the same class, there is no problem of applying the proportioned fine in a given case. It is when they are of different classes that fighting

strength and personality enter into the case as determining factors.

With the Gikuyu, compensation for murder is scaled according to sex. If a man wounds another seriously, he is required to provide a male goat to supply nourishment for the wounded victim. If the wound heals, the matter ends there. If the wounded man dies, the killer is charged with murder because he has admitted his guilt by providing the male goat. Compensation for the killing of a man is fixed at one hundred sheep or goats or ten cows. Compensation for killing a woman is thirty sheep or goats or three cows. In other places, for instance in Africa where Islam has made itself felt, compensation is payable in different degrees depending on whether the killing was unintentional or intentional. The amount of payment assessed for unintentionally killing a person is one hundred camels, male and female. The compensation for deliberate killing of a person is one hundred female camels.

Double, triple, and even greater indemnity is common among preliterates. In some African tribes, the thief is made to give to his victim double the amount he stole from him. With the Nabaloi, a thief stealing an animal is required to pay three times its value to the owner. If the thief returns the animal, it is necessary to pay twice its value. The severer penalties inflicted for stealing animals at night are justified, it is explained, on the grounds that it is more difficult to detect the thief. An animal may be stolen in one village in the early part of the night, taken to another village, and consumed entirely before the next morning. Among some peoples, not only is the thief made to pay double or more but he is beaten besides. In Tswana the man who steals an ox is required to pay the owner two or more oxen, and is also thrashed if he is unable to make restitution or is in the habit of stealing.

Some preliterates distinguish between liability for damage done by straying animals during the night and during the day. No compensation is due for nocturnal damage. Thus among the Kamba if cattle or goats break out at night and enter a neighbor's property, no compensation is payable for damage done or crops destroyed. The reasoning is that, if the animals had broken out and been killed by a lion or hyena, there would have been no recompense for the owner. This would have been the will of "Mulingu." But if the cattle strayed and did the damage in the daytime, compensation could be collected. A man is expected to look after his animals and see that they do not damage other people's property. This can well be done by day. Likewise, if a man's cattle stray and do damage a second or third time at night, the elders assume that the owner is not even trying to keep his cattle enclosed and they will rule that compensation be paid.

The punishments and multiple damages scaled to various offenses, including a distinction between nighttime and daytime theft, were prevalent among peoples other than preliterates. The law of the Hebrews decrees that a thief caught at night could be killed with impunity. If he was apprehended during the day, he could not be killed but was liable for multiple compensation. If he could not pay, he was sold into slavery.[74]

Among some tribes, such as the Bedouin, time limits on retaliation and compensation do not exist, at least in theory. These people live a nomadic life in the desert, drifting over enormous areas and probably never returning to exactly the same place again. Hence, it is difficult if not impossible to fix any hard and fast time limit to liability. Bedouin custom law, therefore, holds that lapse of time does not affect claims to take reprisals and compensation however long that time may be. In practice, if a tribe from which compensation is due returns within "ten years or so," the claimant could probably collect. But if many years more than ten have elapsed and no steps have been taken to collect the money, the probability is that, when the case was tried, some modification of what was payable would be in order.

The value judgment that it is good to employ compensations in the settlement of disputes seems to be general among preliterates.[75]

## 6. Enforcement

The enforcement of decisions is the final step in the process of inculcating respect for others' relations of title. Among preliterates, this is accomplished either by the chiefs and the elders or by the people themselves. Among the Tswana, the chief and the local courts have the power to enforce their decisions. With the Naskapi, members of the council of elders carry out an execution. The condemned man is led out immediately after the sentence. Members of the council bring their guns and three or four of them are designated by the chief to carry out the death sentence. The unshackled convict

walks slowly ahead of his executioners. At a lonely spot, usually said to be near a lake, he is shot from behind. His corpse is left untouched and unburied.

Among the Nandi, some of the convicted person's own relatives perform the execution. The usual method consists of placing a noose of rope made from tree bark around the neck of the convict. Several relatives then pull on the rope with a swaying motion from opposite directions. As he is gradually being strangled, bystanders beat him with sticks and throw stones at him. Some offenders are executed by the community at large. The execution for witchcraft is accomplished by clubbing the convicted person to death. With the Ifugao also the death sentence is enforced by the injured person or his relatives. But here it is potentially dangerous for the executioners to do so. It is usually inflicted from ambush, with the culprit never having been notified that he has been sentenced to death. A good indication of this, though, is the withdrawing of the go-betweens. Because this inflicting of the death penalty by relatives has been the beginning of many interminable blood feuds between families, every effort is exhausted by the injured person to bring about a settlement less than death that is consonant with his station in life.

In some places, for instance among the Bantu, the head of the group may be merely an arbiter with no authority to enforce his own rulings. The force of public opinion, however, can accomplish this enforcement by threats of expulsion and by withdrawal of support for the defiant offender. Sukuma courts sometimes have to rely almost completely on the force of the opinion of the people to ensure the enforcement of its decisions. It is reported that among the Ifugao, the office of monkalun, that is, advocate or adviser, is the most important one in the whole of their society. He is both court and maker of peaceful settlements. If the convicted person is not disposed to listen to the court's decision, the monkalun follows the offender to his house and, "war-knife in hand, sits in front of him and compels him to listen." The monkalun has no authority and his power lies in his ability to persuade albeit, obviously, with the threat of personal force.

Failing all other means of enforcing court decisions, self-help of some kind is an obvious final recourse. If the chief's court cannot enforce its decision, the dissatisfied parties will act. Among the Montagnais, Micmac, and Etchimin, small chiefs or "sagamores" easily adjusted quarrels with the help of friends. These chiefs had no binding authority and all serious offenses were settled by vengeance or composition. With the preliterates of New Guinea, the Bismarck Archipelago and the Manus of the Admiralty Islands, where organized methods of enforcement are strikingly lacking, the people themselves employ counter measures to restore respect for others' relations of title. Anger, threats, sorcery, or attack with spear or club might be used. After it was over, the weaker or defeated person or group simply moved off.

[74] Exodus 22: 1–4.

[75] Compensation: Charles Dundas, "Native Laws of Some Bantu Tribes of East Africa," Jour. Royal Anthropol. Inst. 51 (1921): pp. 238, 248; Robert Lowie, An Introduciton to Cultural Anthropology (2nd ed., New York, 1940), p. 286; Robert Rattray, Ashanti Law and Constitution (Oxford, 1929), pp. 322–323; S. M. Seymour, Native Law in South Africa (Capetown, 1953), p. 236; Robert Hamilton, "East African Native Laws and Customs," Jour. Comp. Legislation 11 (1910): p. 188; Ralph Barton, "Ifugao Law," Amer. Archaeology and Ethnology 15 (1919): pp. 62, 66, 67, 100; Leonard Hobhouse, Morals in Evolution (New York, 1906), p. 76; Kalervo Oberg, "Crime and Punishment in Tlingit Society," Amer. Anthropologist 36 (1934): p. 150; E. Adamson Hoebel, The Law of Primitive Man (Cambridge, Mass., 1954), p. 117; Arthur Diamond, The Evolution of Law and Order (London, 1951), p. 115; Jomo Kenyatta, Facing Mount Kenya (London, 1953), p. 228; James Anderson, Islamic Law in Africa (London, 1954), p. 360; Alfred Radcliffe-Brown, "Primitive Law," Encyc. of the Social Sciences 9 (1933): p. 203; Claude Moss, "Nabaloi Law and Ritual," Amer. Archaeology and Ethnology 15 (1920): p. 263; D. J. Penwill, Kamba Customary Law (London, 1951), p. 103; Austin Kennett, Bedouin Justice (Cambridge, 1925), pp. 47–48; Isaac Schapera, Government and Politics in Tribal Societies (London, 1956), p. 69; Julius Lips, "Naskapi Law," Trans. Amer. Philos. Soc. 37 (1947): p. 476.

The value judgment, therefore, that enforcement of decisions one way or another is good and desirable is general in all preliterate societies.[76]

### B. COMMON

The value judgments regarding living in political association which appear to be common among preliterates concern leaders, self-help, and proportionate retaliation. They also relate to exile as a punishment and the use of confessions in obtaining evidence.

### 1. *Leaders*

Whether there is leadership among preliterates, and what kind it may be, depends on the meaning given to "leadership." If by leadership is meant a "pecking order," as is common among some birds and animals, such a ranking is probably present in all preliterate groups.[77] But such a ranked position is not political. Leadership, as we shall discuss it here, refers to individuals who are at least implicitly chosen by the people to guide them in the fulfillment of their common needs.

When leadership among preliterates is taken in this sense, the question can be raised whether it is present among all preliterate associations. If it is not, to what extent is it present and in what form? Leadership as thus explained is not found among all preliterate societies. There are many groups which have been reported as having no leadership especially in the person of chiefs. The Nuer, the Australian aborigines, the Bushmen of the Kalahari Desert, the Comanche, the Chippewa, the Basin Shoshone, the Hopi of northern Arizona, and many others have no chiefs. Regulative direction of the whole association is achieved in another way. Among the Hopi of northern Arizona, for example, cooperative effort in the fulfilling of their common needs is obtained by the guidance of ritual and religious groups. When each member of these societies becomes an adult, he joins one of these groups. Governmental direction of the whole association comes from the balance maintained between these groups as they meet in their annual cycle of festivals. The Pokot of East Africa also have no formalized government. They have no recognized judges to whom people can go to have disputes settled. Disputes are settled by clan negotiation influenced by neutral elders.

Another example of a preliterate association governing itself without the leadership of a chief is the Tiv of central Nigeria. Disputes are settled within the lineage by the lineage elders. Disputes between lineages are settled by meetings of reconciliation or by fighting. If a man takes back property which he says belongs to him and if he can convince them he has a good case, his kinsmen will back him. They will meet with the other party and try to convince them of the rightness of their kinsman's position. If this fails, they will fight. In cases of divorce, whole lineages will meet together to consider the claims of the parties involved and to work out a just decision. The Tiv give political authority to no one. Every dispute is said to be settled, one way or another, by power and not by authority.

Many other associations of preliterates, however, have leadership in the person of chiefs. They find it difficult to conceive of maintaining protection and security, order and peace, without them. For this reason, and because of the prevalence of leadership among literate peoples, we shall examine briefly value judgments regarding the leadership of chiefs among preliterates.

The chief among many preliterates is the source of cohesion which gives unity to the whole association. The Bantu, for instance, say they cannot imagine a community ordering its affairs without a chief. The Tsonga say that a tribe without a chief is like a woman without a husband—there is no reason, no authority, no peace. Among the Ashanti, there is no particular link between one elder and another. It is only their common allegiance to the chief which unites them. Communication from one to another is possible only through the chief. Because the elders represent the lineages and villages under their control, their union in the chief brings about a political unity of the whole association.

The selection of chiefs and headmen in some places is by heredity, in others by election, and in still others by both inheritance and election. Although chiefs and headmen are distinguishable by the different degrees of their authority, for our present purpose they will be treated together. In Tswana a man becomes chief by heredity in the male line and chiefdom is normally passed from father to son. A chief is never elected. Usurpation, force, trickery have been used to acquire the chieftainship but this is said to be the exception. Ordinarily a man becomes chief by succeeding to the position by claim of birth. In the Transvaal, the chieftainship is also hereditary. Here a chief is said to be chief because he is born to it. Among most Bantu people, it is the "tribal candle," that is, the eldest son of the royal wife, who is heir to chieftainship.

Among some preliterates the chief is selected not only on the basis of lineage but also popular approval. With the Ashanti, where as we have said each lineage is a political unity represented in the council by an elder, the chief is chosen from among these elders by the other

---

[76] Enforcement: Geoffrey Snell, *Nandi Customary Law* (London, 1954), p. 87; Ralph Barton, "Ifugao Law," *Amer. Archaeology and Ethnology* 15 (1919): pp. 94, 100; Anthony Allott, *Essays in African Law* (London, 1960), p. 118; J. P. Moffett, "Foreword," to Hans Cory, *Sukuma Law and Custom* (London, 1953), p. vii; Leonard Hobhouse, *Morals in Evolution* (New York, 1906), p. 93; Margaret Mead, "Some Anthropological Considerations Concerning Natural Law," *Natural Law Forum* 6 (1961): p. 56.

[77] "[L]eadership, in one form or another, not only is omnipresent in human society but goes back to conditions among animals." Alexander Goldenweiser, *Anthropology* (New York, 1937), p. 375. "Almost all closed societies of animals have leaders and in many cases a definite order of rank may be observed." Franz Boas, *Anthropology and Modern Life* (New York, 1928), p. 232.

elders. In this way, hereditary claim and popular selection were both used in the picking of a new chief. Among the Mende, not only age but also suitability to the people is a prerequisite for chiefdom. The chief is supposed to be the oldest and most suitable man in the male line of descent that claims jurisdiction over the various parts of the whole chiefdom.[78]

Ability recognized and approved by the people also plays a central part in the making of a chief among some preliterates. With the Kalinga, if a man showed certain signs of bravery, had successfully intervened in disputes for the good of the people involved, and had not offended too seriously the moral standards of the group, some of the people would begin to call him pangat or leader. If the rest of the people accepted him, he was received by the pangats as one of their own number. If the rest of the people did not accept him, that was the end of the matter and he was no longer considered as a potential leader. Similarly among the Eskimo, as we have had occasion to remark, proven skills recognized by the group are the first step toward leadership. The man with exceptional skills is seen as a potential leader by the people and one whom they will follow.

Proven ability is also important among the Gikuyu as a factor in the selection of a chief. A man of innate gifts and understanding may be selected by his age-group as their leader. If he is, notice will be taken by the elders and he will be marked for public or political leadership after he has had more experience. By the time he is later chosen, he is already the leader of not only his own age-group but also of his family group of relatives and has proven his ability to lead. The Carib choose their headmen by the acclaim of the adult men in the group. Their decision, however, takes several factors into account. Among these are the man's personality, his economic status, and his physical strength. Sometimes a man's relationship to a former headman may be considered, but this is not a controlling factor.

One of the greatest qualifications for leadership among the North American Indians was oratorical ability. Oratory has been said to be the one tool of the Indian leader that was at times more significant and effective than courage. It stimulated and compelled men to be followers. Some of the most famous of Indian chiefs were known for their oratorical skill. Pontiac, known ordinarily as a man of few words, is said to have been

as great an orator as he was a general. Tecumseh likewise was a brilliant speaker, although ordinarily a silent man. Logan and Red Jacket are also described as outstanding orators. The further observation has been made that of all the Indian nations, it was the Iroquois nation that produced the greatest orators. With the Kalinga, too, oratorical ability is one of the requisites for leadership.

No better example can be found, then, of the workng of the peoples' basic political authority than their acceptance or rejection of their leaders. As among the Unalit in the Arctic and many other preliterates, as long as the people accept a man's leadership, he is leader. When they refuse to follow him, he is no longer the leader. This elementary manifestation by preliterates of men's basic authority over their own political destinies, is a phenomenon of first-class political importance.

The authority of chiefs and headmen varies greatly. It ranges from the minimal to the maximal. The Eskimo have a bare minimum of leadership. Among many American tribes the chief is limited by councils of elders. They accept the supreme authority of the chief but limit it by their own influence and power. With the Tswana, the chief's authority is also limited by councils. The chief is not above custom law and must cooperate with his councilors and his people if effective government is to be had. In the event that the chief commits an offense against one of his subjects, complaint can be lodged and the chief is expected to make amends. Among the Iroquois and the Dakota, the chief succeeded to his position by heredity and rose to great personal and social influence. In South American tribes in Mexico and Peru the power and authority of the chief approached the absolute.

The authority of the chief in many places, for instance South Africa, may extend to areas of making law, administering it, judging cases and executing decisions. There is no separation of powers as is known in other parts of the world. All power is concentrated in the one person. Among the Bantu and Hottentot of South Africa, the chief, with the help of his advisers, initiates and promulgates law, sees that justice is done, functions as supreme judge, and helps execute what must be done even to leading the army into battle. With the Bantu the chief is also the high priest and magician of his people. Among the Bergdama and Bushmen also the chief in person directs all the public activities of this group.

Although a chief ordinarily cannot successfully continue in office without the cooperation of his people and his decisions reflect the desires of his people, it would be incorrect to say that this is always the case. The measures introduced by the chief do not always express the wishes of the people. Among the Tswana, it is said that more often than not the decrees of the chief mirror the will of the chief and his advisers and not the will of the people. As a result of this, the people many times are indifferent or even antagonistic to the decisions

---

[78] Among the Ashanti, it is said that at one time women were chiefs. "It is a common belief that in the olden days it was women who were chiefs. The traditional histories of Wenchi, Mampong, Juaben, and other Divisions in Ashanti tell of women who were chiefs. But, according to a well-known tradition, when war broke out and they were sent for, or sometimes when they were required for important meetings, they would say 'My menstrual period is on . . .' and they could not perform their duties. 'So,' said one informant, 'we [Ashanti] asked them to give us men who would be chiefs in their place. That is why the elders asked the queen-mother to nominate a candidate.'" K. A. Busia, *The Position of the Chief in the Modern Political System of Ashanti* (London, 1951), p. 20. See also Kenneth Little, *The Mende of Sierra Leone* (London, 1951), p. 175.

of the chief. Under such circumstances the law may be difficult to enforce and may quickly lapse into desuetude. At times when laws are forced upon a group, it does not necessarily mean that they are not just or desirable. It may be that they are concerned with needed reforms whose worth the people do not recognize.

The function of the chief and headman is, in the main, to promote the common political goals of security and order. Thus the Bantu chief promotes the common welfare and security of his people and watches over their interests in general. He is said to be the father or headman of his people. The Zulu term for governing the people also means making life happy for them. Such also were the duties of the Ashanti chiefs. They kept law and order in the community. They were the custodians of the land and were responsible for its defense both at law and at arms. This meant defending the people from external attack, keeping friendly relations between persons and groups within the community, and also between the community and its ancestors and gods.

The functions of headmen are also directed to the common welfare of the people, sometimes with authority delegated to them by chiefs. With the Sukuma, much of the management of the country is in the hands of the headmen. They judge cases in their own courts, have their own magico-religious functions, and collect the yearly taxes, and in general are powerful men in their district. Sometimes the type of cases which the headman can adjudicate is limited. Among the Shona, serious cases arising from witchcraft, homicide, and stock theft are in principle excluded from his jurisdiction. An appeal always lies from his court to the court of the chief. As a consequence, the headman will not pass judgment in a case unless he is convinced the parties will accept his decision. Otherwise, even cases of small moment will be appealed to the court of the chief.

In other places the duties of the headman may be more subsidiarily related to the public good. In South American tribes, the headman's principal duties were to harangue the people, make suggestions for the day's schedule of hunting and traveling, and let the views of the majority be known. He enjoys no authority and can expect no obedience. Among the Assiniboine and Cree also, the headman was given deference but not obedience.

Regulatory decrees are the principal means used by chiefs in guiding the people in the fulfillment of their common needs. These directives are law. Among the Tswana, it has long been recognized that the chiefs have the power to make laws. It is said that the chiefs have had this right from time immemorial and that such making of laws and publishing of regulations are necessary to meet the needs of the people. In Bechuanaland, the chief governs his people by deciding questions of tribal policy and making regulations which his subjects are obliged to observe. Among the Barama River Carib, the opinions of the headman in matters pertaining to common needs may be construed as law because of the weight they carry owing to his position.

The proportion of preliterates who govern themselves without chiefs and those who are governed by chiefs appears to be about equal. If this is the case, the value judgment appears to be common among preliterate associations that it is good to govern themselves. By the same token, the value judgment seems common that it is good to be governed by chiefs.[79]

## 2. Self-help

Self-help is a claim to prevent or redress a wrong by one's own efforts without recourse to any other aid of law. In literate systems of law, self-help usually comes into play in cases of self-defense, distress, abatement of a nuisance, and the like. Among preliterates it can have a much wider application. It can also include the help of one's own kin. Self-help is the most elemental way of restoring respect for relations of title. When other means have failed, it may be the only way. It is common among preliterates, some examples of which we have already seen.

Among the Nuer, self-help is the primary sanction. The first punishment inflicted for an offense is the retaliatory reaction of the one offended. The first penalty exacted of me for infringing on the claims of another would be to have him bring physical force to bear on me. With the Eskimo, the single murder is an offense against which the relatives of the victim react immediately. When any member of an Ifugao family is harmed, the entire family assists in the punishment of the of-

79 Leaders: Paul Bohannon, *Social Anthropology* (New York, 1963), pp. 280–282; Max Gluckman, "Natural Justice in Africa," *Natural Law Forum* 9 (1964): pp. 36–37; Isaac Schapera, *Government and Politics in Tribal Societies* (London, 1956), pp. 68, 92, 115: quoting from Eugene Casalis, *Les Basutos* (Paris, 1861), pp. 214–228; K. A. Busia, *The Position of the Chief in the Modern Political System of Ashanti* (London, 1951), pp. 21–22, 44, 64–65; Schapera, *A Handbook of Tswana Law and Custom* (London, 1938), pp. 53, 84; C. L. Harries, *The Laws and Customs of the Bapedi and Cognate Tribes of the Transvaal* (rev. ed., Johannesburg, 1929), pp. 80, 85; Ralph Barton, *The Kalingas* (Chicago, 1949), pp. 148–149; E. Adamson Hoebel, *The Law of Primitive Man* (Cambridge, Mass., 1954), p. 82; Jomo Kenyatta, *Facing Mount Kenya* (London, 1953), pp. 315–316; John Gillin, "Crime and punishment Among the Barama River Carib," *Amer. Anthropologist* 36 (1934): p. 333; Jessie Bernard, "Political Leadership Among North American Indians," *Amer. Jour. Sociology* 34 (1928): pp. 296, 313–314; Alexander Goldenweiser, *Anthropology* (New York, 1937), p. 375; Joseph Danquah, *Gold Coast: Akan Laws and Customs* (London, 1938), p. 42; Schapera, "Tribal Legislation Among the Tswana of the Bechuanaland Protectorate," *London School of Economics and Political Science, Monographs on Social Anthropology* 9 (1943): pp. 18–19; Hans Cory, *Sukuma Law and Custom* (London, 1953), p. 8; J. F. Holleman, *Shona Customary Law* (London, 1952), pp. 8, 13–14; Arthur Diamond, *The Evolution of Law and Order* (London, 1951), p. 59; Schapera, "The Political Organization of the Ngwato of Bechuanaland Protectorate," in: Meyer Fortes and Edward Evans-Pritchard, eds., *African Political Systems* (Oxford, 1940), p. 69.

fender. They will also resist any action on the part of the offender's family to help him. Among the Carib, offenses are punished by the victim assisted by specialists who know techniques relating to spiritual powers. At times, his brothers may also help him.

Ways of obtaining satisfaction are numerous. Retaliation by individuals may be by poisoning, sorcery, and violence. Retaliation by the people may be by violence, ostracism, and exile. All methods used by the people as well as the violence of individuals are overt. Poisoning and sorcery are secret. Self-help among other peoples, such as the Tiv, covers several areas. It may be a matter of seeing that a decision of the court is carried out. Or it may concern itself with the protection of one's own claims. Finally, it may be given over to revenge which can involve a feud. Because of the possibility of continuing feud, this type of self-help does not necessarily help restore the balance of justice.

When the people approve of the self-help of an individual who has been aggrieved, it should be noted, they cooperatively participate in the imposition of the punishment or the compensation. Most systems of self-help are endorsed by the people according to the custom law of the place. In doing so, the people make the value judgments of the aggrieved party their own. The people's approval of self-help may take the form of both assistance to individual retaliation and control of it. If the people force an offender to pay for what he has done and punish him if he does not, they are assisting individual retaliation. If they compel the one offended to accept satisfactory payment when offered, they are controlling individual retaliation. When a man, for example, who has caught another committing adultery with his wife takes retaliatory action, if he proceeds according to the rules of custom law he has the tacit approval of all the people. For the moment, he has the authority of the people in back of him and is *pro tempore* a quasi-official of the people.

In some places, a single murder is a matter of individual self-retaliation, but repeated murder calls for action by the people. The one who executes the offender is considered to act in the name of the people and with their authority. Thus, among the Eskimo, no blood revenge may be taken against the executioner, because his act of execution is not looked on as murder. He carried out the people's sentence and the responsibility is their's. A similar situation prevails in other places. Among the Kapauku, an execution cannot be carried out by family authority, even though a relative is asked to administer the punishment. The authority for capital punishment must come from at least the village headman. With Australian tribes, permission of the elders must be sought to engage in retaliatory self-help. A man who has been injured by another receives permission to take his satisfaction by throwing spears or boomerangs at the offender or by spearing him in a non-vital part of the body.

The part played by the people in supporting an offended person is shown in the original meaning of his "complaint." It was a "plaint" before the people to obtain their support. Among the Slavonic and Teutonic people an accusation was made by a plaint or wail before the people of the neighborhood. The injured party implored his neighbors to stand by him. The custom of "hue and cry" in Normandy and England is said to be of this origin. The whole process has been related to the natural cry for help by the victim of an assault.

The value judgment that self-help is good and desirable seems to be common in preliterate societies.[80]

### 3. Proportionate Retaliation

One of the most famous and effective, and perhaps most misunderstood, of preliterate regulations of custom law for controlling self-help is the law of talion.[81] The victim of an offense may have a claim of self-redress, but how far should he be allowed to go in the exercise of this claim. Retaliation cannot be a venture in uncontrolled indulgence of the victim's ire. Unlimited, and therefore disproportionate, redress would itself be unjust.

The need for limitation is clear. Regulation of this primary method of retaliation was recognized early, with the people or their representatives restricting its exercise to what were considered just proportions. As a matter of fact, it is said, in the investigation on the part of the people into the justness of acts of retaliation we have the first germ of legal procedure. The blood feud itself was regulated by rules of its own. Throughout the whole process, there is a discernible rough justice at work. A norm of what was just was not hard to find. The most natural and simple rule is that of equality. An eye for an eye, and a tooth for a tooth, is the natural and normal way in which reaction sets in regarding an offender.

Such a rule of equal reciprocation is common among preliterates. Among the Galla, blood can be wiped out only with blood. This frequently leads to long feuds, which descend from father to son, and to many deaths.

---

[80] Self-help: Paul Howell, *A Manual of Nuer Law* (London, 1954), p. 23; E. Adamson Hoebel, "Law-ways of the Primitive Eskimos," *Jour. Criminology and Criminal Law* 31 (1941), p. 676; Ralph Barton, "Ifugao Law," *Amer. Archaeology and Ethnology* 15 (1919): p. 14; John Gillin, "Crime and Punishment Among the Barama River Carib," *Amer. Anthropologist* 36 (1934): pp. 344, 337; Paul Bohannon, *Justice and Judgment Among the Tiv* (London, 1957), p. 149; Leonard Hobhouse, *Morals and Evolution* (New York, 1906), pp. 72, 96; Hoebel, "Primitive Law and Modern," *Trans. New York Acad. of Sciences* 5, 2 (1942): pp. 38–39; Leopold Pospisil, *Kapauku Papuans and Their Law* (New Haven, 1958), p. 273; Alfred Radcliffe-Brown, "Primitive Law," *Encyc. of the Social Sciences* 9 (1933), p. 204; Paul Vinogradoff, *Outlines of Historical Jurisprudence* (London, 1922), p. 355.

[81] From the Latin word *talis* meaning "such," which in the phrase *talis qualis* implies "such for such." Compare "retaliation."

With the Khan Tevka in Siberia, the law of retaliation occupies the place of first importance. Blood can be avenged only by blood, mutilation only by similar mutilation. Bedouin tribes of large size have been ruled for centuries by this norm. Although it was their custom law at one time for retaliation to be taken at the discretion of the wronged individual, gradually the law underwent a change and now all retaliation must be carried on according to rules approved by the tribe.

The regulations governing retaliation are an important aspect of custom law. The result of such regulations is that recognized procedures are followed in seeking satisfaction, as we said. One of the principal values to be accomplished, along with the seeking of justice, is the removal of the feeling of resentment in the injured person or persons. Until this is brought about, restoration of the respect due to relations of title cannot take place.

Cases are reported, which from some points of view may appear extreme, where satisfaction of the injured parties was had only by a most literal carrying out of the law of talion. A "folk tale," current over the whole of Northeast Africa and the Middle East, recounts how the rigid application of the law of talion works for injustice instead of justice. A man fell out of a tree on top of a member of a different clan. The man on whom he fell was killed. The killer's clan offered compensation money. But the clan of the victim insisted on their claim to kill the killer in exactly the same way as he killed the deceased. So the killer was required to walk to and fro under the same tree while members of the victim's clan repeatedly fell on him until he was dead.

The rule of retaliation is very old. It was a common regulation among the ancient Hebrews. "He who kills a man shall be put to death. He who kills a beast shall make it good, life for life. When a man causes a disfigurement in his neighbor, as he has done it shall be done to him, fracture for fracture, eye for eye, tooth for tooth; as he has disfigured a man, he shall be disfigured." [82] The rule of talion also runs throughout Mohammedan law. "O faithful, retaliation for murder is prescribed for you: a freeman for a freeman, slave for slave, woman for woman." [83] It is also present in the Babylonian Law of Hammurabi. "If a man has put out the eye of a freeman, they shall put out his eye. If he breaks the bone of a freeman, they shall break his bone. . . . If a man knocks out the tooth of a free man equal in rank to himself, they shall knock out his tooth." [84]

In many places the law of strict quantitative equivalency has gradually changed to one of proportionate

compensation and indemnity. Peace within a community may not always be best preserved by strict equal retribution. The Kalinga regard the collection of an indemnity as a retaliation. Among the Tasmanians, the punishment for adultery was beating the offender and driving a spear through his leg. With the Botocudo, the penalty for the woman caught in adultery was a beating and branding by her husband. In Australia adultery is settled by a duel between the contending parties with death seldom ensuing. One of the principle benefits of compensation is its terminating effect on a blood feud, as we have seen. In Nigeria the law of talion was the guiding rule in cases of assault. The brother of the injured man might retaliate on the offender or on one of the offender's brothers. This could lead to a general fight between the two kindreds. To end this, the elders might intervene and order the offender to pay for the expenses involved in the injured man's illness. If he refused to comply, he would be wounded in the same way he wounded the other, or some of his property would be seized. [85]

Among the wild tribes of East Africa, there has been a gradual shift from talion to fine. With the Balla, blood can be wiped out only by blood, but the Wataveta allow an offense to be compensated for by the payment of cattle. In Nigeria, although the traditional punishment is on a talionic basis, most offenses are compensable by payment. In fact it has been reported, apparently in contradiction to other reports, that the law of talion has not been in effect as long as can be remembered. Because of the numerous instances in which the equal retaliation stipulated by the rule of talion was replaced by compensatory damages, it has been said that the *lex talionis* was never strictly enforced anywhere, preliterates included. It is claimed that it was only a rule which in practice was applied to a group of more serious injuries.

The law of talion has been an effective instrument in maintaining some semblance of balance in the justice that has obtained between vast numbers of widely scattered peoples over the centuries. It was only when the governments of political societies became strong enough to keep this balance by means other than compensation to prevent blood feuds, that the *lex talionis* was no longer needed. The law of talion has been replaced by the law of crimes. Underlying this change was the realization that an imbalance of justice had to be corrected by punishment which pertains to the welfare of the people, not by revenge which relates to the

[82] Leviticus 24: 17–20.

[83] Koran, Sura II, 173; quoted by V. A. Riasanovsky, *Customary Law of the Nomadic Tribes of Siberia* (Tsiensin, 1938), p. 24.

[84] Laws of Hammurabi §§ 196, 197, 200, trans. and ed. by Godfrey Driver and John Miles, *The Babylonian Laws* (2 v., Oxford, 1952–1955), **2**: p. 77.

[85] In early England, around the twelfth century, the following limitation and designation of punishments occurs in the laws of William I. "We also forbid that anyone should be slain or hanged for any offence, but let his eyes be gouged out or his feet or testicles or hands cut off, so that the living trunk may remain for a sign of his treachery and ill-doing, for according to the size of the wrong should punishment be inflicted on evildoers." Willelmi Articuli Retractati, caput 17 (1210); quoted by Arthur Diamond, *The Evolution of Law and Order* (London, 1951), p. 291.

wrath of the individual. It was this growing recognition of the fact that many offenses have a direct bearing on the welfare of the people and not merely on the well-being of the individual person, that caused the emphasis in custom law to shift from torts to crimes.

The value judgment, then, that proportionate retaliation is good appears to be common among preliterate associations.[86]

## 4. Exile

All peoples judge that exile is one of the severest of punishments, as we have seen. Most men, regardless of how stubborn they are, will bow before the threat of exile and banishment. But although all people make this judgment concerning exile, not all of them inflict exile as a punishment.

As one of the earliest forms of punishment, exile is common among preliterates. Among the Barama River Carib, a particularly obnoxious individual will be told to leave. If he persists in staying, he and his family will be socially ostracized. He is not invited to parties, is unable to borrow anything, to get help in hunting, fishing, field cutting, canoe building, or in other activities for which male help is needed. His wife will receive no help in her work and all the family will not be allowed to use the waterhole and bathing place. In a word, he and his family are cut off from all the benefits which social living is intended to furnish. In some instances, if he does not leave, he may be beaten or killed. Ordinarily, though, such extreme measures are not necessary as any man with common sense will leave while it is opportune to do so. Among the Albanian mountaineers, exile or death was the punishment for serious offenses.

Some nomadic peoples, instead of banishing an offender and his family and thereby cutting them off from all means of subsistence, simply move away from the offender and his family and leave them with whatever means of livelihood they may have. The Kiowa people sometimes took this way of dealing with offenders. They are said never to have deprived an offender and his family of the necessities of life. In the Trobriand Islands, the manner in which an exiling can take place is graphic and charged with emotion. In the silence of the night an accuser, in a loud and piercing voice that can be heard by the whole village including the offender, charges the offender with his misconduct and demands that he leave the village. Others, too, may shout their charges and demand that the offender leave. The speeches are heard in deep silence, but before the night is over the offender is gone forever.

The idea behind the form of banishment known as outlawry is that the offender by his lawbreaking actions has put himself beyond the pale of politically organized society and should not be allowed to enjoy the benefits he has denied others. Among the Scandinavian tribes, the outlawed were formally expelled from the society of their fellow-tribesmen. They had to go to the forest and live as best they could with not even their wives and families coming to their aid. Outlawry has been said to be one step beyond execution, because it deprives a man of the benefits of common social living. The severity of this form of punishment can be estimated when it is realized that anyone was free to kill the outlawed man with impunity. Anyone who sheltered him was liable for his acts. If he was sheltered, he practically became a slave to his protector.

The notion that in preliterate life banishment is worse than death perhaps needs qualification. Under some circumstances this need not necessarily be so. Banished Cheyenne, it is reported, were received by the Dakota and Arapaho with friendliness and with no questions asked. But, it is also pointed out, homesickness for the home tribe made the separation of a man and his family a severe trial. Time and again this condition of the banished was pleaded as a reason for remitting the punishment of exile. Not only the man but also his family were in the miserable state of being cut off from association with the rest of the tribe.

The value judgment that it is good to use exile as a punishment appears to be common in preliterate societies.[87]

---

[86] Proportionate retaliation: Richard Cherry, *Lectures in the Growth of Criminal Law in Ancient Communities* (London, 1890), pp. 51, 79, 97; Leonard Hobhouse, *Morals in Evolution* (New York, 1906), p. 72; Ellsworth Faris, "The Origin of Punishment," in: Albert Kocourek and John Wigmore, *Primitive and Ancient Legal Institutions* (3 v., Boston, 1915) 1: p. 152; Robert Hamilton, "East African Native Laws and Customs," *Jour. Comp. Legislation* 11 (1910): p. 185; Valintin Riasanovsky, *Customary Law of the Nomadic Tribes of Siberia* (Tsiensin, 1938), p. 9; Austin Kennett, *Bedouin Justice* (Cambridge, 1925), pp. 37–38; Alfred Radcliffe-Brown, "Primitive Law," *Encyc. of the Social Sciences* 9 (1933): p. 204; Max Gluckman, "Natural Justice in Africa," *Natural Law Forum* 9 (1964): p. 37; Ralph Barton, *The Kalingas* (Chicago, 1949), p. 230; Julius Lips, "Government," in: Franz Boas, ed., *General Anthropology* (Boston, 1938), p. 496; C. K. Meek, *Law and Authority in a Nigerian Tribe* (London, 1937), p. 213; Lewis Tupper, "Customary and Other Law in the East Africa Protectorate," *Jour. Soc. Comp. Legislation* 8 (1908): p. 175; James Anderson, *Islamic Law in Africa* (London, 1954), p. 197; Paul Radin, *The World of Primitive Man* (New York, 1953), p. 253; Arthur Diamond, *The Evolution of Law and Order* (London, 1951), pp. 290–292; John Gillin, "Crime and Punishment Among the Barama River Carib," *Amer. Anthropologist* 36 (1934): p. 343; Margaret Hasluck, *The Unwritten Law of the Albanian Mountains* (Cambridge, 1954), p. 10.

[87] Exile: Jane Richardson, "Law and Status Among the Kiowa Indians," *Monograph Amer. Ethnol. Soc.* 1 (1940): p. 63; Leonhard Adam, "Criminal Law and Procedure in Nepal," *Far Eastern Quart.* 9 (1950): pp. 165–167; Bronislaw Malinowski, "The Forces of Law and Order in a Primitive Community," *Proc. Royal Inst. of Great Britain* 24 (1925): pp. 541–542; Paul Vinogradoff, *Outlines of Historical Jurisprudence* (London, 1922): p. 360; Richard Cherry, *Lectures in the Growth of Criminal Law in Ancient Communities* (London, 1890), pp. 37–38; Karl Llewellyn and E. Adamson Hoebel, *The Cheyenne Way* (Norman, 1941), p. 133.

## 5. *Confessions*

Preliterate courts, in their attempt to find the facts of a case, make use of confession. It plays a varying role. Some preliterates think that there is no reason why a guilty man should deny his guilt; others think there is. The Naskapi Indians, for instance, cannot understand how a guilty man can deny his guilt. Admission of guilt is therefore important in the procedure of Naskapi law. The West African Negro, on the other hand, cannot see why he should admit his guilt even though he is guilty. In fact, he is said to resent any verdict, guilty though he may be. This varying attitude regarding confession of guilt is undoubtedly related to the different background assumptions that prevail among preliterates concerning the status of the accused. In some places, the Transvaal for instance, it has been reported however reliably that accusation raises the presumption of guilt and the accused is looked on as guilty until he can prove his innocence.

Against such a presumption, the possibility of proving his innocence may appear so hopeless to the accused that he will readily admit his guilt. Among the Naskapi, for instance, this condition can work against the accused to the extent that he is sometimes given little time in court to prove that he is not guilty. Among some peoples, the accused may be induced to confess his guilt by the prospect of some leniency. With the Ifugao, confession before the infliction of punishment can mitigate it to no little degree, with the exception of murder and adultery. In cases of adultery, confession before evidence has been adduced is looked on as an insulting boast.

Under such conditions, where confession may play an important part in conviction, the danger is always present that it may be forced. Among the Akan, a man charged with violating the Chief's wife either confessed or was made to do so. A man accused of wrongdoing by a woman has little chance of rebutting this testimony unless strong evidence of his innocence could be brought forward. On the other hand, in places where it is presumed that the accused is innocent until he is proven guilty the accused may hold his tongue, bide his time and await the success or failure of the prosecution's attempt to establish his guilt. Cases are on record in Nigeria where the offender thought it amusing that he should be asked whether he pleaded "guilty" or "not guilty." In his mind, the determination of this question was the purpose of the whole proceedings.

The attitude that an accused man is guilty until he can prove his innocence is by no means peculiar to the preliterate, as is well known. Medieval Europe has furnished a satiety of examples of this type of thinking. Officials were more intent on repressing crime and maintaining order than they were with the personal claims of the accused. The tendency was to treat the accused as guilty, and opportunities for proving his innocence were considered to be privileges sparingly conceded rather than as means of defense to which the accused had a right. Insufficient evidence for conviction was freely supplemented by the use of torture.

The value judgment, therefore, among preliterates that it is good to use confession as a means of obtaining the truth in a case appears to be common.[88]

### C. FREQUENT: OATHS

The taking of oaths is another means employed by preliterates in their attempts to learn the facts in a case where confession or testimony of witnesses is absent. An oath is an appeal to a suprahuman power to witness that a statement is true or that a promise will be kept. The meaning of the oath is in direct relation to the belief of the oath-taker in the power involved. The sanction of the oath lies in the swearer's willingness to undergo an unfavorable reaction by the power involved if the oath is not kept.[89]

Oaths are usually used to draw out confessions of guilt, and failure to take the oath can result in the decision being rendered against the refuser. Among the Nandi, oaths were taken before the elders and at their request. Adults only were allowed to take oaths. The party who refused to take the oath, had judgment delivered against him immediately. If both parties took the oath, it brought on a curse against the obligated or guilty party. The taking of oaths also accomplished other effects. With the Gikuyu, oaths prevented false evidence from being given and helped bring out confessions. Oaths likewise are said to rule out bribery and ensure unbiased judgment. Not only the parties to a case were required to take the oath, but the elders too who were to try the case. In the oath they promise not to accept bribery in any form or from any source. Women are not allowed to take oaths. They are considered mentally and physically unfit to undergo this trying experience which involves not only the individual but the whole family group.

---

[88] Confessions: Julius Lips, "Naskapi Law," *Trans. Amer. Philos. Soc.* 37 (1947): pp. 475, 484: quoting Albert Schweitzer, *Zwischen Wasser und Urwald* (Munich, 1926), p. 72; C. L. Harries, *The Law and Customs of the Bapedi and Cognate Tribes of the Transvaal* (rev. ed., Johannesburg, 1929), p. 101; Ralph Barton, "Ifugao Law," *Amer. Archaeology and Ethnology* 15 (1919): p. 66; Joseph Danquah, *Gold Coast: Akan Laws and Customs* (London, 1938), p. 92; T. Olawale Elias, *The Nature of African Customary Law* (Manchester, 1956), p. 299; Leonard Hobhouse, *Morals in Evolution* (New York, 1906), p. 121.

[89] Oaths that are taken without actual belief in the power invoked are a useless travesty. Such is the situation, for instance, in Kenya where preliterates have been required to swear on the Bible. "Europeans have adopted a form of raising hands or kissing the Bible as symbols of oath. It can be definitely said that this form of oath has no meaning at all to the Africans. It has no binding force, moral or religious. The result has been fabrication of evidence in courts of justice, and furthermore, bribery and corruption is the order of the day in many cases that come before a magistrate or a court of elders. It would not be exaggeration to say that in most cases judgment depends entirely on who pays most." Jomo Kenyatta, *Facing Mount Kenya* (London, 1953), p. 225.

The manner of swearing the oath assumes many forms. When the Nabaloi swear before their council, they say, "May I die if what I say is not true." The Waboni swear by stepping over a spear or the tail of a wild animal saying, "May this animal (or spear) kill me if I do not tell the truth." In some localities, Northern Australia for instance, preliminary to taking the oath there is a procedural step. The witness is told that he should tell no lies and that he should "talk straight-fellow." Among the North American Indians, "smoking the pipe" was an oath-taking procedure which is said to have had an immense influence in checking retaliatory wars. The pipe was a basic institution for stopping intratribal conflict and war. To smoke was to swear that no further action would take place. The smoking of the peace pipe implied no judgment as to which party was right or wrong, with the consequence that there was no loss of face on either side. The smoking of the pipe estopped the operation of the law of talion. Any violation of the pact made by smoking the pipe, immediately brought misfortune to the offender and eventually death.

The value of the oath as a means of solving cases of theft and murder can be seen in areas, such as deserts, where no evidence of the offenses is available. Thus among the Bedouin tribes who roam the desert and among whom consequently little evidence is available, the oath is the only means by which even an approximation can be made to the discovery of thieves and murderers. It has been observed that this use of the oath among Bedouin tribes is as old if not older than the oath as found among the Hebrews. According to the Mosaic law, a man suspected of theft was required, in the absence of witnesses, to take an oath that he was not guilty. If a man delivered an animal to a neighbor and it strayed away and no one saw it, the man delivering the animal took an oath that he did not steal the animal. The owner had to accept the oath and no restitution was made.

The value judgment, then, that it is good to use oaths in attempting to find the truth appears to be frequent in preliterate societies.[90]

### D. OCCASIONAL

There are other value judgments which appear to be only occasional among preliterates. These concern changing custom law, equitable fictions, and the punishments of mutilation, wounding, and imprisonment.

[90] Oaths: Geoffrey Snell, *Nandi Customary Law* (London, 1954), p. 81; Jomo Kenyatta, *Facing Mount Kenya* (London, 1953), pp. 223, 225; Claude Moss, "Nabaloi Law and Ritual," *Amer. Archaeology and Ethnology* (1920): p. 265; Robert Hamilton, "East African Native Laws and Customs," *Jour. Comp. Legislation* 11 (1910): p. 186; Adolphus Elkin, "Aboriginal Evidence and Justice in North Australia," *Oceania* 17 (1947): p. 188; Jane Richardson, "Law and Status Among the Kiowa Indians," *Monograph Amer. Ethnol. Soc.* 1 (1940): p. 11; Austin Kennett, *Bedouin Justice* (Cambridge, 1925), pp. 39, 40; Exodus 22: 10–12.

### 1. *Changing Custom Law*

That preliterates desire to see justice done is also manifested in changes they occasionally make in their custom law. Among the Kamba, their custom law held that any children born to a wife belonged to her husband. In a case involving a young girl who was married to an impotent old man and who had children by other men, the elders judged contrary to the then existing custom law, that the children belonged to her and that she should refund the marriage payment to the old man.

The council of elders of the Nabaloi in Luzon also change custom law when necessary, but clearly with the approval of all the people. The custom law held that, if a young man had committed a fault with a young unmarried girl, they were punished and had to kill a carabao, cow, or pig to be eaten by the people. The council of elders decided that, in view of the fact that animals were becoming scarce, the law might well be changed. The people were gathered together and a majority of them decided that it would be well if the custom law were changed. As long as the council followed custom law, the approval of the people was not necessary. It was only when the decision of the council amended custom law that the consent of the people was required. If anyone refused to obey their decisions, the members of the council would ask the people to punish the recalcitrant. Sometimes they would confiscate his property and distribute it to the people.

In places in South Africa, the chief would not attempt to make any decision of any great tribal importance without having first presented the matter to the council for discussion. If a chief did try to change a custom law without asking the advice of his councilors and without allowing public discussion, the dissatisfied part of the tribe would possibly withdraw its allegiance to him and transfer it to some lesser chief in the same clan. Among the Tswana, the chief's court changed the custom law regarding seed-raising. A man died leaving a wife and children. His younger brother refused to follow the custom law and raise his brother's seed. The father of these brothers began to live with the widow and begot two children by her who were held to be the legal offspring of the son who died. The father's first wife complained about the situation to the local headman and finally took the matter to the chief. Although the father contended that he was acting according to custom law, the chief declared that the custom was obsolete and should be discouraged. He ordered the father to stop living with the widow. When the father ignored the order, he was severely punished by the chief.

There are other examples of chiefs' courts changing custom law. According to Ngwaketse custom law, infant betrothals have been given full recognition. But in a matrimonial dispute involving a fourteen-year-old bride, the chief held that the father acted shamefully in allowing his daughter to be married when she was so young and ordered the marriage to be annulled. The court in this instance, moved by considerations of equity and justice, changed the custom law. Among the Southern Bantu, it is said that the chief in general has the power to change custom law and there is a recognized procedure for doing so.

The value judgment, then, that it is good to change custom law when necessity arises appears to be occasional among preliterate societies.[91]

## 2. Equitable Fictions

Preliterates in their application of custom law, as we have seen, show the same concern for just solutions as does the rest of mankind. This is further demonstrated by their use of "fictions" in the adjustment of custom law to common needs. These are fine examples of constructed value judgments.

A fiction in law is the acceptance, for the sake of justice or expediency, of something as a fact that in reality is not so. The equitable nature of legal fiction lies in its purpose. In their desire to avoid unjust and harsh solutions judges often find it easier to broaden the extension of what is to be included under the law than it is to bring about a change in the law itself. Fictions circumvent the shortcomings of the law. Thus in Africa, rigid rules concerning the non-alienability of family land have been modified into conditioned alienability by raising inconvenient or outmoded concepts to a new plane on the ground of expediency or utility. In Indonesia the line of patrilineal inheritance is preserved through a fictional "son" who is adopted. A family without sons will adopt their daughter's husband as a "son" with the result that her children will remain within the clan and the inheritance will remain within their line.

Fiction is also used in situations wherein outsiders are adopted and treated as if they were blood relations. This is said to be a universal practice among preliterates, and outsiders thus taken in by the group are identified as if they were actual kinsmen. Fiction likewise is at work when the children of a second wife, who has been purchased by the first wife who is childless, address the first wife as "father" following the notion that whoever pays for their mother is their father. Thus in Dahomey in West Africa, a childless wife may buy a second wife for her husband and in this way avoid being divorced. In Baganda a fiction accounts for the justification for killing a member of the upper class caught in adultery. Such men usually carry a spear with them in order that they may be able to rid themselves of anyone who might

come upon them in their adulterous pursuits. The fiction, consequently, arose that all adulterers of the upper class were potential murderers who would not hesitate to kill an intruder and death was an appropriate penalty for them.

The Cheyenne did not hesitate to use fiction when necessary. The installation of chiefs traditionally took place in the lodge of the great chief which was in the center of the tribal camp circle. As time went on, camps ceased to be built in such circles. Hence, the chief would declare a certain spot to be the center of the camp and the ceremonies would be held there. Likewise, parched corn was one of the four sacred dishes which were served in the ritual breakfast at sunrise at Peyote meetings. One year after a drought, there was no corn in the country. So, the head priest brought out commercial candied popcorn and declared that this popcorn was the same as the corn they had traditionally used.

The use of legal fiction by preliterates has its counterpart, of course, in written law. In England, for example, the severity of the existing criminal law was mitigated by the growth of the courts of chancery or equity, but it was also moderated by the use of fiction. One such fiction was the "benefit of clergy." The death penalty was imposed for all felonies except petty larceny and mayhem from the Middle Ages down to 1826. Clergymen could only be tried and convicted by an ecclesiastical court and the penalty could be anything but death. An ecclesiastical court never pronounces a death sentence. During this period, practically the only ones who could read and write were clerics, but as time went on this knowledge began to spread rapidly. The "benefit of clergy" was then extended to all those who could read and write. In 1705 the requirement of reading a verse of the Bible was dropped and "benefit of clergy" became a judicial means of showing leniency. The penalty for a "clergyable" offense was branding on the hand and imprisonment for not more than one year. An exception was made in the case of larceny which by the law of 1717 was made punishable by deportation for seven years.

A similar fiction has existed in India and China. The Brahman is a literate man and for this reason cannot be put to death for homicide or any other offense except treason. He can be branded or even blinded or more commonly he can be banished, but he cannot be executed. The privilege is said to be that of literacy and not priesthood. The same procedure is said to have been found in Nepal in the nineteenth century.

The value judgment seems to be occasional among preliterates that it is good to use fiction in the interpretation of custom law.[92]

[91] Changing custom law: T. Olawale Elias, *The Nature of African Customary Law* (Manchester, 1956), p. 202; Claude Moss, "Nabaloi Law and Ritual," *Amer. Archaeology and Ethnology* (1920): pp. 237–239; G. M. B. Whitfield, *South African Law* (2nd ed., Capetown, 1948), p. 3; Isaac Schapera, "Tribal Legislation Among the Tswana of the Bechuanaland Protectorate," *London School of Economics and Political Science, Monographs on Social Anthropology* 9 (1943): pp. 6–7, 65.

[92] Equitable fictions: T. Olawale Elias, *The Nature of African Customary Law* (Manchester, 1956), pp. 187, 297; Barend Ter Haar, *Adat Law in Indonesia* (New York, 1948), pp. 175–176; E. Adamson Hoebel, *The Law of Primitive Man* (Cambridge, Mass., 1954), p. 285; Melville Herskovits, "A Note on 'Woman

### 3. Mutilation—Wounding—Combat

Mutilation as a punishment, especially for habitual offenders, has been used by preliterates. How extensively is uncertain. Some Uganda tribes are reported as punishing theft by mutilation or payment of compensation. In Nepal offenders had each one hand or one ear cut off for theft, the nose cut off for adultery, and the membrum virile cut off for sexual intercourse with outcasts. Siberian tribes inflicted the deprivation of limbs for thefts of a serious nature.

Wounding an offender, instead of killing him or mutilating him, was resorted to by some peoples as a punishment or a means of settling disputes. Among the tribes of Australia, wounding was the punishment inflicted for serious offenses which in other places would be punishable by death. Offenses of murder within the clan, sorcery, adultery, and betrayal of secret rites were punished by wounding the offender with spears, but without killing him. In the tribes of Southeast Australia, a murderer is made to stand out between the two contending groups of the victim's kin and the kin of the offender. The headman fixes a spot where the culprit will stand. He stands out with a shield and receives the spears thrown at him by the kinsmen of the deceased until finally he is wounded. When this occurs, the headman throws a lighted piece of bark into the air and the contest ceases.

Flogging is also a punishment sometimes inflicted. In some places in Africa, it is reported that young offenders are often flogged or whipped. Among the Siberian tribes, robbery and theft are punished by whipping. With the Eskimo, homicidal disputes are settled by various kinds of combat, instead of killing. Buffeting is prevalent among the central tribes along the Arctic Circle from Hudson Bay to Bering Strait. Wrestling is reported as the form of dispute-settling-combat employed in Siberia, Alaska, Baffin Land, and Northwest Greenland. In West and East Greenland there are song duels in which the contestants sing berating and reproving songs at each other. This song duel is accompanied also by head-butting.

As is well known, some of these forms of punishment, especially mutilation, were specified as punishment in the written laws of many countries among which were England, Ireland, Turkey, and India. Composition was always possible. In places under the influence of Mohammedan Law, such as Turkey, theft was originally punished by mutilation. First to be cut off as a suitable retaliation for theft was the hand, the offending member. The second offense of theft was punished by cutting off the thief's foot. Further offenses brought on added mutilations until all his members were amputated.

It was always possible, however, that the owner of the stolen property would compound with the thief and accept whatever he thought was an equitable substitute for revenge. Eventually mutilation as a punishment was discontinued and imprisonment substituted in its stead.

There is a noticeable similarity of value judgments found among widely separated peoples regarding mutilation as a punishment. As has been pointed out, the law of Turkey was almost identical with the law of Ireland as it existed under the Brehon system. This identity of usage could not have been the result of any communications between the Celtic tribes of Ireland and the Semitic races of Asia. The only explanation seems to be "that human nature is very much the same everywhere, and that, consequently, the course of development of Penal Law is extremely like in the most distant countries." [93]

The value judgment, then, that mutilation, wounding, and combat are good as punishments is occasional among preliterates. [94]

### 4. Imprisonment

Confinement of some form is not unknown among preliterates. It appears to be found only occasionally. A modified form of imprisonment always existed among the Albanian mountaineers. Among the Siberian tribes there was imprisonment for fraud concerning property, for non-payment of a debt when there was ability to pay it, and for the first violation of religious rules. With the Yoruba in Nigeria, debtors were sometimes committed to prison. This rarely canceled the debt and was only a way of exacting interest. Every chief is said to have had his own prison wherein he kept those guilty of disobedience, drunkenness, and the like. More serious offenders were kept in the prison of the Obgoni Society wherever it was in control.

The type of confinement used in some places was a stock which impeded escape after the manner of a ball and chain. In Uganda a stock was made by boring a hole through a heavy log of wood and thrusting the offender's foot into it. The log was attached to the offender's leg. He could lift it and walk about within a limited area. Escape was difficult both because of the presence of guards and the fact that the log constantly

Marriage' in Dahomey," *Africa* **10** (1937): pp. 335–341; H. Hone, "The Native of Uganda and the Criminal Law," *The Uganda Journal* **6** (1938): p. 5; Leonard Hobhouse, *Morals in Evolution* (New York, 1906), p. 123; Arthur Diamond, *The Evolution of Law and Order* (London, 1951), pp. 286–287.

[93] Richard Cherry, *Lectures in the Growth of Criminal Law in Ancient Communities* (London, 1890), pp. 54–55.

[94] Mutilation—wounding—combat: T. Olawale Elias, *The Nature of African Customary Law* (Manchester, 1956), pp. 262–263; Leonhard Adam, "Criminal Law and Procedure in Nepal," *Far Eastern Quart.* **9** (1950): pp. 165–166; Valintin Riasanovsky, *Customary Law of the Nomadic Tribes of Siberia* (Tsiensin, 1938), p. 35; Julius Lips, "Government," in: Franz Boas, *General Anthropology* (Boston, 1938), pp. 496–497; Arthur Diamond, *The Evolution of Law and Order* (London, 1951), p. 23; E. Adamson Hoebel, "Law-ways of the Primitive Eskimos," *Jour. Criminology and Criminal Law* **31** (1941): p. 677; Richard Cherry, *Lectures in the Growth of Criminal Law in Ancient Communities* (London, 1890), pp. 54–55.

rubbed against his foot as he walked. Desperate offenders had both arms and one leg put into the stocks. The nearest thing to imprisonment among the Naskapi is tying an offender to a tree. This form of punishment does not make the offender a moral outcast, but he is looked down on if the punishment occurs too often. When a man is punished by being tied to a tree, he stands with his arms hanging down and a rope is tied around his body and arms.

How widespread imprisonment has been among preliterates is most uncertain. Records regarding preliterate prisons are not extensive. Hence, the value judgment that the use of imprisonment is good probably is occasional among preliterates.[95]

## CONCLUSION

We have examined the data of anthropology and found that they support the position of psychology regarding the universality of certain value judgments among all men. Wherever normal men are in society their laws are found to contain value judgments which are universal and almost universal. These value judgments are relatively few. They relate to the specific areas of our basic drives as well as to obligation, rights, and regulations. The data also show that there are other value judgments which are not universal or almost universal. These value judgments are many. They are either general, common, frequent or occasional in all known societies of men.

The data of anthropology, therefore, support what is indicated by our psychological model, namely, that there are some values which are in law necessarily. If some values are in law necessarily, they will be found universally in the laws of all known associations of men. And such is the case. Of course, and this should be carefully noted, the presence itself of certain value judgments in the laws of all societies does not connote that they are there necessarily. There have been judgments made by all societies of men which were afterwards changed. The necessity of certain value judgments comes from the psychology of men, as we have indicated above. But the persistently constant presence of the same value judgments in the laws of all known associations of men and at all times as far as our historical knowledge goes, although not a proof, is the strongest possible corroboration that these values are in the laws of men necessarily.

The data of anthropology have been employed here as confirming support for the position of psychology,

not as a basis of defining ethical right and wrong. The foundation of right and wrong, of good and bad, is contained in our model of values. From this it is obvious that the basis is not consensus of opinion. Some have said that the concepts of right and wrong ultimately derive their meaning from the consensus of approval or disapproval.[1] But this position has been properly characterized as the "besetting error" of those theories of value which pretend to be positive or scientific.[2] Attempts to define value in terms of consensus overlook the fact that consensus itself is based on some definite grounds. Otherwise consensus would be without reasons, that is, irrational. Consensus presupposes objects which in themselves have value and about which value judgments are formed. Such are the objects of the basic drives and the value judgments formed regarding them. Those value judgments which are universal or almost universal, and perhaps even general, inevitably result in a consensus of the people. It is on these grounds that the laws and government of a free association of men reflect the consensus of the people as a reliable guide of what fulfills their common needs.[3]

There are then, universal and almost universal value judgments which are the bedrock of the consensus of any people. Lawmen who are still under the impression that there are no such value judgments would do well to examine the data of psychology and anthropology. For too long have jurisprudents spurned the findings of other fields of endeavor. From what they take to be high ground, they look down on the work of other disciplines. Efforts to bring data from these knowledges into law have been patronizingly labeled as attempts to "psychologize" or "anthropologize" law. Hence, when statements are made to the effect that it has never been shown that there are universal value judgments in law, the only conclusion which can be accurately drawn is that there is in such remarks much less than meets the eye.[4] If men in law are to understand law, they must

---

[95] Imprisonment: Margaret Hasluck, *The Unwritten Law of the Albanian Mountains* (Cambridge, 1954), p. 10; Valintin Riasanovsky, *Customary Law of the Nomadic Tribes of Siberia* (Tsiensin, 1938), p. 35; Percy Talbot, *The Peoples of Southern Nigeria* (London, 1926), pp. 632, 634; T. Olawale Elias, *The Nature of African Customary Law* (Manchester, 1956), p. 262; Julius Lips, "Naskapi Law," *Trans. Amer. Philos. Soc.* 37 (1947): p. 471.

[1] Edward Westermarck, *The Origin and Development of the Moral Ideas* (2 v., London, 1908–1912) 1: pp. 138, 145.

[2] Ralph Perry, *General Theory of Value* (Cambridge, 1926), pp. 130–131. See also Brand Blanshard, *Reason and Goodness* (New York, 1961), pp. 103–138.

[3] The constitution and the government of a free society acknowledges "the moral consensus freely arrived at by its citizens, not because they so decide, but because they are deemed competent to decide *rightly*, as the authentic spokesmen of the social conscience. I know that this runs counter to current legal positivism, which refuses to qualify in any way the ultimate authority of the 'basic norm' of a given legal structure." Michael Polanyi, *Personal Knowledge* (Chicago, 1958), p. 223. The reference is to Hans Kelsen, *General Theory of Law and the State*, trans. by Angers Wedberg (Cambridge, Mass., 1946), pp. 115–118.

[4] Typical of this disregard of data long since reported is the statement that "even at this date no one has established that there is some defining property or properties which all . . . legal systems have in common and which must therefore be present for the term [law] to be correctly applied." T. Summers, "The New Analytical Jurists," *New York Univ. Law Rev.* 41 (1966): p. 884.

make an effort to understand human beings and the needs of human beings which law is intended to serve. When this effort is made and the facts are faced, it is hard to see how the knowledge can be avoided that fundamentally human beings and their basic needs are everywhere the same.[5]

---

[5] "We need a consensus to erect the bridge [between the totalitarians and the libertarians] and to maintain it. Finding the materials out of which it can be built is a difficult task. But the self-interest in survival is as great among other people as it is among our own. The jurisprudes from the several continents are the ones who can find the strands common to all systems of law. Only after they find them can the diplomats and other men of public affairs reach the consensus necessary for a Rule of Law in World Affairs." William Douglas, "Foreword," *Columbia Law Review* Board of Editors, *Essays on Jurisprudence* (1963) : pp. vii–viii.

There may be those who feel impelled to conclude that in this study I am implicitly confirming "natural law" or that I am implicitly refuting it. If such there be, I suggest that they suspend judgment until the publication (by Appleton-Century-Crofts) of my forthcoming book *Ethics in the Situation*.

ABERLE, DAVID F. 1966. *The Peyote Religion Among the Navaho* (Chicago).

ABRAHAM, ROY. 1933. *The Tiv People* (Lagos).

ADAM, LEONARD. 1950. "Criminal Law and Procedure in Nepal." *Far Eastern Quart.* 9: pp. 146–168.

AIKEN, HENRY. 1962. *Reason and Conduct* (New York).

AJISAFE, A. K. 1924. *Laws and Customs of the Yoruba People* (London).

ALLEN, CARLETON K. 1951. *Law in the Making* (Oxford).

ALLOTT, ANTONY. 1960. *Essays in African Law* (London).

ALLPORT, GORDON. 1961. *Pattern and Growth in Personality* (New York).

—— 1937. *Personality* (New York).

—— 1966. "Traits Revisited." *Amer. Psychologist* 21: p. 8.

ANDERSON, JAMES N. 1954. *Islamic Law in Africa* (London).

ARNOLD, MAGDA B. 1954. "Basic Assumptions in Psychology." *The Human Person* (Magda Arnold and John Gleason, eds., New York).

—— 1960. *Emotion and Personality* (2 v., New York).

ARNOLD, MAGDA, and JOHN GLEASON, eds. 1954. *The Human Person* (New York).

ASCH, SOLOMON E. 1952. *Social Psychology* (New York).

ASHTON, EDMUND. 1952. *The Basuto* (London).

AUSTIN, JOHN. 1875. *Lectures on Jurisprudence* (5th ed., London).

—— 1954. *The Province of Jurisprudence Determined* (London).

—— 1954. "Uses of the Study of Jurisprudence." *The Province of Jurisprudence Determined and the Uses of the Study of Jurisprudence* (Herbert L. A. Hart, ed., London).


BARON, SALO, ERNEST NAGEL, KOPPEL PINSON, eds. 1951. *Freedom and Reason* (Glencoe).

BARTON, RALPH F. 1930. *The Half-Way Sun* (New York).

—— 1919. "Ifugao Law." *Amer. Archaeology and Ethnology* 15: pp. 1–186.

—— 1949. *The Kalingas, Their Institutions and Custom Law* (Chicago).

BASTIAN, ADOLF. 1895. *Ethnische Elementargedanken in der Lehre vom Menschen* (Berlin).

BAUMANN, H. 1936. *Schöpfung und Urzeit des Menschen im Mythus der Afrikanischen Völker* (Berlin).

BEAGLEHOLE, ERNEST. 1932. *Property, A Study in Social Psychology* (New York).

BEALS, RALPH L., and HARRY HOIJER. 1953. *An Introduction to Anthropology* (New York).

BENEDICT, RUTH. 1934. *Patterns of Culture* (New York).

—— 1938. "Religion." *General Anthropology* (Franz Boas, ed., Boston).

BERLIN, ISAIAH. 1964. "Rationality of Value Judgments." *Nomos* 7: p. 233.

BERNARD, JESSIE. 1928. "Political Leadership among North American Indians." *Amer. Jour. Sociology* 34: pp. 296–315.

BERNARD, LUTHER L. 1924. *Instinct: A Study in Social Psychology* (New York).

BEST, ELDON. 1924. *The Maori* (Wellington).

BIDNEY, DAVID. 1962. "The Concept of Value in Modern Anthropology." *Anthropology Today: Selections* (Sol Tax, ed., Chicago).

—— 1954. "The Ethnology of Religion and the Problem of Human Evolution." *Amer. Anthropologist* 56: pp. 1–18.

—— 1953. *Theoretical Anthropology* (New York).

BIRKET-SMITH, KAJ. 1936. *The Eskimos* (New York).

BLACKWOOD, BEATRICE. 1935. *Both Sides of Buka Passage* (London).

BLANSHARD, BRAND. 1961. *Reason and Goodness* (New York).

BOAS, FRANZ. 1928. *Anthropology and Modern Life* (New York).

—— 1930. "Culture." *Encyclopedia of the Social Sciences* 2: pp. 79–110.

—— 1907. "The Eskimo of Baffinland and Hudson Bay." *Amer. Museum Nat. Hist.* 15.

—— 1938. "Invention." *General Anthropology* (Franz Boas, ed., Boston).

—— 1938. *The Mind of Primitive Man* (New York).

—— ed. 1938. *General Anthropology* (Boston).

BOHANNON, PAUL. 1960. *African Homicide and Suicide* (Princeton).

—— 1957. *Justice and Judgment Among the Tiv* (London).

—— 1963. *Social Anthropology* (New York).

BRECHT, ARNOLD. 1941. "The Myth of Is and Ought." *Harvard Law Rev.* 54: p. 811.

—— 1959. *Political Theory* (Princeton).

BRIGHTMAN, EDGER S. 1940. *A Philosophy of Religion* (New York).

BRONOWSKI, JACOB. 1965. *Science and Human Values* (New York).

BUNZEL, RUTH. 1938. "Art." *General Anthropology* (Franz Boas, ed., Boston).

BURCHELL, W. J. 1953. *Travels in the Interior of Southern Africa* (2 v., London).

BUSIA, K. A. 1951. *The Position of the Chief in the Modern Political System of Ashanti* (London).

BUXTON, L. H. DUDLEY, ed. 1936. *Custom is King* (London).


CAHN, EDMUND. 1949. *The Sense of Injustice* (New York).

CAIRNS, HUNTINGTON. 1931. "Law and Anthropology." *The Making of Man* (Victor F. Calverton ed., New York).

—— 1935. *Law and the Social Sciences* (New York).

CALHOUN, GEORGE M. 1927. *The Growth of Criminal Law in Ancient Greece* (Berkeley).

CALVERTON, VICTOR F. 1931. *The Making of Man* (New York).

CANTRIL, HADLEY. 1950. *The "Why" of Man's Experience* (New York).

CARDOZO, BENJAMIN N. 1924. *The Growth of the Law* (New Haven).

CASALIS, EUGENE. 1859. *Les Basutos* (Paris).

CHAPPLE, ELIOT D., and CARLETON S. COON. 1942. *Principles of Anthropology* (New York).

CHASE, STUART. 1956. *The Proper Study of Man* (New York).

CHERRY, RICHARD R. 1890. *Lectures in the Growth of Criminal Law in Ancient Communities* (London).

CHRISTENSEN, JAMES B. 1954. *Double Descent among the Fanti* (New Haven).

COHEN, MORRIS. 1933. *Law and The Social Order* (New York).

COON, CARLETON S. 1931. "Tribes of the Rif." *Harvard African Studies* 9.

CORY, HANS. 1953. *Sukuma Law and Custom* (London).

CROSBY, K. H. 1937. "Polygamy in Mende Country." *Africa* 10: pp. 249–250.


DANQUAH, JOSEPH B. 1938. *Gold Coast: Akan Laws and Customs and the Akim Akuakwa Constitution* (London).

DAVIE, MAURICE R. 1929. *The Evolution of War* (New Haven).

DAVITT, THOMAS E. 1960. "Criminal Responsibility and Punishment." *Nomos* 3: pp. 143–152.

—— 1959. *The Elements of Law* (Boston).

—— 1951. *The Nature of Law* (St. Louis).

DEVEREUX, GEORGE. 1954. "A Typological Study of Abortion in 350 Primitive, Ancient, and Pre-Industrial Societies." *Therapeutic Abortion* (Harold Rosen, ed., New York).

DIAMOND, ARTHUR S. 1951. *The Evolution of Law and Order* (London).

—— 1935. *Primitive Law* (London).

DRIBERG, JACK H. 1928. "Primitive Law in East Africa." *Africa* 1: pp. 63–72.

DRIVER, GODFREY R., and JOHN C. MILES, eds. and trans. 1952, 1955. *The Babylonian Laws* (2 v., Oxford).

DUBLIN, LOUIS I., and BESSIE BUNZEL. 1933. *To Be or Not To Be: A Study of Suicide* (New York).

DUBOIS, CORA. 1944. *The People of Alor* (Minneapolis).

DUNDAS, CHARLES. 1921. "Native Laws of Some Bantu Tribes of East Africa." *Journal Royal Anthropol. Inst.* 51: pp. 217–278.

—— 1915. "The Organization and Laws of Some Bantu Tribes." *Journal Royal Anthropol. Inst.* 45: pp. 234–306.

DURKHEIM, EMILE. 1915. *The Elementary Forms of the Religious Life* (Joseph W. Swain trans., 1947, Glencoe).

—— 1963. *Suicide: A Study in Sociology* (Glencoe).

DuSHANE, GRAHAM. 1962. "The Proper Study of Mankind." *Science* 135: pp. 697.

EDEL, ABRAHAM. 1964. *Ethical Judgment* (Glencoe).

ELIADE, MIRCEA. 1965. *Rites and Symbols of Initiation* (William R. Trask trans., New York).

ELIAS, T. OLAWALE. 1956. *The Nature of African Customary Law* (Manchester).

ELKIN, ADOLPHUS P. 1947. "Aboriginal Evidence and Justice in North Australia." *Oceania* 17: pp. 173–210.

EVANS-PRITCHARD, EDWARD E. 1931. "An Alternative Term for 'Bride-Price.'" *Man* 31: pp. 36–39.

—— 1951. *Kinship and Marriage Among the Nuer* (Oxford).

—— 1940. "The Nuer of the Southern Sudan." *African Political Systems* (Meyer Fortes and Edward E. Evans-Pritchard, eds., Oxford).

—— 1956. *Nuer Religion* (Oxford).

—— 1956. "Religion." *In:* Evans-Pritchard and others, *The Institutions of Primitive Society* (Glencoe).

—— 1951. *Social Anthropology* (Glencoe).

—— 1956. *The Institutions of Primitive Society* (Glencoe).

FARIS, ELLSWORTH. 1915. "The Origin of Punishment." *Primitive and Ancient Legal Institutions* (Albert Kocourek and John H. Wigmore, eds., 3 v., Boston), pp. 151–161.

FARIS, ROBERT E. L. 1952. *Social Psychology* (New York).

FEIBLEMAN, JAMES. 1946. *The Theory of Human Culture* (New York).

FIRTH, RAYMOND. 1956. "Function." *Current Anthropology* (William L. Thomas, ed., Chicago).

—— 1957. *We, The Tikopia* (London).

FORTES, MEYER. 1940. "The Political System of the Tallensi of the Northern Territories of the Gold Coast." *African Political Sytems* (Meyer Fortes and Edward E. Evans-Pritchard, eds., Oxford).

—— 1949. "Time and Social Structure: An Ashanti Case Study." *Social Structure* (Oxford).

FORTES, MEYER and EDWARD EVANS-PRITCHARD, eds., 1940. *African Political Systems* (Oxford).

FORTUNE, ROBERT F. 1947. "Law and Force in Papuan Societies." *Amer. Anthropologist* 49: pp. 244–259.

FRANK, LAWRENCE. 1940. "Science and Culture." *Scientific Monthly* 50: p. 492.

—— 1948. "The Concept of Inviolability in Culture." *Society as the Patient* (New Brunswick), pp. 143–150.

FRANKENA, WILLIAM. 1963. *Ethics* (Englewood Cliffs).

FRAZER, JAMES G. 1927. *The Golden Bough* (New York).

FRIEDRICH, CARL J. 1963. *Man and His Government* (New York).

GENY, FRANÇOIS. 1921–27. *Science et Technique en Droit Privé Positif* (4 v., Paris).

GILLIN, JOHN P. 1934. "Crime and Punishment Among the Barama River Carib." *Amer. Anthropologist* 36: pp. 331–334.

—— 1948. *The Ways of Men, An Introduction to Anthropology* (New York).

GLASS, BENTLEY. 1965. *Science and Ethical Values* (Chapel Hill).

GLUCKMAN, MAX. 1965. *The Ideas in Barotse Jurisprudence* (New Haven).

—— 1953. *The Judicial Process Amongst the Barotse of Northern Rhodesia* (Glencoe).

—— 1964. "Natural Justice in Africa." *Natural Law Forum* 9: pp. 25–44.

—— 1956. "Political Institutions." *In:* Evans-Pritchard and others, *The Institutions of Primitive Society* (Glencoe), pp. 66–80.

GOLDENWEISER, ALEXANDER. 1937. *Anthropology* (New York).

GOLDSCHMIDT, WALTER R. 1959. *Man's Way: A Preface to the Understanding of Human Society* (Cleveland).

GOODHART, ARTHUR. 1953. *English Law and the Moral Law* (London).

—— 1951. "The Importance of a Definition of Law." *Jour. African Administration* 3: pp. 106–109.

GRAY, JOHN C. 1921. *The Nature and Sources of the Law* (New York).

GRAY, ROBERT. 1960. "Sonjo Bride-Price and the Question of African 'Wife-Purchase.'" *American Anthropologist* 62: pp. 34–57.

HALLOWELL, A. IRVING. 1943. "The Nature and Function of Property as a Social Institution." *Jour. Legal and Political Sociology* 1: pp. 115–138.

HAMILTON, ROBERT W. 1910. "East African Native Laws and Customs." *Jour. Comparative Legislation* 11: pp. 181–195.

HARRIES, C. L. 1929. *The Laws and Customs of the Bapedi and Cognate Tribes of the Transvaal* (Johannesburg).

HART, HERBERT L. A. 1961. *The Concept of Law* (Oxford).

HARTLAND, E. SIDNEY. 1910. "Introduction" to: Hugh O'Sullivan, "Dinka Laws and Customs." *Jour. Royal Anthropol. Inst.* 40: pp. 171–172.

—— 1924. *Primitive Law* (London).

HASLUCK, MARGARET. 1954. *The Unwritten Law of the Albanian Mountains* (Cambridge, England).

HERSKOVITS, MELVILLE. 1948. *Man and His Works* (New York).

—— 1937. "A Note on 'Woman Marriage' in Dahomey." *Africa* 10: pp. 335–341.

HILGER, INEZ. 1939. *A Social Study of One Hundred Fifty Chippewa Indian Families* (Washington).

HILL, WILLARD W. 1936. "Notes on Pima Land Law and Tenure." *Amer. Anthropologist* 38: pp. 586–589.

HOBHOUSE, LEONARD T. 1906. *Morals in Evolution* (2 v., New York).

HOBHOUSE, L. T., and others. 1915. *The Material Culture and Social Institutions of the Simpler Peoples* (London).

HOEBEL, E. ADAMSON. 1948. "Anthropology of Inheritance." *Social Meaning of Legal Concepts* 1: pp. 5–26.

—— 1942. "Fundamental Legal Concepts as Applied in the Study of Primitive Law." *Yale Law Journal* 51: pp. 951–966.

—— 1954. *The Law of Primitive Man* (Cambridge, Mass.)

—— 1941. "Law-Ways of the Primitive Eskimos." *Jour. of Criminology and Criminal Law* 31: pp. 663–683.

—— 1949. *Man in the Primitive World* (New York).

—— 1940. "The Political Organization and Law-Ways of the Comanche Indians." *Mem. Amer. Anthropol. Assoc.* 54.

—— 1942. "Primitive Law and Modern." *Trans. N. Y. Acad. of Sci.* 5, 2: pp. 30–41.

—— 1961. "Three Studies in African Law." *Stanford Law Rev.* 13: pp. 418–442.

HOGBIN, H. IAN. 1934. *Law and Order in Polynesia: A Study of Primitive Legal Institutions* (London).

—— 1939. "Social Reactions to Crime: Law and Morals in the Schouten Islands, New Guinea." *Jour. Royal Anthropol. Inst.* **68**: pp. 223–262.

HOLLEMAN, J. F. 1952. *Shona Customary Law: With Reference to Kinship, Marriage, the Family and the Estate* (London).

HOLMES, OLIVER W. 1897. "The Path of Law." *Harvard Law Rev.* **10**: pp. 457–461.

HONE, H. 1938. "The Native of Uganda and Criminal Law." *Uganda Jour.* **6**: p. 5.

HOWELL, PAUL P. 1954. *A Manual of Nuer Law* (London).

HUNTINGFORD, GEORGE W. B. 1953. *The Nandi of Kenya* (London).

HUXLEY, THOMAS, and JULIAN HUXLEY. 1947. *Touchstone for Ethics* (New York).

IHERING, RUDOLF VON. 1879. *The Struggle for Law* (John J. Lalor trans., Chicago).

JACKSON, JUSTICE ROBERT H. 1955. "Forward" to: Majid Khadduri and Herbert J. Liebesny. *Law in the Middle East* (Washington).

JAMES, EDWIN O. 1955. *The Nature and Function of Priesthood* (London).

JARVIE, I. C. 1965. "Limits of Functionalism and Alternatives to It in Anthropology." *Functionalism in the Social Sciences* (Donald A. Martindale, ed., Philadelphia).

JENKS, ALBERT E. 1905. *The Bantoc Igorot* (Manila).

JENSON, ADOLF E. 1963. *Myth and Cult Among Primitive Peoples* (Marianna Choldin and Wolfgang Weissleder trans., Chicago).

JONES, HARRY. 1966. "Legal Realism." *The Nature of Law* (M. P. Golding, ed., New York).

KAGAME, ALEXIS. 1956. *La Philosophie bantu-rwandaise de l'Être* (Brussels).

KANT, IMMANUEL. 1949. "Critique of Practical Reason." *Immanuel Kant: Critique of Practical Reason and Other Writings in Moral Philosophy* (Lewis W. Beck trans., Chicago).

—— 1956. *The Critique of Pure Reason* (Norman Kemp Smith trans., London).

—— 1949. "Foundations of the Metaphysics of Morals." *Immanuel Kant: Critique of Practical Reason and Other Writings in Moral Philosophy* (Lewis W. Beck trans., Chicago).

—— 1949. "An Inquiry into the Distinctness of the Principles of Natural Theology and Morals." *Immanuel Kant: Critique of Practical Reason and Other Writings in Moral Philosophy* (Lewis W. Beck trans., Chicago).

—— 1836. *The Metaphysics of Ethics* (John W. Semple trans., Edinburgh).

KELSEN, HANS. 1946. *General Theory of Law and State* (Anders Wedberg trans., Cambridge, Mass.).

KENNETT, AUSTIN. 1925. *Bedouin Justice* (Cambridge).

KENYATTA, JOMO. 1953. *Facing Mount Kenya—The Tribal Life of the Gikuyu* (London).

KHADDURI, MAJID, and HERBERT LIEBESNY. 1955. *Law in the Middle East* (Washington).

KLINEBERG, OTTO. 1954. *Social Psychology* (New York).

KLUCKHOLM, CLYDE. 1949. *Mirror for Man* (New York).

—— 1962. "Universal Categories of Culture." *Anthropology Today: Selections* (Sol Tax, ed., Chicago).

—— 1959. "Values and Value-Orientation in the Theory of Action: An Exploration in Definition and Classification." *Toward a General Theory of Action* (Talcott Parsons and Edward Shils, eds., Cambridge, Mass.).

KOCUREK, ALBERT, and JOHN H. WIGMORE eds. 1915. "Primitive and Ancient Legal Institutions." *Evolution of Law: Select Readings of the Origin and Development of Legal Institutions, Volume II* (Boston).

KOHLER, JOSEPH. 1914. *Philosophy of Law* (Adalbert Albrecht trans., Boston).

KOPPERS, WILLIAM. 1952. *Primitive Man and His World Picture* (Edith Raybould trans., New York).

KROEBER, ALFRED L. 1948. *Anthropology* (New York).

KROEBER, ALFRED L., and THOMAS T. WATERMAN, eds. 1931. *Source Book in Anthropology* (Berkeley).

LADD, JOHN. 1957. *The Structure of a Moral Code* (Cambridge, Mass.).

LAYARD, JOHN. 1956. "The Family and Kinship." *In*: Evans-Pritchard and others, *The Institutions of Primitive Society* (Glencoe), pp. 50–65.

LEACH, EDWARD R. 1956. "Aesthetics." *In*: Evans-Pritchard and others, *The Institutions of Primitive Society* (Glencoe), pp. 25–38.

LEEUW, GERARDUS VAN DER. 1938. *Religion in Essence and Manifestation* (John E. Turner trans., London).

LEPP, IGNACE. 1963. *Atheism in Our Time* (Brenard Murchland trans., New York).

LEWIN, JULIUS. 1948. *Studies in African Native Law* (Philadelphia).

LIENHARDT, GODFREY. 1956. "Modes of Thought." *In*: Evans-Pritchard and others, *The Institutions of Primitive Society* (Glencoe), pp. 95–106.

LINTON, RALPH, ed. 1945. *The Science of Man in the World Crisis* (New York).

—— 1936. *The Study of Man* (New York).

LIPS, JULIUS E. 1938. "Government." *General Anthropology* (Franz Boas, ed., Boston).

—— 1947. "Naskapi Law." *Trans. Amer. Philos. Soc.* **37**: pp. 379–487.

LISSNER, IVAR. 1961. *Man, God, and Magic* (J. Maxwell Brownjohn trans., New York).

LITTLE, KENNETH L. 1951. *The Mende of Sierra Leone* (London).

LLEWELLYN, KARL N., and E. ADAMSON HOEBEL. 1941. *The Cheyenne Way* (Norman).

LOWIE, ROBERT. 1929. *Are We Civilized?* (New York).

—— 1928. "Incorporeal Property in Primitive Society." *Yale Law Jour.* **37**: pp. 551–563.

—— 1940. *An Introduction to Cultural Anthropology* (New York).

—— 1927. *The Origin of the State* (New York).

—— 1920. *Primitive Society* (New York).

—— 1943. "Property Rights and Coercive Powers of Plains Indian Military Societies." *Jour. Legal and Polit. Sociology* **1**: pp. 59–71.

McCALL, RAYMOND J. 1963. "Invested Self-Expression: A Principle of Human Motivation." *Psychol. Rev.* **70**: pp. 289–303.

McDOUGALL, WILLIAM. 1908. *Introduction to Social Psychology* (London).

—— 1937. "Tendencies as Indispensible Postulates of All Psychology." *Proc. Internatl. Cong. on Psychology* **11**, *passim*.

MacIVER, ROBERT M. 1946. "Government and Property." *Jour. Legal and Polit. Sociology* **4**: p. 5.

—— 1947. *The Web of Government* (New York).

MacIVER, ROBERT M., and CHARLES H. PAGE. 1949. *Society* (New York).

MAINE, HENRY. 1879. *Ancient Law* (New York).

—— 1883. *Early Law and Custom* (New York).

MAIR, LUCY P. 1934. *An African People in the Twentieth Century* (London).

MALINOWSKI, BRONISLAW. 1951. *Crime and Custom in Savage Society* (New York).

—— 1925. "The Forces of Law and Order in a Primitive Community." *Proc. Royal Inst. of Great Britain* **24**: pp. 529–547.

—— 1934. "Introduction" to: H. Ian Hogbin, *Law and Order in Polynesia* (New York).

—— 1948. *Magic, Science and Religion* (Boston).

—— 1942. "A New Instrument for the Interpretation of Law—Especially Primitive." *Yale Law Jour.* **51**: pp. 1237–1254.

—— 1944. *A Scientific Theory of Culture and Other Essays* (Chapel Hill).

—— 1927. *Sex and Repression in Savage Society* (London).

MARETT, ROBERT R. 1911. *Anthropology* (New York).

MARINER, WILLIAM. 1817. *An Account of the Natives of the Tonga Islands* (2 v., London).

MASLOW, ABRAHAM H. 1954. *Motivation and Personality* (New York).

—— 1943. "A Theory of Human Motivation." *Psychol. Rev.* **50**: pp. 370–396.

—— 1962. *Toward a Psychology of Being* (New York).

MEAD, MARGARET. 1931. "The Role of the Individual in Samoan Culture." *Source Book in Anthropology* (Alfred L. Kroeber and Thomas T. Waterman, eds., New York).

—— 1961. "Some Anthropological Considerations Concerning Natural Law." *Natural Law Forum* **6**: pp. 51–64.

MEEK, C. K. 1937. *Law and Authority in a Nigerian Tribe* (London).

MEEK, THEOPHILE J. 1950. *Hebrew Origins* (New York).

MESSING, SIMON. 1957. *The Highland-Plateau Amara of Ethiopia* (Ann Arbor).

MIDDLETON, JOHN. 1953. *The Kikuyu and Kamba of Kenya* (London).

MILLER, NATHAN. 1928. *The Child in Primitive Society* (New York).

MOFFETT, J. P. 1953. "Forward" to: Hans Cory, *Sukuma Law and Custom* (London).

MONTAGU, ASHLEY. 1957. *Man: His First Million Years* (Cleveland).

MOSS, CLAUDE R. 1919–1922. "Kankaney Ceremonies." *Amer. Archaeology and Ethnology* **15**: pp. 343–384.

—— 1919–1922. "Nabaloi Law and Ritual." *Amer. Archaeology and Ethnology* **15**: pp. 207–342.

MUNTSCH, ALBERT. 1934. *Cultural Anthropology* (Milwaukee).

MURDOCK, GEORGE. 1945. "The Common Denominator of Culture." *The Science of Man in the World Crisis* (Ralph Linton, ed., New York).

—— 1959. *Africa* (New York).

—— 1949. *Social Structure* (New York).

MURPHY, GARDNER, LOIS B. MURPHY and THEODORE NEWCOMB, 1937. *Experimental Social Psychology* (New York).

MURRAY, EDWARD J. 1964. *Motivation and Emotion* (Englewood Cliffs).

MURRAY, HENRY A. 1959. "Toward a Classification of Interaction." *Toward a General Theory of Action* (Talcott Parsons and Edward Shils, eds., Cambridge, Mass.).

NADEL, SIEGFRIED F. 1961. *A Black Byzantium* (London).

—— 1947. *The Nuba* (London).

NEWCOMB, THEODORE M. 1950. *Social Psychology* (New York).

NOON, JOHN A. 1949. "Law and Government of the Grand River Iroquois." *Viking Fund Pub. in Anthropology* **12**: (New York).

NORTHRUP, F. C. S. 1949. "Jurisprudence in the Law School Curriculum." *Jour. Legal Education* **1**: p. 489.

OAKLEY, FRANCIS. 1961. "Mediaeval Theories of Natural Law: William of Ockham and the Significance of the Voluntarist Tradition." *Natural Law Forum* **6**: p. 83.

OBERG, KALERVO. 1934. "Crime and Punishment in the Tlingit Society." *Amer. Anthropologist* **36**: pp. 145–146.

—— 1940. "The Kingdom of Ankole in Uganda." *African Political Systems* (Meyer Fortes and Edward E. Evans-Pritchard, eds., Oxford).

O'SULLIVAN, HUGH. 1910. "Dinka Laws and Customs." *Jour. Royal Anthropol. Inst.* **40**: pp. 171–191.

OTTO, RUDOLPH. 1958. *The Idea of the Holy* (John W. Harvey trans., New York).

OVERSTREET, HAROLD. 1951. "The Growth Imperative." *Freedom and Reason* (Salo Baron, Ernest Nagel, Koppel Pinson, eds., Glencoe).

PARSONS, TALCOTT, and EDWARD SHILS, eds. 1959. *Toward a General Theory of Action* (Cambridge).

PAUL, LESLIE. 1957. *Nature into History* (London).

PENWILL, D. J. 1951. *Kamba Customary Law* (London).

PERISTIANY, J. G. 1956. "Law." *Evans-Pritchard and Others, The Institutions of Primitive Society* (Glencoe), pp. 39–49.

PERRY, RALPH BARTON. 1926. *General Theory of Value* (Cambridge, Mass.).

—— 1954. *Realms of Value* (Cambridge, Mass.).

PETER, PRINCE. 1963. *A Study of Polyandry* (The Hague).

PIAGET, JEAN. 1948. *The Moral Judgment of the Child* (Marjorie Gabain trans., Glencoe).

PIDDINGTON, RALPH. 1950. *An Introduction to Social Anthropology* (London).

POLANYI, MICHAEL. 1958. *Personal Knowledge* (Chicago).

—— 1959. *The Study of Man* (Chicago).

POSPISIL, LEOPOLD. 1958. *Kapauku Papuans and Their Law* (New Haven).

POSTMAN, LEO, JEROME BRUNER and ELLIOT McGINNIES. 1965. "Personal Values as Selective Factors in Perception." *Readings for Introductory Psychology* (Richard Teevan and Robert C. Birney, eds., New York).

POUND, ROSCOE. 1959. *Jurisprudence* (5 v., St. Paul).

PREJEVALSKY, NIKOLAS M. 1876. *Mongolia* (2 v., London).

RADCLIFFE-BROWN, ALFRED R. 1933. *The Andaman Islanders* (Cambridge).

—— 1940. "Preface" to: *African Political Systems* (Meyer Fortes and Edward E. Evans-Pritchard, eds., Oxford).

—— 1933. "Primitive Law." *Encyclopedia of the Social Sciences* **13**: pp. 202–206.

—— 1935. "Social Sanctions." *Encyclopedia of the Social Sciences* **13**: 531–534.

—— 1952. *Structure and Function in Primitive Society* (London).

RADIN, PAUL. 1927. *Primitive Man as Philosopher* (New York).

—— 1953. *The World of Primitive Man* (New York).

RADIN, MAX, and A. M. KIDD, eds., 1935. *Legal Essays* (Berkeley).

RAMSEY, T. D. 1941. *Tsonga Law in the Transvaal* (Pretoria).

RATTRAY, ROBERT S. 1929. *Ashanti Law and Constitution* (London).

REDFIELD, ROBERT. 1950. "Maine's Ancient Law in the Light of Primitive Societies." *Western Polit. Quart.* **3**: pp. 574–589.

—— 1953. *The Primitive World and Its Transformations* (Ithaca).

—— 1952. "The Primitive World View." *Proc. Amer. Philos. Soc.* **96**: pp. 30–36.

REICHARD, GLADYS. 1938. "Social Life." *General Anthropology* (Frank Boas, ed., Boston).

RIASANOVSKY, VALENTIN A. 1938. *Customary Law of the Nomadic Tribes of Siberia* (Tsiensin).

RICHARDS, AUDREY I. 1956. *Chisungu—A Girl's Initiation Ceremony among the Bemba of Northern Rhodesia* (New York).

RICHARDSON, JANE. 1940. "Law and Status Among the Kiowa Indians." *Amer. Ethnol. Soc.* **1**.

RIVERS, WILLIAM H. R. 1914. *The History of Melanesian Society* (Cambridge).

—— 1924. *Social Organization* (New York).

RODNICK, DAVID. 1937. "Political Structure and Status Among the Assiniboine Indians." *Amer. Anthropologist* **39**: pp. 408–416.

ROSCOE, JOHN. 1915. *The Northern Bantu* (Cambridge).

ROSE, HERBERT J. 1936. "The Wiro Sky-God." *Custom is King* (L. H. Dudley Buxton, ed., London).

ROSEN, HAROLD. 1954. *Therapeutic Abortion* (New York).

SAKSENA, R. N. 1962. *Social Economy of a Polyandrous People* (New York).

SARBAH, JOHN MENSAH. 1897. *Fanti Customary Laws* (London).

SARBIN, THEODORE R. 1952. "Preface to Psychological Analyses of the Self." *Psychol. Rev.* **59**: pp. 11–22.

SCHAPERA, ISAAC. 1956. *Government and Politics in Tribal Societies* (London).

—— 1938. *A Handbook of Tswana Law and Custom* (London).

—— 1930. *The Khoisan Peoples of South Africa* (London).

—— 1940. "The Political Organization of the Nguato of Bechuanaland Protectorate." *African Political Systems* (Meyer Fortes and Edward E. Evans-Pritchard, eds., London).

—— 1955. "The Sin of Cain." *Jour. Royal Anthropol. Inst.* **85**: pp. 33–43.

—— 1943. "Tribal Legislation Among the Tswana of the Bechuanaland Protectorate." *London School of Economics and Political Science, Monographs on Social Anthropology* 9, pp. 1–67.

SCHECHTER, FRANK I. 1935. "The Law and Morals of Primitive Trade." *Legal Essays* (Max Radin and A. M. Kidd, eds., Berkeley).

SCHMIDT, WILHELM. 1931. *Origin and Growth of Religion* (Herbert J. Rose trans., New York).

—— 1926–1935. *Der Ursprung der Gottesidee* (Münster).

SCHMIDT, WILHELM, and WILLIAM KOPPERS. 1924. *Völker und Kulturen* (Regensburg).

SCHNEIDER, DAVID M. 1957. "Political Organization, Supernatural Sanction and Punishment for Incest on Yap." *Amer. Anthropologist* **59**: p. 797.

SCHNEIDMAN, EDWIN S., and NORMAN L. FARBEROW. 1961. "Some Facts About Suicide." *U. S. Department of Health, Education and Welfare* 852, 101: p. 5.

SCHWEITZER, ALBERT. 1926. *Zwischen Wasser und Urwald* (Munich).

SEYMOUR, S. M. 1953. *Native Law in South Africa* (Capetown).

SIMMONS, LEO W. 1945. *The Role of the Aged in Primitive Society* (New Haven).

SIMPSON, GEORGE G. 1966. "Naturalistic Ethics and the Social Sciences." *Amer. Psychologist* **21**: p. 28.

SMITH, W. ROBERTSON. 1907. *Kinship and Marriage in Early Arabia* (London).

—— 1927. *The Religion of the Semites* (London).

SNELL, GEOFFREY S. 1954. *Nandi Customary Law* (London).

SPENCER, ROBERT. 1965. "The Nature and Value of Functionalism in Anthropology." *Functionalism in the Social Sciences* (Donald A. Martindale, ed., Philadelphia).

SPIRO, MELFORD E. 1954. "Human Nature in its Psychological Dimensions." *Amer. Anthropologist* **56**: pp. 19–30.

STONE, JULIUS. 1950. *Province and Function of Law* (Sidney).

TALBOT, PERCY A. 1926. *The Peoples of Southern Nigeria* (London).

TAX, SOL. 1962. *Anthropology Today* (Chicago).

TEEVAN, RICHARD, and ROBERT C. BIRNEY, eds. 1965. *Readings for Introductory Psychology* (New York).

TER HAAR, BAREND. 1948. *Adat Law in Indonesia* (New York).

THOMAS, W. ISAAC. 1937. *Primitive Behavior* (New York).

THOMAS, WILLIAM L., ed. 1956. *Current Anthropology* (Chicago).

TITIEV, MISCHA. 1959. *Introduction to Cultural Anthropology* (New York).

—— 1954. *The Science of Man: Introduction to Anthropology* (New York).

TOLMAN, EDWARD C. 1955. "A Psychological Model." *Toward a General Theory of Action* (Talcott Parsons and Edward Shils, eds., Cambridge, Mass.).

TROTTER, WILFRED. 1916. *Instincts of the Herd in Peace and War* (London).

TUPPER, LEWIS. 1908. "Customary and Other Law in the East Africa Protectorate." *Jour. Soc. Comparative Legislation* 8, pp. 172–184.

TYLOR, EDWARD B. 1916. *Anthropology* (New York).

VEATCH, HENRY. 1962. *Rational Man* (Bloomington).

VINOGRADOFF, PAUL. 1920–22. *Outlines of Historical Jurisprudence* (New York).

WACH, JOACHIM. 1944. *Sociology of Religion* (Chicago).

WADDINGTON, C. H. 1960. *The Ethical Animal* (London).

WAGNER, GUNTER. 1949. *The Bantu of North Kavirondo* (London).

—— 1940. "The Political Organization of the Bantu Kavirondo." *African Political Systems* (Meyer Fortes and Edward E. Evans-Pritchard eds., London).

WESTERMARCK, EDWARD. 1922. *The History of Marriage* (3 v., New York).

—— 1908–1912. *The Origin and Development of the Moral Ideas* (2 v., London).

WHITFIELD, G. M. B. 1948. *South African Law* (Capetown).

WILLIAMS, F. E. 1941. "Group Sentiment and Primitive Justice." *Amer. Anthropologist* **43**: pp. 523–539.

WILSON, GODFREY. 1937. "Introduction to Nyakyusa Law." *Africa* **10**: pp. 16–36.

WINFIELD, PERCY H. 1926. "The History of Negligence in the Law of Torts." *Law Quart. Rev.* **42**: pp. 184–201.

—— 1926. "The Myth of Absolute Liability." *Law Quart. Rev.* **42**: pp. 37–51.

WISSLER, CLARK. 1923. *Man and Culture* (New York).

WOLFLE, DALE. 1966. "The Spirit of Science." *Science* **152**: p. 1699.

WOODWORTH, ROBERT S., and HAROLD SCHLOSBERG. 1954. *Experimental Psychology* (New York).

WRIGHT, LORD. 1936. "Ought the Doctrine of Consideration be Abolished from the Common Law?" *Harvard Law Rev.* **49**: pp. 1225, 1229.

WRIGHT, QUINCY. 1942. *A Study of War* (2 v., Chicago).

YOUNG, KIMBALL. 1956. *Social Psychology* (New York).

# INDEX

Aberle, David, 75

Abortion, 45; general value judgment, 46; motives, 45; prevalence, 45; value judgment of, 45

Accession, relations of title, 20

Accident, distinct from negligence, 85; immaterial in collective responsibility, 84

Accounts of origins, man and world, 78

Acquired drives, 16

Adair, J., 55

Adam, Leonhard, 55, 110, 113, 116, 124, 128

Adat law, 35

Adultery, described, 54; in-group versus out-group, 54; punishments, 54; universal value judgments in all societies with rare exceptions, 52, 55

Adverse possession, relations of title, 20

African tribes, 56, 58, 61, 85, 86, 91, 92, 93, 95, 103, 108, 111, 112, 116, 117, 123, 125, 126, 127, 128

Aggressive drive, different from drive to distinguish mine from thine, 86

Agreements, exchange, 91, relations of title, 20; gifts, 91; inheritance, 91; keeping, 93

Ahats, 94

Aiken, Henry, 23

Ajisafe, A. J., 49, 56, 61, 91, 105, 106

Akamba, 83, 95

Akan, 71, 92, 105, 106, 107, 108, 111, 125

Ala, 54

Alacaluf, 95

Albanian mountaineers, 47, 103, 110, 111, 112, 115, 128

Algonquin, 96

Allen, Carlton K., 23

Allott, Anthony, 35, 75, 102, 103, 107, 111, 112, 119

Allport, Gordon, 7, 9, 12, 14, 15, 16, 18, 19, 79, 80

Almost universal value judgments, see Value judgments, almost universal

Alorese, 45, 67, 84

Alur, 115

Amara, 67

American Law Institute, 21

American town meeting, 103

Ammassalik, 90

Andaman Islanders, 48, 59, 62, 71, 76, 89, 92, 95, 99, 100

Anderson, James, 82, 94, 113, 118, 124

Anglo-Saxons, 58

Animals, leadership, 119; monogamy, 62; no property, 22; polygyny, 60

Ankole, 86

Annam, 46

Anthropology, conceptions of Supreme Being, 77; data of, 38; not basis of defining right and wrong, 129; relation to law, 30; supports psychology, 129; false notions of religion, 74

Aquinas, Thomas, 8, 23, 95, 97

Arabs, 47, 58, 113

Arapaho, 124

Arapesh, 90

Aristotle, 8, 71, 86, 97, 98

Arnold, Magda, 9, 79

Art, described, 65; form of communication, 65; process of making, 65

Artifacts, tools, 65

Artistic creation, universal value judgment, 67

Asch, Solomon, 12

Ashanti, 44, 47, 48, 56, 61, 69, 71, 82, 85, 89, 93, 95, 103, 104, 105, 109, 114, 116, 119, 120, 121

Ashton, Edmund, 47

Asin, 117

Asis, 73, 78

Assiniboine, 49, 59, 110, 121

Association, basic drive for, 96; innate, 98; human, different from animals, 97; lawless, no evidence, 99; political, 97; described, 101; necessity of sanctions, 101; universal, 99; protection and security, 96; required, for fulfillment of common needs, 97; for mental development, 97; value of, universal postulate, 101

Atomistic living, no evidence, 98

Auni of New Mexico, 48

Austin, John, 26, 27, 28, 29, 30, 32

Australian tribes, 44, 45, 48, 49, 54, 57, 90, 95, 98, 99, 100, 107, 109, 110, 119, 123, 126, 128

Authority, chief, 107; claim to direct, 103; delegated distinguished from substitutional, 24; elders', 107; people's, 106

Azande, 66

Babylonian law of Hammurabi, 123; law of talion, 123

Bad, as wrong, 8

Baffin Islanders, 90, 92, 128

Baganda, 127

Bagesu, 56, 57

Bali, 46, 66

Balla, 123

Baluba, 82

Bansang, 94

Bantu, 44, 45, 56, 59, 61, 62, 68, 73, 81, 93, 95, 99, 107, 110, 113, 115, 116, 118, 119, 120, 121, 127

Banyika, 46

Bapedi, 60, 81, 82, 109, 112

Barnard, Jessie, 121

Barotse, 40

Barter, form of exchange, 91; secondary to gift-giving, 91

Barton, Ralph, 35, 44, 56, 61, 75, 83, 84, 85, 86, 88, 90, 94, 96, 101, 107, 109, 113, 115, 116, 118, 119, 121, 122, 124, 125

Basic drive, associate, 96; innate, 98; basic values in lawmaking, 11; communicate, 65; connatural value judgments, 10; decide, 79; distinguish mine from thine, 86; establish relations of title, 19; grounds of personal rights, 18; inter-operative, 16; know, 62; controlling, 15; learn, 67; mouldable, 13; normal men, 15; observable constants, 11; opinions regarding, 13; plasticity of, 17; position taken regarding, 14; pre-

serve self, 42, 47; related to basic values, 8; unite sexually, 50; source of personal rights, 19; unequal, 16; value judgments without reasoning process, 10

Basic ethical commandment, respect for life, 11

Basic motives, basic values, 9

Basic values, 7; basic drives in lawmaking, 7, 10; basic motives, 9; in law necessarily, 10; related to basic drives, 8; sexes and lawmaking, 11; source of obligation, 16

Basoga, 44, 48

Basonge, 85

Bastian, Adolph, 39

Basuto, 75

Batwa of Ruanda, 71

Beaglehole, Ernest, 59

Beals, Ralph, 51, 55, 56, 57, 60, 62, 67, 72, 75, 76, 79, 90, 107, 114

Beauty, described, 66; urge to create, 66

Bechuanaland, 121

Bedouin Arabs, 103, 118, 123, 126

Bemba, 68, 69, 70

Benedict, Ruth, 50, 59, 60, 73, 75, 101

Benefit of clergy, equitable fiction, 127

Bentham, Jeremy, 27

Bergdama, 120

Berlin, Isaiah, 15

Bernard, Luther, 12

Best, Eldon, 50

Bhote, 115

Bidney, David, 13, 16, 40, 41, 44, 52, 70, 78, 79, 80, 97, 98

Birket-Smith, Kaj, 115, 116

Bismarck Archipelago, 103, 118

Blackwood, Beatrice, 49

Blanshard, Brand, 8, 12, 14, 129

Boas, Franz, 22, 34, 41, 47, 59, 64, 67, 68, 69, 70, 71, 87, 90, 92, 96, 100, 110, 115, 119

Bodenheimer, Edgar, 36

Bohannon, Paul, 11, 21, 36, 39, 45, 47, 48, 49, 52, 53, 60, 61, 62, 64, 76, 79, 84, 87, 106, 108, 115, 116, 121, 122

"Bootless," derivation, 116

Botocudo, 92, 123

Brahmans, 127

Brazilian tribes, 98

Brecht, Arnold, 18, 77, 86

Brides, persons, 58; price, 58; property, 58; protectorship, 58

Brightman, Edgar, 73

British Columbia, 63

Bronowski, Jacob, 33

Bruner, Jerome, 80

Buddhism, relation to polyandry, 53

Bunzel, Bessie, 47, 49, 67

Burchell, W. J., 47

Buriat law, 35, 94

Bushmen, 46, 47, 49, 92, 98, 99, 100, 119, 120

Bushongo, 56, 57

Busia, K. A., 72, 104, 105, 110, 120

Caesar, Julius, 95

Cahn, Edmund, 88

Cairns, Huntington, 21, 42, 52, 59, 88, 90, 92, 93
Calhoun, George, 108
California tribes, 93
Cape Nguni, 61
Cardozo, Benjamin, 28
Carib, 54, 64, 81, 82, 89, 90, 109, 120, 121, 122, 124
Casalis, Eugene, 121
Categories of value judgments, 38
Causation, predominant in collective responsibility, 84
Chandler, W., 55
Chapple, Eliot, 34, 51, 65, 103
Charms, use of, 75
Chase, Stuart, 40
Chastity belt, Cheyenne girls, 57
Cherokee, 46, 48, 55
Cherry, Richard, 42, 83, 102, 109, 124, 128
Cheyenne, 57, 68, 83, 114, 124, 127; girls, chastity belt, 57
Chief, authority, 107; destooling of, 105; grounds for, 105; function, 121; government by common value judgment, 121
Childbirth, premarital, 56
Children, learning from example of adults, 68; value judgments regarding, 52
Chinese, 58, 61, 62, 127
Chippewa, 67, 119
Choroti, 45
Christensen, James, 68
Chukchee, 49, 59
Cicisbeism distinguished from polandry, 53
Circumcision, part of initiation rites, 69; socio-economic results of, 70
Claim to direct, authority, 103; basically with the people, 103
Claims, basis, others' obligation, 20
Coercion, does not constitute law, 35; not basis of obligation in law, 24
Collective responsibility, causation predominant, 84; culpability not predominant, 84; for decisions, 83; extent, 84; general value judgment, 84; Hebrew code, 84; motive, intention, accident, negligence are immaterial, 84; prevalence, 83
Comanche, 47, 54, 58, 59, 89, 94, 95, 96, 106, 119
Combat as punishment, 128; occasional value judgment, 128
Command, not basis of obligation in law, 24; versus directive judgment, 23
Common needs, fulfilled by regulations, 80; fulfilled by regulative judging, 103; demand association, 96, 97; presuppose universal postulates, 102; require cooperative effort, 102; universal value judgment, 102; offenses directly and indirectly against, 108
Common values, communicable to all, 23, 97; deprivation of, earliest punishment, 102; severest punishment, 102; distinguished from proper values, 23; offenses against, directly and indirectly, 107
Communal property, primordial, no evidence of, 88

Communicability, essence of common values, 23, 97
Common value judgments, see Value judgments, common
Communication, 65; basic drive for, 65; expressed in art, 65; value of, presupposed by science, 33; postulated in all societies, 65
Comparative values, 39
Compensation, African, effected by Islam, 117; compensabiles, 116; lists of, 117; described, 116; diurnal damage, 117; double and triple, 117; intentional or accidental killings, 82; gradations, 117; Hebrew law, 118; in-group versus out-group, 117; nocturnal damage, 117; non-compensabiles, 116; prevalence, 116; torts, 108; use of, general value judgment, 118
Comte, Auguste, 27
Concubinage distinguished from polyandry, 53
Confessions, common value judgment, 125; presumptions behind, 125; role, 125
Connatueral value-judgments, 10
Consensus of opinion, not basis of defining right and wrong, 129
Constitution of the United States of America, no punishments specified, 105
Contract, marriage, 58; relation of title, 20
Control of events described, 75; general value judgments, 76
Constructed judgments and givens, 19; relations of title, 19; values, 10
Contraception among preliterates, few data, 62
Coon, Carleton, 34, 51, 65, 68, 103
Cooperative effort, based on self-interest, 102; needed in political association, 101; requisite, fulfillment of common needs, 102; value of reciprocity, 102
Copleston, Fredrick, 26
Cordozo, Benjamin, 42
Cory, Hans, 121
Councils, elders, 107; general value judgment, 111; make laws, 111; membership, 111; qualifications, 111; prevalence, 111
Counting coup, meaning of, 68
Court theory of law inadequate, 41
Creation, origins, 78; symbolized by light, 78
Creative actions, establish relations of title, 88
Cree, 121
Crimes, distinguished from torts, 108; law of, replaces law of talion, 123; offenses directly against common needs, 108; origin of concept, 108; versus torts, 23
Crosby, K. H., 59, 61
Crow, 59, 74, 89, 114
Culpability not predominant in collective responsibility, 84
Cultural value, religion, 74
Culture, fountainhead of plasticity of drives, 13; postulated value judgments, 36; self-evident value judgments, 36
Custom law, changing of, 126; examples, 126; occasional value judgment, 127;

definite and effective, 104; described, 35; different from customary law, 35; known from people's reaction, 35; result of trial and error, 104
Customary law different from custom law, 35
Customs, law, relating to common needs, 34, 35; not law, not relating to common needs, 34, 35; people-made law, 24

Dahomey, 127
Dakota, 45, 120, 124
Danquah, Joseph, 72, 93, 105, 106, 113, 121, 125
Davie, Maurice, 44
Davitt, Thomas, 22, 30, 32, 58, 86, 97, 99, 102, 106, 107, 108
Death, offenses punished by, 115; as punishment, 115, general value judgment, 116; in-group—out-group basis, 115; prevalence, 115
Deciding, 62; distinction between premeditated and unpremeditated, general value judgment, 83; freedom from determination, 79; motivated, 79; reacted to by sanctions, 81; regulated, 80; responsibility for, individual, 80; collective, 83; unique type of freedom, 79
Delegated authority, distinguished from substitutional, 24; executives, 24; judges, 24; legislators, 24
Dependence on a supreme power, 73; universal value judgment, 75
Deprivation, common values, severest punishment, 102; essence of punishment, 102, 106; physical and non-physical, 106
Destooling of chief, 105
Deuteronomy, 83
Devereaux, George, 45, 46, 49
Diamond, Arthur, 22, 42, 51, 52, 55, 61, 72, 73, 76, 77, 83, 95, 96, 101, 109, 118, 121, 123, 124, 128
Dinka, 54, 81
Directive judging, government, 103; participation in, universal value judgment, 105; law, 22, 41; the people's delegates, 24; the people themselves, 23; versus command, 23
Distinction between mine and thine, basic drive for, 14, 86; prelegal fact, 96
Distinction between intention and accident, general value judgment, 83
Divorce, causes, 59; general value judgment, 60; not the ideal, 59; prevalence, 59
Dobu, 59, 99, 100
Douglas, William, 130
Driberg, Jack, 22, 58, 102
Drives, appetites, 7; basic, anchor of values, 8; establish relations of title, 19; grounds of personal rights, 18; inter-operative, 16; mouldable, 13; opinions, 13; plasticity, 17; position taken, 14; unequal, 16; different from instinct, 12; described, 13; influenced by ideas, 13; innate and acquired, 16; for knowing, controlling drive, 15; master, happiness, 15; obligation, 17; self-actualization, 15; self-development, 15; self-

realization, 14; nature, 11; not instinct, 11; plastic tendencies, 12; plasticity, fountainhead of culture, 13; shaped by knowledge and decision, 12; source of values, 7; tendencies, 7
Dublin, Louis, 47, 49
DuBois, Cora, 68, 85
Dundas, Charles, 44, 49, 52, 53, 55, 56, 57, 59, 60, 61, 62, 83, 88, 93, 94, 96, 104, 113, 116, 118
Durham versus M'Naghten, 85
Durkheim, Emile, 47, 48, 49, 74, 75
DuShane, Graham, 14

Eastern Torres Straits Islanders, 89
Edel, Abraham, 8, 11
Education, source, initiation rites, 69
Egypt, 55
Elders, age, 110; authority, 107; councils, 107; general value judgment, 111; make laws, 111; membership, 111; qualifications, 111; judges, value of, 107; political leaders, 110; respect for, 110; acquired, not innate, 110; grounds, 110; related to mores, 110
Eliade, Mircea, 69, 70
Elias, T. Olawale, 22, 23, 35, 41, 42, 56, 58, 81, 85, 91, 93, 96, 97, 103, 104, 107, 109, 113, 116, 125, 127, 128, 129
Elkin, Adolphus, 126
Enforcement, general value judgment, 119; methods, 118; persuasion in, 118; self-help, 118
Engels, Friederich, use of primordial, communal ownership theory, 88
England, 128
English county meeting, 103
Enterprising activities, 19, 20; establish relations of title, 88
Equitable fictions, benefit of clergy, 127; described, 127
Eskimo, 49, 53, 54, 59, 62, 63, 66, 67, 89, 90, 92, 95, 99, 100, 108, 109, 114, 115, 116, 120, 121, 128
Etchimin, 118
Ethnology, data of, 38
Etiquette, importance, 68; offenses against, no punishment, 108; rules, 34
Evans-Pritchard, Edward, 42, 46, 51, 52, 56, 59, 61, 68, 71, 72, 73, 75, 76, 77, 78, 79, 103
Events, control of described, 75
Evidence, anthropological and ethnological, 38; reliability, 38; witnesses, general value judgment, 112
Example of adults, relation to children's learning, 68; general value judgment, 58
Exchange, items at marriage, 57, 58
Exchange agreements, described, 91; methods of confirming, 91; relations of title, 20; silent trade, 91; universal value judgment, 91
Executives, delegated authority, 24
Exile, early form of punishment, 124; outlawry, 124; severest of punishments, 124; punishment worse than death, needs qualifications, 124
Exodus, 118, 126
Explanations of life, prevalence, 70; universal value judgment, 70

Faith, value presupposed by science, 33
Fallacy, naturalistic, 8
Family, ownership, land, 95; universal value judgment, 52; value of, universal postulate, 52
Fanti, 67, 68
Farberow, Norman, 47
Faris, Ellsworth, 43, 68, 115, 116, 124
Faris, Robert, 7, 12, 13, 14
Feibleman, James, 14, 15, 40, 52, 63, 67, 74
Fictions, equitable, examples, 127; necessity, 127; at Peyote meetings, 127; purpose, 127; use of, occasional value judgment, 127
Fiji, 58
First-wife, importance of, 60; polygyny, 60; relation to monogamy, 61; rights of inheritance, 61
Firth, Raymond, 68, 69, 93, 96
Flatheads, 46
Flogging, punishment, 128
Fortes, Meyer, 61, 101, 103
Fortune, Robert, 56
Fox, 100
Frank, Lawrence, 68, 88
Frankena, William, 7
Frazer, James, 76, 77
Freedom, power of self-determination, 79; requires regulation, 40; value presupposed by science, 33
Frequent value judgments, see Value judgments, frequent; use of oaths, 126
Freud, Sigmund, 10
Friedrich, Carl, 23
Functionalism, 39

Galla, 122
General value judgments, see Value judgments, general
Geny, François, 11, 37, 50
Germanic tribes, 94
Gerung, 115
Gestures, type of symbolic language, 65
Gift-giving, described, 91; establishes relations of title, 20; implies reciprocity, 91; importance, 91; potlatch, 92; prevalence, 91; primary form of exchange, 91; universal value judgment, 92
Gikuyu, 44, 46, 47, 57, 62, 67, 68, 69, 73, 74, 76, 77, 78, 81, 83, 95, 104, 106, 108, 111, 115, 117, 120
Gillin, John, 12, 13, 14, 55, 62, 63, 64, 65, 67, 83, 90, 109, 121, 122
Gilson, Etienne, 27
Gisu, 115
Givens and constructs, show plasticity of basic drives, 11; relations of title, 19; values, 10; value of two sexes, 50
Glass, Bentley, 33, 34
Gluckman, Max, 36, 40, 56, 86, 87, 97, 121
Goldenweiser, Alexander, 20, 39, 40, 56, 62, 63, 87, 88, 89, 90, 94, 103, 119, 121
Goldschmidt, Walter, 13, 14, 35, 42, 50, 76
Good, as coterminus with being, 8; described, 8; different from value, 8; history of word, 8; of life, scientific question, 11; "naturalistic fallacy," 8; as right, 8; same as value, 8; survival, 8
Goodhart, Arthur, 23, 42
Government, directive judging, 103

Gray, John, C., 27, 28, 29, 32
Gray, Robert, 59
Great Spirit, 78
Greeks, 58
Greenlanders, 44, 62, 128
Group ownership, land, 95
Gunantuana, 45

Hallowell, A. Irving, 20, 21, 22, 38, 39, 40, 87, 88, 90, 96, 114
Hamilton, Robert, 53, 58, 83, 112, 118, 124
Hammurabi, laws of, 123
Happiness, described, 15; master drive, 15; as motive, 15
Harlow, Harry, 63
Harlow, Margaret, 63
Harries, C. L., 59, 61, 83, 110, 113, 121, 125
Hart, Herbert L. A., 16, 29, 30, 32
Hartland, E. Sidney, 34, 42, 59, 88
Hasluck, Margaret, 42, 104, 110, 111, 113, 116, 124, 129
Hauer, L., 75
Hawaii, 55
Head-butting, punishment, 128
Headman, function, 121
Hebrew law, collective responsibility in, 84; compensation, 118; law of talion, 123; oaths, 126; places of refuge, 83
Herskovits, Melville, 13, 42, 58, 65, 70, 83, 112, 118, 124, 127
Hill, Willard, 90
Hillger, Inez, 68
Hindus, 58, 89
Ho, 58
Hobbes, Thomas, 32, 98
Hobhouse, Leonard, 45, 82, 83, 102, 107, 113, 116, 118, 119, 122, 124, 125, 128
Hoebel, A. Adamson, 21, 36, 42, 46, 49, 51, 54, 55, 57, 68, 70, 76, 87, 89, 94, 101, 107, 110, 115, 118, 124, 128
Hogbin, Ian, 8, 35, 39, 41, 55, 56, 57, 68, 71, 72, 87, 95, 102
Hoijer, Harry, 51, 55, 56, 57, 60, 62, 67, 72, 75, 76, 79, 90, 107, 114
Holleman, J. F., 111, 121
Holmes, Oliver W., 28
Holy, described, 76; other-than-human spirits, 76
Homosexuality, among preliterates, few data, 62
Hone, H., 128
Hopi, 119
Hot blood versus cold blood, responsibility for decisions done in, 83
Hottentots, 46, 47, 107, 120
Howell, Paul, 42, 83, 84, 122
Huntingford, George, 47
Huxley, Julian, 8, 13
Huxley, Thomas, 8, 13
Hypothesis, value of, presupposed by science, 33

Iban Khaldun, 97
Ibo, 49, 72, 73, 74, 95, 111
Ideas, influence drives, 13
Ifugao, 35, 61, 75, 82, 83, 85, 89, 93, 95, 99, 100, 104, 109, 112, 114, 115, 116, 118, 121
Igorot, 56, 57

Imprisonment, methods, 128; occasional value judgment, 129; prevalence, 128

Incest, described, 55; no inherent aversion, 56; prevalence, 55; punishment for, 56; universal value judgment, in all societies with rare exceptions, 52, 56; value judgment not innate, 56

India, 62, 127, 128

Indians, 55, 63, 66, 67, 68, 89, 90, 92, 94, 100, 107, 108, 120, 121, 126

Individual ownership, land, 95

Indonesia, 84, 127

Inebriates, less responsible, common value judgment, 85

Infanticide, 49; motives, 49; occasional value judgment, 49; prevalence, 49

Inferences, licit and illicit, 39

In-group versus out-group, adultery, 54; compensation, 117; killing, 46, 47; punishment by death, 115; punishment for killing, 46; taking of things, general value judgment, 95; varied meaning, 94

Inheritance, by custom law, older than wills, 94; relation of title, 20; rights of first-wife to, 61; tangibles and intangibles, 94; title by, not pristine form, 93; title to things, 93

Initiation rites, classes of, 69; compared to psychoanalysis, 70; demand sign of maturity, 70; described, 69; hand down traditions, 69; include circumcision, 69; source of education, 69

Innate drives, 16

Insanes, less responsible, common value judgment, 84, 85; meaning, 84; treatment of, 84

Insanity, not necessarily in suicide, 47; promoted by solitude, 97

Instinct, described, 12; different from drives, 11, 12

Intangibles, inheritance, 94; product of labor, 89; relation of title, 19

Intention, immaterial in collective responsibility, 84

Intention versus accident, distinguished and not distinguished, 81

Intercourse, premarital, 56

Intrinsic relations of title, 20

Ireland, 128

Iroquois, 69, 120

"Is," demands of, basis of "ought," 18; interpreted according to "ought" in zones of uncertainty, 31; factually linked with "ought," 18

Islamic law, 62, 82, 93, 112, 117

Jackson, Robert, 75

James, Edwin, 73, 75, 76

James, William, 18, 20

Jarvie, I. C., 39

Jaunsaris, 53

Java, 57

Jealousy, in polygyny, 61

Jehova's Witnesses, 31

Jenks, Albert, 57

Jensen, Adolf, 76, 78

Jews and Nazis, 23

Jones, Harry, 31

Judges, delegated authority, 24

Judging cases, people, councils, chiefs, 106

Jurisprudence, and lawmaking, 32; and philosophy of law, 32

Just law, fulfills people's common needs, 32

Justice, based on distinction between mine and thine, 86; described, 21, 86; elemental restoration of self-help, 121; law of talion effective instrument of, 123; prevalence of concept, 86; universal postulate, 96, 107; universal value judgment, 107

Justinian, 21

Juvenal, 30

Kababuyan, 117

Kaffir, 46, 116

Kai, 59, 61, 62

Kalinga, 44, 55, 84, 99, 100, 113, 120, 123

Kamba, 54, 60, 81, 84, 85, 95, 106, 117, 126

Kamchadal, 48

Kammalan, 53

Kant, Immanuel, 25, 26, 28, 29

Kantianism, half-way house to positivism, 26

Keeping agreements, demand for re-exchange, 93; general value judgment, 93; time limits, 93; variations, 93

Keller, A. G., 14, 98

Kelsen, Hans, 28, 29, 32, 129

Kennett, Austin, 113, 118, 124, 126

Kenyatta, Jomo, 45, 51, 57, 68, 70, 75, 76, 78, 79, 83, 96, 105, 109, 111, 118, 121, 125, 126

Kgatla, 46

Khadduri, Majid, 94

Kham, 53

Khan Tevka, 123

Killing, in-group versus out-group, 46; intentional or accidental, compensation for, 82; regulated, all societies, 43; self-defense, general value judgment, 44; unjustified, murder, 43; war, 44

Kimdunba, 116

Kiowa, 42, 106, 114, 124

Kirghiz, 35, 58, 59, 60, 62

Kirikiri, removal of leaders, 105

Kiwai Papuans, 68

Klineberg, Otto, 10, 14, 16, 38, 42, 49, 51, 56, 98

Kluckhohn, Clyde, 9, 11, 36, 39, 44, 45, 50, 64, 70

Knowledge, 62; and decision mold drives, 12; drive for controlling, 15; human distinguished from animal, 63; regulations regarding transmission of, 64; symbolic and abstract, 63; universal value judgment, 64; value of, postulate in all societies, 64

Kohler, Joseph, 37

Koppers, Wilhelm, 51, 67, 77, 78

Koran, 123

Kroeber, Alfred, 40

Kubu, 95

Kutubu, 54

Kwena, 104

Kwoth, 73, 77

Labor, creates relations of title, 19; described, 19, 88; Hindu law, 89; products of, intangible and tangbile, 89

Laborer in his product, 89

Ladak, 53

Ladd, John, 76

Lahul, 53

Lamba, 73

Land, individual, family, and group ownership, common value judgment, 95, 96; owned by, families, 95, groups, 95, individuals, 95; permanency of, 96; territorial exclusiveness, 95

Langan, Thomas, 27

Lango, 89

Language, described, 65; function, 65; partial transmission by, 65; prevalence, 65; universal value judgment, 65; value of, 65

Laski, Harold, 99

Law, adat, 35; allied with religion, 74; and anthropological data, 30; Buriat, 94; content, absolute and relative, 24, duties rather than rights among preliterates, 22, rights, 22; court theory inadequate, 41; criminal, originating in retaliation, 41; custom, changing of, 126; description, 22; directive judgment, 22, 41; just, fulfills people's common needs, 32; Hammurabi, 123; Hebrew, compensation, 118; Hindu, labor, 89; inadequately conceived, 41; Islamic, 82, 93, 112; model of, 22, 23, 41; making of, councils of elders, 111; motivation, evaluated goals, 10; necessary values in, 10; not constituted by, coercion, 35, sanction, 35; not a science, 32; no societies without, 41; obligation of, from means-end relation, 24, implies necessity, 30, not from command or coercion, 24; people-made customs, 24; promulgation, not part of, 23, prerequisite condition, 23, prudence not science, 32; as regulations, 34; value-areas, 38, values in, more than minimal, 31, necessary, 30, psychological necessity, 30, values postulated in, see Postulated values; unwritten, values in, 38; unwritten regulations, 35; written and unwritten, 34; zones of uncertainty, "is" interpreted according to "ought," 31

Law of talion, Babylonian law of Hammurabi, 123; derivation, 122; effective instrument of justice, 123; Hebrew law, 123; limitation of self-help, natural norm, 122; Mohammedan law, 123; proportionate retaliation, 123; replaced by law of crimes, 123

"Lawless societies," 42

Lawmaking, basic values, from basic drives, 11, from fact of two sexes, 11; and jurisprudence, 32

Layard, John, 52, 56

Leach, Edmund, 67

Leaders, among animals, 119; described, 119; elders, 110; in many groups, 119; meaning, 119; minimal to maximal, 120; not in all groups, 119; political, 119; qualifications, 120; removal of, grounds, 104; kirikiri, 105, people's authority, 104–105; selection, 119; "tribal candle," 119; women, uncertain, 120

Learning, basic drive for, 67; oral instruction, 67; preliterate, for life here and now, 69; universal value judgment, 70; value of, universal postulate, 70
Legislators, delegated authority, 24
Leinhardt, Godfrey, 79, 85
Leopard-skin chief, political function, 100
Lepp, Ignace, 77
Lesa, 73
Leve, 77, 78
Leviticus, 123
Lewin, Julius, 113
Liability, strict or absolute, 86
Lidum, 75
Liebesny, Herbert, 94
Life, 42; basic drive to preserve, 42; explanations of, 70; a good, scientific question, 11; regulations protecting, 43; respect for, basic ethical commandment, 11; self-preservation, 42; title to, 43
Life after death, described, 71; origin of, 72; prevalence of concept, 71; universal value judgment, 72
Life principle, described, 71; prevalence of concept, 70; as soul, 70; universal value judgment, 71
Light, symbol of creation, 78
Linton, Ralph, 36, 43, 44, 51, 52, 53, 60, 62, 87, 96, 97, 115
Lips, Julius, 46, 49, 56, 68, 70, 83, 88, 90, 91, 92, 93, 102, 104, 105, 107, 115, 118, 124, 125, 128, 129
Lissner, Ivar, 67, 74, 77
Lists of universal values, 39
Little, Kenneth, 69, 70, 78, 79, 93
Llewellyn, Karl, 57, 68, 83, 110, 115, 124
Locke, John, 98
Logan, Chief, orator, 120
Lowie, Robert, 13, 39, 46, 50, 53, 56, 60, 65, 72, 83, 86, 90, 96, 99, 101, 104, 115, 118
Luo, 60, 61
Luyia, 115
Lying, common value judgment, 76; prevalence, 76

McCall, Raymond, 7, 9, 14, 15
McDougal, William, 7, 12
McGinnies, Elliot, 80
Machakos District of Kenya, 82
MacIver, Robert, 41, 96, 98, 99
M'Naghten versus Durham, 85
Madagascar, 59, 98
Magdalenian period, art, 66
Magic, positive and negative, 75; and religion, 75; white and black, 75
Maine, Henry, 94, 102
Mair, Lucy, 68
Making custom law, people's governing authority, 104
Malinowski, Bronislaw, 8, 22, 35, 36, 41, 49, 50, 51, 55, 57, 64, 65, 67, 76, 80, 90, 92, 98, 100, 102, 103, 104, 105, 124
Manitou, suprahuman power, impersonal, 72
Manu, 59, 118
Maori, 49, 63, 96
Maoto, 104
Marett, Robert, 55, 109
Margi, 72

Mariner, William, 41, 68
Maritain, Jacques, 10
Marriage, basic institution, 51; contract, 51, 58; exchange of items at, 57; and family, 52; group, no evidence, 51; permanence the ideal, 51; prevalence, 51; regulations, universal, 52; state of, 51, 58; universal postulate, 52
Marshall, Alfred, 20
Marshall Islanders, 63
Martel, Charles, 75
Marx, 75
Marxism, embraced theory of primordial, communal ownership, 88
Masai, 54, 56, 61, 83
Master drive, happiness, 15; root of obligation, 17; self-actualization, 15; self-development, 15; self-realization, 14
Maurer, Armand, 27
Mead, Margaret, 44, 56, 58, 59, 87, 88, 90, 104, 119
Means-end relation, basis of law's obligation, 24; necessity of, precedes law, 24
Meek, C. K., 49, 50, 55, 56, 57, 68, 69, 72, 73, 75, 94, 95, 96, 104, 110, 111, 124
Melanesians, 47, 91
Mende, 68, 69, 77, 78, 92, 120
Menger, Anton, 20
Menomini, 100
Mental development, requires association, 97
Mesakin, 46, 47
Messing, Simon, 68
Mexico, 120
Micmac, 118
Middleton, John, 47
Mill, John S., 27
Miller, Nathan, 50
Mine, not coextensive with property, 21; extension of self, 20
Mine and thine, distinction between, basic to every man's world view, 86, basic to justice, 86, universal value judgment, 86; drive to distinguish, 14, 86, different from aggressive drive, 86; value of distinguishing, universal postulate, 86
Mitchell Islanders, 45
Model, of law, 22, 23, 41; of value, 7, 38
Mohammedan law, law of talion, 123; mutilation, 128
Mongols, 60
Monogamy, all societies, 61, 62; among animals, 62; common value judgment, 62; described, 61; implied in polygyny, first-wife, 61; motives, 62
Monotheism, primordial, 77
Montagnais, 118
Montagu, Ashley, 13, 39, 40, 41, 50, 51, 52, 55, 65, 67, 73, 74, 79, 97, 102, 106, 107
Montesquieu, Charles, 98
Moore, G. E., 8
Morgan, Lewis, 51, 88
Moss, Claude, 45, 46, 55, 59, 71, 76, 79, 85, 90, 92, 94, 107, 113, 118, 126, 127
Motivation, happiness, 15; needs, 9; from values, 9
Motives, cause of decisions, 79; described, 9; infanticide, 49; immaterial in collective responsibility, 84; monogamy,

62; polyandry, 53; polygyny, 60; suicide, 48; war, 45
Muganda, 67
Muhammadanism, 75
Muntsch, Albert, 77
Murder, unjustified killing, 43
Murdock, George, 40, 52, 102
Murphy, Gardner, 14
Murphy, Lois, 14
Murray, Henry, 7, 14
Mutilation, Mohammedan law, 128; punishment, occasional value judgment, 128
Myth, account of origin, 78, 79; analogy, 79; fiction versus history, 78

Nabaloi, 44, 45, 48, 54, 59, 71, 72, 76, 79, 85, 89, 92, 94, 104, 107, 112, 113, 117, 126
Nadel, Siegfried, 39, 47, 68
Nandi, 46, 47, 59, 69, 73, 78, 82, 83, 84, 85, 109, 111, 114, 118
Naskapi, 45, 48, 56, 68, 70, 91, 92, 107, 114, 118, 125, 129
"Natural law" neither confirmed nor refuted, 130
"Naturalistic fallacy," 8; misconception, 8
Navaho, 46, 48, 76
Nazis and Jews, 23
Necessity, absolute and relative, 17; basis of obligation, 17; in universal value judgments, from psychology not anthropology, 3, 10, 129
Needs, basis of values, 8; and motivation, 9; related to value judgments, 7
Negligence, distinct from accident, 85; immaterial in collective responsibility, 84; responsibility for, common value judgment, 85, 86
Negritos, 91, 95
Nepal, 109, 112, 115, 127, 128
New analytical jurists, 29
Newar, 115
Newcomb, Theodore, 9, 12, 14
New England town meeting, people governing selves, 23
New Guinea, 103, 118
New Stone Age, 44
Ngai, 77, 78
Ngarigo, 90
Nguni, 109
Ngwato, 103, 104, 126
Nigeria, 48, 54, 56, 67, 69, 93, 110, 112, 114, 123
Noon, John, 70
"No political association," no evidence, 100
"No political organization," no evidence, 99
Normal men, 15, 39; basic drives, 15; psychology and psychiatry, 15; sensitive to others' suffering, 15; in society form universal and almost universal value judgments, 129; symbolic and abstract reasoning, 64
Northern Spain, art, 66
Northrop, F. C. S., 37
Nsukka, 56, 103
Nuer, 45, 56, 61, 67, 71, 73, 76, 77, 78, 79, 82, 83, 84, 99, 100, 103, 119, 120
Numbers, 83

Nurmi, 115
Nyakyusa, 45, 103, 106, 112, 114
Nyoro, 115

Oakley, Francis, 30
Oaths, described, 125; forms of, 126; among Hebrews, 126; necessity, 126; purpose, 125; smoking the pipe, 126; travesty of, 125; use of, frequent value judgment, 126; women exempt, 125
Oberg, Kalervo, 47, 56, 86, 90, 95, 115, 116, 118
Obgoni, 128
Obligation, from basic values, 16; basis, drive for self-realization, 17; described, 17; in law, from means-end relation, 24; necessarily, 30, not from command or coercion, 24; from master drive, 17; of others, basis of my claims, 20; stressed by preliterates over claims, 87; type of necessity, 17; universal, 40; value-relation of means to end, 17
Observable constants, basic drives, 11
Occasional value judgments, see Value judgments, occasional
Occupation, described, 92; establishes relation of title, 20, 92; by "twig-in-turf," 92; value judgment in all societies with rare exceptions, 92
Offenses, bearing and not bearing on common welfare almost universal value judgment, 106; against common values, directly and indirectly, 107; lists of, 109; not distinguished by punishment, 107; among preliterates, mostly torts not crimes, 108; reaction to, sanctions, 105; against the whole community, directly and indirectly, 105
Ojibwa, 45, 48
Older analytical jurists, 29
Old Stone Age, 44, 66
Omaha, 100
Ona, 62, 63
Oral instruction, source of learning, 67
Orang-Laut, 45
Ordeals, advantage over oath, 112; described, 112; explanations of, 113; kinds, 112; refused, consequences of, 112; use of, general value judgment, 113
Orenda, suprahuman power, impersonal, 72
Orient, 44
Origin of man and world, variously described, 78
Origins, creation, 78; myth, 78; related to Supreme Being, common value judgment, 79
Orinoco, 54
Ossete, 95
O'Sullivan, Hugh, 55, 83
Other-than-human spirits, described, 76; extent of conviction, 76; holy, 76
Otto, Rudolph, 73
"Ought," from demands of "is," 18
"Ought" and "Is," factually linked, 18
Outlawry, see Exile
Overstreet, Harold, 15

Ownership, primordial, communal, embraced by Marxism, 88, Engels use of, 88; property, 22
Ownership of land, individual, family, group, common value judgment, 96

Page, Charles, 99
Paleolithic cultures, 66
Papuans, 82, 108, 109, 114
Passing love affairs distinguished from polyandry, 53
Paul, Leslie, 55, 56, 73, 79
Pelew Islanders, 59
Penwill, D. J., 61, 83, 85, 96, 118
People, authority of, 106; common values of, 23; customs of, as law, 24; directive judgments of, 23; governing selves, New England town meeting, 23; Swiss cantons, 24; reactions of, indicates custom law, 35
Peristiany, J. G., 46, 107, 111
Permanence in sex, absolute and relative, 51; universal postulate, 51; universal value judgment, in all societies, 50
Perry, Ralph B., 8, 129
Peru, 55, 120
Peter, Prince, 53
Peyote meetings, equitable fictions at, 127
Peyote religion, 75
Philosophy of law and jurisprudence, 32
Piaget, Jean, 18, 40, 86
Piddington, Ralph, 14, 35, 40, 41, 50, 51, 52, 56, 71, 72, 75, 88, 90, 99, 103
Pima, 45, 89
Pipe smoking, form of oath, 126
Places of refuge, Hebrew code, 83; indicate distinction between intentional and accidental, 83
Plasticity of basic drives, 12, 17; fountainhead of culture, 13; meaning, 12; related to given and constructed value judgments, 11; shaped by knowledge and free decision, 80
Plateau tribes, 94
Poitiers, 75
Pokot, 119
Polanyi, Michael, 7, 33, 34, 63, 129
Political association, 97; described, 101; prevalence, 97; protection, common value, 101; requires cooperative effort, 101; requires sanctions, 101; security, common value, 101; universal, 99; value of, universal value judgment, 96
Polyandry, 52; and Buddhism, 53; described, 52; distinguished from cicisbeism, 53, concubinage, 53, passing love affairs, 53; wife-lending, 53; motives, 53; universal value judgment in all societies with rare exceptions, 53
Polygyny, in animals, 60; common value judgment, 61; described, 60; first-wife in, 60; implies monogamy, 61; jealousy in, 61; motives, 60; prevalence, 60; property rights, 60; sign of wealth, 60; source of esteem, 60
Polynesians, 53, 54, 55, 71, 72
Ponape, 46
Pontiac, Chief, orator, 120
Position taken, basic drives, 14

Positivism, Kantianism half-way house to, 26; legal, 129; main assumptions, 30; meaning, 29, 129; mistake, of, 34; root kinship, voluntarism and scholasticism, 30
Pospisil, Leopold, 35, 83, 103, 110, 115, 122
Postman, Leo, 80
Postulated values, 37; association, 101; basic values, 36, 37; common needs, fulfillment of, 102; communicating, 65; culture, 36; deciding, 79, 80; distinguishing mine from thine, 86; drives, 7; family, 52; given value judgments, 36; justice, 86, 96, 107; knowing, 64; language, 65; learning, 70; marriage, 52; order, 102; owning some things, 87–88; peace, 102; prelegal facts, 96; protection, 102; regulations, 43, 80; relative permanence in sex, 51; responsibility relating to doer, 80; in science, 33; security, 102; selectivity in sex, 51; self-defense, 43; self-evident value judgment, 36; self-preservation, 42, 47; sexes, difference in, 50; sexual union, 51
Potlatch, gift-giving, 92; significance, 92
Pound, Roscoe, 37
Power, suprahuman, 72
Prejevalsky, Nikolas, 55
Prelegal fact, distinction between mine and thine, 96; postulates, 96; relations of title, 96
Preliterates, stress obligations rather than claims, 87; value judgments regarding children, 52
Premarital intercourse and childbirth, 56
Pre-Mousterian times, art, 66
Prescription or adverse possession, relations of title, 20
Price paid for bride, 58
Primordial monotheism, explained, 77; variously evaluated, 78
Process of making, art, 65
Product of labor, related to laborer, 89, 90; universal value judgment, 90
Promiscuity, primeval, no evidence of, 51
Promulgation of law, not part of law, 23; prerequisite condition of law, 23
Property, see also Mine and thine; described, 21, 87; exclusive use of, from others' respect, 21; from Latin "proprium," 21; none among animals, 22; not coextensive with mine, 21; ownership, 22; prevalence of concept, 87; primordial, communal, no evidence of, 88; private, relative, 87; security, basis of, 20; triadic concept, 21; web of relations, 21, 96
Proper values distinguished from common values, 23
Prostitution, among preliterates, few data, 62
Protection, political association, common value, 101; through association, 96; universal value judgment, 101
Prudence, act of, law, 32; described, 33
Psychiatry, standard of normal men, 15
Psychoanalysis compared with initiation rites, 70

Psychology, source of necessary value judgments, 129; standard of normal men, 15; supported by data of anthropology, 129

Public opinion, see also Ridicule; punishment, non-physical, 41

Pueblos, 63

Punishment, for adultery, 54; combat, 128; distinguishing offenses, not basis of, 107; earliest, deprivation of common values, 102; early form of, exile, 124; essentially deprivation, 102, 106; exile, common value judgment, 124; flogging, 128; head-butting, 128; for incest, 56; for in-group—out-group killing, 46; mutilation, 128; non-physical, more efficient than physical, 41, public opinion, 41, ridicule, 41; not without reason, 39; for rape, 59; sanctions, 105; severest, deprivation of common values, 102, exile, 124; severity of, related to offense, 106; wounding, 128

Purpose, value of presupposed by science, 33

Pygmies, 62, 91, 98

Radcliffe-Brown, Alfred, 35, 42, 43, 44, 73, 75, 93, 98, 100, 101, 118, 122, 124

Radin, Paul, 41, 46, 64, 124

Rai, 115

Ramsey, T. D., 55, 61

Rape, described, 59; general value judgment, 59; prevalence, 59; punishment, 59

Rattray, Robert, 45, 49, 56, 69, 83, 85, 87, 90, 95, 104, 115, 118

Reasoning described, 64

Reciprocity, dynamic of gift-giving, 92; gift-giving, 91; promotes cooperative effort, 102

Redfield, Robert, 39, 40, 42, 70, 88, 90, 92, 99, 100, 104, 115

Red Jacket, Chief, orator, 120

Refuge, places of, 83

Regulations, all societies, 41; concerning knowledge, 64; of deciding, 80; directive of the common good, universal value judgment, 103; fulfill common needs, 80; marriage, universal, 52; may or may not be laws, 34; necessary for freedom, 40; protective of life, 43, no societies without, 43; regarding decisions, prevalence, 80; regarding title to things, 87; of retaliation, 123; universal, 40; universal postulate, 43, 80; unwritten, may be law, 35; value of, universal postulate, 80

Regulative judging fulfills common needs, 103

Reichard, Gladys, 41, 43, 47, 50, 52, 56, 60, 62, 68, 93, 94, 97

Rejang, 59

Relationship with suprahuman power, religion, 73

Relations of title, accession, 20; adverse possession, 20; constructed, 19; contracts, 20; created by labor, 19; creative actions, 88; enterprising activities, 88; established by basic drives, 19; exchange agreements, 20; gifts, 20; given,

19; inheritance, 20; intangibles, 19; intrinsic, 20; occupation, 20; prelegal fact, 96; prescription, 20; tangibles, 19; ways of establishing, 88

Religion, absence of, false reports on, 74; allied with law, 74; authority of, from greater than human source, 73; cultural value, 74; described, 73; and magic, 75; Peyote, 75; preliterate, invalid interpretation, 74, objective basis of, 74; prevalence, 73; relationship with suprahuman power, 73; sacrifice, integral part of, 73

Removal of leaders, 104

Respect for elders, see Elders

Responsibility based on, fault, 81; cause, 81; collective, 83, Hebrew code, 84, extent, 84, motive, intention, accident, negligence immaterial, 84, prevalence, 83; decisions made in hot blood or cold blood, 83; extenuating circumstances, 80; individual, 80; individual and collective, 83; insanes, 84; negligence, 85; related to doer of deed, 80; shift in grounds of, 81

Retaliation, common value judgment, 124; origin of criminal law, 41; proportionate, law of talion, 123; regulation of, 123

Riasanovsky, Valintin, 35, 45, 61, 81, 85, 94, 115, 116, 124, 128, 129

Richards, Audrey, 69, 70

Richardson, Jane, 42, 107, 115, 124, 126

Ridicule, legal sanction, 114; prevalence, 114; public forms of, 114; punishment, non-physical, 41; sanction, non-physical, 113; use of, general value judgment, 115

Right and wrong, basis of distinction, psychology and not anthropology, 129

Rights, see also Mine and thine; from basic values, 16, 19; complex connotations, 21; content of law, 22; as good, 8; personal, grounded on basic drives, 18; property, in polygyny, 60; triadic concept, 21, 87; viability of, 20; web of relations, 21

Rites, see Initiation rites

Rivers, William, 88, 90

Rodnick, David, 50, 110

Rombo, 54

Root kinship, voluntarism, scholasticism, and positivism, 30

Roscoe, John, 57

Rose, Herbert, 73, 78

Rousseau, Jean-Jacques, 98

Rules of etiquette, 34

Rupchu, 53

Sacrifice, integral part of religion, 73; qualifications for offering, 73

Sakai, 95

Saksena, R. N., 53

Samoa, 45, 57, 58, 59, 83, 90, 104, 106

Samoyeds, 114

Sanction, does not constitute law, 35; extrinsic, not necessary for law, 105; intrinsic, necessarily in law, 105; intrinsic and extrinsic, 105; necessity of, political associations, 101; non-physical

as effective as physical, 114; physical and non-physical, 113; physical or psychological, 35; prevalence, 105; reaction to offenses, 81, 105; rewards and punishments, 105

Sapao, 117

Sarbin, Theodore, 19

Sauk, 100

Scandinavians, 76, 93, 124

Schapera, Isaac, 35, 42, 47, 49, 55, 61, 70, 83, 86, 99, 101, 107, 115, 118, 121, 127

Schechter, Frank, 91, 92, 93

Schlosberg, Harold, 12

Schmidt, Wilhelm, 71, 77

Schneider, David, 75

Schneidman, Edwin, 47

Scholasticism, root kinship, voluntarism and positivism, 30

Schouten Islanders, 54, 67

Schweitzer, Albert, 125

Science, permeated by values, 32, 33; communication, 33; faith, 33; freedom, 33; hypothesis, 33; purpose, 33; standards, 33; truthfulness, 33

Scientific question, life, a good, 11

Seagle, William, 35, 42

Security, through association, 96; common value in political association, 101; property, basis of, 20; universal value judgment, 101

Selectivity in sex, universal postulate, 51; universal value judgment, in all societies, 50, 51

Self-actualization, master drive, 15

Self-defense, 45; aspect of self-preservation, 43; value of, postulate in all law, 43

Self-development, master drive, 15

Self-government, common value judgment, 121; prevalence, 103

Self-help, community's participation in, 122; described, 121; elemental restoration of justice, 121; methods, 122; natural norm of limitation, law of talion, 122; need of limitation, 122

Self-interest, basis of cooperative effort, 102

Self-preservation, expressed in self-defense, 43; universal postulate, 42; universal value judgment, 42

Self-realization, drive for, root of obligation, 17; master drive, 14

Semang, 71, 89

Semites, 58

Senilicide, motives, 49; occasional value judgment, 49, 50; prevalence, 49

Sex, 42; determines values, 11; permanence in, absolute and relative, 51; universal postulate, 51; universally regulated, all societies, 50; value of, postulate in all societies, 50

Sexes, fact of two, source of given values, 50

Sexual union, basic drive, 50; title to, 50

Seymour, S. M., 61, 63, 86, 118

Shaman, function, 76

Shame, see Ridicule

Shills, Edward, 7

Shona, 111, 121

Shoshone, 58, 119

Siberian tribes, 44, 61, 85, 90, 115, 128
Silent trade, exchange agreements, 91; pygmies of the Congo, 91
Simmons, Leo, 60, 68, 110
Simpson, George, 18
Sinhalese, 53
Smith, Adam, 91
Smith, W. Robertson, 47
Snell, Geoffrey, 49, 59, 70, 73, 79, 83, 84, 85, 86, 110, 111, 115, 119, 126
Social-contract rejected, 98
Societies, "lawless," 42, no evidence, 41; none without regulation, 41
Soga, 115
Solitude leads to insanity, 97
Sotho, 46
Soul, see Life principle
Southern France, art, 66
South Sea Islanders, 66
Spencer, Robert, 39
Spiro, Melford, 14
Standards, value of, presupposed by science, 33
"State," unclear usage, 99
"State of nature," no historical support, 40, 98
Stone, Julius, 37
Stonehenge, 63
Substitutional authority distinguished from delegated, 24
Suicide, 47, 49; common value judgment, 47, 48; described, 47; desire for, limited by poverty, 48; integration-segregation in, 48; motives, 47, 48; not necessarily implying insanity, 47; prevalence, 47
Sukuma, 118, 121
Sumbwa, 57, 115
Summers, Robert, 29
Summers, T., 129
Sumner, William, 14, 98
Sundra Islanders, 114
Supernatural, meaning, 72
Suprahuman power, impersonal, orenda, 72, wakan, 72, Manitou, 72; impersonal and personal, 72; personal, 72; prevalence of concept, 72; religion, relationship with, 73; universal value judgment, 73
Supreme being, common value judgment, 77; conceptions of anthropology, 77; origin of concept, 77; prevalence of concept, 77
Survival, a good, 8
Swiss canton meeting, 103; people governing selves, 24

"Taboo," oceanic derivation, 55
Taking of things, see also Theft; ingroup versus out-group varied meaning, 94
Talbot, Percy, 129
Tallensi, 94, 99, 100
Tangibles, inheritance, 94; products of labor, 89; relations of title, 19
Tasmanians, 123
Tecumseh, Chief, orator, 120
Teda, 98, 100
Tendencies, drives, 12; linked with values, 7; necessary postulates, 7; related to value judgments, 7

Tenimber, 46
Ter Haar, Barend, 42, 57, 74, 85, 127
Territorial exclusiveness, land, 95
Teutons, 58
Thandans, 53
Theft, 39; prevalence, 95; universally disapproved, 87
Theraka, 115
Thomas, Isaac, 57
Tibetans, 53
Tikopia, 68, 92, 96
Timor-Laut, 46
Titiev, Mischa, 41, 43, 49, 50, 55, 61, 63, 72, 73, 87
Title, from basic drives, 88; to associate, 97; to decide, 80; given relations of, 19; by inheritance, prevalence, 93; to know, 64; to life, 43; relations of, ways of establishing, 88; to sexual union, 50; to things, 87; by occupation, 92
Tiv, 47, 84, 103, 106, 114, 115, 119, 122
Tlingit, 47, 48, 56, 89, 95, 114, 115
Tlokwa, 105
Toda, 53
Tollman, Edward, 7
Tonga Islanders, 59
Tools, artifacts, 65
Torts, compensation for, 108; distinguished from crime, 108; most offenses among preliterates, 108; offenses indirectly against common needs, 108; versus crimes, 23
Traditions, passed on by initiation rites, 69
Transvaal, 119
Triadic concept, right, property, 21
"Tribal candle," as leader, 119
Trobrianders, 90, 91, 104, 114, 124
Trotter, Wilfred, 12, 14, 97
Truk, 45
Truthfulness, value presupposed by science, 33
Tsang, 53
Tsonga, 61, 119
Tswana, 35, 45, 49, 54, 61, 67, 69, 82, 83, 85, 104, 109, 111, 117, 118, 119, 120, 126
Tubu, 98
Tungunse, 94
Tupinamba, 45
Tupper, Lewis, 55, 83, 96, 109
Turkey, 128
"Twig-in-turf," occupation, 92
Tylor, Edward, 41, 43, 46, 73, 77, 95

U, 53
Ubena, 54
Uganda, 128
Uhehe, 54
Ukamba, 89, 112, 115
Umnak, 44
Unalaska, 44
Unalit, 120
Ungoni, 54
Unique relations of title to things, universal value judgments, 87
Universal obligation, 40
Universal postulates, see Postulated values
Universal recognition, obligation, 40
Universal values, lists, 39

Universal value judgments, see Value judgments, universal
Universality of regulations, 40
Unjust law is law, means-end view, 32; is not law, positivist view, 32
Unyamwesi, 54
Upare, 56, 113
Useguha, 54
Uzigua, 113

Values, anchored in basic drives, 8; basic, 7, source of obligation, 16, source of rights, 16; from basic drives, in lawmaking, 11; common to all the people, 23; comparative, 39; constructed, 10; described, 8; different from good, 8; from drives, 7; family, 52; given, 10, by fact of two sexes, 11, 50; history of word, 8; imply standard, 7; in law, more than minimal, 31, necessarily, 10, 30, psychological necessity, 30; linked with tendencies, 7; meaning, 7; model of, 7, 38; motivation, in law, 10; from needs, 8; not self-evident, 36; permeate science, 32, 33; of persons, 7; postulated, 37; prerequisite to motivation, 9; proper and common, 23; same as good, 8; self-evident, 36, absolutely and relatively, 36; of things, 7; universal, lists, 39; in unwritten law, 38
Value-areas in law, 38
Value judgments, according to drives, 10; almost universal, 38, adultery, 52, 54, 55, distinguishing crimes and torts, 109, distinguishing offenses directly and indirectly against common values, 106, 107, incest, 52, 55, 56, polyandry, 52, respect for elderly, 110, title by occupation, 92; categories of, explanation, 38; common, 38, confessions, 125, exile as punishment, 125, government by chiefs, 121, individual, family, group ownership of land, 96, insanes and inebriates less responsible, 85, land, 95, leaders, 119, lying, 76, monogamy, 61, 62, negligence, 85, origin of man and world, 78, origins related to supreme being, 79, other-than-human spirits, 76, polygyny, 60, 61, proportionate retaliation, 124, responsibility for negligence, 86, retaliation, 122, self-government, 121, self-help, 121, suicide, 47, Supreme Being, 77, connatural, 10; constructed and given, 10, frequent, 38, oaths, 125, 126; general, 38, 44, abortion, 44, 46, collective, responsibility, 83, 84, compensation, 116, 118, control of events, 75, 76, councils, 111, of elders, 111, death as punishment, 115, 116, distinguishing between intention and accident, 83, distinguishing between premeditated and unpremeditated decisions, 83, divorce, 59, 60, enforcement, 118, 119, evidence through witnesses, 112, exchange of items at marriage, 57, 58, hot blood versus cold blood, 13, ingroup versus out-group killing, 46, ingroup versus out-group taking of things, 94, 95, intention versus accident, 81, keeping agreements, 93, killing in

self-defense, 44, ordeals, 111, 113, pre-marital intercourse and childbirth, 56, 57, rape, 59, ridicule, 115, title by inheritance, 93, war, 45, witnesses, 111, given, 10, postulates, 36, given and constructed, plasticity of basic drives, 11, by inclinations, 10, necessity of, from psychology, 129; occasional, 38, changing custom law, 126, 127, fictions, 127, imprisonment, 128, 129, mutilation, wounding, combat as punishment, 128, regarding children, among preliterates, 52, related to needs and tendencies, 7, self-evident, every culture, 36; universal, 38, 42, 43, artistic creation, 65, 67, association, 101, communication, 65, cooperative effort, 102, dependence on a supreme power, 75, distinction between mine and thine, 14, 86, example, 68, exchange agreements, 91, explanations of life, 70, family, 52, fulfillment of common needs, 102, gift-giving, 92, individual responsibility for decision, 80, initiation rites, 69, judging cases, 106, killing, 43, knowledge and decision, 14, 62, 64, 79, language, 65, less than, not scientific, 10–11, 38; learning, 67, 70, life after death, 71, 72, life principle, 70, 71, marriage, 51, murder, 43, necessity from psychology not anthropology, 3, 10, 129, oral instruction, 67, participation in directive judging, 105, product of labor uniquely related to laborer, 90, protection and security, 101, reactions to decisions, 81, regulations, 43, 50, 64, 80, 87, 103, regulative judging, 103, relationship with suprahuman power, 73, relative permanence in sex, 50, sanctions, 104, scientific, 10–11, 38, security, 101, seeking what is just, 107, selectivity in sex, 50, 51, self-defense, 43, self-preservation, 14, 42, sexual union, 14, 50, suprahuman power, 72, 73, theft, 87, unique relations of title to things, 87, unjust repression of action, 80, unjust repression of thought, 64, ways of establishing relations of title, 88; without reasoning process, 10

Value of deciding, universal postulate, 79, 80

Value-relations, absolute and relative necessity, 17

Van Der Leeuw, Gerardus, 75, 78, 79

Veach, Henry, 8

Vedda of Ceylon, 44, 57, 92, 95

Viability of rights, 20

Vinogradoff, Paul, 41, 42, 102, 108, 109, 122, 124

Virginity, premium put on, 68

Voluntarism, root kinship, scholasticism and positivism, 30

Von Jhering, Rudolph, 20

Vugusu, 46, 47

Wabena, 115

Waboni, 82, 126

Wabunga, 46, 54, 56

Wach, Joachim, 73, 76

Waddington, C. H., 13

Wadigo, 83, 95

Wagner, Gunter, 47, 69, 72, 75, 97, 110

Wakitusika, 46, 57, 60, 72, 93

Walluvanad Taluk, 53

Wamakonda, 56, 115

Wanyamwesi, 46, 115

Wanika, 58

Wapare, 115

War, general value judgment, 45; motives, 45; not necessarily a moral evil, 45; prevalence, 44

Wasove, 46, 54

Wataveta, 53, 54, 82, 123

Waziguha, 57

Westermarck, Edward, 42, 43, 44, 51, 53, 56, 62, 70, 71, 76, 87, 95, 103, 129

Whitfield, G. M. B., 111, 127

Wife-lending distinguished from polyandry, 53

Williams, F. E., 47, 55, 86, 109

Wilson, Godfrey, 45, 104, 105, 107, 113, 114, 115

Winfield, Percy, 81

Winnebago, 64, 100

Wissler, Clark, 13, 40, 44, 50, 65, 67, 70, 71, 75

Witnesses, evidence from, general value judgment, 112; passing strangers, testimony of, 112; prime source of evidence, 111; qualifications, 112; relevance of number, 112

Wogeo, 94

Wolfle, D., 63

Wonevaro, 94

Woodworth, Robert, 12

World view, every man's, based on mine-thine distinction, 86

Wounding as punishment, 128

Women, unsatisfactory leaders, 120

Wright, Lord, 58

Wright, Quincy, 44

Wrong as bad, 8

Xosa, 68

Yahgans, 48

Yamana, 71, 91

Yap, 45, 75

Yoruba, 48, 56, 60, 91, 128

Yurok, 81, 99, 100, 104, 114, 116

Zones of uncertainty in statutes, "is" interpreted according to "ought," 31

Zulu, 121

Zuni, 59, 62